Program Evaluation

METHODS AND CASE STUDIES

SEVENTH EDITION

Emil J. Posavac

Loyola University of Chicago

Raymond G. Carey

R. G. Carey and Associates

PEARSON

Prentice
Hall

Upper Saddle River, New Jersey 07458

Library of Congress Cataloging-in-Publication Data

Posavac, Emil J.
   Program evaluation : methods and case studies / Emil J. Posavac, Raymond G. Carey. — 7th ed.
      p. cm.
   ISBN-13: 978-0-13-227560-6 (hardcover)
   ISBN-10: 0-13-227560-0 (hardcover)
   1. Evaluation research (Social action programs)—United States. I. Carey, Raymond G. II. Title.
   H62.5.U5P62 2007
   361.6'1072—dc22

                                                                                    2006012136

Executive Acquisitions Editor: Jeff Marshall
Editorial Director: Leah Jewell
Editorial Assistant: Jennifer Puma
Senior Marketing Manager: Jeanette Moyer
Assistant Managing Editor: Maureen Richardson
Production Liaison: Fran Russello
Manufacturing Buyer: Sherry Lewis
Art Director: Jayne Conte
Composition/Full-Service Project Management: Babitha Balan/GGS Book Services
Printer/Binder: RR Donnelley & Sons Company

Credits and acknowledgments borrowed from other sources and reproduced, with permission, in this textbook appear on appropriate page within text.

Pearson Education LTD. London
Pearson Education Singapore, Pte. Ltd
Pearson Education, Canada, Ltd
Pearson Education–Japan
New Jersey
Pearson Education Australia PTY, Limited

Pearson Education North Asia Ltd
Pearson Educación de Mexico, S.A. de C.V.
Pearson Education Malaysia, Pte. Ltd
Pearson Education, Upper Saddle River, New Jersey

10 9 8 7 6 5 4 3 2 1
ISBN: 0-13-227560-0

To

Wendy, Steve, Heidi, Austin, and Brett
(Emil J. Posavac)

Rita, Mike, and Mark
(Raymond G. Carey)

Contents

Preface   xiv

1 Program Evaluation: An Overview   1

EVALUATION TASKS THAT NEED TO BE DONE   3
Verify That Resources Would Be Devoted to Meeting Unmet Needs   4
Verify That Implemented Programs Do Provide Services   4
Examine the Outcomes   4
Determine Which Programs Produce the Most Favorable
    Outcomes   5
Select the Programs That Offer the Most Needed Types
    of Services   5
Provide Information to Maintain and Improve Quality   6
Watch for Unplanned Side Effects   6

COMMON TYPES OF PROGRAM EVALUATIONS   7
Assess Needs of the Program Participants   7
Examine the Process of Meeting the Needs   7
Measure the Outcomes of the Program   8
Integrate the Needs, Costs, and Outcomes   9

ACTIVITIES OFTEN CONFUSED WITH PROGRAM EVALUATION   10

DIFFERENT TYPES OF EVALUATIONS FOR DIFFERENT KINDS OF PROGRAMS   11
Organizations Needing Program Evaluations   11
Time Frames of Needs   12
Extensiveness of Programs   13

PURPOSE OF PROGRAM EVALUATION   14

THE ROLES OF EVALUATORS   16
A Variety of Work Settings   16
Comparison of Internal and External Evaluators   17
Evaluation and Service   19
Evaluation and Related Activities of Organizations   20

Summary and Preview   21

Study Questions   22

Additional Resource   22

2 Planning an Evaluation   23

AN OVERVIEW OF EVALUATION MODELS   24
The Traditional Model   24
Social Science Research Model   25

Industrial Inspection Model   25
Black Box Evaluation   25
Objectives-Based Evaluation   26
Goal-Free Evaluation   26
Fiscal Evaluation   26
Accountability Model   27
Expert Opinion Model   27
Naturalistic or Qualitative Model   27
Success Case Method   28
Empowerment Evaluation   28
Theory-Driven Evaluation   28
An Improvement-Focused Approach   29

STEPS IN PREPARING TO CONDUCT AN EVALUATION   **30**
Identify the Program and Its Stakeholders   30
Become Familiar with Information Needs   31
Plan the Evaluation   35

DYSFUNCTIONAL ATTITUDES TOWARD PROGRAM EVALUATION   **40**
Assume That the Program Is Perfect   41
Fear That the Evaluation Will Offend the Staff   41
Fear That the Evaluation Will Inhibit Innovation   42
Fear That the Program Will Be Terminated   42
Fear That Information Will Be Misused   42
Fear That Qualitative Understanding May Be Supplanted   43
Fear That Evaluation Drains Program Resources   43
Fear of Losing Control of the Program   43
Fear That Evaluation Has Little Impact   44
The Effect of These Attitudes   45

Summary and Preview   45

Study Questions   45

Additional Resource   46

3 Selecting Criteria and Setting Standards   **47**

USEFUL CRITERIA AND STANDARDS   **48**
Criteria That Reflect a Program's Purposes   48
Criteria That the Staff Can Influence   49
Criteria That Can Be Measured Reliably and Validly   50
Criteria That Stakeholders Participate in Selecting   50

DEVELOPING GOALS AND OBJECTIVES   **52**
How Much Agreement on Goals Is Needed?   52
Different Types of Goals   53
Goals That Apply to All Programs   55

EVALUATION CRITERIA AND EVALUATION QUESTIONS   **55**
Does the Program or Plan Match the Values of the
Stakeholders?   56

Does the Program or Plan Match the Needs of the People
   to Be Served?   56
Does the Program as Implemented Fulfill the Plans?   57
Do the Outcomes Achieved Match the Goals?   58
Using Program Theory   60
Is the Program Accepted?   64
Are the Resources Devoted to the Program Being Expended
   Appropriately?   65

SOME PRACTICAL LIMITATIONS IN SELECTING EVALUATION CRITERIA   68
Evaluation Budget   68
Time Available for the Project   68
Criteria That Are Credible to the Stakeholders   69

Summary and Preview   69

Study Questions   69

Additional Resource   70

4 Developing Measures   71

SOURCES OF DATA FOR EVALUATION   71
Intended Beneficiaries of the Program   72
Providers of Services   74
Observers   75
Which Sources Should Be Used?   77

GOOD ASSESSMENT PROCEDURES   79
Use Multiple Variables   79
Use Nonreactive Measures   80
Use Variables Relevant to Information Needs   80

CASE STUDY 1: USING MULTIPLE MEASURES IN AN EVALUATION OF A SUMMER
COMMUNITY PROGRAM FOR YOUTH   81
Use Valid Measures   81
Use Reliable Measures   82
Use Measures That Can Detect Change   84
Use Cost-Effective Measures   85

TYPES OF MEASURES OF EVALUATION CRITERIA   86
Written Surveys and Interviews with Program Participants   86
Checklists, Tests, and Records   88

PREPARING SPECIAL SURVEYS   90
Format of a Survey   90
Preparing Survey Items   91
Instructions and Pretests   92

Summary and Preview   92

Study Questions   92

Additional Resource   93

5 Ethics in Program Evaluation   94

STANDARDS FOR THE PRACTICE OF EVALUATION   95

ETHICAL ISSUES INVOLVED IN THE TREATMENT OF PEOPLE   96
    Compensating for Ineffective, Novel Treatments   96
    Obtaining Informed Consent   97
    Maintaining Confidentiality   98

ROLE CONFLICTS FACING EVALUATORS   98

RECOGNIZING THE NEEDS OF DIFFERENT STAKEHOLDERS   100
    Program Managers Are Concerned with Efficiency   100
    Staff Members Seek Assistance in Service Delivery   101
    Clients Want Effective and Appropriate Services   101
    Community Members Want Cost-Effective Programs   101

THE VALIDITY OF EVALUATIONS   102
    Valid Measurement Instruments   102
    Skilled Data Collectors   103
    Appropriate Research Design   103
    Adequate Descriptions of Program and Procedures   104

AVOIDING POSSIBLE NEGATIVE SIDE EFFECTS OF EVALUATION
    PROCEDURES   105
    Can Someone Be Hurt by Inaccurate Findings?   105
    Consider Statistical Type II Errors   106
    Pay Attention to Unplanned Effects   107
    Analyze Implicit Values Held by the Evaluator   107

INSTITUTIONAL REVIEW BOARDS AND PROGRAM EVALUATION   108

ETHICAL PROBLEMS EVALUATORS REPORT   110

Summary and Preview   111

Study Questions   111

Additional Resource   112

6 The Assessment of Need   113

DEFINITIONS OF NEED   114

SOURCES OF INFORMATION FOR THE ASSESSMENT OF NEED   115
    Describing the Current Situation   116
    Social Indicators of Need   117
    Community Surveys of Need   119
    Services Already Available   121
    Key Informants   122
    Focus Groups and Open Forums   123

INADEQUATE ASSESSMENT OF NEED   125
    Failing to Examine Need   125
    Failing to Examine the Context of Need   126
    Failing to Relate Need to Implementation Plans   127
    Failing to Deal with Ignorance of Need   127

USING NEEDS ASSESSMENTS IN PROGRAM PLANNING   **128**
Summary and Preview   129
Study Questions   130
Additional Resource   130

7 Monitoring the Operation of Programs   **131**

MONITORING PROGRAMS AS A MEANS OF EVALUATING PROGRAMS   **132**
WHAT TO SUMMARIZE WITH INFORMATION SYSTEMS   **134**
    Relevant Information   134
    Actual State of Program   134
    Program Participants   135
    Providers of Services   135
PROGRAM RECORDS AND INFORMATION SYSTEMS   **135**
    Problems with Agency Records   135
    Increasing the Usefulness of Records   136
    How Records Can Be Used to Monitor Programs   136
    Reporting Information Separately for Each Therapist   143
    Developing Information Systems for Agencies   144
    Threatening Uses of Information Systems   146
AVOIDING COMMON PROBLEMS IN IMPLEMENTING AN
    INFORMATION SYSTEM   **148**
    Guard Against the Misuse of the Information   149
    Avoid Setting Arbitrary Standards   149
    Avoid Serving the Needs of Only One Group   149
    Avoid Duplicating Records   150
    Avoid Adding to the Work of the Staff   150
    Avoid a Focus on Technology   150
Summary and Preview   150
Study Questions   151
Additional Resource   151

8 Qualitative Evaluation Methods   **152**

EVALUATION SETTINGS BEST SERVED BY QUALITATIVE EVALUATIONS   **153**
    Admission to Graduate Studies   154
    Dissatisfaction with a Library Collection   154
    Evaluating a Political Campaign   155
GATHERING QUALITATIVE INFORMATION   **156**
    The Central Importance of the Observer   156
    Observational Methods   157
    CASE STUDY 2: USING QUALITATIVE METHODS IN AN EVALUATION
    OF A UNIVERSITY LIBRARY   **160**
    Interviewing to Obtain Qualitative Information   160

CARRYING OUT NATURALISTIC EVALUATIONS   163
Phase One: Making Unrestricted Observations   163
Phase Two: Integrating Impressions   164
Phase Three: Sharing Interpretations   164
Phase Four: Preparing Reports   164
Are Qualitative Evaluations Subjective?   165

COORDINATING QUALITATIVE AND QUANTITATIVE METHODS   166
The Substance of the Evaluation   166
Getting Insights from the Most Successful Participants   167
Changing Emphases as Understanding Expands   167
The Evaluation Questions   167
Cost of Evaluation   168

PHILOSOPHICAL ASSUMPTIONS   168

Summary and Preview   169

Study Questions   170

Additional Resource   170

9 Single-Group, Nonexperimental Outcome Evaluations   171

SINGLE-GROUP EVALUATION DESIGNS   171
Observe Only After the Program   171
Observe Before and After the Program   172

USES OF SINGLE-GROUP, DESCRIPTIVE DESIGNS   173
Did the Participants Meet a Criterion?   173
Did the Participants Improve?   173

CASE STUDY 3: A PRETEST-POSTTEST DESIGN TO EVALUATE A PEER-BASED
PROGRAM TO PREVENT SKIN CANCER   174
Did the Participants Improve Enough?   174
Relating Change to Service Intensity and Participant
Characteristics   177

THREATS TO INTERNAL VALIDITY   180
Actual but Nonprogram-Related Changes in the Participants   180
Apparent Changes Dependent on Who Was Observed   181
Changes Related to Methods of Obtaining Observations   184
Effects of Interactions of These Threats   185
Internal Validity Threats Are Double-Edged Swords   185

CONSTRUCT VALIDITY IN PRETEST-POSTTEST DESIGNS   186

OVERINTERPRETING THE RESULTS OF SINGLE-GROUP DESIGNS   187

USEFULNESS OF SINGLE-GROUP DESIGNS AS INITIAL APPROACHES
TO PROGRAM EVALUATION   188
Assessing the Usefulness of Further Evaluations   188
Correlating Improvement with Other Variables   189
Preparing the Facility for Further Evaluation   189

Summary and Preview   190
Study Questions   190
Additional Resource   191

10 Quasi-Experimental Approaches to Outcome Evaluation   192

MAKING NUMEROUS OBSERVATIONS   193

TIME-SERIES DESIGNS   196
Patterns of Outcomes Over Time Periods   197
Analysis of Time-Series Designs   198

OBSERVING OTHER GROUPS   201
Nonequivalent Control Group Designs   201
Problems in Selecting Comparison Groups   202

CASE STUDY 4: NONEQUIVALENT CONTROL GROUPS USED TO EVALUATE AN EMPLOYEE INCENTIVE PLAN   205

REGRESSION-DISCONTINUITY DESIGN   206

OBSERVING OTHER DEPENDENT VARIABLES   209

COMBINING DESIGNS TO INCREASE INTERNAL VALIDITY   209
Time-Series and Nonequivalent Control Groups   209
Selective Control Design   211

Summary and Preview   213
Study Questions   214
Additional Resource   214

11 Using Experiments to Evaluate Programs   215

EXPERIMENTS IN PROGRAM EVALUATION   215
Benefits of Experiments   215
Experimental Designs   216

OBJECTIONS TO EXPERIMENTATION   218
Don't Experiment on Me!   218
We Already Know What Is Best   218
I Know What Is Best for My Client   219
Experiments Are Just Too Much Trouble   220

THE MOST DESIRABLE TIMES TO CONDUCT EXPERIMENTS   220
When a New Program Is Introduced   221
When Stakes Are High   221
When There Is Controversy About Program Effectiveness   222
When Policy Change Is Desired   222

CASE STUDY 5: TEACHING DOCTORS COMMUNICATION SKILLS: AN EVALUATION WITH RANDOM ASSIGNMENT AND PRETESTS   223
When Demand Is High   223

GETTING THE MOST OUT OF AN EXPERIMENTAL DESIGN   224
Take Precautions Before Data Collection   224
Keep Track of Randomization While the Experiment
Is in Progress   226
Analyze the Data Reflectively   227

Summary and Preview   229

Study Questions   229

Additional Resource   230

12 Analyses of Costs and Outcomes   231

COST ANALYSES AND BUDGETS   232
Types of Costs   232
An Example Budget   234
The Necessity of Examining Costs   234

COMPARING OUTCOMES TO COSTS   235
The Essence of Cost-Benefit Analysis   236
The Essence of Cost-Effectiveness Analysis   238
When Outcomes Cannot Be Put into the Same Units   240

SOME DETAILS OF COST ANALYSES   240
Units of Analysis Must Reflect the Purpose of the Program   240
Future Costs and Benefits Are Estimated   241
Who Pays the Costs and Who Reaps the Benefits?   243
CASE STUDY 6: THE VALUE OF PROVIDING SMOKING CESSATION CLINICS
FOR EMPLOYEES ON COMPANY TIME   244
Using Cost-Benefit and Cost-Effectiveness Analyses   245

MAJOR CRITICISMS OF COST ANALYSES   246
The Worth of Psychological Benefits Is Hard to Estimate   246
Placing a Value on Lives Seems Wrong   246
Cost-Benefit and Cost-Effectiveness Analyses Require
Many Assumptions   248

Summary and Preview   248

Study Questions   249

Additional Resource   249

13 Evaluation Reports: Interpreting and Communicating
Findings   250

DEVELOPING A COMMUNICATION PLAN   251
Explore Stakeholder Information Needs   251
Plan Reporting Meetings   251
Set a Communication Schedule   253

PERSONAL PRESENTATIONS OF FINDINGS   253
Need for Personal Presentations   253
Content of Personal Presentations   254

Audience for the Personal Presentations   256
Distributing Drafts of Reports   256

CONTENT OF FORMAL WRITTEN EVALUATION REPORTS   **257**
Remember the Purposes of the Formal Report   257
Provide an Outline and a Summary   258
Describe the Context of the Evaluation   258
Describe the Program Participants   260
Justify the Criteria Selected   260
Describe the Data-Gathering Procedures   260
Provide the Findings   261
Develop Recommendations   264
Formal Reports Should Look Attractive   265

PROVIDE PROGRESS REPORTS AND PRESS RELEASES   **266**

Summary and Preview   266

Study Questions   266

Additional Resources   267

14 How to Encourage Utilization   268

OBSTACLES TO EFFECTIVE UTILIZATION   **269**
Constraints on Managers   269
Value Conflicts Among Stakeholders   269
Misapplied Methodology   270
Evaluating a Program at Arm's Length   270

DEALING WITH MIXED FINDINGS   **271**
Don't Abdicate Your Responsibility   271
Don't Take the Easy Way Out   271
Show How to Use the Evaluation to Improve the Program   272

USING EVALUATIONS WHEN AN INNOVATIVE PROGRAM SEEMS NO BETTER THAN
OTHER TREATMENTS   **273**
When Can Evaluators Be Sure Groups Do Not Differ?   273
Are Evaluations Valuable Even When No Advantage for the Innova-
tion Is Found?   274

CASE STUDY 7: EVALUATIONS OF THE OUTCOMES OF BOOT CAMP PRISONS:
THE VALUE OF FINDING NO DIFFERENCES BETWEEN PROGRAM AND
COMPARISON GROUPS   **275**

DEVELOPING A LEARNING CULTURE   **275**
Work with Stakeholders   275
Adopt Developmental Interpretations   276
Frame Findings in Terms of Improvements   277
Treat Findings as Tentative Indicators, Not Final Answers   278
Recognize Service Providers' Needs   278
Keep Evaluation Findings on the Agency's Agenda   279

THE EVALUATION ATTITUDE   **280**

Summary and Possible Trends for Program Evaluation   281
Study Questions   282
Additional Resource   283

APPENDIX: ILLUSTRATIVE PROGRAM EVALUATION REPORT   **284**

REFERENCES   **297**

NAME INDEX   **325**

SUBJECT INDEX   **332**

Preface

Program evaluation is an activity that organizations do routinely, formally and informally, because we want to know how well human services serve people in need. Evaluation was a new and rather threatening idea not too long ago. Initially it was viewed with skepticism, even hostility; sometimes it still is. We show, first, that evaluations are performed for many good reasons other than to root out sloth, incompetence, and malpractice; second, that organized efforts to provide human services (that is, programs) can be evaluated; and, third, that evaluations conducted cooperatively can serve to improve programs and, thus, the quality of life.

To communicate those ideas, we include many illustrations based on our experiences, the experiences of our students, and published material. The Case Studies and Evaluator Profiles show that there really are program evaluators conducting evaluations in private service agencies, foundations, universities, and federal, state, and local governments. Sometimes the abstract material in textbooks does not do enough to help readers visualize the real people who use the skills described in the book. We hope that these short descriptions help students to see program evaluation as a field that they might consider for themselves. The profiles also reveal the range of disciplines represented in the evaluation community.

Another reason to tie the concepts into specific settings is because program evaluation is still not a household word even though the daily newspapers of any large city refer to many efforts to evaluate services—Are the schools teaching well? Are crimes being solved? Are the homeless cared for? Will the latest change in interest rates have the desired effect on the economy? These activities are seldom called "program evaluations," but they are. We trust that after reading this text, you will appreciate the wide range of activities that are part of the evaluation effort.

This is an introductory book. Program evaluations can be quite simple when done with a small program offered at a single site or very ambitious when carried out to learn about a federal policy with participants in every state or province. We have concentrated on smaller projects because we feel that new evaluators can develop a better sense of the meaning of program evaluation when the scale is more manageable. We have written this text at an introductory level; however, in several chapters you will gain more if you have completed a statistics course. Other courses that would be helpful (but not essential) include courses in social science research methods and principles of psychological or educational measurement.

Soon after the first edition appeared, many federally funded evaluation activities were curtailed. The era of big evaluations of large-scale demonstration projects came to an end. Many evaluators were apprehensive: Would organized, objective assessments of the effectiveness of government-funded social, medical, and educational programs end? Although federal support had given program evaluation a major boost in its infancy, decreased federal support did not reduce interest in evaluating programs. We believe that evaluating our organized activities is inherently helpful if done with an open mind for the purpose of adjusting our work in the light of the findings; consequently, evaluation survived federal cutbacks. In fact, it blossomed in ways that early evaluators had not foreseen. The degree of this blossoming is easy to see if one searches for "program evaluation" on the Internet.

Evaluation is as natural as a chef tasting vegetable soup or a basketball player watching to see if a hook shot goes into the basket. Of course, evaluation gets more complicated when we seek to evaluate the impact of efforts of a team rather than a solitary individual, when success is harder to define than getting the ball through the hoop, and when scarce resources are used to support a program.

We wish you well as you begin your study of program evaluation. We hope it will help you to participate actively and productively in the effort to develop a more effective, just, and healthy society—after all, that is what program evaluation is all about.

Acknowledgments We would like to thank the following reviewers for reviewing the manuscript for the publisher: Brian Stipak, Portland State University; Sandra Emerson, California State Polytechnic University, Pomona; John Kelley, Villanova University; Karol Kumpfer, University of Utah.

Emil J. Posavac
Loyola University of Chicago

Raymond G. Carey
R. G. Carey and Associates

About The Authors

Emil J. Posavac (Ph.D., University of Illinois, Champaign) is Professor Emeritus of Psychology at Loyola University of Chicago where he served as director of the Applied Social Psychology Graduate Program and chairman of the Psychology Department. He has consulted with a number of public and private organizations. He has published over sixty papers and chapters, edited or co-edited six volumes on program evaluation and applied social psychology, and written numerous evaluation reports for health care and educational institutions. He has written a textbook (with Eugene B. Zechmeister) on statistical analysis based on emerging orientations that emphasize a more complete understanding and presentation of data. In 1990, he was awarded the Myrdal Award by the American Evaluation Association for his contributions to the advancement of program evaluation practice.

Raymond G. Carey (Ph.D., Loyola University of Chicago) is principal of R. G. Carey Associates. He was the vice president of Parkside Associates, Inc., a member of the Lutheran General Health Care System (now Advocate Health Care). Widely published in the fields of health services and quality assurance, Dr. Carey has consulted on employee attitudes and quality assurance with hospitals throughout the United States. In addition, he was a member of the Technical Advisory Panel of the Post-Acute Care Study for the U.S. Department of Health and Human Services. He has taught quality improvement procedures for hospital managers seeking to improve the quality of their health services. Carey is the author of *Managing to Win: Evaluating the Use of Human Resources in Health Care Organizations* and *Measuring Quality Improvement in Healthcare: A Guide to Statistical Process Control Applications* (with Robert C. Lloyd).

Program Evaluation: An Overview

Suppose you are working for the Student Counseling Center at Western Tech a year or two from now. The center plans to offer a Sexual Assault Prevention Program to women and men in the following month, and you have been asked to develop a plan that will permit the center's staff to decide whether (a) to offer the program again if it is successful, (b) to alter the program in order to make it more useful to participants, or (c) to drop the program if it fails to meet a need. You might stop reading for a moment and write down the steps you think are necessary to measure the success of such a program.

Because the center wishes to maintain and promote useful services to students, evaluating a program that might reduce sexual assaults on campus is an important assignment. On the other hand, the staff of the center would not want to devote resources from its tight budget to a program that does not meet the needs of students on campus; in such a case, something more helpful should be offered instead. So, if the program is good, you would want your plan to detect its strengths; but if it needs improvement, you would want to detect its limitations. When you are finished with this text, we think that you will be ready to tackle this project. To begin, we first discuss what program evaluation is.

The practice of evaluating one's own efforts is as natural as breathing. Cooks taste their gravy and sauce and basketball players watch to see whether their shots go in. Indeed, it would be most unwise after turning on the hot water to neglect to check the water temperature before stepping into a shower stall. At a basic level, program evaluation is nothing more than employing this commonsense practice to settings in which organized efforts, called programs, are devoted to helping people who need education, medical treatment, job training, safe streets, welfare assistance, safety while traveling in airplanes, recreational services, or any of the thousands of services provided in a modern society. Program evaluation is a collection of methods, skills, and sensitivities necessary to determine whether a human service is needed and likely to be used, whether the service is sufficiently intensive to meet the unmet needs identified, whether the service is offered as planned, and whether the service actually does help people in need at a reasonable cost without unacceptable side effects. Utilizing research methods and concepts from psychology, sociology, administration and policy sciences, economics, and education, program evaluators seek to contribute to the improvement of programs.

There are several crucial differences between the natural, almost auto-matic, evaluations we carry on as we work and play compared to the practice of program evaluation in organizational settings. These differences make pro-gram evaluation harder than the self-evaluation that we all do. First, organiza-tional efforts are nearly always carried out by a team—whether that be a school team of teachers, coaches, and administrators; a hospital team of physi-cians, nurses, and technicians; or a welfare department team of social workers, counselors, and file clerks. This specialization means that the responsibility for program evaluation is diffused among many people. Furthermore, the end product of a program—an educated student, a cured patient, or an effective young mother—is not the sole responsibility of any individual.

Second, most programs attempt to achieve objectives that can only be observed sometime in the future rather than in a matter of minutes, as is the case with a cook adding a spice to a simmering pot or a painter repairing a scrape mark on a wall. In other words, as the time between an activity and the desired outcome of that activity lengthens, it becomes less clear what we are to observe in order to decide that the activity is being carried out appropriately or not and what could be done to improve the result of the activity. Furthermore, the choice of criteria to use in deciding whether a program is working well creates debates among evaluators, program personnel, clients, and funding agencies. How to respond when a problem is detected is often just as controversial.

Third, when evaluating our own ongoing work, a single individual fills many roles—worker, evaluator, beneficiary of the work being done, and recipient of the feedback, to name just four roles. When programs are evaluated, these roles are distributed among many different individuals. Consequently, the effectiveness of teaching in a school is assessed by evaluators who work for the central administration or the school board. It would not be surprising that individual staff members might feel threatened if the evaluators do not have the total trust of the teaching and administrative staff since, in an extreme case, the livelihood of the teachers might be harmed by an incompetently done program evaluation.

Last, programs are usually paid for by parties other than the clients of a program. Funds for the salaries of nurses are obtained from payments to hospitals by insurance companies and government agencies, and school teachers are paid through taxes collected by school districts. Although nearly all nurses and teachers want to do effective work, in a sense being favorably evaluated is more closely dependent on keeping the program funders satisfied than serving their patients and students well.

Such complications as these make program evaluation considerably more difficult to do than the evaluations of our own activities that we perform so easily and naturally. This text focuses its discussion on evaluations of programs in human services, such as education, medical care, welfare, rehabilitation, or job training. Program evaluation is one form of the general discipline of evaluation that includes employee assessment, quality control in manufacturing, policy analysis, among other activities (Scriven, 2003). The various kinds of evaluation get confused with each other. Although all forms of evaluation involve discovering the value and worth of something, the purposes and methodologies are quite different.

EVALUATION TASKS THAT NEED TO BE DONE

Although organized human services supported by public or private funds have been provided in some form for centuries, the discipline of program evaluation became formalized only during the past several decades. Some early innovators, including the nineteenth-century reformer of hospital nursing, Florence Nightingale, argued that governments ought to track their efforts to help people lest the efforts fail to achieve their goals (Cronbach, 1980). However, the regular use of social science methods to assist in monitoring and assessing the quality of services only began in the 1960s when the U.S. federal government sought to make its planning more rational, effective, and accountable (Levitan, 1992). Rational planning became a concern in the 1960s because the rapid expansion of government-funded programs made traditional, unsystematic approaches untenable. In 2002 the Federal budget included $352 billion for education, training, social services, and health (*A citizen's guide to the Federal budget FY 2002*, 2001). This figure did not include Medicare. When federally funded interventions are questioned, credible program evaluations are critical to maintaining or increasing support for human services.

The use of program evaluation has grown rapidly because information is needed to meet the obligation of providing effective services. Stufflebeam (2001) emphasizes that program evaluations are designed to help some audience to assess a program's merit or worth. In the following paragraphs we divide that purpose into seven responsibilities of planners and managers and outline how the methods of program evaluation can be used in meeting those responsibilities.

Verify That Resources Would Be Devoted to Meeting Unmet Needs

When human service programs are planned, it is important that they be directed to meet unmet needs. While this may sound like an obvious point, services are sometimes offered without a careful dialogue with the people the program planners believe will want the program's services. The more distance between the planners and the potential clients of the program, the greater the possibility of misunderstanding. Critics of a plan for a federal agency to buy and distribute all childhood immunization drugs pointed out that most children have all the immunization that they need. Furthermore, some argued that although the program was designed to reduce the cost of immunization, costs were seldom a barrier for most poor people; the problem, they argued, was that some parents seem unmotivated to have their children immunized before school regulations require them to do so (Chan, 1994, 1995). In contrast, it appears that more people would take part in drug treatment programs if more such programs were available (Dennis, Ingram, Burks, and Rachal, 1994; Sabin, 1998).

Verify That Implemented Programs Do Provide Services

The most fundamental problem with programs is that some are either never implemented as planned or are implemented in such a diluted fashion that people in need receive no or minimal benefit. Consequently, it is essential that evaluators confirm that program personnel have been hired, offices have been opened, services are being provided, and clients have found the program. Although the monitoring function of program evaluation may at first strike the reader as unnecessary, there are many examples of programs that, although funded, were never put into practice. Sometimes fraud was the reason, but more often the programs were poorly planned or the needs of target populations were misunderstood and, as a result, the programs either never got off the ground or they faded away when people did not make use of them (see Rossi, 1978, for vivid examples).

Examine the Outcomes

The monitoring task described above stresses that managers, funders, and legislators should expect to see activity when a program is begun. Activity must occur if outcomes are to be observed; however, human needs are not met by activities per se. Instead, programs should lead to improved levels of accomplishment, health, or well-being. Speer and Trapp (1976) commented that "the assumptions that operating a service is equivalent to rendering service, and that both are equivalent to rendering quality service are no longer being honored as inherently valid" (p. 217). In a commercial setting, a new product is deemed a success if enough people buy it to cover development, production, and marketing expenses. Since few people purchase human services directly, program planners must develop criteria for defining successful outcomes before they can decide whether the results are valuable. Well-meant, expensive, and ambitious programs planned during the middle and late 1960s to overcome the effects of poverty did not measure up to the optimistic expectations held by the federal government, program developers, and the general public (Cook and Shadish, 1986). Intensive evaluations of the drug use prevention program, DARE, have shown mixed results. Some evaluations show positive effects (Ullman, Stein, and Dukes, 2000) while others show no long-term effects (Rosenbaum and Hanson, 1998). One program that seems to have consistently good results is the Special Supplemental Food Program for Women, Infants, and Children (WIC). An evaluation revealed that WIC participants had fewer low birth-weight babies, a strong correlate of health problems. The results were not only good for the families involved, but the program even saved welfare funds that otherwise would have gone to treat the problems of the sick babies (Wholey, 1991).

Determine Which Programs Produce the Most Favorable Outcomes

Although a particular program may produce good outcomes, human services can be provided in a number of ways, some more effective than others. For example, numerous theories attempt to explain why some teenagers join urban gangs and commit crimes. It can be argued that the adolescents involved are merely seeking a substitute family, that the fruits of crime are the attraction, or that a gang offers protection from other gangs (see Gruber, 2001). These different theories suggest different approaches to efforts at keeping adolescents out of gangs. In a mental health setting, treatment alternatives include inpatient versus outpatient care, individual versus group therapy, and social cognitive versus behavioral approaches to psychotherapy. If the outcomes of various programs are roughly equivalent, the less expensive choice would be selected since that would permit more people to be served or additional services to be offered.

Select the Programs That Offer the Most Needed Types of Services

In addition to alternative approaches to achieving a specified outcome, many types of services might conceivably be offered. Unfortunately, a society cannot possibly provide all services that every person might want. Which is needed more—treatment of alcoholics in the workforce or park programs for potentially delinquent children? Evaluators seek to help government planners compare the benefits of programs aimed at the very different needs of a variety of potential beneficiaries. Traditionally such choices were made on the basis of a program supporter's political clout. Although political influence will continue to exist in a democracy, tools to compare different alternatives can assist in making ethical and socially just choices when resources are limited, as they usually are.

Provide Information to Maintain and Improve Quality

It is one thing to provide a program that benefits its participants and quite another thing to maintain the quality of a program over time. Evaluators have developed approaches to monitoring programs both to verify that services were delivered, satisfying the first obligation, and to assure clients and staff that program quality has been maintained.

Rather than show that a program had a beneficial effect when begun or that quality has been maintained, the new emphasis in evaluation concerns itself with seeking improvements in services. Continuous quality improvement has become a watchword in manufacturing firms (Dobyns and Crawford-Mason, 1991). Compared with Japanese manufacturers, U.S. firms were slower to adopt management practices that encourage frequent incremental improvements even though the techniques for detecting the need for such improvements were developed by an American, W. Edwards Deming, during the 1940s (Dobyns and Crawford-Mason, 1991). Although initially developed for quality improvement in manufacturing, these techniques are now being applied to education (Brigham, 1993; Fehr, 1999), medical services (Carey and Lloyd, 1995; Marszalek-Gaucher and Coffey, 1993), and mental health care (Eckert, 1994; Green and Newman, 1999; Mawhinney, 1992).

Watch for Unplanned Side Effects

Efforts to solve problems usually create some undesirable side effects (Sieber, 1981). For example, medications that relieve one health problem may create additional problems in other systems of the body; sometimes these side effects are minor, sometimes they require medical attention or a change in medication, and sometimes, though rarely, they are fatal. Patients and physicians must therefore weigh the dangers of side effects, neither minimizing their importance nor avoiding necessary treatments because of them. A parallel situation occurs in the area of educational and social service programs. Welfare policies can help people get through crises with dignity and regain their productive roles in society; on the other hand, welfare policies can create long-term dependency (McKnight, 1995). Programs to provide social support to isolated people can have negative effects that have typically been ignored according to Lincoln (2000). Special education classes permit children with unique needs to learn at a comfortable pace, yet being in such a class carries a stigma. Consequently, program planners seek to develop services that provide benefits but minimize negative side effects. At times, program advocates have denied that unwanted side effects have occurred, thus making it harder to improve the program. On the other hand, unforeseen side effects are occasionally positive: When people learn new skills, self-esteem often increases (Dawes, 1994; Felson, 1984).

Program evaluation can contribute to the well-being of society only if evaluators successfully meet their obligation to help government agencies and private organizations focus on important needs, plan effectively, monitor carefully, assess quality accurately and justly, nurture improved practices, and detect unwanted side effects.

COMMON TYPES OF PROGRAM EVALUATIONS

The primary goals of program evaluation, just discussed, can be met using a number of different types of program evaluations; the major ones involve studies of need, process, outcome, and efficiency.

Assess Needs of the Program Participants

An evaluation of need seeks to identify and measure the level of unmet needs within an organization or community (Gaber, 2000). Assessing unmet needs is a basic first step before any effective program planning can begin. Program planning involves the consideration of a variety of alternative approaches to meet needs. In selecting some alternatives and discarding others, planners engage in a form of program evaluation, one that occurs before the program is even begun. The close association between program planning and program evaluation is indicated in the title of the journal *Program Planning and Evaluation.*

As part of the assessment of need, evaluators may examine the socioeconomic profile of the community, the level of social problems within the community, and the agencies and institutions currently serving the community. Through close contact with residents and local leaders, evaluators can determine which aspects of a program are likely to be useful and which might be unacceptable, thus adding depth to the inferences drawn from statistical summaries suggesting critical unmet needs.

Examine the Process of Meeting the Needs

Once a program has been developed and begun, evaluators turn to the task of documenting the extent to which implementation has taken place, the nature of the people being served, and the degree to which the program operates as expected. Evaluations of process involve checking on the assumptions made while the program was being planned. Do the needs of the organization or community match what was believed during planning? Is there evidence to support the assessment of needs made during the planning stage? Do the activities carried out by the staff match the plans for the program? What evidence can be found that supports the theoretical assumptions made by the program planners? It is crucial to learn how a program actually operates before offering the same services at additional locations or with other populations.

The importance of verifying program implementation was evident when it was discovered that a Russian tractor factory said to have been a model of efficiency did not exist. Severe construction problems prevented it from ever being built. To avoid criticism for failure, those responsible for construction claimed that the factory was completed and even fabricated glowing production records ("Potemkin Factor," 1980).

Under normal situations the information necessary for an evaluation of process is available in the agency sponsoring the program; however, the information may be recorded in a way that is hard to use. For example, information on application forms often is not summarized, and records of actual services received may not permit easy analysis. In a later chapter on program monitoring and information systems, we illustrate some very simple methods of developing an information system for a human service setting. In addition to quantitative information, an evaluation of process may well benefit from unstructured interviews with people using and not using the service. Such qualitative information often provides points of view that neither evaluators nor service providers had considered.

Evaluators occasionally draw different conclusions about the degree to which a program has been implemented because they disagree about what constitutes the program. For example, the PUSH/Excel program, designed to raise the aspirations of inner-city youth through a variety of local initiatives, was unfavorably reviewed by its original evaluators. However, House (1988, 1990) argued that the evaluators treated PUSH/Excel as if it were a set of standardized services that could be offered at different sites. The original evaluators concluded that there was no national program when, in fact, the program was designed to encourage local initiatives. Since local initiatives are bound to differ from each other, no common criteria indicating successful implementation could be applied; however, this did not mean that there was no program.

Measure the Outcomes of the Program

If a study of implementation shows that a program has been implemented well and that people seek its services, an assessment of the program's outcome may become a focus of an evaluation. An evaluation of outcome can take on several levels of complexity. The most elementary level concerns the condition of those who have received services: Are program participants performing well? A more challenging evaluation would compare the performance of those in the program with those not receiving its services. An even more challenging evaluation would show that receiving the program's services caused a change for the better in the condition of those participating in the program (Boruch, 1997).

Although program managers hope that their programs will elicit positive changes in people, the causes of behavioral changes are difficult to pin down. For example, many people begin psychotherapy during a life crisis. If after several months of counseling they feel better, the change could be due to the counseling, the natural resolution of the crisis (or a combination of both), or something else entirely. In a work setting, a change in procedures may result in better morale because of increased efficiency or because the workers feel that management cares about their well-being. Or perhaps an improved national economic outlook reduced the workers' anxiety about possible job loss. Discovering the causes of behavioral changes requires sophisticated techniques since an organization must continue to provide services while the evaluation is being conducted. Experienced evaluators are not surprised by conflicts between evaluators gathering information and program staff providing services. In later chapters we suggest some approaches to minimize problems related to such conflicts.

Besides the limitations on the choice of research design, evaluators seeking to assess the outcome of a program often discover that people hold different opinions about what constitutes a successful outcome. A job-training program paying unemployed people to learn job skills may have been planned so that they can later obtain jobs with private companies. City officials may view the training as a reward for people who have worked in local election campaigns, and the trainees may view the program as a good, albeit temporary, job. Whose definition of outcome is to be used?

Assessing the maintenance of improvement creates another problem when evaluating outcomes. People leaving a drug rehabilitation program typically return to the same community that contributed to their problems in the first place. Despite their good intentions, people treated for alcoholism are often unable to withstand the social pressure of their peers. Changing long-standing behaviors is difficult. Although positive changes may be observed after a person's participation in a program, the changes may be only superficial and disappear in a matter of months, weeks, or days. If so, was the program a failure?

Integrate the Needs, Costs, and Outcomes

Even when evaluators can show that a program has helped participants, they must also deal with the question of costs. Just as a family must make choices in how a budget is spent, governments and agencies must select from those services that might be supported. A successful program that requires a large amount of resources simply may not be a good choice if a similar outcome can be achieved with markedly less cost. If an evaluator is asked to compare two or more programs designed to effect similar outcomes, efficiency can be assessed in a fairly straightforward manner; this would be called a cost-effectiveness analysis (Levin and McEwan, 2001). Real difficulties occur when evaluators are asked to compare the efficiency of programs designed to achieve different outcomes, sometimes for different groups of people. For example, should a university spend funds to reduce alcohol abuse among students or to increase the number of tutors available? Although competing purposes are seldom contrasted in such a stark fashion, no organization can do everything that might be worthwhile; choices have to be made.

Note that there is a logical sequence to these four general types of evaluations. Without measuring need, planning cannot be rational; without effective implementation, good outcomes cannot be expected; and without achieving good outcomes, there is no reason to worry about efficiency. A premature focus on an inappropriate evaluation question is likely to produce an evaluation with little value (Wholey, 1983).

ACTIVITIES OFTEN CONFUSED WITH PROGRAM EVALUATION

Sometimes it is easier to understand a concept when one understands what the concept does not include. Program evaluation is often confused with basic research, individual assessment, and program audits. Although these activities are valuable, when program evaluation work is confused with one of these other activities, the evaluation becomes all the more difficult to carry out.

Basic research concerns questions of theoretical interest, without regard to the information needs of people or organizations. In contrast, program evaluators gather information to help people improve their effectiveness, to assist administrators to make program-level decisions, and to enable interested parties to examine program effectiveness. Evaluators, of course, are very interested in theories of why a service might help its participants. Understanding theories helps in planning programs and selecting variables to observe. However, contributing to the development of theories can only be a delightful side benefit of a program evaluation. Evaluation findings should be relevant to the immediate or short-term needs of managers and must be timely. If program staff members believe that evaluators are collecting information primarily to serve their research interests, cooperation may well be lost.

Human service staff members often confuse program evaluation with individual assessment. Educational psychologists, personnel workers, and counseling psychologists administer intelligence, aptitude, interest, achievement, and personality tests for the purpose of evaluating a person's need for service or measuring qualifications for a job or a promotion. These activities are not part of the work of a program evaluator. In program evaluation, information about the level of job performance, educational achievement, or health may well be gathered. However, the purpose is not to diagnose individuals. Instead, the purpose is to learn how well a program is helping people improve on those variables.

Last, the methods and objectives of program evaluation differ from those used by program auditors examining government-sponsored programs to verify that they operate in compliance with laws and regulations. When Congress supports a program, it is important that the funds be spent as Congress intends. If the appropriation was for the enrichment of elementary schools, spending the funds for high school laboratories constitutes fraud. If 10,000 students were to be served, documentation of services for close to that many children ought to be available. Program evaluators are concerned that the program serve the right number of children, but in addition, evaluators would be particularly interested in how the services have affected the children.

The work of program auditors is closely related to accounting, whereas program evaluators tend to identify with education and other social sciences. Davis (1990) and Wisler (1996) point out that these two fields have moved toward each other in recent years because neither can give a complete picture of a program. Nevertheless, the different training and orientation of program auditors and program evaluators lead to differences in variables examined, emphases in analyses, and types of recommendations offered. If a program evaluator seeking to help a program make improvements in its services is viewed as a program auditor seeking to verify compliance with laws, it is easy to imagine that the evaluator will not have easy access to complete information.

DIFFERENT TYPES OF EVALUATIONS FOR DIFFERENT KINDS OF PROGRAMS

Evaluators who are sensitive to the needs of program staff members and sponsors realize that when designing a program evaluation, it is definitely wrong to assume that "one size fits all." Programs differ in many ways: There are great differences among the organizations that offer services, the needs of program participants require different types of services, and evaluations are needed for programs ranging from complex national efforts through those that are offered by one agency at one location.

Organizations Needing Program Evaluations

Education. Schools and colleges should regularly evaluate the quality of the education provided to students as well as special services such as enrichment and remedial programs (Astin, 1993). Calls for accountability for student learning led to the No Child Left Behind Act of 2002. Higher education accrediting bodies require colleges to gather information that will reflect how students have benefitted from attendance (McMurtrie, 2000; Schuh and Upcraft, 2001).

Health care. The requirements to monitor quality of treatment and to develop improvements in care and the results of care have increased for hospitals and outpatient clinics. In order for facilities to qualify for continued accreditation, health care facilities must now demonstrate that high quality care is being provided and that improvements are being made (Carey and Lloyd, 1995; Hsia, 2003).

Criminal justice. The best ways to organize police forces, the more effective types of probation services, and better approaches to pretrial negotiations should be found and implemented. Criminal justice agencies are politically sensitive and function under more restrictive regulations than most other organizations in our society; this makes designing changes and evaluating those changes complicated (see Wilson, Gallagher, and MacKenzie, 2000).

Business and industry. A quality revolution has swept through American businesses and industries. Programs such as Total Quality Management and Continuous Quality Improvement have become central to the survival of manufacturing concerns (Dobyns and Crawford-Mason, 1991). Although some of the needs of for-profit organizations are quite different from those of non-profit service organizations, many of the concepts being implemented have clear parallels to the tools that program evaluators have developed for human service organizations (Morell, 2000).

Government. Governmental agencies at all levels sponsor many services to citizens; these services range from wetlands preservation to school lunches to space exploration. Citizens and organizations are asking for greater levels of accountability from government agencies (Wye and Sonnichsen, 1992). The Government Performance and Results Act (GPRA) of 1993 was an attempt to improve the effectiveness of agencies of the U.S. federal government by requiring reports showing the level of activities and the degree to which agencies were meeting their assigned objectives (Levine and Helper, 1995). The degree to which the act itself is effective is a controversial issue (Bernstein, 1999; Perrin, 1998). Such efforts by governments are widespread (Russon and Russon, 2005).

Time Frames of Needs

Short-term needs. Many programs are set up to help people in crises. For example, health care is needed for injuries or illnesses, and emotional and financial support are often needed after a crime, a natural disaster, or a home fire. Some educational services are designed to meet specific needs of employees required to learn new skills. To be effective, such services should be available on short notice.

Long-term needs. To meet some needs, services must be available for a long period of time. Children need education for many years. Psychotherapy, treatment for chronic illnesses, training for prison inmates, and rehabilitation for alcoholism and drug abuse are examples of programs that focus on problems that cannot be resolved in a short time period.

Potential needs. Ideally, potential problems can be averted. Preventive programs are supported so that problems can be avoided or at least postponed. Immunization, health education, or business security programs are judged by the degree problems do not occur. Clearly, evaluations of prevention programs must differ from evaluations of programs developed to relieve current problems.

Extensiveness of Programs

Some programs are offered to small groups of people with similar needs, others are developed for use at many sites throughout a county or a state, and yet others are written into federal laws to be offered throughout a nation. Although tools useful in program evaluation apply to evaluations carried out at all levels, there are considerable differences between an evaluation of a day hospital program in Memorial Hospital and an evaluation of psychiatric services supported by Medicaid. Although it would be quite reasonable for these evaluations to use some of the same measures of adjustment, the decisions faced by the administrators of the local program differ so greatly from those faced by Medicaid managers that the evaluations must differ in scale, focus, and type of recommendations.

We have concentrated our discussions throughout this text on evaluations of smaller programs likely to be encountered by evaluators working for school districts, hospitals, personnel departments, social service agencies, city or state governments, and so on. Although some national programs are mentioned, the focus on smaller programs is useful in an introductory text because most readers are more familiar with local government or educational programs than they are with national programs. Johnston (1983) envisioned evaluators working with local agencies carrying the major responsibilities for program evaluation as the number of national evaluation projects decreased. Political trends, an appreciation of the difficulties in carrying out and interpreting national-level program evaluations (Lincoln, 1990a), and attention to incremental program improvement (Vermillion and Pfeiffer, 1993) have led to the situation Johnston anticipated. Organizations with support from local governments, foundations, and federal agencies are expected to carry out program evaluations and submit them to the funding source.

For studies done at a local level, statistical procedures seldom need to be particularly complicated partially because many administrators find statistics to be an incomprehensible—if not intimidating—topic. Complicated analyses require data from larger numbers of people than are usually available to evaluators working with local organizations. Evaluators can often show how to improve data summaries and presentations so that program information can be used to answer questions faced by program administrators.

Purpose of Program Evaluation

There is only one overall purpose for program evaluation activities: contributing to the provision of quality services to people in need. Program evaluation contributes to quality services by providing feedback from program activities and outcomes to those who can make changes in programs or who decide which services are to be offered. Without feedback, human service programs (indeed, any activity) cannot be carried out effectively. Our bodily processes require feedback systems; similarly, feedback on behavior in organizations is also crucial for the success of an organization. Delayed feedback, not clearly associated with the behavior being examined, is not very informative. Some writers have argued that environmental problems are hard to solve because of the long delay between environmentally destructive activities and feedback indicating a weakening of natural systems (Meadows and Perelman, 1973).

Figure 1.1 illustrates the place of program evaluation as a feedback loop for a human service program. Assessing needs, measuring the implementation of programs to meet those needs, evaluating the achievement of carefully formed goals and objectives, and comparing the level of outcome with the costs involved relative to similar programs serve to provide information from which to develop program improvements (Wholey, 1991; Zammuto, 1982) or to make wise choices among possible programs (Levin and McEwan, 2001). Michael Hendricks' comments on the role of evaluation are given in Evaluator Profile 1.

Feedback can be provided for different purposes. First, evaluations can strengthen the plans for services and their delivery in order to improve the outcomes of programs or to increase the efficiency of programs; such evaluations are called formative evaluations (Scriven, 1967) because they are designed to help form the programs themselves. Second, evaluations can help us decide whether a program should be started, continued, or chosen from two or more alternatives; such evaluations are called summative evaluations (Chambers, 1994; Scriven, 1967). There is a finality to summative evaluations;

FIGURE 1.1   The place of evaluation as a feedback loop for a human service program.

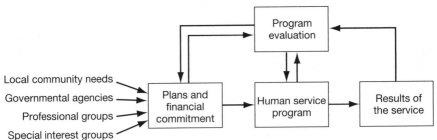

Michael Hendricks: The Role of Program Evaluators

Michael Hendricks is an independent evaluation consultant in Bethesda, Maryland specializing in program evaluation, organizational development, and training. Previously, he was with the Office of Inspector General of the U.S. Department of Health and Human Services. His Ph.D. is in Social Psychology (Northwestern University).

In the light of his wide experiences in program evaluation, Dr. Hendricks was asked about what changes in evaluation he had seen. He answered: "I'm an incurable optimist, but I really do think that the field has blossomed and is still blossoming. . . From a fairly narrow technical specialty which basically wrote 'report cards' on programs, we've grown to fill many different roles during all phases of a program—planning, implementation, operationalization, as well as after (the program was over). We have a much more sophisticated understanding of the importance of the environment, and, . . . we recognize much more the need to be useful."

Adapted from: Sporn, D. L. 1989b. A conversation with Michael Hendricks. *Evaluation Practice*, *10* (3), 18–24.

once the value and worth of the program have been assessed, the program might be discontinued. In actuality, very few single evaluations determine whether or not a program will be continued (Cook, Leviton, and Shadish, 1985). Many sources of information about programs are available to administrators, legislators, and community leaders. Because program evaluation is only one of these sources, evaluators are not surprised when clear evaluation findings are not followed by specific decisions. Chelimsky (1997) uses the terms "evaluation for development" and "evaluation for accountability" to refer to the formative and summative purposes, respectively.

Once a program has been carefully refined using feedback from formative evaluations and found to be effective using a summative evaluation, frequent feedback is still needed to maintain the quality of the program. This third form of evaluation is called monitoring; its purpose is quality assurance (Schwartz and Mayne, 2005; Wholey, 1999). This can be as simple as checking the speedometer from time to time while on a highway and as complicated as examining how international aid is used (Svensson, 1997). Monitoring critical process and outcome variables to verify that an effective program stays effective is a crucial activity after programs have been successfully implemented (Lee and Walsh, 2004). Furthermore, monitoring can be expected to isolate problems occurring when the social environment changes. As efforts are made to resolve those problems, monitoring feedback takes on a formative function as well. If problems cannot be resolved, monitoring can come to serve a summative purpose also.

Some evaluations are also carried out to learn about programs; Chelimsky (1997) calls this "evaluation for knowledge." This purpose is seldom part of the work of evaluators working on specific programs. Their work might be used by others to deepen our understanding of, for example, rehabilitation programs, but this occurs only after evaluations are completed and shared with others. We recognize the need to develop better understandings of programs and intervention strategies; however, this text does not focus on such types of evaluation because they involve more ambitious undertakings than most evaluators deal with regularly.

THE ROLES OF EVALUATORS

A Variety of Work Settings

Most program evaluators are employed by one of three types of organizations. Some work as internal evaluators for the agencies providing the services to be evaluated. In this situation, an evaluator should not work directly under the manager of the service being studied, since explicit or implicit pressure to provide favorable summative evaluations would be very severe (Cook, Leviton, and Shadish, 1985). However, working for the central administration of a large organization that sponsors the services being evaluated helps to insulate the internal evaluator from such pressure.

Other evaluators are employed by governmental or regulatory agencies. The U.S. Government Accountability Office, for example, carries out many evaluations at the request of members of Congress. GAO reports can influence any area of federal legislation. The Office of Inspector General completes evaluations for the Secretary of Health and Human Services. Some states have created evaluation units, often in the offices of the state auditor. The act creating the Office of the Legislative Auditor in Minnesota stated that this office is to

> ... determine the degree to which the activities and programs entered into or funded by the state are accomplishing their goals and objectives, including the evaluation of goals and objectives, measurement of program results and effectiveness, alternative means of achieving the same results, and efficiency in the allocation of resources ("Spotlight," 1982, p. 2).

In 2001 the Office issued a report on insurance for behavioral health care in Minnesota; the report included data on need, processes, outcomes, and costs, all issues central to program evaluation (Office of the Legislative Auditor, 2001). Adding evaluation to the job of auditors is an example of the trends to merge the activities of financial auditing with program evaluation described by Davis (1990) and Wisler (1996). Since states have responsibilities in the areas of education, health care, welfare, safety, and transportation, evaluators in state offices work on a variety of topics. Since government-sponsored programs have supporters who carefully guard their turf, evaluations of government-based programs can be "explosive" (Nienstedt and Halemba, 1986).

Private research firms are a third common work setting for program evaluators. Some firms are very large; others are small enough to be run from the evaluator's home. Such firms submit proposals in response to Requests for Proposals announcing competitions for contracts to evaluate government-funded or privately funded programs. Open information sessions are held for potential evaluators to learn about what is needed. Evaluators then submit proposals that are judged on the basis of cost, the evaluator's professional reputation, and the quality of the methods proposed. Such proposals are evaluated in much the same way as are competitive bids for construction projects: A contract to do the project is offered to the firm or evaluator group that has submitted the highest quality proposal within the allotted budget. Some university faculty members conduct evaluations independently; they work in much the same way as evaluators who work with research firms.

In addition to professional evaluators, many individuals holding positions in educational, personnel, medical, training, rehabilitation, and corrections organizations perform evaluations as part of their responsibilities. Readers who currently fill or intend to seek positions in such settings may find that the concepts and methods presented in this text are valuable in their work even if they never have a position labeled "evaluator."

Comparison of Internal and External Evaluators

There are two primary ways evaluators relate to organizations needing an evaluation services: (1) Evaluators can work for the organization itself and do a variety of evaluations in that setting, or (2) they can work for a research firm, a university, or a government agency to evaluate a specific program. In this book, the terms internal evaluator and external evaluator refer to these two types of evaluators, respectively. Although there are great similarities in what all evaluators do, the affiliation of an evaluator has implications for the manner in which evaluations are done.

Factors related to competence. In terms of knowledge about a program, internal evaluators have an advantage since they have better access to program directors and to the administrators of the organization. A person who is physically present on a regular basis is likely to see the program in action, to know its staff, and to learn about its reputation from other people in an organization. Such information is unavailable to an external evaluator. The more that is known about the actual operation of programs, the easier it is to ask relevant questions during the planning and interpretation of evaluations.

The technical expertise of an evaluator is important. An internal evaluator often works with a small group of two or three; some evaluators work alone. An external evaluator, however, can often draw upon the resources of a greater number of people, some of whom are very skilled in sampling, qualitative analysis, or statistics. Some independent evaluators, however, essentially work alone and do not have access to such resources.

A different facet of the question of technical expertise is suggested by the need to perform evaluations of programs in different areas of an organization. Moving from topic to topic is stimulating; however, there is also a risk that inexperience with the services being evaluated could limit an internal evaluator's insight into the most crucial issues involved in some of the programs. By selecting external evaluators with experience in the type of program being evaluated, organizations might avoid errors due to inexperience.

Personal qualities. In addition to technical competence, an evaluator's personal qualities are also important. Evaluators can do more effective work if they are objective and fair, trusted by administrators, and concerned that program improvements be encouraged. Being well known and, let us hope, having been found worthy of trust (Taut and Alkin, 2003), internal evaluators usually find program directors and staff more willing to devote time to the evaluation, to admit problems, and to share confidences than they would be with an evaluator not affiliated with the organization. Being trusted increases the likelihood that a competent evaluator can fill the organizational educator role suggested by Cronbach (1980). Since credibility can be easily lost, evaluators avoid acting in ways that might suggest that they have allowed personal biases to determine their conclusions.

An internal evaluator can also be expected to want to improve the organization sponsoring the program and paying the evaluator's salary. External evaluators, being less dependent on the organization sponsoring the program, might not have the same level of commitment to working for program improvements. On the other hand, being dependent on the organization could affect the objectivity of an evaluator. Knowing program directors and staff members might make it difficult for an internal evaluator to remain objective (Scriven, 1997a); it is not easy to criticize a friend. An external evaluator, however, is less likely to experience conflicting pressures when an evaluation reveals problems in a program. Internal evaluators might find it easier to remain objective if they remember that their value to an organization depends on their work being credible. Developing a reputation for tackling sensitive issues is somewhat easier when evaluators emphasize that most deficiencies in programs are due to system problems rather than personal inadequacies. Deming (1986), an early champion of the quality revolution in industry, insisted that 85 percent of problems in workplaces are due to limitations in organizational procedures or work setting designs and 15 percent due to staff problems. Since many people mistakenly believe that evaluations focus on finding bad apples, evaluators should refer to Deming's point often because acting on that assumption will help them maintain their objectivity and develop their credibility with others in the organization.

Factors related to the purpose of an evaluation. Earlier in this chapter the purposes of evaluation were discussed—formative, summative, and quality assurance. Both internal evaluators and external evaluators can perform all types of evaluations; however, internal evaluators may have an advantage in performing formative and quality assurance evaluations. This seems true because such evaluations cannot lead to a traumatic decision to end a program. In fact, the internal evaluator's rapport with managers and staff may encourage nondefensive communications, which are essential if avenues to improve programs are to be found. If, in contrast, a summative evaluation is wanted because support for a program might be withdrawn, it may be best if an external evaluator is used instead of an internal evaluator. For example, if a small elementary school district knows that it must close one of three schools, it may be wise to have an external evaluator perform an evaluation of the schools and select the one to close. No matter which one is selected, some residents will object. It could be hard for an administrator to serve in the school district if a sizable portion of the residents were dissatisfied with the decision; however, the external evaluator need never set foot in the school district again.

Evaluation and Service

An evaluator's job falls somewhere between the role of the social scientist concerned about theory, the design of research, and the analysis of data (but for the most part uninvolved with the delivery of services) and the role of the practitioner dealing with people in need (but seldom interested or trained in the methods of data collection and analysis). Evaluators are able to use the language and tools of the research scientist; however, they must also be sensitive to the concerns and style of the service delivery staff. In addition, evaluators are called upon to communicate with organization administrators who have different priorities, such as balancing a budget and weighing competing demands for services. Since the role of program evaluator is still fairly new, it is likely that the evaluator will at times seem out of step with everyone.

Participating in such a new field has advantages and disadvantages. The advantages include the intellectual stimulation provided by exposure to people serving various roles in human service settings and the satisfaction of seeing research methods used in ways that can benefit people. The disadvantages include being viewed as intrusive and unnecessary by some service delivery personnel. The most effective evaluators show that they are allies of service providers, while at the same time asking challenging questions and insisting that answers be supported by data.

Of course, at times even the most skilled evaluator will be in conflict with an organization. It was reported that some military planners ignored the findings of their own research and those of internal evaluators when ambitious officers wanted their pet projects funded (Isaacson, 1983). Campbell (1983), one of the early leaders in evaluation, became particularly concerned about the possibility that the perceived threat of evaluation would make it impossible to collect data of sufficient validity to draw useful conclusions. In contrast, more recent observers (Johnston, 1983; Lincoln, 1990a, McClintock, 1983; Vermillion and Pfeiffer, 1993) predict that staff members themselves will more frequently use evaluation methods to develop improvements in programs. When evaluation systems are developed that clearly distinguish data collected for the purpose of program improvement from individual performance appraisals for salary increases (Astin, 1993), conflicts among evaluation, service delivery, and administration may be minimized. That happy day has not yet come, but when evaluation is built into program management and all agree that program improvement is both possible and desirable, the potential for conflict will be reduced (Donaldson, Gooler, and Scriven, 2002).

Evaluation and Related Activities of Organizations

Some agencies may combine evaluation with another activity of the agency. Five functions that sometimes include evaluation are research, education and staff development, auditing, planning, and human resources.

Research. Some human service organizations routinely sponsor research directly with operating funds or indirectly through grants. For example, a police department was awarded a grant to study the effect of providing emotional support to victims of crimes. The social scientists responsible for such research would be excellent colleagues of an evaluator. University-affiliated hospitals carry on research; researchers working with psychiatric problems or emotional issues related to medical care deal with research problems sufficiently similar to those faced by evaluators to serve as colleagues.

Education and staff development. Some organizations have joined the functions of education and evaluation. There is a long-standing precedent for this marriage in educational psychology. New study materials and curricula are evaluated before being widely used by school districts. Universities have combined faculty development and program evaluation into one office. Many organizations besides schools sponsor educational programs that need monitoring. For example, industries have developed major educational programs to train employees to qualify for more responsible positions.

Auditing. As mentioned earlier in this chapter, some states have combined the functions of program evaluation and program oversight often carried out by state auditors. There are important differences in the assumptions and roles of auditors and evaluators, but there is precedent for coordinating these efforts in the inspector general offices in the federal and state governments.

Planning. Planning is an activity in which people with skills in program evaluation are needed because many service providers are not data oriented, feel uncomfortable constructing surveys, and may be unable to analyze the information obtained. Megan Deiger's comments on her first job in program evaluation, given in Evaluator Profile 2, show this connection between planning

EVALUATOR PROFILE 2

Megan Deiger: Getting Started in Program Evaluation

During her graduate program, Megan Deiger served as Summer Intern in the Policy and Planning Group of the Teachers Academy for Mathematics and Science, a Chicago-based center for the improvement of public education. Dr. Deiger earned her Ph.D. in Applied Social Psychology from Loyola University Chicago.

When asked about her work, she commented: "Working in the Policy and Planning Group has been a wonderful introduction to the world of program evaluation. After having finished my first course in program evaluation, I was thrilled to encounter the Academy's online* advertisement for a summer quantitative researcher. In addition to internal evaluations, the Academy enlists its Policy and Planning Group to analyze and interpret relevant data concerning the efficacy and betterment of the program. My first project was one in which my colleagues and I examined the effect of a student's mobility, or movement from school to school, on his or her academic achievement. The project allowed me to see firsthand the ways in which qualitative and quantitative data can compliment one another."

*Dr. Deiger found the position notice on EVALTALK, the Internet discussion group sponsored by the American Evaluation Association (AEA). Directions for joining EVALTALK are given on AEA's home page (www.eval.org).

and evaluation. Evaluators can contribute to the task of estimating the level of community acceptance. Sometimes evaluators can help planners simply by posing probing questions about the assumptions implicit in the plan or about the steps involved in its implementation.

Human resources. Large businesses have offices of human resources. The office oversees all hiring, compensation, and professional development of employees. Policy development, compensation plans, training programs, and management effectiveness seminars all require evaluation if an organization is to be as effective as possible.

Summary and Preview

This chapter outlines the major questions and purposes of program evaluation: assess unmet need, document implementation, measure results, compare alternative programs in terms of the best results and the most needed services, provide information to maintain and develop quality, and detect negative side effects. Such activities are undertaken to help plan and refine programs, to assess their worth, and to make corrections in ongoing services. Some ways in which evaluators fit into the activities of agencies are described.

Chapter 2 deals with steps in planning an evaluation. Working with program staff and sponsors will often reveal that some people fear program evaluations; when an evaluation must have the cooperation of staff, it is necessary to allay these fears before beginning.

Study Questions

1. One of the interesting aspects of program evaluation is its relevance to a variety of activities and agencies. Gather some examples of activities related to program evaluation from newspapers or news magazines. You might find material on medical care, education, or a public policy in any area. The material might concern advocacy of new proposals or criticisms of current activities. Consider what information might illuminate the debates.

2. Illustrate how program evaluation activities could be applied in an organization with which you are familiar.

3. List the advantages and disadvantages of making program evaluation a part of human service delivery systems. Save your lists; when you are finished with the course, consider how you might change them.

4. Some people have suggested that while people want to believe that something is being done about social problems, most people don't really care if the programs have a measurable impact on the problems. In other words, social programs are symbols, not real efforts. Consider the validity of such comments in the context of the reports you found in response to the first question.

5. Compare your ideas on evaluating the Sexual Assault Prevention Program mentioned in the introductory paragraph of this chapter with those of other students. What reasons lie behind different choices of outcomes considered relevant?

Additional Resource

STUFFLEBEAM, D. L. 2001. Evaluation models. *New Directions for Evaluation, no. 89.* San Francisco: Jossey-Bass.

This work is a compact presentation of many different approaches to program evaluation. Stufflebeam provides an overview of 22 models of program evaluation. He then compares the different approaches on numerous characteristics as he seeks to find strengths and weakness of the models.

Planning an Evaluation

P reparation precedes production; it is often harder to plan well than to follow a good plan. Experienced evaluators know that the time put into planning an evaluation is well spent. Program evaluations begin in a variety of ways: Program personnel may initiate an evaluation, the central administration or a funding agency may require an evaluation, an internal evaluation team may suggest an evaluation of a program, or public dissatisfaction might prompt calls for evaluation. Regardless of who initiates an evaluation, evaluators need to become familiar with the nature of the program, the people served, and the goals and structure of the program, and, above all, learn why an evaluation is being considered. Evaluators seek to meet with program personnel, program sponsors, and groups that may question the need for an evaluation. Then, in consultation with these groups, evaluators must decide whether it is appropriate to evaluate the program. If these initial discussions reveal that an evaluation would be useful, consideration is given to the timing of an evaluation, the manner of conducting it, and its costs.

In the first part of this chapter, we provide an overview of major models of program evaluation. Next we outline the approximate sequence and manner in which issues can be addressed, identifying the steps to be taken between the time of the initial proposal and the beginning of data collection. The time and effort devoted to completing each step varies, depending on the complexity of the program, the relationship of the evaluator to the program personnel and sponsors, and the urgency of time constraints. Some steps, such as selecting or developing measures, are major tasks in themselves. Chapter 3 treats the complicated and sensitive issue of specifying the criteria that are to be used to decide whether a program has been implemented as planned, or shows the level of effectiveness that is desired. Chapter 4 deals with the more technical questions of the qualities of good measures of the criteria selected for assessment.

AN OVERVIEW OF EVALUATION MODELS

A number of different approaches to evaluation have been put forward to guide the planning and implementation of program evaluations. At times, disagreements over the best way to carry out an evaluation have been based on conflicting, unexamined assumptions about the best or proper way to evaluate a program. This overview highlights some of these assumptions. Each of the models discussed includes emphases that are valid aspects of program evaluation. One value of thinking about models lies in developing an appreciation of the range of questions evaluators can consider. The specific questions being addressed by an evaluation or the specific aspects of the program setting often make one or another of the models especially useful. It is crucial for evaluators and stakeholders to avoid selecting a model as the approach to use before thoroughly analyzing the setting and the questions that are to be answered by the evaluation. Most evaluations, in fact, use features from several of the models. Readers should not view the order in which these models are discussed as indicating a progression on any single dimension. Many of these descriptions have been adapted from House (1980), Scriven (1991), Shadish, Cook, and Leviton (1991), Stufflebeam, Madaus, and Kellaghan (2000), and Stufflebeam (2001).

The Traditional Model

In the not-very-distant past, those who provided services in schools, hospitals, or justice systems were free to work as they felt best, with few concerns about formal evaluation of the results of their efforts. Evaluations of their work were confined to impressionistic evaluations made informally by supervisors or, in the case of physicians, only self-evaluations were made. It is not surprising that such evaluations tended to serve the interests of the organization providing the service and did little to challenge the program directors and staff. This is not to say that human service professionals were dishonest or uninterested in providing quality care or education, but without the disciplined analysis encouraged by formal models of evaluation, cognitive biases (Heath et al., 1994; Kahneman, Slovic, and Tversky, 1982) may have influenced even well-intentioned informal evaluators.

Social Science Research Model

In an effort to make evaluations more rigorous and to control for self-serving biases, some evaluators came to view program evaluation as a specialized form of social science research: The way to determine a program's degree of success was to form two random groups, providing one with a service and using the other as a control group. After the program was completed, the members of both groups were observed or they described themselves on appropriate dependent variables. Boruch (1997) argues that experimental approaches have great promise when applied faithfully. However, in program evaluation contexts, experimental designs were analyzed in the same way as laboratory research is and, consequently, promising programs were labeled as failures because sample sizes were too small for the level of impact realistically attainable. The failure was often on the part of the evaluator, not the program (Lipsey, 1990). The social science approach to program evaluation served well to introduce greater rigor and objectivity into program evaluation, but its inherent limitations in applied settings and the potential for misuse have become evident. More attention will be paid to these issues in later chapters.

Industrial Inspection Model

An approach to evaluation sometimes used in manufacturing depends on inspecting the product at the end of the production line. When problems are found, the item is fixed before it is delivered to customers (Dobyns and Crawford-Mason, 1991). This approach is inefficient and leads to high costs; it is usually less expensive to do the job right the first time. In some ways, this model is similar to using a single examination after four years of unevaluated work to determine whether a student merits a college degree. Although a negative evaluation reveals that something is wrong, the inspection model does not provide information soon enough to correct problems that will ultimately yield a defective product (or a less than well-functioning client). It is easy to see that such an approach is very inefficient as an approach to making improvements to a program, yet evaluators often discover that many program managers mistakenly assume that evaluations are carried out using the industrial inspection model.

Black Box Evaluation

Black box (or closed box) evaluation refers to those evaluations that examine the output of a program without examining its internal operation. Other names for this approach are the consumer model or product evaluation (Scriven, 1994). In some situations this is precisely the form of evaluation that is needed. Before purchasing a car, many people examine *Consumer Reports*, a magazine reporting tests of consumer products. Since car buyers are not in a position to correct the faults of automobiles, knowing why a transmission shifts roughly or why an engine is hard to start on cold mornings is irrelevant. Consumers need to know which cars perform better than others, not why. Black box evaluations serve well when consumers evaluate manufactured objects like cars or TVs. Such evaluations do not serve well when evaluating social programs for which an evaluation is expected to lead to program improvement.

Objectives-Based Evaluation

In an effort to design an evaluation for a specific program, some approaches emphasize working with clearly stated program goals and objectives so that the degree to which such goals and objectives are achieved can be measured. This has been the most prevalent model used for program evaluation (Stufflebeam, 2001). Examining goals and objectives seems to be an essential aspect of evaluation; it is important to judge a program relative to its particular structure and what it is designed to achieve. However, some evaluators become so focused on the stated goals that they neglect to examine why programs succeed or fail, to consider any additional positive effects or undesired side effects of the programs, or to ask whether the goals were the best ones for the people served.

Goal-Free Evaluation

An attempt to avoid a premature focus on goals led to the suggestion that evaluators work more effectively if they do not know the stated goals of a program (Scriven, 1973). Evaluators who know the goals of the program might unintentionally focus on information that supports the goals and not observe how the program is actually administered or assess the total impact on the program's clients. A goal-free evaluator spends a considerable amount of time studying the program as administered, the staff, the clients, the setting, and the records to identify all the positive and negative impacts of the program. The evaluator observes in a way that is similar to how an anthropologist works while living in a particular culture for the first time. Later the program staff and financial supporters decide whether the evaluator's findings reveal that the program meets the needs of the clients. There is much to recommend about this approach; however, it would be expensive and its open-ended nature would make it very threatening to staff members.

Fiscal Evaluation

Potentially, the most objective evaluations require calculations of the financial investment needed to support a program and the return on that investment (Levin and McEwan, 2001). When a company introduces laborsaving machines, it expects to save on labor costs or to increase output in order to pay for the equipment and provide a return on the funds invested. When deciding to make an investment, planners project how the change may affect the amount of money coming into the organization. While such projections cannot be completely accurate, the final evaluation of the investment is based strictly on financial considerations. Fiscal evaluations remind evaluators that services require resources and that costs can never be ignored. On the other hand, many decisions about selecting the services to offer cannot be made strictly in a bottom-line manner since it is hard to place dollar values on pain relief for an ill patient or a child's improved skill in multiplying fractions.

Accountability Model

The accountability or audit models developed from fiscal evaluations (Davis, 1990; Wisler, 1996). Publicly funded programs must devote resources to the activities that were mandated when the programs were approved. Large programs, such as most federally funded programs, involve many managers, in numerous sites, scattered across many regions. The Office of Inspector General (IG) of the U.S. Department of Health and Human Services is the evaluation and audit arm of the department's Secretary. The IG's primary mission is to verify that the federal government's funds support effective services for the groups identified in the legislation that created the service. Because accountability evaluations focus so much on compliance with regulations, they cannot be applied universally.

Expert Opinion Model

An approach that seeks to remove self-serving biases in the traditional approach and to avoid the limitations of black box and fiscal evaluations involves having experts examine the program. Art and literary criticism are forms of evaluation in which a learned person carefully examines a work to render a judgment about its quality. Although art criticism is subjective, expert opinion evaluation can make use of objective data. Observations made in post-occupancy evaluations of recently completed buildings include how well buildings were designed and constructed, how efficiently the heating and air-conditioning systems functioned, and whether a building was conducive to effective work (Bechtel, 1997). Some decisions in such studies are based on objective, quantified information as well as qualitative impressions. Expert opinions are often used when the entity being evaluated is large, complex, and unique. University accreditation decisions are based on the recommendations of a team of experts who examine quantitative records, inspect buildings, and talk with students, administrators, staff, and faculty (see, for example, Middle States Commission on Higher Education, 2000). Since a set of numbers cannot reveal the overall quality of a college, expert opinion is used.

Naturalistic or Qualitative Model

When evaluators want to develop a deep and thorough understanding of a program, they sometimes use qualitative methods to conduct a naturalistic evaluation (Patton, 2002; Shaw, 1999). In doing so, the evaluator becomes the data-gathering instrument, not surveys or records. By personally observing all phases of the program and holding detailed conversation with stakeholders, the evaluator seeks to gain a rich understanding of the program, its clients, and the social environment. Because of the detail included, reports often become quite lengthy. Regardless of the overall model used, personal observations are often necessary to understand the meaning of numerical information about programs.

Success Case Method

Most evaluations are planned to gather information from all or a random selection of participants in a program. In some situations a very different approach is taken. It might be very informative to seek detailed information from those participants who have benefitted the most from the program. Those people, the successes, might well provide clues about how others could benefit as well. This approach has been called the success case method (Brinkerhoff, 2003). It would be important that one distinguish those who participated in the program faithfully and therefore succeeded from those who entered the program already equipped to succeed. In a classroom setting, students who were well-prepared when they started a program may be successful, but less well-prepared students may well have gained more relative to their starting point. This suggests that applied naively, the success case method could tempt program managers to engage in "creaming," tailoring the program to those most likely to succeed rather than to those most in need of the program.

Empowerment Evaluation

Some evaluators have sought to complete program evaluations in a way that helps the people for whom a service has been developed to become more competent in dealing with community problems and public and private agencies (Fetterman, Kaftarian, and Wandersman, 1996). The name is a little misleading because it implies that the evaluator is somehow responsible for giving power to the clients of programs; in fact, evaluators cannot give power to anyone. The point of the empowerment model is to discourage evaluators from collecting data without close contact with the community stakeholders. Instead, evaluators invite stakeholders to participate actively and assist them to gain skills from the process. It is hoped that after the evaluation, the clients will be more informed citizens, possess more skills, and have greater self-confidence enabling them to work at improving their own families and communities. There are some who argue that the validity of this approach to evaluation can be easily compromised (for example, Scriven, 1997b).

Theory-Driven Evaluation

An approach to evaluation that is another response to the difficulty of conducting program evaluations that meet the criteria of carefully controlled research is called the theory-driven model (Chen, 1994; Donaldson, 2003).

Theory-driven evaluations are based on a careful description of the services to be offered to people in need. Then, the ways these services are expected to change the participants are specified. Finally, the outcomes the program is expected to affect are listed. The analysis consists of discovering the relationships (a) among the services and the characteristics of participants, (b) among the services and the immediate changes, and (c) among immediate changes and outcome variables. Complex correlational techniques are used (Lipsey and Cordray, 2000). Most evaluators strongly endorse examining these associations among variables; however, critics argue that such analyses are not as valid as evaluations involving random assignment to program groups and control groups (Cook, 2000).

An Improvement-Focused Approach

The authors have adopted an approach to evaluation in which program improvement is the focus rather than particular methodologies. Improvements can be made in programs when discrepancies are noted between what is observed and what was planned, projected, or needed. Evaluators help program staff to discover discrepancies between program objectives and the needs of the target population, between program implementation and program plans, between expectations of the target population and the services actually delivered, or between outcomes achieved and outcomes projected. Finding discrepancies is not a perverse trait of evaluators. If the point of evaluation is to improve the program—which we think is nearly always the point—then discrepancies provide a place to seek to effect improvements. To learn how to improve a program, staff members need to discover what has been occurred as planned and what has not: Do the clients have needs that were anticipated or different ones? Do the staff have the needed skills or has it been difficult to teach the staff needed skills? Has the promised support materialized? Does the operation of the program suggest that the conceptual basis of the program is sound or that it can be improved? To deal with such questions, objective information is needed, but such information should be interpreted using qualitative information as well. We have found that personal observations provide direction in selecting what to measure and in forming an integrated understanding of the program and its effects.

The improvement-focused approach—we believe—best meets the criteria necessary for effective evaluation: serving the needs of stakeholders, providing valid information, and offering an alternative point of view to those doing the really hard work of serving program participants. To carry this off without threatening the staff is the most challenging aspect of program evaluation. This approach is not to be interpreted as implying that evaluators are not to celebrate successes. After all, evaluators are to look for merit and worth in programs. Managers of programs are going to pay close attention to evaluation reports when evaluators demonstrate that they recognize the strengths of programs, not just the ways in which the program has fallen short and can be improved.

We now turn to the practical steps of planning a program evaluation. Our comments are particularly aimed at the work of an internal evaluator; however, these steps must be followed by external evaluators in similar ways.

STEPS IN PREPARING TO CONDUCT AN EVALUATION

Before discussing steps in planning an evaluation, we want to stress that when working in an applied setting with emotionally sensitive issues—like health, justice, and work success—it is necessary that the communication be clear and agreements made be explicit. Oral agreements between evaluators and administrators should be followed up with memos outlining the discussion and the evaluator's understanding of the agreements. Depending on memory is very unwise; evaluators need to recognize that since a program administrator deals with many problems during each day, the evaluation merits the administrator's attention during only brief moments during a week. Putting an agreement on paper serves to remind all parties about the plans and is a record if disagreements occur later. Furthermore, seeing developing plans described on paper can suggest implications that neither evaluators nor administrators had considered previously.

Identify the Program and Its Stakeholders

Obtain a complete program description. The first thing effective evaluators do is obtain descriptions of the program. It makes quite a difference whether an evaluation is proposed for a new program or a well-established one; whether it is locally managed or offered at many sites; whether people seek to participate voluntarily or are assigned to complete it; whether participants are functional or suffer cognitive, emotional, or physical problems; whether it serves 25 or 25,000 people; and whether the program theory is well-articulated or based on common sense.

Meet with stakeholders. The second thing effective evaluators do is identify the stakeholders. Stakeholders are those people who are personally involved with the program, derive some of their income from it, sponsor it, or are clients or potential recipients of the program's services (Bryk, 1983; Sieber, 1998).

Program personnel are usually more personally involved in the program than either the sponsors or the clients. The program director is a key person with whom the evaluators relate during the entire project. It helps to learn as much as possible about the director's training, program philosophy, vision for the program, and reputation. The people who deliver the services need to be involved as well. Such involvement should begin early so that they can add specific and detailed insights that only they can provide because only they know what happens hour by hour. Rapport between the director and the staff is also critical so that consensus on the need for an evaluation develops. Such cooperation increases the chances that all groups will cooperate in planning the evaluation, collecting data, and finally using the findings.

Program sponsors should be considered. At times program personnel are the sponsors; in other situations sponsors are foundations, government agencies, or central administrators of the institution housing the program. Often specific individuals are responsible for the evaluation. For example, a member of the school board or the vice-president of a hospital might be the person who must be satisfied with the evaluation. It is important that evaluators meet with sponsors early during the planning phase to answer questions about the evaluation; however, such people will seldom be involved in detailed planning. As the evaluation proceeds, sponsors appreciate progress reports. Suggestions for keeping sponsors informed and helping sponsors use the information gained through the evaluation are given in Chapters 13 and 14.

The clients or program participants also need to be identified. The type of contact with clients will vary with different types of evaluations and programs. Evaluations of services directed to whole communities might require contact with just a small sample of eligible residents, those of school-based programs might depend on work with parents, and evaluations of small programs might involve all participants in some way. Having a good understanding of the needs of participants is necessary because, after all, it is for their welfare that the program has been developed.

Become Familiar with Information Needs

After learning what the program is and meeting stakeholders, an evaluator should answer the following questions: (1) Who wants an evaluation? (2) What should be the focus of the evaluation? (3) Why is an evaluation wanted? (4) When is an evaluation wanted? (5) What resources are available to support an evaluation?

Who wants an evaluation? Ideally, both program sponsors and program personnel want to have the program evaluated. In such situations evaluators usually interact with cooperative people secure in their professional roles who want to verify that the program meets their expectations and who wish to improve or extend the program.

If the sponsors have initiated the proposed evaluation, the evaluators are faced with helping program personnel become comfortable with the goals and methodology of the evaluation before data collection begins. If this effort fails, evaluators face the possibility of active opposition or passive resistance; either way, they will not gain the cooperation essential to carry out the project (Donaldson, Gooler, and Scriven, 2002). When program personnel think of

EVALUATOR PROFILE 3

Gerald L. Barkdoll: Working Closely with Stakeholders

Gerald Barkdoll directed strategic planning, program evaluation, and economic analysis for the Food and Drug Administration. After working as an industrial engineer and consultant, he came to the FDA in 1971. His B.S. is in engineering. He earned an MBA (Drexel) and a Doctor of Public Administration (University of Southern California). Dr. Barkdoll was with the FDA evaluation staff when its mission was enlarged to carry out evaluations of programs making up the FDA. He was asked how he handled the change in role. He replied: "We did three things to make the evaluations a positive experience for the program managers. First, we used teams including people from the program selected by the program managers to do the evaluation. Each team was headed by a member of the evaluation staff. Second, we had a 'no surprise' rule. We shared our plans, our schedule, our activities, and our preliminary insights and findings with the program manager on a real-time basis. And, last, we finished each evaluation in three months. One program manager told us that this was most important since he knew he could tolerate almost anything for three months."

Adapted from Sporn, D. L. 1989a. A conversation with Gerald L. Barkdoll. *Evaluation Practice, 10*(1), 27–32.

the evaluation as a means of improving the effectiveness of their work, they are more likely to give the evaluators assistance in data collection and to volunteer valuable insights into the interpretation of the data. The importance of working with stakeholders is described by an evaluator who worked with the Food and Drug Administration in Evaluator Profile 3.

If the program personnel initiate the proposed evaluation, the evaluators need to be sure that sponsors are convinced of its usefulness. Sponsors who are disinterested in the evaluation during the planning stages are not likely to pay attention to the findings nor to lend support to improvements that might be recommended.

What should be the focus of the evaluation? During meetings with the sponsors and personnel, evaluators often learn that the term "program evaluation" does not have the same meaning for everyone. Although it would be better for them to think in terms of formative evaluations that would help them to retain positive features of the program and modify or improve other aspects of their work, sometimes program personnel merely seek affirmation of their current efforts. Program sponsors may want a summative evaluation if they are under pressure to divert resources to another program. Others might confuse program evaluation data collection instruments with measurements of individual accomplishments similar to employee appraisals (Bauer and Toms, 1989).

At this point, evaluators help stakeholders to learn what types of evaluations best meet their needs and resources. The choice is seldom between one type of evaluation or another. Incorporating some elements of various types of evaluations is often desirable, depending on the complexity of the goals of the program and the resources available for the project. For example, in an early evaluation of "Sesame Street" a number of issues were addressed in the overall evaluation (Cook, Appleton, Conner, Shaffer, Tamkin, and Webber, 1975). These issues included (1) the degree to which the program reached its target audience; (2) learning effectiveness; (3) effectiveness relative to the need that led to the program; (4) the ratio of benefits to costs; (5) the aspects of home viewing situations that foster learning; (6) the value of program objectives, and (7) the degree the program was effective in reducing the preschool academic gap between advantaged and poor children.

Why is an evaluation wanted? Closely tied to the previous question is the issue of why evaluation is wanted. People seldom commission an evaluation without a specific reason. Effective evaluators put a high priority on identifying the reasons why an evaluation is wanted. Are there some groups in the organization who question the need for the program? Is the foundation that provided the funds expecting an evaluation? What level of commitment is there to use the results of an evaluation to improve decision-making? Ideally, program personnel seek answers to pressing questions about the program's future: How can it be improved? Are we serving the right people? Should we expand? Evaluators expect that different stakeholder groups have differing priorities. Some want a smoothly functioning program, others want tips on making their work more effective, and still others want to see services expanded (Cook et al., 1985). One aspect of an evaluator's role is to help both the sponsors and program personnel arrive at a consensus on the purposes of evaluations.

Some reasons for evaluating programs are undesirable. For example, an administrator may use program evaluation as a ploy to postpone or avoid making a decision. Evaluations are also inappropriate when administrators know what decision they will make but commission a program evaluation solely to give their decision legitimacy.

When is an evaluation wanted? Stakeholders often want an evaluation completed quickly. Part of the planning process involves agreeing on a balance between the preferences of the stakeholders and the time needed for carrying out the best evaluation possible. When setting a viable completion date, evaluators must consider the time it takes to prepare a proposal, access records, arrange meetings, develop measures of the criteria for intermediate and long-term outcomes, find and observe a reasonable number of program participants and sites, and draw together the observations and prepare written and oral reports. Internal evaluators are often restricted in how many observations they can make because schools, hospitals, and businesses include only a limited number of students of a certain age, patients of a given diagnosis, or employees in a specific job. Furthermore, the type of evaluation requested leads to different constraints on the time needed to plan and complete an evaluation.

There is no formula to determine how long a project will take. With experience, however, evaluators develop a sense of the relationship between the scope of a project and the time needed for its completion. A good technique is to break the overall project down into small steps and then estimate how much time each step in the project needs. Using the list of considerations in the previous paragraph might help in estimating the time needed to complete an evaluation (see Card, Greeno, and Peterson, 1992).

What resources are available? Besides time, another factor that can limit an evaluation is the availability of resources. Grants include a specified amount for an evaluation. Of course, internal evaluators cannot be reckless with resources either. The assistance of program personnel can hold down the expense of data collection. Even if no formal contract is to be signed, listing in writing what is to be done as part of the evaluation is advisable.

Assess the evaluability of the program. After coming to understand the program and learning what information the stakeholders need, evaluators must consider the resources available for meeting those needs. This process, called an evaluability assessment (Smith, 1989; Wholey, 1979, 1997), is intended to produce a reasoned basis for proceeding with an evaluation. It is best if the stakeholders agree on both the objectives of the program and the criteria that would reveal when successful outcomes have been achieved. If stakeholders cannot agree on what makes the program a success, evaluators are faced with a particularly difficult situation because they would need to provide a greater variety of outcome data and may be unable to draw clear conclusions. A program is also not ready for a thorough evaluation until its conceptual basis has been developed. One review showed that less than 30 percent of published evaluations described programs with theoretical formulations linking the program to the desired outcomes (Lipsey, Crosse, Dunkle, Pollard, and Stobart, 1985). Others agree that many programs do not have an explicit statement of how the program is expected to affect people (see Bickman, 2000; Cook, 2000; Leeuw, 2003). Upon questioning, it may turn out that some implicit program theories are no more complicated than "we tell them what to do, and they do it" (see reviews by Posavac, Sinacore, Brotherton, Helford, and Turpin, 1985; Posavac, 1995). From what you know about the health effects of regular exercise and a balanced diet low in fat, refined sugar, and salt, would you agree that knowledge of what to do is sufficient to motivate people? Many steps intervene between the provision of knowledge and actions; such steps can include social support, reinforcing appropriate behaviors, reminders, skill in applying knowledge, belief in the personal applicability of information, and so forth. Discussions with evaluators can reveal that planners had not developed a clear rationale on which to base a program or do not have the freedom to make changes in response to an evaluation. Recognizing such situations even before gathering any data is a contribution that evaluators can make (Cook and Shadish, 1986).

When deciding whether a program has a useful theoretical basis, it is helpful to construct an impact model showing how the elements of the program lead to the expected changes in the program participants (Lipsey, 1993). Impact models are mentioned at several points in this text. In brief, an impact model is a diagram listing the activities making up a program across the top of a page and the outcomes the program is expected to produce at the bottom. See Figure 2.1 for an impact model of a hypothetical program to increase the competence of science faculty in teaching ethical issues. The activities are at the top. The objectives of the workshop concern the students of the faculty workshop participants; these are listed in the bottom. In the middle of the diagram are intermediate outcomes that the workshop leaders believe must occur for the objectives to be achieved. The impact model helps the evaluator to decide what to observe and measure. The best evaluations involve assessing the quality of the program's activities (i.e., faithful implementation), the degree to which the intermediate outcomes were achieved (e.g., the quality of the lesson plans that were prepared during the workshop), and the extent to which the participants' own students mastered ethical issues. If one focused only on the objectives for students (the points in the bottom boxes) and did not find improvements, one would not know what went wrong. Figure 2.1 is a very simple impact model, but it still is valuable because it prompts the stakeholders to look at the elements of the program and trace the process by which the outcomes are expected to be obtained. It also tells the evaluator what to consider measuring.

Plan the Evaluation

Once it is decided to conduct an evaluation, planning begins in earnest. Examining published research and evaluations of similar programs, determining the best methodology, and preparing a written proposal complete the preparation phase.

Examine the literature. When evaluators work in an area that is new to them, making a careful search of the literature before designing or developing new instruments is important. Evaluators can learn from the successes and failures of others and get a picture of the methodological, political, and practical difficulties that must be overcome. Searching published materials is much easier than in the past. University and public libraries provide access to the research literature through Internet searches. For medical, mental health, and educational program evaluations, MEDLINE, PsycINFO, and ERIC are readily available. Many other specialized systems have also been developed that have taken much of the drudgery out of literature searching. Once some

FIGURE 2.1   Simple impact model for a workshop for science faculty on ethics in research and policy.

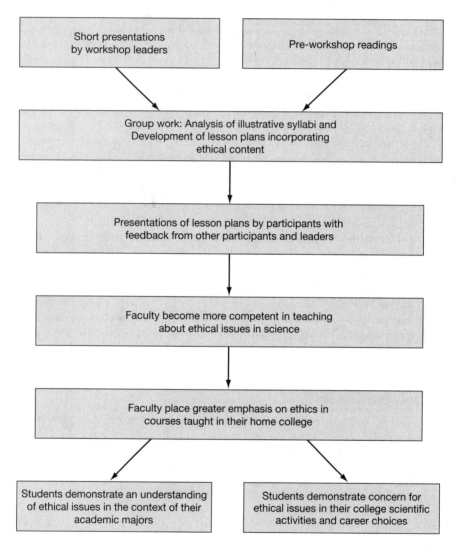

Impact Model for Workshop for Science Faculty on
Ethical Issues in Scientific Research and Policy

reports are found, the bibliographies of these articles provide additional references. Figure 2.2 provides just a hint of the sites available on the Internet for help in planning program evaluations.

While reading reports of previous work, evaluators keep several key questions in mind: In what ways is the program evaluated similar to the program

FIGURE 2.2   There are many Internet sites that can help in planning a program evaluation. Here are some illustrative sites. It is worthwhile to spend some time searching because there is a wealth of information.

Illustrative Internet Sites for Help in Planning Program Evaluations

U.S. Federal Government	Agency for Healthcare Research and Quality	www.ahrq.gov
	Centers for Disease Control	www.cdc.gov/eval
	Department of Education	www.ed.gov
	Department of Health and Human Services (Planning and Evaluation)	aspe.os.dhhs.gov/pic/index.cfm
	Educational Resources Information Clearinghouse	www.eric.ed.gov/
	Substance Abuse and Mental Health Services Administration	www.samhsa.gov
	U.S. Census	www.census.gov
Illustrative State Government Sites	Florida Department of Juvenile Justice	www.djj.state.fl.us/research/research_index.html
	Minnesota Office of the Legislative Auditor	www.auditor.leg.state.mn.us
Foundations	Kellogg Foundation	www.wkkf.org/
	Robert Wood Johnson Foundation	www.rwjf.org/research/index.jsp
Universities	Harvard University	www.gse.harvard.edu/hfrp/eval.html
	Western Michigan University	www.wmich.edu/evalctr/ess.html
Organizations	American Evaluation Association	www.eval.org/
	UNICEF	www.unicef.org/publications/index.html
	United Way of America	national.unitedway.org/outcomes/
	World Bank	www.worldbank.org/ieg/

being considered for an evaluation? What research designs were used? Can some of the measures of the outcome criteria be adapted? How reliable and valid were the measures? What statistical analyses were used? Is there a consensus among the reports? If there are conflicting findings, are these conflicts due to different approaches to sampling, design, or interpretation? What issues were not addressed?

Plan the methodology. After reviewing the literature, the evaluators are ready to make decisions regarding sampling procedures, research design, data collection, and statistical analysis. Later chapters are devoted to some of these topics, but it is helpful to preview the main issues now to show how these decisions contribute to planning an evaluation.

Once the program's target population has been identified, evaluators need to consider whether to use the entire population, a random sample, or a sample selected for other reasons. One argument for including the entire population is political: Some people may be offended if they are not included. Evaluations within a large organization will be more readily accepted if all employees have an opportunity to participate rather than a random sample only. If a state auditor's office is evaluating a statewide program, gathering information from every county, or at least from every congressional district, would be wise.

When there are concerns about particular types of participants, it is wise to be sure that those types are represented in the sample. If a program is offered in different communities, confidence in the findings of the evaluation is enhanced when evaluators take special care to be sure that participants from a variety of program locations are included (Campbell, 1986). For example, an evaluation of a reading program in a large urban school system could be based on schools whose students represent different ethnic and economic backgrounds rather than just taking a random sample of students from all schools.

To minimize expenses and to complete an evaluation on time, it is often necessary to sample participants rather than observe an entire population. The strategy of selecting a representative sample and devoting resources to obtaining data from as many from that sample as possible produces a more representative sample than a halfhearted attempt to include the whole population would yield. For example, a 75 percent response from a random sample of 100 would provide more valid information than a 15 percent response from a sample of 1,000 even though the second sample would be twice as big as the first. Observers untrained in social science research methods frequently emphasize a sample's size rather than its representativeness; this misperception may require the evaluator to teach a little sampling theory to stakeholders.

No matter how sampling is to be done, evaluators know that some people do not cooperate and some cannot. Thus, it is advisable to seek a larger sample than is essential. Identifying the characteristics of nonparticipants and those who drop out at various points in time is important. Both the attrition rate and the reasons for attrition have a bearing on the conclusions the data can support.

The Success Case Method would not employ a representative sample, but only include those who showed particular success in achieving the objectives held for the participants. In a formative evaluation there may well be very good reasons for seeking a nonrepresentative sample in order to develop insights into what pattern of participation is needed to achieve success. Many stakeholders might not be comfortable with a sample of participants that was chosen in this selective manner. It is critical to keep the purpose of the evaluation in mind when planning it. The Success Case Method is probably unsuitable for a summative or a quality assurance evaluation. Furthermore, it is critical that successful participants be selected because they followed the activities of the program, not because they were already much better off than other participants when the program began.

Another crucial step in selecting a methodology is choosing a research design. The choice depends on such constraints as the purpose of the evaluation, the preferences of the stakeholders, the time when the project must be completed, and the funds available. Some evaluations simply require a series of interviews conducted by a knowledgeable evaluator, others require a creative examination of existing records (see Evaluator Profile 6, in Chapter 7), and still others require a design similar to those used in basic research involving random assignment to program and control groups. We stress that evaluators should remain flexible, selecting the methodology that matches the needs of stakeholders rather than routinely using a favorite method. The evaluation project proceeds more smoothly when the stakeholders have participated in the selection of the methodology and understand the reasons for whatever approach is ultimately chosen.

Using multiple criteria from different sources yields the best information for an evaluation. The program participants themselves are one of the most important and accessible data sources. They can describe their reactions to the program and their satisfaction with it, and they can describe their current behavior. People close to the participants, such as family members, may sometimes provide information, especially when the participants are very young or incapacitated. Program personnel and records are often essential. For some programs, community-level variables are the most relevant. Last, evaluators must not overlook their own observations; this point is expanded in Chapter 8 on qualitative methods.

The day-to-day mechanics of data collection usually involve an on-site coordinator who keeps track of program clients, personnel, and other individuals supplying data for the evaluation. Surveys must be administered at appropriate times, addresses need to be updated, and relationships must be maintained with program staff. Because data collection is critical, yet tedious, only a responsible person can handle the task.

In quantitative evaluations, appropriate statistical analyses need to be completed. Using simple statistical procedures whenever possible is desirable because the findings will be presented to stakeholders who may not have a great deal of statistical expertise. Stakeholders ideally should be able to understand the interpretation of the results; they should not merely be impressed by statistical sophistication. One approach is to use statistical analyses that are as powerful and complex as necessary, but to illustrate the findings using percentages or—even better—graphs. Some ways in which analyses of evaluations differ from those that are used in basic research are mentioned at several points in later chapters.

During the planning phase careful thought must be given to how an evaluation is to be reported to the stakeholders. Often evaluators have erred in focusing on a single report. Instead, a plan for reporting throughout the evaluation better serves the interests of the stakeholders and the need of the evaluator for constructive feedback as the project progresses. Chapter 13 contains an extended description of the variety of reporting avenues evaluators use to maintain support for the evaluation and to encourage the use of findings.

Present a written proposal. After reviewing the literature and thinking through the various methodological considerations outlined above, the evaluators are ready to prepare a written proposal. The acceptance of a proposal indicates that evaluators, program personnel, and perhaps the funding agency have agreed on the nature and goals of the program, the type of evaluation wanted, the criteria and measures to be used, and the readiness of the program for evaluation. It is psychologically and practically important for the program personnel to understand the evaluation process, feel comfortable with it, and even to be enthusiastic about having the information that will be obtained.

Formal contracts are required for external evaluators. Such contracts will specify the tasks that the evaluator is to complete and any tasks for which the program staff is responsible. Items that went into the estimate of the costs should be specified. Internal evaluators probably cannot insist on formal written agreements; however, listing agreements in memos with copies to program directors and central administrators helps in assuring that the various stakeholders hold similar expectations for the evaluation. Expectations for an evaluation can be renegotiated if necessary. Using written communications ought not to be interpreted as a lack of trust because honest misunderstandings occur when memories differ. Such differences have created problems after evaluations have been completed.

DYSFUNCTIONAL ATTITUDES TOWARD PROGRAM EVALUATION

Political and emotional factors can undermine an evaluation project. Effective evaluators seek to identify these factors, discuss conflicts, and reassure stakeholders that the program evaluation is planned to serve their needs. Some concerns simply represent misunderstandings of program evaluation. Other concerns may reflect real conflicts within the organization that the evaluation has brought to the surface.

Assume That the Program Is Perfect

Most people seem to think that they are better than average in lots of ways (Epley and Dunning, 2000) even though on the average that cannot be. In a similar way program planners are generally enthusiastic and confident about the effects of their work; indeed, many expect their new program to have dramatic, positive results. Mendez and Warner (2000) showed that the goal published by the U.S. Public Health Service concerning the percentage reduction in adult smoking rates by 2010 is "virtually unattainable." Program planners and staff might feel betrayed when evaluators find programs to be less than perfect. Difficulties are especially likely when a new program is expected to improve on a reasonably good existing program.

It may be necessary to assist the stakeholders in estimating the amount of practicable improvement. For example, if elementary school children are reading at appropriate levels, a new reading program cannot raise reading levels very much. The new reading program might be considered successful if reading levels increase just a little or if students like reading better. Furthermore, a small improvement experienced by many people could be very valuable (Cook and Shadish, 1986; Rosenthal, 1990).

There are other reasons why a dramatic effect seldom occurs. Whenever a group of people is compared with a group of program participants, the comparison group will usually be receiving some kind of service. Program participants rarely can be compared with a group that receives no service at all. Similarly, when evaluators compare two versions of the same service, both of which are considered good, large differences between groups are unlikely. For example, if psychosomatic patients treated in a special unit are compared with psychosomatic patients being treated by their own physicians but without the benefit of the special program, both groups should improve because both are receiving treatment for their immediate problems.

Fear That the Evaluation Will Offend the Staff

O'Doherty (1989) described an evaluation of a mediation program. Mediation is a negotiation procedure that can serve as an alternative to resolving a dispute in court; it is cheaper, reduces hostile feelings between the protagonists, and reduces the load on the courts. O'Doherty discovered that some program directors felt that asking clients about the quality of the mediators' work would detract from their professional image. Some university faculty members seem to show a similar distaste for student comments about the quality of their teaching (Astin, 1993). Most people who seek the services of physicians, lawyers, and other professionals would be pleased to know that people in these roles are trying to learn how to meet their patients' and clients' needs better.

Fear That the Evaluation Will Inhibit Innovation

Staff members may worry that evaluation will interfere with innovation by inhibiting them from experimenting with new techniques. In both process and outcome evaluations, the staff may believe that after beginning an evaluation no variation in the program is permitted until data collection is complete. This is partially true because major structural changes in the program would alter the essential goals or nature of the program. In such a case the evaluation would need to be revised. However, this does not mean that clinicians or program personnel cannot be flexible in the day-to-day operation of the program within broad structural boundaries. Every program has some flexibility; evaluation will not limit this. However, it is wise not to attempt to conduct an outcome evaluation of a program that is just getting started; major changes can occur as staff become clearer about their objectives.

Fear That the Program Will Be Terminated

Although a negative evaluation seldom leads to a program's cancellation (Cook and Shadish, 1986), it is possible that an evaluation could result in the curtailment or elimination of a program when findings show that a given approach simply is not working as expected. However, before sponsors can eliminate a program designed to meet a specific problem, they are ordinarily under some pressure to decide what to put in its place. Therefore, an unfavorable evaluation will more likely result in the refinement of a program than its elimination.

Early in the planning phase, effective evaluators will try to have program personnel view them as partners who share the goal of providing quality education, service, or care. Evaluators can assist program personnel in meeting accountability standards that may be a condition for continued funding. One practice that allays some anxiety is to promise the program managers that they will see the final draft of the report and be asked for their suggestions and clarifications (see Chapter 13). The comments of program administrators are appended to many reports done by evaluation and audit offices of local and federal governments. Of course, evaluators cannot eliminate anxiety completely when a program does not have the full support of central administrators or when there are valid concerns about the quality of the program.

Fear That Information Will Be Misused

Besides the fear that the program will be canceled, there might be some concern that information gained about the performance of the staff may be misused. Even competent clinicians, administrators, teachers, and other personnel are concerned about merit reviews, future promotions, and career advancement. It is an absolute necessity to keep formative program evaluations distinct from assessments conducted to reward the more effective staff members. This point is emphasized by writers in education (Astin, 1993), medical care (Berwick, 1989), and industry (Dobyns and Crawford-Mason, 1991).

Fear That Qualitative Understanding May Be Supplanted

Service personnel rightly feel that their observations are valuable sources of ideas both for improving the functioning of a program and for evaluating its effects. They may feel that the evaluators' questionnaires, complicated research designs, and statistical techniques are less sensitive than their own observations and evaluations. At times they are right.

Although the subjective evaluations of the staff can be biased (see Dawes, 1994), the ideas of program personnel are a very valuable source of evaluation data. Evaluations can be improved by both quantitative and qualitative data gathered from many sources. The staff's subjective observations will be very important when the data are being interpreted. The ideal is not to eliminate either quantitative or qualitative approaches but to integrate the findings from both methodologies as described in Chapter 8.

Evaluators gain the confidence of managers and staff not only by recognizing this problem but also by articulating this awareness in such a manner that program staff members are reassured that the richness of human services have been appropriately respected (Taut and Alkin, 2003). Early in the planning phase, program personnel can be assured that the evaluation will not begin until they have had the opportunity to review the evaluation proposal carefully and are confident that their concerns have been addressed properly.

Fear That Evaluation Drains Program Resources

The six concerns described so far are focused on various aspects of evaluation but not on the concept of evaluation itself. Some objections to evaluation strike at the very idea of program evaluation. The staff may charge that program evaluation drains money and energy away from direct service (Botcheva, White, and Huffman, 2003). As the statement stands, it is true. However, the main question is whether evaluation can improve service. The alternative to spending money on evaluation is to risk spending money on services that are of unknown value. Today it would be hard to find a program funded either by government agencies or by private foundations that is not required to evaluate its services. Those who are not convinced by the accountability argument may be persuaded by a more pragmatic one: Evaluations, if done well, may help in attracting more support and resources into the program. Furthermore, a favorable evaluation could lead to additional settings adopting an effective program.

Fear of Losing Control of the Program

No matter whether an evaluation is conducted by external or internal evaluators, staff and managers may fear that their right to make decisions about the way the program is offered will be reduced. Such a fear may be groundless but is quite common. Staff members realize that they probably cannot control the information about the program that will be available to administrators of the organization housing the program. Unless the staff knows that the program is grossly inadequate or fraud has occurred, this fear may be reduced by working closely with the program so that an evaluation shows strengths as well as weaknesses. Sometimes programs can use evaluations to increase control since the evaluation will give evidence to use in presenting the case for a larger allotment of resources for the program.

Fear That Evaluation Has Little Impact

Some critics point out that evaluations frequently have had very little impact on programs. There is a good deal of validity to this objection; evaluators have often been frustrated by seeing their reports set aside. However, evaluators should remember that when evaluations are used, their results will be only one of many factors behind decisions. Because evaluators work in a complex organizational context, the results of their work must be timely and relevant to decision making (Cronbach, 1982). Well-designed and carefully executed studies are valuable only when they speak to issues that are important to the

---

EVALUATOR PROFILE 4

Robin Turpin: Reducing the Effects of Political Influences on Methodology

Robin Turpin conducts evaluations for Merck & Co., Inc. (a pharmaceutical and other health products company). Dr. Turpin earned her Ph.D. in Applied Social Psychology from Loyola University of Chicago. Her work has included studies on the quality of life and managing multisite evaluations, delivery of healthcare to female veterans, and discharge planning.

These comments were excerpted from her winning answer to the American Evaluation Association President's Problem of 1988. The problem had asked for suggestions about avoiding or countering political pressures that would cause evaluators to make nonoptimal decisions in planning an evaluation. Dr. Turpin recognized the potential for pressures on evaluators to guarantee results that conform to the expectations of powerful groups in a large organization. She recommended that instead of ignoring or trying to work around political pressure, evaluators should assess the potential for pressure and then seek to counter it. "For example, if an evaluator is being pressured to use a method that most likely would produce favorable results, insisting on a review (of the method) by a consultant or an expert panel would give the evaluator enough leverage to defend another (better) method." By countering inappropriate pressure, Dr. Turpin hopes to produce as credible an evaluation as possible; evaluations without credibility will not be used.

Source: Winner of the 1988 President's Problem. 1989. *Evaluation Practice*, *10* (1), 53–57.

organization. When evaluators show how evaluation is relevant to pending decisions, they raise the odds of the evaluation being used.

The Effect of These Attitudes

Working closely with stakeholders who fear evaluations of their work might lead stakeholders to attempt to determine the methods to be used. A stakeholder may press evaluators to use marginally valid methods that are likely to produce a preordained result. Ideally, discussions among stakeholders and evaluators will reveal that better procedures are available and should be used. Open discussion ought to reduce or resolve unreasonable fears; however, evaluators ought not to ignore the threatening nature of evaluation. At times, an organizationally powerful stakeholder may seek to control an internal evaluation. One way for an internal evaluator to resist that influence is to seek outside support in the form of a review panel. Robin Turpin describes how she would resist such pressure in Evaluator Profile 4.

Summary and Preview

Careful planning of an evaluation project serves to get an evaluation off to a good start. Note that the steps are suggested to help evaluators respond to the needs of the people most affected by the evaluation. Responsive evaluators have fewer problems with the fears outlined in the second part of this chapter than do evaluators who seem to ignore stakeholder needs.

The next chapter focuses on a central concern—specifying the implementation and outcome criteria of wisely planned and successful programs. A thoughtless selection of criteria will negate efforts to conduct a useful evaluation.

Study Questions

1. Apply the evaluation planning steps to the hypothetical sexual assault prevention program mentioned at the beginning of Chapter 1. Make a list of what needs to be done if you were to contemplate evaluating such a program.
2. What models of evaluation would you think are most appropriate for the program to prevent sexual assault on campus?
3. One can think of a college course as a program. (In fact, a three-hour class requires more time and energy than many social service programs.) The elements of the program consist of (a) reading assignments, (b) class discussions, (c) lectures, and (d) projects such as term papers. The outcomes that university and future employers value include (a) the mastery of content, (b) the development of information management skills such as writing, analysis of arguments, and synthesis of information, and (c) the development of meta-skills such as organization, self-discipline, and maintaining good interpersonal relationships. What are some intermediate steps needed to get from the elements of the program to outcome skills?
4. Imagine that you are part of an evaluation team in the institutional research office of a large university. The chairperson of the department of psychology asks you to

evaluate a graduate program called "Community Psychology." List the stakeholders. What are the first questions to ask the chairperson? What models of evaluation seem most appropriate to such an evaluation?

5. What models of evaluation are implied if an administrator asks an evaluation office to conduct an evaluation of a program specifying that the program manager and staff are not to be aware that the evaluation is being done?

Additional Resource

CARD, J. J., GREENO, C., AND PETERSON, J. L. 1992. Planning an evaluation and estimating its cost. *Evaluation & the Health Professions, 15,* 75–89.

> When asked to estimate how much to charge for conducting a program evaluation, most new evaluators have little to go on. When pressed, most people will greatly underestimate how much time is necessary to complete even a very modest project. These authors suggest how long it is likely to take to complete various steps in the process. Evaluators making a cost estimate need to remember that they ought to be paid for the initial discussion and the preparation of the proposal itself. Proposing a cost would become even harder if one were asked to estimate what it would cost to maintain and run an office.

Selecting Criteria and Setting Standards

W hat is the best measure of a good intercollegiate athletic program? Some would say the proportion of games won; others would say the number of tickets sold; others, the devotion of the alumni to the team; others, the success of the student athletes after graduation; and still others, the favorable media attention attracted to the university through its teams. Some college presidents and faculty have argued that the criteria of a good sports program have shifted too much toward winning and away from the academic and life successes of the athletes after graduation. In fact, at some well-known schools, only small percentages of basketball and football players graduate. For the few who become professional athletes, failing to complete college may not seem to matter that much in terms of earning power. For the others, not graduating limits their future vocational opportunities. Some people argue that this is irrelevant; basketball and football proceeds earn enough to support the entire athletic program, and, since no one compels the students to participate, the academic administration should not disrupt a good thing ("Graduation Rates," 1999; "Students Cheated," 1990).

Disputes over the choice of the criteria to use in evaluation also lie beneath many disagreements over government policies. For example, is the overall level of a nation's economic well-being more important than improving economic conditions specifically for poor people? Judgments and preferences in daily life similarly depend on the choice of criteria;

however, the criteria we use are often implicit. If we test-drive a car, we use degree of comfort, ease of operation, clear vision of the road, perhaps what our friends think is cool, and other criteria, even though we have never written those standards down. When people disagree over the desirability of different automobiles, it is often because they are using different criteria to make their choices. For some people, an attractive exterior design is more important than a reputation for reliability; for parents with several children, a larger rear seat would be more important than it is for single people holding their first jobs.

Whether we think about them or not, we do have criteria that permit us to make distinctions and to form preferences as we make our choices of foods, friends, churches, automobiles, and politicians. When conducting an evaluation of a program or a product, we need to develop or select criteria and standards in a fashion that is far more explicit than we need for daily life. Without the development of clear, appropriate criteria and specific standards, we might never be able to agree on the value of a counseling program for students who fear math, food stamps for poor families, or training for people who have lost jobs. As mentioned in Chapter 1, the traditional model of evaluation had been a subjective assessment by the people offering or funding services. Such informal assessments are no longer acceptable, especially when programs are paid for with public funds. This chapter describes the need to specify criteria of value for program evaluations, defines different types of criteria, and illustrates a variety of evaluation questions and how they can be answered more easily after specifying what makes a program a success.

USEFUL CRITERIA AND STANDARDS

Merely selecting a quantitative tool in order to substitute numbers for a subjective judgment does not satisfy the need for a standard. The point is to choose criteria and develop standards of program quality that will permit us to carry out useful program evaluations. Many evaluators have emphasized the importance of sound research design (and we do as well in later chapters); however, just as a chain is only as strong as its weakest link, the thoughtless selection of criteria can lead to a failed evaluation just as surely as an inappropriate research design can. Ill-considered choices of standards could make it impossible to draw any conclusions from an evaluation even when the evaluation was well planned in other ways.

Criteria That Reflect a Program's Purposes

Without very careful planning and a thorough understanding of a program, it is quite easy to select criteria that do not reflect its purposes. Many observers believe that the first evaluation of Head Start (Cicarelli, Cooper, and Granger, 1969), a popular, federally funded preschool program for children of poor families, was mortally wounded by the decision to use measures of the improvement of intellectual skills as the primary criteria of success. Instead, Lazar (1981) argued that the most important aspect of Head Start was the involvement of parents in the education of their children. It was hoped that the involvement of low-income parents, many of whom typically participate only minimally in the education of their children, would continue as their children grew. Thus, Head Start would increase the likelihood that low-income parents would encourage the development of their children, help with doing homework, and make sure their children were in school. If parents adopted such practices, such activities could have a long-term positive effect on the children, an effect far more important than the specific knowledge that the children gained in Head Start classes (Leik and Chalkley, 1990).

What should the criteria for success be for a recycling program? Since it is necessary for residents to separate their garbage before it can be picked up, it might seem reasonable to measure the amount of recyclable material collected as an outcome criterion. But there have been reports of materials being collected, but then simply added to the regular garbage landfill. The real criterion of success is that the materials be reused in some way. A recycling program is actually quite complex. For such an effort to achieve desirable outcomes, the cooperation of residents is needed, along with an efficient collection system that meshes with sorting facilities that in turn distribute materials to appropriate manufacturers who find customers for their products. Criteria of success may look valid but yet not measure success in achieving the real objectives of the program.

The time when an evaluation criterion is measured could be chosen in a way that fails to reflect the program's purposes. A program could have positive immediate or short-term effects, but a marginal long-term one. A physical fitness program can be quite effective in improving muscle tone without having an effect on program participants' physical condition or health ten years later. On the other hand, some college alumni remark how helpful a faculty member was for their development even though the faculty member was perceived as critical and overly difficult when they were in school. Here, the long-term effect seems more favorable than the short-term one. Evaluators seek to make observations at a time that correctly reflects the objectives of the program and the needs of the participants.

Criteria That the Staff Can Influence

Evaluators can expect considerable resistance to an evaluation when program staff feel that their program will be judged on criteria that they cannot affect (Torres, 1994). For example, employees in manufacturing firms may feel that their effectiveness is limited by the quality of the equipment they use. Such limits need to be considered in evaluating whether they are doing as good a job as possible. Some college faculty object to the use of tests of student skills to evaluate teaching effectiveness because they fear that student achievement levels reflect student effort at least as much as faculty skills and effort. Furthermore, students enter college with different levels of developed skills; thus, the more well-prepared students graduate with better skills. Astin (1993) has sought to develop methods of assessments that focus on improvement during college rather than achievement at graduation. He includes suggestions for taking account of the hours students spend on jobs that cannot be devoted to academic work. Those whose success depends on the performance of others—as is the case for teachers, counselors, coaches, or managers—face a more uncertain situation than do people who are more directly in control of the results of their efforts. The challenge to evaluators is to find ways to identify measures and criteria that do reflect the efforts of the staff and are agreed to be central to the program's purpose.

Criteria That Can Be Measured Reliably and Validly

When repeated observations under the same conditions yield essentially the same values, a measurement tool is said to be reliable. Reliability even of physical measurements cannot be perfect. Evaluators are concerned about measuring variables that are far less stable than physical variables; consequently, observations made by evaluators are less reliable, often far less, than we would like. Suppose we had wanted to use parental participation as a criterion in evaluating Head Start. Parental participation would be affected by work schedules, transportation problems, health, responsibilities for other children, among other issues that will sometimes make participation more difficult; at other times participation will be more convenient. Parental participation is quite different from stable variables such as weight, reading level, or health.

On the community level, trying to measure unreliable criteria can make it hard to learn if a crime prevention program has an effect. Beyond the actual frequency of crime, official crime rates are influenced by the willingness of victims to report crimes, the way police officers record the reports, the weather and time of the year, and media coverage of recent heinous crimes. These factors could cause the apparent level of community crime to go up or down. Evaluators seek variables to reflect program outcomes that are as stable as possible yet reflect the outcomes desired. Below and in later chapters we discuss methods that serve to increase the reliability and validity of measurement procedures.

Criteria That Stakeholders Participate in Selecting

The criteria for a specific evaluation are selected in close consultation between the evaluator and the stakeholders involved with the project. If the stakeholders do not accept the criteria selected, even when they are appropriate, the evaluation cannot have the impact that it would otherwise have. This does not mean that evaluators simply use whatever criteria and standards stakeholders want. Stakeholders are seldom trained in evaluation methodology. When there is disagreement about the appropriate criteria and standards, evaluators spend

EVALUATOR PROFILE 5

Joseph S. Wholey: Stakeholders and Evaluation Criteria

Joseph Wholey earned his Ph.D. in Philosophy at Harvard University and is a faculty member of the University of Southern California (Washington Center). He has focused his work on improving the performance and accountability of public and nonprofit organizations. He coined the term *evaluability assessment* to describe the process of examining program plans and structure in order to enable evaluators to judge whether a program can be evaluated.

During an interview, Dr. Wholey commented on the need to have stakeholders agree on the criteria of an evaluation. He said, "I recall working as an evaluator for the Tennessee Health Department, working with program (delivery) people who thought the prenatal care program objective was to deliver services while the politicians who appropriated the money thought that the objective was to reduce infant mortality. The evaluator's role . . . was helping people at different levels (the program coordinator at the state level, local program coordinators, the bureau chief, and the deputy commissioner of health) decide what it was that their program was trying to accomplish. . . ." "The program objective that we came to was that delivery of prenatal services would lead to (a) reduction (in the) incidence of low birth weight. Reduction of the incidence of low birth weight babies would lead to a reduction of infant mortality. (The program people and the politicians) could agree that the intermediate objective, reducing the incidence of low birth weight, was a suitable objective . . ."

Adapted from: Johnson, P. L. 1990. A conversation with Joseph S. Wholey about the Program for Excellence in Human Services. *Evaluation Practice, 11*(1), 53–61.

many hours in dialogue with the stakeholders to assure that all parties agree on the standards discussed (McGarrell and Sabath, 1994). Note the comment on this process in Evaluator Profile 5.

The selection of criteria and standards also varies depending on what aspect of the program development process is to be studied. Programs go through a number of phases: proposal preparation, planning, initial implementation, actual operation, expansion, contraction, or accreditation and reaccreditation. Criteria and standards to evaluate a plan will differ markedly from those used to evaluate the implementation of an operational program.

In addition, the criteria differ according to the type of program being evaluated. Programs in education, health, criminal justice, marketing, and training differ in their emphases, the relative power of different stakeholder groups, the traditional types of information found useful, and the financial support available for evaluation studies. These differences play a part in the development of standards of program success and are taken into consideration in designing program evaluations. Although employed by a specific organization, internal evaluators study different organizational functions and thus may experience considerable variety in their work. Many evaluators find that the opportunity to work with many different programs is a rewarding feature of their work.

DEVELOPING GOALS AND OBJECTIVES

In order to know how well we have achieved our goals, we need to know what we wanted to achieve. Sometimes people set out on an automobile trip without a destination in mind. If driving is pleasurable and if a change in scenery is what is desired, having no destination is fine. But most people want to travel to some specific location. If stakeholders are unable to decide what a training or service program is supposed to achieve, there is little reason to begin the program or to evaluate it. A number of issues related to goals need to be addressed: Are there clear ideas about objectives? Are there disagreements about objectives? If so, are these disagreements mutually incompatible or could they complement each other?

How Much Agreement on Goals Is Needed?

Sometimes people are very unclear about what might be accomplished through a program (Cook, 2000; Mathison, 1994). Community groups may sense that there is a problem and wish to provide some service, but simply saying that we want people to be educated, healthy, and happy will not permit us to develop a program to assist them. In other words, stating goals only in the most abstract terms may attract supporters, but it will provide little assistance in designing a program or in evaluating a program once it is under way. Abstract goals may be appropriate in the U.S. Constitution or in the mission statements of organizations, but will not do once people try to produce an operational program. There really is no reason to begin to plan if no one can describe goals any more specifically than saying that "we want to empower people," "we want to provide excellent medical care," or "we want excellence in education."

When stakeholders can describe the specific goals they hold, even if the goals are dissimilar, progress has been made and negotiations may begin. Progress will be stalled if the goals conflict with each other to the extent that achieving one goal makes it impossible to achieve the other; a family cannot vacation on Baja beaches and in the Canadian Rockies at the same time. Similarly, a basketball coach cannot develop a high energy, high scoring offensive while demanding a tight defense, and cancer care cannot make patients as comfortable as possible while using aggressive treatment with experimental medications. Planners can work with stakeholder groups to find mutually agreeable alternatives or to define situations in which one would use one policy rather than another. There might be ways to define a patient's condition that would determine when aggressive (but uncomfortable) treatment would be used versus situations when the goal would be simply to maintain comfort and to minimize pain while suspending intensive medical treatment.

Sometimes people have goals that are different but not incompatible. No college faculty is unified about what students are expected to achieve. Some professors expect detailed knowledge, others conceptual clarity. Some are concerned about the development of employable graduates; others are more concerned that students develop a sound philosophy of life. In most colleges, these different views exist side by side while students are exposed to a variety of professors and courses. In such a setting, mutual respect for differing points of view permits the organization to function.

Different Types of Goals

Once a program has been planned and started, there are different types of goals whose achievement can be evaluated. It is important to verify that the program has gotten underway as planned and to learn whether short-term outcome goals as well as long-term outcome goals have been achieved.

Implementation goals. All programs involve some level of activity before it is possible to achieve any outcomes (Durlak and Ferrari, 1998). For example, equipment must be purchased and staff members must be hired and trained before any service is given. If these activities do not occur, there is no point in seeking to learn if the desired results have been achieved. Figure 3.1 includes a number of goals that the evaluator needed to examine in an evaluation of the effectiveness of a new computerized system to keep track of the inventory

FIGURE 3.1   Objectives for a program should refer to all levels of the program. Implementation, intermediate, and outcome goals are reflected in this illustration. (Adapted from Marshall, 1979)

Various Types of Goals for an Inventory Control System

Implementation. An example of goals that refer to the acquisition of basic hardware and personnel for computerizing an inventory control system. (This is a "start-up" objective. Nothing can happen without this being achieved.)

- The system will be installed in all forty-two company locations in a six-year period—four in the first year, six in the second, and eight each year after.

Intermediate. The ways to recognize that the inventory system is working well are included in this second level of goal statements. (The achievement of Implementation goals does not guarantee achievement of Intermediate goals.)

- The system can handle 15,000 inventory items.
- Items can be located using the system in an average of 2 seconds, with no more than 5 percent of searches taking more than 8 seconds.

Outcome. Although achieving goals at the first two levels is crucial for the ultimate success of the project, there are additional goals that should be considered. (The real reason for computerizing an inventory system is to make a difference for customers. These goals reflect whether the customers are getting better service from the company.)

- Delivery times will be reduced by 20% compared to the current system.
- There will be 50% fewer items out of stock as compared to the current system.
- Formal customer complaints about out-of-stock items and slow responses to customer requests for information will be reduced by 50%.

---

of a large merchandiser. Implementation goals refer to goals that focus on the timely installation of the hardware. Other implementation goals could focus on employee training.

Although it may seem obvious to verify that the program exists before seeking to evaluate its effectiveness, some stakeholders and evaluators have ignored this step. They seem to believe that if a program developer says that something will be done, then it is safe to assume that it would occur as planned. One university vice president for research challenged the assertion that the evaluation of implementation goals must be part of a program evaluation by rhetorically asking, "Can't we assume that these are honorable people? Can't we assume that if they say they will do something, they will do it?" The potential evaluator responded that it is seldom a question of personal integrity. Instead, it is usually a question of unforeseen problems making it impossible to carry out plans. It is crucial to verify that program plans have been carried out before seeking to learn if the program affected the participants.

A graduate student team sought to evaluate the effectiveness of a program in which faculty members volunteered to invite freshman commuter college students into their homes for dinner in an effort to encourage the students to identify more closely with the college. Each faculty volunteer was given the names and addresses of 10 to 12 new students. The evaluators learned that 40 percent of the volunteer faculty members did not invite any students to their homes. Of the students invited, only 60 percent showed up. This means that, at best, only 36 percent of this phase of the program was implemented. The faculty members' good intentions are not in question. Scheduling problems may have come up; for some faculty members the task may have been more difficult than they had imagined; others may have misunderstood what they agreed to do; and perhaps some volunteered before checking with their spouses. Without including an implementation phase in this evaluation, the evaluators would have been unaware that the program was only one-third as strong as planned.

Intermediate goals. By intermediate goals we refer to things that are expected to occur as a result of the proper implementation of the program, but that do not constitute the final goals intended for the program. For example, all students should have textbooks (an implementation goal) and they should read the assignments on time (an intermediate goal), but the actual criteria of success go beyond reading the assignments. In Figure 3.1 the performance of the inventory system is the focus of the intermediate goals. If the efficiency of the organization is to be improved, the performance of the new system needs to meet certain standards. If it does, then there is a better chance of attaining an improvement in program quality and a reduction in complaints.

Outcome goals. Even if the inventory system in Figure 3.1 is working as planned, it is still necessary to learn whether customer service is indeed better. We cannot be satisfied with simply verifying that the equipment works: We must also examine the outcome goals. The most ideal finding would be that the program was implemented as planned, that the intermediate goals were achieved, and that the outcomes were favorable. Even then we would still not have conclusive proof that the program caused the achievement of the valued outcomes. However, finding that good results followed faithful implementation is compatible with believing the program was responsible.

There are other possible patterns of findings. Suppose that the intermediate goals were met (the inventory system worked as planned), but customer satisfaction did not improve? That would mean that the initial diagnosis of the reason for dissatisfaction was in error. Thus, the causes of customer complaints must be sought in aspects of the organization not involved with the inventory system. The limitations of the black box model of evaluation become obvious whenever the findings of an evaluation are mixed in some way. Information on the implementation and intermediate goals provides clues to where to look for what went wrong and how the program might be improved.

Goals That Apply to All Programs

Critics argue that those who use objectives-based program evaluations limit the focus of evaluations to the explicitly stated goals of the program being evaluated, and devote little attention toward other factors (Scriven, 1991; Stufflebeam, 2001). If other aspects of a program were not examined, then objectives-based evaluation would have major limitations. One way to avoid this problem is to recognize that there are many goals that apply to all programs even though such goals are not listed during program planning. Program planners seldom need to state that people are to be treated with respect, that school children are not to be treated in a way that fosters dependence, or that people are not to be discriminated against on the basis of race or sex. Since criteria such as these do not appear in lists of program goals, some evaluators have not treated these issues in program evaluations.

All programs also have the usually unstated goal of no negative side effects. Evaluators should strive to become sufficiently familiar with the program and participants so that they can recognize any serious negative side effects. The negative side effects of Prozac, the anti-depressant medication, became apparent (Glenmullen, 2000) in spite of enthusiastic advocacy of its widespread use (Kramer, 1993). At times evaluators have avoided personal exposure to the program in a misguided quest for objectivity, depending on surveys and records to provide evaluation data. Evaluators who do not become extremely familiar with the program, its staff, and its customers, clients, students, or patients run the risk of overlooking side effects.

EVALUATION CRITERIA AND EVALUATION QUESTIONS

Since criteria and standards are chosen for specific programs, it is impossible to list the criteria that evaluators might use in conducting specific program evaluations. However, a number of general evaluation questions are central to program evaluation; most evaluations would include some of these questions. The value of dealing with these questions and the costs of poor choices of criteria are illustrated in the following sections.

Does the Program or Plan Match the Values of the Stakeholders?

Educational and social service programs are designed to fulfill purposes that are laced with values. For example, what should be included in sex education classes for junior high students? Should the government provide funding for abortions? Should welfare recipients be required to perform public service work? These questions cannot be answered by listing facts.

Evaluators provide a valuable service when they help stakeholders clarify their values and assumptions. For example, most citizens believe that the U.S. federal income tax should be progressive; that is, the more income people have, the greater their tax rate should be. The maximum federal income tax rate in 2006 was 35 percent. The lowest rate was 10 percent (Neikirk, 2001). Is the difference between 35 percent and 10 percent too large or too small? The maximum rate was lowered in recent years. The effects of the changes in tax rates are hard to pinpoint, but the effort would be worthwhile to help in deciding whether the rate change was wise. The data will not affect fundamental value disagreements. However, identifying the value disagreements permits gathering data that speak to the central issues rather than to those merely peripheral to the arguments.

Turning to a different example, public housing programs are designed to make adequate housing available to poor people at affordable costs. Most people would agree that this goal matches the values of society. However, the way public housing policies had been implemented in large cities led to the clustering of poor people, often in high-rise buildings that neither foster a sense of community nor provide safe settings for residents (see "High-rise brought low at last," 1998). An evaluation of public housing ideally would include information on the conflict between the values on which public housing policies were based and the results that have occurred. While a program evaluation cannot tell anyone what values to hold, the demonstration of the discrepancy between what occurred and what was hoped for could be an important motivator for improvement.

Does the Program or Plan Match the Needs of the People to Be Served?

The unmet needs of some segment of the population usually form the basis for the development of a program. The most useful program evaluations compare the unmet needs of people with the services available through the program. Unemployed people need skills that lead to employment. An excellent training program for a skill that is not in demand would not fulfill a need.

Programs cannot be evaluated in isolation from the community characteristics and the people being served.

In order to verify that a program plan meets the needs of the people to be served, evaluators conduct a needs assessment as part of the development of the program (McKillip, 1987). An introduction to the methodology of the assessment of need is provided in Chapter 6. At this point, we want to stress the importance of examining the needs of program participants in all program evaluations. Since program resources are always limited, a particularly important phase of the evaluator's job in laying the groundwork for a program is to provide some suggestions for balancing competing needs during the program selection process.

Does the Program as Implemented Fulfill the Plans?

Evaluators first examine a program plan to learn if its likely impact will match the values of the stakeholders and meet the needs that motivated the development of the program. Next, evaluators compare the operation of the program to the plan. Observers provide numerous examples of situations in which the match between program plan and operation left much to be desired: The blood tests of only 8 of 31 alcoholics who were to be getting Antabuse by surgical implant showed the presence of a therapeutic level of medication (Malcolm, Madden, and Williams, 1974), a low-income population proved too hard to reach so a publicly funded family planning center served nearby college students (Rossi, 1978), and shopping mall cholesterol tests have been found to be exceedingly unreliable and, thus, of little use to people wanting to know whether they needed medical attention ("Cholesterol Screening," 1990). A quantitative measure of fidelity to program plans can be developed (Mowbray, Holter, Gregory, Teague, and Bybee, 2003). A large proportion of implementation failures can be traced to two major problems: The staff discovers that the program cannot be offered as planned, and value conflicts reduce the cooperation among major stakeholder groups.

Programs that cannot be implemented as planned. A program cannot be offered as planned when the population to whom the program was directed rejects the service. The community mental health system was proposed to serve chronically ill psychiatric patients in community settings rather than keeping them confined to large state mental hospitals. It was believed that antipsychotic medication would permit such patients to live independently or with family members and that community mental health centers would provide supportive care and medications. Unfortunately, many discharged patients rejected the treatment. Since people cannot be compelled to go to the centers and since funding was not as generous as expected, the program could not be implemented as envisioned. Community mental health centers therefore broadened their concerns and sought clients who were more functional than those the centers were originally designated to serve.

Sometimes the theory underlying a program is not sensitive to local conditions. A curriculum to teach mathematics in elementary schools (dubbed the "New Math") was well-planned, mathematically sophisticated, and evaluated favorably during development. However, the teachers who used it during development were better trained than the teachers who used it after widespread implementation. Accustomed to drilling children in multiplication tables, elementary teachers were expected to teach set theory. In addition, the new terminology made it impossible for most parents to offer their children any help. After a few frustrating years the new curriculum was discarded (Kolata, 1977). An objectives-based evaluation that focused only on the degree to which the children learned the concepts covered could not detect the reason why the New Math curriculum was ineffective: Many elementary school teachers fear and dislike mathematics.

Value conflicts can make thorough implementation impossible. People seeking to change the economic systems in Eastern Europe and the former USSR met with great resistance from people who benefited from the older, centrally planned systems. Furthermore, many people preferred guaranteed employment and artificially maintained low food prices over the promises of better economic conditions in a more free economy. These ingrained attitudes placed rather effective restraints on changes envisioned by national leaders. An example closer to home occurs when college deans ask faculty members to spend more time doing one-on-one academic counseling with undergraduates and to report on the counseling done. Faculty members who feel pressure to make progress with their research or who may be more interested in graduate education have found ways to feign compliance with a dean's request while not changing actual behavior, perhaps by describing brief hallway contacts as academic counseling.

Do the Outcomes Achieved Match the Goals?

Evaluations of operating programs usually examine at least some results of the programs. Developers of innovative curricula would include measures of student achievement, and planners of an advertising campaign often depend on sales information. Even programmers of religious events deal with outcomes when they report the number of people who say that important behavioral changes took place as a result of participation.

The level of outcome achieved. Deciding whether the outcome observed is good or only marginal depends on an estimate of what should have been achieved. In other words, after a year of reading instruction, third graders can read better than when they started school in September; however, school boards and parents will not be satisfied with just any level of improvement. The improvement should be commensurate with nine months of instruction in third grade. Similarly, football fans may want to see their favorite team do more than improve; they want to see victories. Thus, when evaluators and stakeholders specify goals and objectives, attention must be paid to how much improvement they expect.

When evaluators first begin to work with stakeholders to develop statements of outcome objectives, sometimes they borrow the style of writing hypotheses that they learned in statistics classes. In statistical analyses the alternative hypothesis is often presented as the mean of the program group exceeding the mean of the control group, H_a: $M_p > M_c$. In the social sciences, the amount of difference between the groups is often not specified. This is not the way statistics is used in the physical sciences (Meehl, 1978, 1990). In more developed sciences, the expected numerical value of an observation is compared to the actual observation in the statistical test to learn if the observed difference is smaller than sampling error (a desirable finding) or larger than sampling error (an undesirable finding). Statements of objectives that are modeled after hypotheses used in basic social science research are not as useful as objectives that list the actual level of achievement desired for students, patients, and trainees. For example, in Figure 3.1, intermediate goals do *not* only say that the new system would be *faster* than the old system. Instead, a minimum performance level is specified. If the new system is not at least that fast, then the system is not working as well as planned. Evaluators trained in social science research methods often have difficulty committing themselves to a specific goal because basic research in the social sciences is not carried out that way. There are some alternative approaches to statistics for evaluators (see E. J. Posavac, 1998, and Chapter 13).

How to specify levels of outcome expected. Education and health measures are among the most well developed for setting specific goals. Norms for academic skills are available for standardized achievement tests, and normal ranges are well known for many laboratory tests used by physicians. The outcome of on-the-job training programs could be specified in terms of the trainees' skill in carrying out the tasks needed by the employer. However, tests with norms that have been validly developed can be misused. Critics of the use of standardized achievement tests to evaluate school districts (Cannell, 1987; Shepard, 1990) suggest that when schools are repeatedly evaluated using standard tests, teachers come to tailor their teaching to the test and may even teach specific aspects of the test to their students. Linn (2000) showed that when a new test is used in a school district scores initially fall, but then rise each following year as teachers learn about the test.

When programs are in areas for which extensive norms do not exist, evaluators are often tempted to permit program staff members to specify the objectives of the program. Although evaluators need the contributions of staff stakeholders in all phases of evaluations, experienced evaluators frequently discover that staff members are *too optimistic* about the level of success that will be observed. When one can find completed evaluations of similar programs, the outcomes achieved in those programs can provide information on what might be achieved by the program to be evaluated. The more closely an evaluated program matches the program to be evaluated, the more relevant the previous findings will be. Such information provides some rationale for the levels of outcome specified in the objectives.

Outcomes and black boxes. Readers may well feel that we are beating a dead horse when we mention again the limitations of black box evaluations; however, the ease with which staff, government auditors, and the general public fall into the black box trap leads us to continue to emphasize the issue. The Auditor General of Illinois criticized *Parents Too Soon,* a state-funded program whose objectives included reducing the rate of teenage pregnancy (Karwath, 1990). In defense, the program's administrator described the difficulty of evaluating a prevention program, and mentioned the reduced number of live births to Illinois teenagers between 1983 and 1988. (By using these figures, note that the administrator had adopted a black box evaluation.) Since the number of Illinois teenagers dropped between those years and since the numbers of abortions were not known, the decreased birth rate was not seen as support for the program. Furthermore, there are so many influences on the rate of teenage pregnancy that the use of a black box evaluation model places insurmountable limitations on the interpretation of any findings. If the program had specified implementation goals and intermediate goals as well as the final, bottom-line outcome goal, the administrator may well have been in a better position to respond to the criticism. The following section will suggest some approaches to relating implementation, intermediate, and outcome goals to each other as a way to show that the program works as hypothesized which, consequently, will strengthen the evaluation.

Using Program Theory

Whenever people develop service or intervention programs, assumptions about the causes of the problems and the best ways to change problem behavior are made. Unfortunately, these assumptions are often implicit (Cook, 2000; DeFriese, 1990; Lipsey, 1993; Posavac, 1995; Posavac et al., 1985). When there is no explicit statement of the theory behind the choice of intervention or when there is no conceptual framework linking the interventions to the projected outcomes, it is hard to do an effective evaluation or to improve the intervention (Pion, Cordray, and Anderson, 1993).

Why a program theory is helpful. Initially, many evaluations were carried out without an explicit statement of the theory behind the program design. DeFriese (1990) lamented that a sizable portion of the descriptions of proposed health-related treatment programs did not include credible descriptions of how the interventions are supposed to work. The value of articulating the logic of programs offered in community mental health agencies has been demonstrated (Yampolskaya, Nesman, Hernandez, and Koch, 2004). Increasingly, it has become clear that program design is less effective without theory and evaluations are less informative when carried out in a conceptual vacuum (Chen and Rossi, 1989; Donaldson, 2003; Lipsey, 1993).

Specifying the theory behind the program provides assistance for planners, staff members, people responsible for obtaining funding, as well as for evaluators. In a comment on failed social welfare programs Etzioni reminded us that people "are not very easy to change after all." Yet governments and agencies frequently propose policies that are based on the assumption that interventions can motivate people to make major changes in their lifestyles in short periods of time. We act as though threatening shoplifters with jail will keep them from taking clothes from stores; telling patients with diabetes to lose weight will lead them to do so; showing teenagers how to recycle soda cans will stop them from discarding cans on the beach. Information is important; without knowledge of adaptive behavior people cannot change. Yet, there is ample evidence that such information alone is very weak compared to the major influences in life, such as peer pressure, family practices, media models, and simple convenience. Sometimes evaluators when working with a program planning committee can lead the planners to clarify their assumptions and implicit theories and perhaps refocus their plans. Perhaps the plans should focus on more realistic objectives rather than spreading program funds too thin by attempting too much.

A second value of thinking theoretically is that we can identify the intermediate results of a program rather than just the final outcome. We are also reminded that different people might respond to different forms of a program. Teenagers might respond if a music or sports figure endorsed the program; on the other hand, business managers might want to see a financial approach to a social concern. Before participating, most people need to learn how to visualize themselves carrying out the recommended behaviors. A neighbor was overheard arguing with her husband about a newly announced community recycling program. Citizens were to place cans, bottles, and newspapers into orange-colored containers on Friday mornings. She was not enthused and asked her husband, "Are you going to sort through the garbage every night?" For decades she had put apple peels, the morning newspaper, coffee grounds, and empty soda cans into the kitchen garbage basket. Although keeping recyclable items separate from other garbage may have seemed to be a small matter to planners, the idea of separating garbage was initially novel for some people. Publicity about a recycling program should include illustrations of how to participate in the most convenient manner. Describing the processes for people to follow in making changes in their lives can lead to more effective programs.

A third benefit of having a program theory is that theory helps us to know where to look in conducting an evaluation. Lipsey and Pollard (1989) remark that adopting "the basic two-step" in program planning and evaluation would improve common practice. Planners can specify (a) what should happen right after participation in a program as a prerequisite for change and (b) a more ultimate outcome behavior that reflects a goal of the program. Evaluators would then develop methods to measure both. Learning about success or failure while the program is being provided is more informative than learning that the final outcome was or was not achieved. Particular attention would be paid to why the program did not lead to the intermediate result; perhaps additional resources are needed or the original theory was not valid. If the intermediate outcome was achieved but the final outcome was not, it would seem that the theory linking program activities to the intermediate step is valid, but that there must be strong nonprogram influences limiting the achievement of the desired ultimate outcomes.

How to develop a program theory. It is easier to agree that a program theory should be developed than to develop one. There are a number of approaches to developing a program theory. First, evaluators talk with the staff of the program. At times the staff will have a fairly clear idea of how the parts of the program affect the participants and how the intermediate stages lead to the final desired outcomes. If the staff members are not too helpful, evaluators turn to the research literature on similar programs. Perhaps there is research showing that a program is more effective with people of higher or lower educational levels. The characteristics of programs that seem to be well regarded can be summarized and compared to the tentative plans for a new program.

The research literature contains two kinds of material that might prove helpful. First, evaluations of similar programs might describe program theories. For example, peer leadership might lead to favorable outcomes more consistently in antismoking campaigns in junior high schools than do teacher-led classes (see Evans and Raines, 1990). Since junior high children are especially sensitive to the attitudes of peers, program planners might try to use peers in any program that attempts to influence adolescents (Turner, 1999). Another example comes from energy conservation research. Writers have noted that electricity use is not easy for people to monitor; few people ever look at their meters and, when they do, it is hard to relate the spinning disk to kilowatts of electricity. In fact, few people know what a kilowatt is. On the basis of these observations, programs have been developed to provide new ways to give people feedback about their use of power in terms that are understandable (see Seligman and Finegan, 1990). Examining basic research is a second way published research can help to develop program theory. Social support is often believed to be related to health and positive adjustment. Approaches to help people obtain social support are discussed in social and clinical psychology research studies (e.g., Glasgow, Terborg, Strycker et al., 1997). Some of those ideas might be appropriated to enrich the theory of some social service programs. Unfortunately, writers of basic research often provide only brief descriptions of the independent variable, that is, the treatment, thus making it difficult to apply their work to other settings ("The Trouble with Dependent Variables," 1990).

A particularly good example of the development of program theory was provided by Cook and Devine (1982), who described the expected processes whereby a psychoeducational intervention would help postsurgery patients recover more quickly and experience fewer side effects. Figure 3.2 has been adapted from Cook and Devine to illustrate some of the processes that connect the nurses' teaching to the desired outcome, having patients able to leave the hospital sooner without ill effects. Note that there are numerous criteria that may be observed by someone evaluating the program, including many intermediate variables as well as the final outcome criteria of program success.

Implausible program theories. In the process of selecting the criteria of program success sometimes it becomes clear that program theories are implausible. We don't want to suggest that a great proportion of program theories are implausible, but some are, and wise evaluators don't dismiss the idea that the conception of the program that they have been asked to evaluate might be based on implausible assumptions. Owners of swamp land were selling alligator hides to shoe manufacturers at a rate that led naturalists to worry about

FIGURE 3.2   Illustration of an impact model showing the intermediate steps that are expected to be observed between the intervention and the desired outcomes. (Illustration prepared on the basis of the findings presented by Cook and Devine, 1982.)

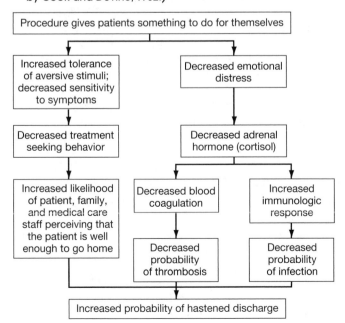

FIGURE 3.3   Sometimes programs are planned without a carefully thought-through impact model; when that happens there may be unstated assumptions in the model. At times unstated assumptions are implausible. When that happens the program can have an effect that was not imagined when the program was designed and implemented. (Adapted from Sieber, 1981)

Policy	Immediate Objective	[Unstated Assumption]	Stated Desired Outcome
Forbid the sale of alligator hides	Reduce the number of alligators killed for their hides	[Landowners will maintain land as alligator habitat.]	Alligators will continue to thrive.
		[Plausible Reaction to the Ban]	**Plausible Outcome**
		[Landowners will seek an alternative use of the land, such as draining it to develop farms.]	Alligators will have less habitat and will not thrive.

the disappearance of alligators in Florida. To protect alligators, the Florida state legislators passed a law forbidding the sale of alligator hides. This seemed like a straightforward decision. The goal was to have alligators thrive in Florida. We diagramed the impact model in Figure 3.3. The outcome of the policy could have been evaluated by estimating the number of hides sold in spite of the ban. A comparison to the sales in years prior to the ban might well have shown that the new law successfully reduced the number of hides available. However, the real objective was not to have fewer hides sold; the real objective was to have alligators thriving in Florida. There was an unstated assumption in the impact model. It was assumed that landowners who were unable to sell alligator hides would maintain their land as alligator habitat. If that happened the goal of the legislation would have been obtained; however, what happened was that landowners sought alternative uses of their land. By draining the land they were able to develop new farm land. When they did, the amount of habitat for alligators was reduced thereby negating the desired outcome of the legislation (Sieber, 1981). Detecting implausible program theories is more likely when impact models are developed with particular attention to discovering unstated assumptions.

Is the Program Accepted?

Good ideas are seldom adopted immediately. Mosteller (1981) described the astonishing lag in applying the sixteenth-century finding that citrus fruits (vitamin C, of course) would protect seamen from scurvy. On some long voyages, over 60 percent of the crew members died. One might have expected officials to immediately implement a policy that would have reduced this staggering loss of life, but 198 years elapsed between the first of several published descriptions of how to protect crews from scurvy and the adoption of the knowledge by the British Navy in 1795.

People for whom a program is designed may also reject it. The rejection of community mental health centers by chronically ill patients was mentioned already. There is a long line of research that clearly shows that physically ill patients often reject or ignore the treatment prescribed for their conditions (Posavac et al., 1985). Attempts to understand noncompliance with medical treatment suggest that better communication between physicians and patients promotes compliance. Some patients misunderstand the recommended treatment. It is especially hard for some patients with chronic illnesses such as diabetes to maintain the motivation to make lifestyle changes for the rest of their lives. Involving supportive family members is often an effective approach.

Many programs request participants to complete surveys at the end of a service to measure how much the participants were satisfied with the program. We believe that such surveys have a role to play in program evaluation, but it is important to recognize that such surveys cannot provide a sufficient means to assess the degree to which the program was effective. Some people are very satisfied with worthless treatments because they feel respected and valued by the people offering the service. However, a program that is disliked and rejected may not have a chance to be effective because participants who dislike a program or its staff are unlikely to participate fully. Marketing research firms focus on learning the preferences of potential customers and then matching products to those preferences. Although human service fields cannot base service design only on what students, clients, and patients think they need, program staff who are aware of client preferences have a better chance of designing and offering a service that will be accepted and utilized.

Are the Resources Devoted to the Program Being Expended Appropriately?

There are many ways in which program costs can be used in program evaluations. Elementary procedures that relate cost to program outcomes are introduced in Chapter 11. The range of the evaluation questions that can be treated are reviewed here.

Using program costs in the planning phase. When a government program is developed to provide a service to all who qualify, it is difficult to project its ultimate cost because it is difficult to estimate how many people will apply. However, when a specific program such as a new curriculum or a counseling service for a set number of participants is being planned, the costs can be fairly well estimated. Sometimes it may be possible to project the value of the results. For example, job training should result in better jobs at salaries that can be estimated. Then, the taxes those people will pay and the amount of welfare assistance they will not use can be estimated. One could ask whether that result justifies the use of the amount of government funds needed to provide the program. If such a program succeeded in providing job skills and leading people to be self-sufficient, there may be additional benefits to which dollar values cannot be assigned.

A second issue in the planning phase concerns whether alternative uses of the funds would provide a more desired result. Since resources are limited, it is important that critical stakeholders agree that the services to be supported are needed more than other services that could be supported instead. Such decisions are based partially, not totally, on the basis of costs and the value of benefits.

Is offering the program fair to all stakeholders? The use of ethnic origin to target educational aid is an attempt to give minorities a boost to overcome past discrimination. Many people endorse this policy (Dawes, 1994); however, some writers argue that such programs primarily assist children of middle-class minority parents who do not need the assistance (McWhorter, 2000; Steele, 1990). Evaluations of some programs aimed at increasing the skill levels of minorities have found that the programs actually increased the difference in skills between the children from low-income families and those from the middle class (Cook et al., 1975), possibly because middle-class parents made special efforts to expose their children to programs such as "Sesame Street." If so, is it fair to continue to use public funds to support the program?

A second illustration concerns support for public education. Because American public education has been funded largely through local property taxes, wealthy communities and communities with large numbers of businesses and industries can spend far more per pupil than can poor communities without industrial firms. Some critics then argue that it would be more fair if school funds were dispersed on the state level so that all school districts can offer school programs of a similar quality. The evaluator cannot answer these questions of fairness using research methods. However, the use of standards of social justice in evaluation has been encouraged by some writers (see Sirotnik, 1990) who argue that a value-free evaluation methodology is neither possible nor desirable. It would be critical to be explicit about how such values are being used; evaluators with hidden agendas do not serve stakeholders well (Scriven, 1997a).

Is this the way the funds are supposed to be spent? Another question about the use of program funding concerns whether the funds are being spent in a way that is compatible with the intention of the funding stakeholder. This question is related to the traditional accountability issue, which is designed to reduce the possibility of the misappropriation of funds. In the past, Congress and state legislators were often more interested in the question of whether funds had been spent as intended rather than the more difficult-to-answer questions of whether the funds had been spent wisely and whether the activities supported had met the needs that prompted the interest of the legislators.

Do the outcomes justify the resources spent? Once the results of a program are known, it is possible to examine the program costs to determine whether the outcomes were worth what it cost to attain them. If it is possible to place a dollar value on the outcome, then we can ask if the return was worth more than the cost of the program. Business-based financial analysts do this all the time. If the expected return on a company's investment does not exceed the investment, then there is probably something better to do with the investment. If there does not seem to be something better to do with the money, then the business should be sold off and the money distributed to the stockholders. Sometimes U.S. businesses are criticized for demanding a return on investments too soon; it may be that sizable returns require a long-range perspective. In human service and educational fields it is quite hard to place a dollar value on the results of programs. In this case, evaluators seek to compare programs that are designed to affect similar behaviors, such as developing employment or reading skills, and to ask which program is the most efficient. Unless there are other constraints, the most efficient would be the best program to offer.

Has the evaluation plan allowed for the development of criteria that are sensitive to undesirable side effects? If it were possible to predict specific side effects, program plans would be changed to reduce the chance of these negative outcomes. Since evaluators and managers expect some unanticipated outcomes to occur, observation procedures are planned to permit side effects to become apparent. This means that evaluators will allot time for visiting program sites and talking with representatives of all stakeholder groups. An organizational consultant remarked that although the management of a company hired him, he accepted a project only after it was agreed that the union would codirect the project. There is no point in carrying out an evaluation if the evaluator only hears one view of the strengths and weaknesses of a program or an organization.

Our improvement-focused approach to evaluation includes attention to unplanned results, whether positive or, as is often the case, negative. Overlooking side effects is more likely when evaluators plan an evaluation on the basis of official program descriptions (rather than the program as implemented), obtain information from only one stakeholder (usually the manager), and then carry out the evaluation at arm's length from the program. A professor of community nursing described how one evaluation team tried to evaluate a program designed to provide medical care to dispersed poor families in suburban areas. From the comfort and security of their offices they prepared a questionnaire based on the official objectives presented in the grant proposal and simply mailed the survey to a list of participants. These evaluators never visited any of the sign-up centers, never interviewed any participants, and never contacted any of the cooperating physicians. This mechanical application of objectives-based evaluation has contributed to negative reactions to evaluation in general and objectives-based evaluation in particular.

When evaluators believe that they have detected negative side effects, they will share their observations with stakeholders to obtain confirmation of their views or additional information to explain the observations. More careful observation procedures can then be developed to examine the unanticipated problem. Finding negative side effects is not done to discredit programs, but to assist in improving programs. Perhaps the program theory can be improved (Fitzpatrick, 2002). A director of training in a large city department once called a consultant "a self-appointed pin pricker." Pin pricking is not the mission of program evaluators; program improvement is. Sometimes it helps to have an outside observer call attention to overlooked problems, but calling attention to a problem is merely the first step; for effective evaluators, a harder and more important step involves developing recommendations.

SOME PRACTICAL LIMITATIONS IN SELECTING EVALUATION CRITERIA

Textbook authors have the freedom to describe ideal practices without being limited by the practical realities of specific evaluations. Three important restrictions on the selection of criteria are: the evaluation budget, time constraints, and the degree to which various criteria are accepted by the stakeholders.

Evaluation Budget

Evaluation is not free; evaluators and their staffs need to be paid, surveys need to be duplicated and mailed, costs for phones and computers add up quickly, and getting around to various program sites can be expensive. Evaluators estimate the amount of time they will need to do a credible job in the light of the stakeholders' needs. It is usually necessary to negotiate the parameters of the evaluation since few stakeholders know how much time is involved in completing a valid evaluation. Since the funds for an evaluation will be fairly inflexible, the focus of the evaluation is often adjusted during these negotiations. It is better to carry out a modest evaluation whose findings one can be trusted than to plan an ambitious project that can only be done poorly given the resources available.

Time Available for the Project

Since evaluation is an applied discipline, the use of findings is often tied into budget cycles, academic years, or the meeting schedules of governmental bodies. Some years ago the federal government commissioned a study of an innovative approach to welfare. By the time the demonstration project and evaluation were completed, the political climate had changed and Congress was no longer interested in the original idea or the evaluation. Often, projects are of a much shorter duration than expensive multisite demonstration projections costing tens of millions of dollars, but the principle is the same: There is a time when information can be used and a time after which it is no longer relevant and will not contribute to decisions (Sonnichsen, 2000). Before evaluators accept a project or begin to plan seriously, they ask about the project deadline. If the deadline and the stakeholders' evaluation needs are incompatible, the evaluator must bow out or the project must be renegotiated. There simply is no reason to begin a project that cannot be completed when it is needed.

Criteria That Are Credible to the Stakeholders

Evaluators seek to collect valid data in ways that permit valid interpretations; in addition, it is crucial that stakeholders accept those interpretations. While planning the evaluation, evaluators ascertain that the stakeholders have agreed that the jointly selected criteria fit the goals of the program and are appropriate for the participants in the program. We talk about stakeholders "buying into" the criteria: It is helpful to have agreements in writing. The stakeholders need not sign a statement of acceptance; however, the evaluator can keep careful notes during meetings as an evaluation is planned. After each meeting copies of these notes can be distributed to critical stakeholders. At the beginning of each meeting the agreements summarized in the notes can be reviewed to be sure that stakeholders still agreed on the criteria of the program and the focus of the evaluation.

Summary and Preview

The importance of the criteria selected for an evaluation is hard to overemphasize. They are the windows through which users of the evaluation see the program. If the windows distort the view, the program would be misrepresented, either favorably or unfavorably. Ideally, evaluators observe more than just the final outcome of programs that require the cooperation and effort of the participants as do programs in educational, psychological, criminal justice, and other settings. Evaluators and their clients benefit by examining the processes whereby a service is thought to lead to the expected outcomes. Even a very simple program theory that specifies program activities, expected intermediate outcomes, and final outcomes greatly improves the evaluator's ability to understand the program.

The next chapter focuses on the specific steps that one takes in measuring the criteria selected. Although a textbook separates the selection of criteria from a discussion of measurement issues, evaluators consider whether criteria can be measured validly and reliably at the same time they are making choices of criteria to measure.

Study Questions

1. Consider a setting with which you are familiar: school, work, church, team, dormitory. Each has rules or procedures to meet certain objectives. Try to analyze the assumed impact model to learn how the procedures might lead to the objectives.

For example, there are required courses or area requirements for most college curricula. How might these requirements lead to educated graduates? What intermediate outcomes need to occur? How much validity does your impact model seem to possess? Drawing an impact model often helps to detect implausible assumptions. Try to find a few implausible assumptions underlying a public policy.

2. This chapter suggested that different stakeholders have very different views of how intercollegiate athletes should be evaluated. Make a list of some public policies or programs that would be likely to be seen as having quite different purposes depending on the stakeholder group evaluating the policy. You might consider the views of different groups regarding traffic flow, casino gambling, or drinking laws.

3. Show how an evaluator might select criteria of program success that are easily measured, but that miss the central point of the program. If you have trouble starting, think about the criteria of success for a little league baseball team or a volleyball coach in a junior high. Those should be easy; now work with the meaning of success for college teaching, counseling, law enforcement, or other important community activities.

4. A local health care center participated in a program to teach volunteer community residents to how to use computers to find health information posted by the center on its Internet site. Some stakeholders postulated that this effort would result in fewer cases of low birth weight babies in the community. Is this a plausible result of such a program? What might be more plausible outcomes from such a program?

5. What are some values and some limitations to the contributions that potential participants can make to specifying the criteria of successful programs from which they might receive services?

Additional Resource

SHADISH, W. R., COOK, T. D., AND LEVITON, L. C. 1991. *Foundations of program evaluation: Theories of practice.* Newbury Park, CA: Sage.

This is a major work describing major theoretical approaches to program evaluation. The authors are prominent theorists and methodologists themselves. In the second paragraph of Chapter 1 the authors write: ". . . we have few clear, agreed-upon criteria for judging the worth of social activities" (p. 19). Their comment underscores the importance of working carefully while planning an evaluation in order to begin on the right foot with a wise choice of criteria by which to assess unmet needs or the implementation and outcomes of a program. Looking up "criteria of merit" in the index will lead to eight discussions of the way to choose the criteria of successful programs from the point of view of influential theorists.

Developing Measures

— So many stakeholders in the french department

A fter evaluators and stakeholders have agreed on criteria that would indicate successful implementation and outcome, evaluators face the task of developing methods to measure those criteria. Psychologists gather data from individuals; sociologists gather data on a community or neighborhood level; and economists focus attention on larger groups. These differences reflect the questions treated by these disciplines. Programs are designed to affect individuals (e.g., education or rehabilitation), or communities (e.g., crime prevention, building improvement), or states or regions (e.g., clean air policies, economic stimulation). Depending on the program being evaluated, program evaluators gather data in ways similar to the methods used by psychologists, sociologists, business managers, or economists. Regardless of the focus of the program, each type of data has strengths and weaknesses; consequently, evaluators should use multiple sources and methods. We cannot cover all approaches in one chapter. Instead we discuss the most frequently used sources and methods as well as the characteristics of good measures of evaluation criteria. Last, some measurement tools are presented to illustrate the principles.

Sources of Data for Evaluation

A dilemma for evaluators is that the stakeholders who know the program best may be biased toward seeing program success, whereas those who have the least self-interest know little about the program. This dilemma leads evaluators to seek data from a variety of sources using different types of measurement techniques.

Intended Beneficiaries of the Program

Educational, training, medical, and welfare programs that focus on individuals usually involve information from individual participants. On the other hand, programs in economic development, preventive medicine, and criminal justice focus on community-level variables rather than on specific, identifiable individuals. With such programs, all members of a community are, in a sense, recipients of the service; consequently, data that reflect the state of the community will be most relevant.

Program participants. Program participants can provide information that is not available from other sources. In some situations participants spend more time with program staff than managers who are responsible for assessing the competence of the staff. College students, for example, often know more about the quality of a professor's teaching than does a department head or dean. Furthermore, only the program participants know what their reactions are to the program. For many programs, participants are the best source of information on their own condition. After interviewing deinstitutionalized chronically ill psychiatric patients, Shadish, Orwin, Silber, and Bootzin (1985) concluded that for many patients, discharge damaged their sense of well-being. An advantage of participant-provided information is that it is often relatively inexpensive to gather and is at least as accurate as other assessment approaches for a variety of behavioral and emotional dimensions (Shrauger and Osberg, 1981). There are, however, surprising limitations to what people can report about themselves. For example, people have difficulty recalling what they ate the previous week and most people report eating medium-sized servings even though the definitions of "medium" varied by 200 percent in different versions of the same survey ("On a Diet?", 1989). Schwarz and Oyserman (2001) have shown how small differences in the phrasing of questions can affect what people report about themselves or their surroundings.

It is valuable to recognize that most participants can provide good data on many objective aspects of a program but not on other aspects. General hospital patients usually know if rooms are clean, whether nurses and resident physicians treat them politely, and how long they have to wait in radiology (see Brown and Adams, 1992). However, they cannot evaluate the choice of medication or the competence of their surgeons. Similarly, college students can report on whether a teacher returned tests promptly, held classes as scheduled, and lectured or led class discussions. There are few undergraduates who can evaluate the accuracy of information presented in lectures unless the professor is grossly incompetent.

Experienced evaluators do not forget that an evaluation is not a high priority for program participants because they have sought the services of the program in order to meet a need, not to provide data. Many people will share their views if they believe that their efforts can help improve services for others. However, few are so altruistic that they will put effort into struggling with a poorly organized survey. Our experience is that the participants who have the most favorable impressions of a program or facility are the most likely to cooperate with data collection. The 86 percent who responded to a lengthy survey on a chaplaincy internship were independently evaluated by their former supervisors as having performed better than the 14 percent who did not return the survey (Posavac, 1975). Hogan (1985) found that college alumni who returned a mailed survey had earned higher GPAs than those who did not.

Participants will need to be assured that their answers to surveys or interviews will be treated confidentially. Many people do not understand the social scientist's disinterest in facts about individuals, nor do they understand the necessity of using group averages and proportions in evaluation reports. They are familiar with the case study approach often used in newspaper and television discussions of medical, correctional, counseling, and educational programs. At times, however, details on an individual level can play a role in an evaluation report by giving vivid illustrations of very good or very bad program performance. Using case studies of teenagers, Love (1986) showed that troubled adolescents were unlikely to fit into the mental health and welfare systems of a large city. Although a case study cannot show the extent of a problem, it can show how specific program failures occur and can help policy makers visualize a need for program development or change. Success stories can help planners as well because the way participants succeeded may suggest how to improve the program for others (Brinkerhoff, 2003; Kibel, 1999).

Artifacts. In some settings, evaluators can use things that program participants or community members produce. In schools, students write essays, term papers, theses, school newspapers, and yearbooks. These artifacts reflect the quality of the curriculum, the teaching staff, and, indirectly, the school administration. In vocational settings, it might be useful to track the quality of items made and the amount of material wasted. The success of morale-boosting efforts might be revealed by a greater use of coffee cups and caps marked with a company or university logo. Turning to unwanted artifacts, the need for a community vandalism prevention program might be demonstrated by high rates of broken windows, unkempt yards, and doubly or triply bolted doors. Success of a community program might be indicated by a lower rate of such artifacts.

Community indexes. Some programs are designed to improve community-level variables. Examples include a crime prevention program to increase citizen participation in an effort to reduce theft, and a citizen-developed program to monitor housing code violations to increase or maintain the quality of housing in a neighborhood. Since such programs are delivered to a community, they must be evaluated differently than programs aimed at individuals. Instead of seeking data from people gathered for classes or group therapy, a representative sample of the residents of communities may have to be obtained or community records, such as crime reports, fire losses, or immunization rates may be summarized.

A major difficulty with community-level indexes is that there are many steps between the program and the desired end results (Cook, Leviton, and Shadish, 1985). So many nonprogram events, policies, and even habits may have such strong effects on the behavior to be changed that even a well-conceived program may not create a detectable effect. Such influences are, of course, beyond the control of the program staff. An evaluator who measures community-level indexes for an outcome evaluation of, say, a media-based preventive health effort while ignoring the integrity of program implementation and intermediate outcomes may be left quite in the dark about the reasons for apparent failure or success.

Providers of Services

The staffs of programs have information that is crucial to program evaluations. Programs also maintain records that, when summarized, can provide important cues concerning a program's operation and the outcomes achieved.

Program staff. Staff members have been trained and are expected to assess participants' needs and improvement. Also, staff members know how well a program is managed and run on a day-to-day basis. On the negative side, staff members expect to see improvement; after committing themselves to helping people improve their skills, health, or adjustment, it becomes easy to overlook program problems.

Beyond a concern over the expectations of staff, evaluators need to recognize that evaluating a program is in some ways an evaluation of the staff's performance. Few staff members unhesitatingly welcome an evaluation of the effectiveness of services they provide; in fact, most will have questions about how an evaluation is to be used. If they are worried, they may resist the evaluation. Some college professors try to bar students conducting course evaluations from entering classrooms, and some psychotherapists argue that checklists of symptoms and rating forms are not sensitive enough to detect subtle, yet crucial, changes in clients that only therapists can sense. Although it may be hard to counter all concerns, program managers can assure staff that program evaluations are designed to evaluate programs, not individuals, and evaluators can assure staff of confidentiality. Furthermore, evaluators can include staff members in a thorough discussion of the findings of the evaluation as part of the report preparation process; providing scheduled progress reports as well as a final report can assure staff members that they will receive feedback throughout the evaluation process (Posavac, 1992).

Program records. Evaluators often begin developing specific methods to assess the criteria by asking about a program's records (Hatry, 1994). Records should include client characteristics, types and amounts of services provided, costs of services, and workloads of staff members. When the variables are objective, these records can be very reliable. When the variables are less objective, as is the case with diagnoses or comments on progress, evaluators must exercise caution in using the information. There are several important advantages of using the program's archives: The measurement process cannot affect the program participant, there can be no participant loss due to refusal or inability to cooperate, and data collection is less costly than would be the case when gathering data in the field. However, the quality of records may be poor. For example, a jail-based drug rehabilitation treatment program had such poor records that attempts to match treatment information with other information about clients had to be abandoned (Lurigio and Swartz, 1994); hospital discharge records to be used in an evaluation contained many coding errors (Green and Wintfeld, 1993). Furthermore, records have been deceptively altered in anticipation of an evaluation as the Inspector General of the Pentagon did (Margasak, 2001).

When working as an agent of the service provider, an evaluator has legal authority to use confidential records; however, the importance of maintaining confidentiality cannot be overestimated. Program records often contain material which, if released, could harm the program participant or staff member. Even the accidental release of critical information could leave the evaluator open to legal challenge; if insufficient care is taken when handling program or agency records during an evaluation, the evaluator would provide a very unprofessional image, would lose credibility, and could be denied further access to records.

Observers

Observers who are not part of a program often provide perspectives that neither participants nor staff can. Observers could be (a) experts who are familiar with a wide range of similar programs or the needs the program is designed to meet, (b) people especially trained to rate the variables that describe the process or outcomes of a program, (c) people with relationships with participants such as family members or work associates, or (d) the evaluators themselves.

Expert observers. Very complicated programs with abstract goals are often evaluated by having a team of experts examine the program's structure and products (Averch, 1994). Accreditations of hospitals, rehabilitation facilities, and colleges are handled by experts who examine much information and talk with staff and participants before rendering a judgment. A basic research program must be evaluated before it can be provided with financial support. It is hard to think of a way to evaluate a proposed research program that does not use expert opinion. Experts not involved in the program being evaluated may be the least biased sources of information (Endicott and Spitzer, 1975). Expert opinions may be essential to clarify the meaning of quantitative information describing the program.

Trained observers. Many programs can be evaluated using people who have been trained to rate well-defined criteria of program success. A municipal program to repair and clean parks might be evaluated by training a team of employees to examine parks using checklists with objectively defined levels of maintenance (Greiner, 1994). An evaluation of treatment services for severely mentally disabled clients may utilize ratings of psychological function by trained observers using a social adjustment scale (Green and Jerrell, 1994).

Significant others. If a program is designed to change behavior (as correction and counseling programs are) or to improve health or work skills, people who have contact with the participants outside of program settings often can provide important information on improvements or problems (e.g., Katz and Warren, 1998). With the exception of hospital patients or prisoners, staff members see participants for far fewer hours per week and in fewer settings than family members who see participants in natural situations. However, significant others also have biases; they want to see improvement in troubled family members. Evaluators seeking information from significant others would want to learn about specific changes in participants; general subjective opinions would be less useful.

When requesting information about participants from significant others, it is necessary to have the participants' permission beforehand. People differ in their willingness to have spouses or others provide personal information to an evaluation staff. Requests for cooperation can emphasize the potential to improve services for others. Care should be taken to avoid implying that good treatment for the participant is contingent on giving permission to contact a significant other or on providing information for an evaluation.

Evaluation staff. In some situations information is gathered by people playing the role of clients (Turner and Zimmerman, 1994). The number of busy signals, time to answer telephone calls, and time on hold can indicate business and agency responsiveness to citizen needs (Jason and Liotta, 1982). The Chicago city Consumer Services Department placed calls for taxi service to learn if companies were honoring a requirement to serve disabled riders; it was learned that 47 percent of such requests were ignored (Washburn, 2001). Some forms of qualitative evaluations are based on the thorough observations by an evaluator familiar with social science methods and intervention programs, but not with the specific program being evaluated. When a disinterested observer examines the program, traditional practices and assumptions made by the staff may be questioned (Guba and Lincoln, 1989). Fresh insights into side effects of the program may be detected. Both the goal-free and the naturalistic models of evaluations depend on information gathered by the evaluators themselves. Figure 4.1 summarizes the primary strengths and weaknesses of the various sources of information just introduced.

Which Sources Should Be Used?

The choice of data sources depends on the cost of obtaining data, the type of decision to be made on the basis of the evaluation, the size of the program, and the time available to conduct the evaluation. If an agency needs information to satisfy a state auditor's office, it is likely that a summary of records, a sampling of participants' attitudes, and a fiscal report will suffice. If a decision to expand (or eliminate) an expensive, controversial service is anticipated, a thorough analysis of the needs and progress of the participants coupled with the judgments of outside experts may be essential. Such decisions must be made on the basis of an evaluation of considerable rigor and credibility.

Regardless of the reason for an evaluation, evaluators should strive to use multiple measures from more than one source (Shadish, 1993). In choosing multiple measures, it is especially important to select measures that are not likely to share the same biases. For example, a client's subjective assessment of the success of a program may be mirrored by the subjective feelings of the client's spouse. If subjective measures of a program's success are supplemented by objective measures, evaluators are less likely to obtain sets of data affected by the same biases. When a conclusion is supported from a variety of sources, it becomes more plausible to stakeholders.

It is, however, possible that the different sources will not agree. Shipley (1976) conducted an evaluation of a program in which college students served as volunteer companions to discharged psychiatric patients. The volunteers, patients, and hospital staff all viewed the program in quite glowing terms. However, more objective measures of the patients' behavior (staff ratings and records of frequency and duration of rehospitalizations) revealed highly variable outcomes. Some patients apparently benefitted; others did not. The use of multiple measures led Shipley to a conclusion different from that drawn in evaluations of similar companion programs using only subjective ratings. In a similar vein, Sullivan and Snowden (1981) found that staff, clients, standard tests, and agency files did not agree about the nature of the clients' problems. Massey and Wu (1994) showed that patients, family members, and case managers in a mental health facility assess the patients' level of functioning differently. While evaluating publicly funded job-training programs, Hougland (1987) found that subjective satisfaction was not highly correlated with objective outcomes, such as income level. Evaluators must therefore be sensitive to the possibility that their selection of data sources and measurement methods can affect their conclusions.

FIGURE 4.1   Different sources of information used in program evaluations have different strengths and weaknesses. Using multiple sources is the best approach to obtain comprehensive information.

Sources of Information	Strengths	Weaknesses
Intended Beneficiaries of the Program		
Individual participants (surveys or interviews)	Can provide information on the operation of the program. Have unique information on reaction to the program. Can demonstrate changes in accomplishments.	Are not an expert on programs. Could be biased to see improvement.
Community residents (surveys or interviews)	Unique information on the visibility of programs planned to affect communities. Not likely to be predisposed to report improvements.	Are not experts on programs. May be unaware of the program (that, of course, could be valuable information).
Providers of Services		
Program staff	Can provide information on the operation of the program.	Likely to be favorably disposed to the program.
Program records	Unique information describing the program and participants. No problem with nonresponses.	Sometimes have been doctored to support the program.
Observers		
Expert observers	Familiar with programs similar to the one being evaluated. Not likely to be biased in favor of the program.	Visits are brief and observers could be misled.
Trained observers	Can focus on the variables of particular interest. Not likely to be biased.	Could be expensive to train and maintain on the program site.
Significant others	Best source of observations of the day-to-day behavior of participants.	Could be biased to see improvement.
Evaluation team	Can provide targeted information. Not likely to be biased.	Could be an expensive form of data collection.

Since evaluators frequently work with people trained in service delivery techniques, not in research methods, evaluators often are surprisingly free to choose the criteria of effectiveness and the analyses of those criteria. Some observers go so far as to say that evaluators can determine the findings of an evaluation before it is conducted through their choice of criteria and analytic methods (Berk, 1977; Berk and Rossi, 1976; Zigler and Trickett, 1978). Fairness to all stakeholders requires evaluators to examine their own attitudes as they design evaluations. The following section describes the most important issues to consider when choosing assessment procedures.

GOOD ASSESSMENT PROCEDURES

When making choices among possible data sources and approaches to measurement, evaluators strive to use techniques that will contribute to valid, sensitive, and persuasive evaluations. Using measures with the qualities discussed below will help achieve this goal.

Use Multiple Variables

Evaluators usually recommend using multiple sources of information (Mark and Shotland, 1987) and multiple variables from each of the data sources. The elevation of a single variable as the criterion of success can obscure an effect (Lipsey, Crosse, Dunkle, Pollard, and Stobart, 1985) and will probably lead to its corruption (Sechrest, 1984). Elliott (1989) showed how advancement in grade and standard test scores became corrupted when used to the exclusion of other variables; teachers began to promote a greater proportion of students and begin to teach to the test. Barbour and Wolfson (1973) provide a different example of how variables become corrupt—in this case, measures of police productivity. Concentrating on number of arrests may unintentionally encourage poor evidence-gathering practices and police officers may make arrests when the interests of justice would be better served without an arrest. Measuring police performance by the number of miles police cars were driven led police officers to cruise highways rather than congested city streets (Chen, 1994). A performance criterion of mental health workers (i.e., "90 percent of referred clients actually make contact with the new agency") led to less service, not better service (Turner, 1977). The evaluator learned that in order to reach this 90 percent criterion, mental health workers were escorting clients to the second agency while other duties were left unfinished. These illustrations are not presented to suggest that teachers, police officers, or mental health workers shirk their duties. But because people tend to behave in ways that are rewarded, a naive focus on a specific criterion thought to indicate program success could instead adversely affect the program.

Using multiple variables reduces the likelihood of corrupting variables and distorting the operation of an agency. It is especially helpful when the variables serve as a check on one another. Thus, both arrest rate and conviction rate should be used as measures of police productivity. Percentage of successful referrals and number of clients interviewed could be used as criteria for assessing the work of mental health workers who screen people seeking care.

An additional reason for using multiple variables is that different variables are affected by different sources of error. Multiple variables measured in very similar ways from one source may be affected by the same biases. When this happens, the extra effort is of little value. By using several variables, assessed in different ways from different sources of data, evaluators can draw conclusions from the convergence of these variables and thus add considerable strength to the evaluation. Case Study 1 illustrates how the convergence of multiple measures provided strong support for a summer program for teenagers.

Use Nonreactive Measures

Nonreactive measurement refers to procedures of gathering information that do not prompt the respondent to give invalid information. For example, whenever it seems obvious that certain answers are desired by interviewers, some respondents tend to give those answers. The previous section hinted at the problem of reactive measures: Merely focusing attention on a variable can lead people to change their behavior. Even surveys can be reactive because they may prompt respondents to think about issues they may have never concerned themselves with before. Clearly when an evaluation leads to changes in the behavior of staff or clients, the evaluation does not reflect the program in operation. Unless the evaluation depends solely on existing records, totally nonreactive measurement is an ideal seldom achieved, although care in designing evaluations can reduce reactivity (Webb, Campbell, Schwartz, Sechrest, and Grove, 1981).

Use Variables Relevant to Information Needs

Because program evaluation is an applied discipline, the variables selected must be relevant to the specific informational needs of facility management, community representatives, those responsible for budgets, and other stakeholders. In planning an evaluation, evaluators seek to learn what issues are pressing but not understood. Discussions with staff and managers often reveal the important variables. If no decisions can be affected by a variable, or if no program standards mention the variable, then it probably is not essential to the evaluation. Evaluators take care not to measure variables that some stakeholders might think would be "interesting" but which would not affect the operation of the program or agency; such variables raise the cost of an evaluation but do not contribute to its value. There are times when evaluators expect that a variable would be seen as important once summarized for agency leaders; experienced evaluators act in the role of educator at times. Furthermore, evaluators seek to be sure that they are sensitive to good and bad side effects that cannot be anticipated.

CASE STUDY 1

Using Multiple Measures in an Evaluation of a Summer Community
Program for Youth

The value of making observations from a variety of perspectives was illustrated by an evaluation of a community policing project (Thurman, Giacomazzi, and Bogen, 1993). Note that participant observations, focus groups, telephone surveys, and written questionnaires were used and program cost was presented. Note also that the interests of four stakeholder groups—participants, parents or guardians, staff, and taxpayers—were examined.

Police officers worked with a program designed to help 325 high-risk children develop a sense of responsibility, envision occupational roles, recognize the relationship between education and finding a good job, and hold positive images of police officers. The children, whose median age was 13, were nominated by school counselors from the most economically disadvantaged neighborhoods. The week-long program included: (a) work periods spent removing trash, weeds, and graffiti; (b) lunches in parks; (c) tours of businesses and museums; (d) a $40 bank account for program completion; and (e) contact with role models, including police officers.

Five focus groups were used to assess immediate reactions of the children. Each session was held near the end of the week and lasted one hour. The children volunteered comments that seemed to match the goals of the program: They said that they learned responsibility, were encouraged to complete their education, and for the most part reported positive feelings toward the police officers.

The parents or guardians were randomly selected for structured telephone interviews after the program ended; 94 percent agreed to be interviewed. All said that their children had talked about positive aspects of the program and wanted to participate again in the following summer. Nearly all respondents (90 percent) said there were no negative aspects of the program and about half said that their child did gain a sense of responsibility.

At the end of the summer all program staff received surveys. Respondents were aware of organizational problems; however, nearly all had a very positive perception of the program, all recommended that the program be repeated the next summer, and all said that they wanted to be involved if it were offered again.

The cost of the program was $46,311, or $142.50 per child. There was no way to compare this cost to the long-term benefits; however, if such efforts motivate only a small number of high-risk children to avoid gangs and drugs, considerable suffering would be avoided and society would save significant future law enforcement, legal, and rehabilitation funds.

Use Valid Measures

In an evaluation, the instruments must validly measure the behaviors that the program is designed to change. These behaviors may be the ultimate criterion behaviors (such as a healthy life, developed skills, employment) or more immediate behaviors believed to be useful in achieving the planned long-term outcomes (such as more consistent adherence to prescribed medical treatment, higher quality work, or improved leadership practices). In order to increase the credibility of the evaluation, evaluators make sure that staff members have approved the measures. But because program staff members are often inexperienced in social science methodology and cannot judge how feasible it is to measure a particular variable, evaluators do not depend on them to suggest all the measures and variables.

In general, the more a measurement tool focuses on objective behavior rather than on ill-defined or vague terms, the more likely it is to be valid. Objective behaviors (such as "late to work less often than once a week" or "speaks in groups") can be more validly measured than traits (such as "punctual" and "assertive"), regardless of the specific measurement approach chosen (Mager, 1972).

Even when the variables seem quite objective, information taken from official records may not be as valid as it first appears. Changing definitions and differing levels of care in preparing records can introduce changes in the meaning of variables that could influence an evaluation. At least twice Chicago's crime records appeared to reveal a crime wave when the real cause of the changes was better recordkeeping by the police. Campbell (1969) showed that after a well-respected person was installed as chief of police, thefts under $50 increased dramatically. Instead of ushering in a crime wave, the new chief simply insisted on better reporting procedures, and may have reclassified some crimes. Since homicides are usually recorded accurately and completely and cannot be reclassified into a different category, homicide rates were used to determine that the crime rate did not increase once the new chief took over. In 1983 a similar increase was observed when recording standards were again strengthened ("Good News," 1983). After the renorming of the SAT ("Notebook," 1994), average SAT scores of college freshmen showed an increase between 1994 and 1995, a result solely due to a change in scaling by the Educational Testing Service. The national jobless rate increased in 1994 because the Bureau of Labor Statistics changed the survey used to assess joblessness to better reflect the participation of women in the workforce ("Survey's Overhaul," 1993). In 2000 the U.S. Census revised the categories used by respondents to indicate their race (Lee, 2001). This change means that information on race from the 2000 Census cannot be directly compared with previous census data. Using records is efficient and often less expensive than making observations specifically for an evaluation, but whenever one uses data collected by someone else for a purpose other than the evaluation, a critical examination of the validity of the data is always in order.

Use Reliable Measures

The concept of reliability. Reliability refers the consistency of the information that a measure produces for the same person in the same situation (Murphy and Davidshofer, 2005). There are many ways to think about reliability. If different observers describing the same thing report similar levels of a variable, we say that the observation procedure is reliable. If different levels are reported, we say that the procedure is unreliable. Reliability is calculated using the correlation coefficient, r. If two observers agreed completely after making a number of observations, a correlation of the two sets of data would be 1.00, perfect reliability. To the extent that they do not agree with each other, the correlation would be smaller; 0.0 would indicate that knowing one observer's reports would tell us nothing about the other observer's reports.

If an outcome measure is a 50-item test of knowledge gained from, say, a job training program, there is another way to estimate reliability. The scores that a group of trainees got on half of the items can be correlated with the scores on the other half of the items; such a correlation is called a "split-half" reliability. Note that the focus of interest is still consistency just as in the first example concerning interobserver reliability. For split-half reliability the issue is inter-item consistency.

Reliability is higher when the measurement procedure is minimally affected by the passing moods of the observer or the individuals observed. Like validity, reliability is likely to be higher when observations are based on objective behaviors rather than on inferences. Reliability is also higher when the measurement instrument contains more items. You may well have a sense of the higher reliability produced by using many questions if you think of a classroom test. A single item forms a larger portion of a short test than it would of a long test. If you had happened to be unable to master the topic covered by a certain question, your score would be affected much more in the context of a short test than in the context of a long test. Because a single question can have major effect, short tests are less reliable than long tests. The more reliable a measure is, the more likely it is to detect an effect of a program (Lipsey, 1990).

Evaluators trained in disciplines in which the individual assessment is important are familiar with the reliability of classroom, achievement, or job selection tests. It is crucial that evaluators recognize that using tests to evaluate individuals is markedly different from using tests to evaluate programs. Since evaluators focus attention on groups, not individuals, surveys and observational techniques that would not be useful for individual assessment are quite acceptable to estimate the mean score of a group. By using the standard deviation of a measure and its reliability, it is possible to calculate a range of values likely to include a person's true score. For example, assume a person scored 105 on an IQ test whose standard deviation is 15 and reliability is 0.95. The true scores of 68 percent of the people getting 105 will be between $105 \pm 15 \sqrt{(1-0.95)}$, or 101.6 and 108.4. The value added and subtracted to the person's score is called the standard error of measurement and applies when measuring an individual's score (Murphy and Davidshofer, 2005).

In contrast, when estimating a group's mean score, the standard error of the mean should be used to calculate confidence intervals instead of the standard deviation. Suppose a group of 81 students are selected at random from a school. Suppose further that they have an average of 105 on the same IQ test mentioned above. For a group, we work with the sampling error of the mean;

sampling error is given by the standard error of the mean which, in this case, is $15\sqrt{81}$, or 1.67. We can conclude that 68 percent of such groups have true mean scores between $105\pm1.67\sqrt{(1-.95)}$, or 104.6 and 105.4. Compare this confidence interval with the one found for an individual in the paragraph above. We can be more certain of the likely value of a group mean than the score of any one of the individuals in the group. Even a measure with a reliability of only 0.40 would yield a sufficiently precise estimate for program evaluation purposes because evaluators are concerned about groups, not individuals. Astin (1971, 1993) makes much the same point when he points out that even three-item scales are often sufficiently reliable for evaluating the effects of college experiences when samples are large.

Different forms of reliability. Some reliability indexes are less relevant to evaluation than to individual assessment. A crucial distinction relates to the difference between assessing a personality trait that is thought to be a stable characteristic of an individual versus measuring a behavior that can change, depending on the intentions of people or the situations in which they act. For personality assessment, a high test–retest reliability shows that the measure reliably produces consistent estimates of a trait. The items on such measures have been chosen because they produce stable results; however, *stability is not the focus of evaluators.* Programs are designed to change people or communities; program success cannot be evaluated with measures that were selected to be stable. Evaluators seek measures that are sensitive to change (Lipsey and Cordray, 2000).

A form of reliability that evaluators seek in scales is homogeneity, that is, the degree to which a scale measures one thing rather than a mixture of behaviors. If a reading program is to be evaluated, the instrument should measure reading improvement, not general knowledge or quantitative skills. Cronbach's *alpha* is available in many statistical programs and is often reported when several items are placed together to form a scale. In essence, this index is a generalization of the traditional *split-half reliability* coefficient without the need to divide the scale into arbitrary halves (Pedhazur and Schmelkin, 1991).

When observer ratings are used, evaluators also seek high interobserver reliability. An instrument that yields similar values when used by different people has more credibility than one that yields different values. Obviously, if the ratings are done in different settings—at home versus at school—a low interobserver reliability index may be due to real differences between the settings themselves. Interobserver reliability can be increased through the development of a detailed instruction manual, observer training, and periodic monitoring of observers (Greiner, 1994).

Use Measures That Can Detect Change

Sensitivity to change was mentioned above, but its importance needs to be stressed. Before a course, few students are expected to do well on a test covering the course material. After the course, however, students who mastered the material will do well. Classroom tests are good if they are sensitive to changes that occur as the skills of the students improve. Fairly stable characteristics of the students (such as intelligence) should not be the primary factors leading to differences among the students' classroom test scores. In contrast, the developers of intelligence tests seek to minimize the effects of specific learning experiences on intelligence scores and maximize the effect of general skills developed over a long time period. This is nearly opposite to the approach evaluators take when seeking to detect the impact of a specific program (Meier, 2004).

Furthermore, care must be taken to be sure that measures of outcome are affected by the program, not by a great number of other influences. Community-level performance indicators were used in an evaluation of crime prevention efforts in Victoria, Australia (van den Eynde, Veno, and Hart, 2003). Unfortunately, the programs appeared totally ineffective because the outcome measures were not closely linked to program activities. For example, some programs (such as, drama, wilderness experiences, training skills needed for circus performances) were designed to change youth culture; even if effective, such an outcome would hardly effect emergency hospital visits a month or two after the program began.

Several methods can be used to check on the expected sensitivity of a measure. Previous effective use of a measure with evaluations of similar programs would increase confidence that it is sufficiently sensitive. If the measure has been developed specifically for an evaluation, perhaps existing groups can be found who differ on the variable. For example, a newly developed measure of scientific reasoning that reveals differences between physics and humanities majors is a better measure of an outcome of an innovative science curriculum than a measure that cannot discriminate between such groups (Lipsey, 1993). In estimating the sensitivity of a measure, evaluators must consider the typical score of the participants before a program begins. It is hard to detect improvements among program participants if most of them are already in a desirable condition when the program begins. This problem is called a ceiling effect. For example, in a given week very large proportions of hospital patients are discharged alive and most automobile drivers are accident-free; consequently, even when medical care improves or drivers become more careful, it is hard to detect changes in such variables unless observations are made on very many people. If appropriate, one way to increase statistical sensitivity to small changes is to observe the same people both before and after participation in a program. Repeated measures designs increase statistical sensitivity and should be considered when practical (Lipsey, 1990; Shaughnessy, Zechmeister, and Zechmeister, 2005).

Use Cost-Effective Measures

In planning program evaluations, the cost of developing and producing data collection instruments must be considered. Several principles are important to remember. First, efforts devoted to making test material attractive and easy to use reap higher response rates; computers make this job rather easy. Second, funds devoted to obtaining copyright materials are small compared to the costs of gathering, analyzing and interpreting data. Third, because interviews are a much more expensive form of data collection compared to surveys, interviews should not be routinely planned. Some evaluation questions, however, cannot be answered using records or written surveys. At times, program participants are unable to use written forms (e.g., children, elderly or very ill patients), need prompting to obtain complete information (poorly educated participants), do not respond to written surveys (physicians), or might be defensive when answering written surveys (addicts). Last, the relationship between the instruments and participant loss needs to be considered. An instrument that is in itself inexpensive may not be cost-effective if evaluators must spend a considerable amount of time following up tardy potential respondents or if so few respond that the results do not represent any group.

TYPES OF MEASURES OF EVALUATION CRITERIA

It is impossible to catalog the wide variety of measures of unmet needs or the implementation and outcomes of programs. In this section several of the strengths and weaknesses of the most widely used techniques are described. Some ways to speed your access to the literature are illustrated.

Written Surveys and Interviews with Program Participants

Written surveys. Probably the single most widely used method of gathering data for evaluation is the written survey administered to program participants. The written survey provides the most information for the cost and effort required. Depending on the nature of the questions addressed, surveys differ in their reliability and validity. Asking clients of psychotherapy about the overall quality of the service they received is not likely to yield particularly reliable or valid responses. However, the reliability of a survey that focuses on current specific behaviors is likely to be fairly high. Evaluators and stakeholders often draft surveys that are longer than they need to be and more complicated than participants are likely to complete. Gathering information that cannot be used is a poor use of evaluation resources and an imposition on the potential respondents.

Using surveys developed by others saves evaluators' time in writing and pretesting items. Furthermore, previous users of such surveys may have published the means and standard deviations that will provide comparisons to the program being evaluated, thus making the interpretation of findings more valid. When the program is indeed unique, evaluators are required to develop new surveys to measure attitudes toward the program. Evaluators must be realistic about how much time they can afford to put into the construction of new instruments; like playing a guitar, writing survey items is easy to do badly.

Evaluators plan on reminding potential respondents to complete surveys. Reminder letters or telephone calls can be made soon after mailing a survey (Anderson and Berdie, 1975). Mangione (1998) recommends repeated reminders because with each reminder more surveys are returned. If too much time elapses before sending a reminder, many people who received the survey will have forgotten about it. The proportion of people who will complete a survey varies with the effort required to complete it, the nature of the program, and the degree to which individuals identify with the program. Receiving less than 50 percent of the surveys back makes drawing most conclusions highly tentative. Even when participants respond at respectable rates, those who do not respond are probably different from those who do. In one study the 66 percent who returned a survey about their experience in counseling had participated in a mean of 20.2 sessions, but those who did not respond participated in a mean of only 9.5 sessions (Posavac and Hartung, 1977).

Interviews. Interviews are used when it seems that the members of the target population are unlikely to respond to a written survey, when respondents may not answer difficult or sensitive questions unless an interviewer is at hand to encourage them, or when evaluators are not at all sure what is most important to potential respondents (Guba and Lincoln, 1981). The most compelling advantage that interviewing has over a written survey is the opportunity for the interviewer to follow up on the points made by the respondent. Interviewing is a difficult task requiring concentration and considerable familiarity with the interview questions and the program under study; it is not shooting the breeze with program participants. Group interviews permit program participants or community residents to respond to the ideas of others; it is felt that such interaction yields richer and more well-thought-out ideas. Initial stages of needs assessments can often be profitably based on group interviews called focus groups (Krueger and Casey, 2000). Sometimes focus groups are used to gain information that can be used to design written surveys (Mitra, 1994). Interviews used in qualitative evaluations are less formal than is described here (see Chapter 8).

An alternative to face-to-face interviews is interviewing over the telephone (Lavrakas, 1998). Because telephones are a necessity of life in developed countries, an interviewer can contact just about anyone. Furthermore, telephone interviews do not involve travel, so their cost is lower than in-person interviews. However, the interviewer may have to make repeated calls and must establish rapport quickly before the person who answers the phone classifies the caller as a salesperson and hangs up. A letter received before the telephone call explaining the need for the study and requesting cooperation may increase an interviewee's receptivity. Since both face-to-face and telephone interviews are more expensive than written surveys, choosing among them should not be done without careful consideration of cost and the nature of the evaluation being planned.

Checklists, Tests, and Records

Checklists. A checklist permits people to select any items that describe themselves or a program. A complex observational checklist approach to evaluating the effectiveness of residential mental health treatment facilities was developed by Paul (1986). By carefully defining the variables of interest, Paul and his co-workers developed lists of specific behaviors (such as pacing) that are objective and visible. Paul's checklists are reliable and can be used very efficiently once observers have been trained and know the definitions of the target behaviors thoroughly. Greiner (1994) describes checklists used in the evaluation of municipal programs such as street and building maintenance.

Individuals can be asked to use checklists to describe less objective behaviors in themselves or others. For example, family members might be asked to indicate the degree to which discharged rehabilitation patients perform various behaviors thus indicating the how well people are able to take care of themselves. Mental health staff members might be asked to describe a patient's social functioning by checking one of several possible levels ranging from totally dependent on others to provide a supportive environment, through partially dependent (i.e., able to function with frequent therapeutic interventions), to totally independent (i.e., functioning well with no need to continue contact with a mental health center) (Carter and Newman, 1976).

Tests. In many educational settings, measurements of cognitive achievement are frequently used to measure both needs and outcomes. Published achievement tests with high reliability are well developed and widely accepted in educational settings (Murphy and Davidshofer, 2005). As mentioned already, educational program evaluators should avoid choosing measures of aptitude or intelligence when looking for a measure of achievement. Evaluators in mental health settings can often find standard tests that reflect a patient's stress, anxiety, and depression, emotional states that should be relieved by most therapies. The rapid development of computerized databases has made the search for potential measures possible for an evaluator with access to a university library. A particularly useful database for evaluators seeking measures related to mental health is the Health and Psychosocial Instruments (HAPI), a database produced by Behavioral Measurement Database Services and increasingly available in university libraries. Figure 4.2 contains illustrative citations obtained from HAPI. Each of the citations listed was just one of many that appeared to be relevant to the type of program listed.

Agency records. Detailed records are kept for employees of all businesses; medical care providers are required to keep incredibly detailed information on patients; in order to run manufacturing firms, orders, inventories, and

FIGURE 4.2 Illustration of information on scales obtained from the Health and Psychological Instruments database. This database of scales greatly reduces the effort required to search for measurement tools.

Focus of the Program Being Evaluated	Name of Illustrative Measure	Example Citation Discussing or Using the Measure
Drug rehabilitation	Women in Recovery Questionnaire	TURNER, N. H., O'DELL, K. J., WEAVER, G. D., RAMIREZ, G. Y., AND TURNER, G. 1998. Community's role in the promotion of recovery from addiction and prevention of relapse among women: An exploratory study. *Ethnicity and Disease, 8,* 26–35.
Juvenile delinquent rehabilitation	Multidimensional Anger Inventory	HEMPHILL, J. F., AND HOWELL, A. J. 2000. Adolescent offenders and stages of change. *Psychological Assessment, 12,* 371–381.
Depression among children	Children's Depression Inventory	SILVERMAN, W. K., KURTINES, W. M., GINSBURG, G. S., WEEMS, C. F., LUMPKIN, P. W., AND CARMICHAEL, D. H. 1999. Treating anxiety disorders in children with group cognitive-behavioral therapy: A randomized clinical trial. *Journal of Consulting and Clinical Psychology, 67,* 995–1003.
Suicide prevention	Reasons for Living Inventory	DEAN, P. J., RANGE, L. M., AND GOGGIN, W. C. 1996. The escape theory of suicide in college students: Testing a model that includes perfectionism. *Suicide and Life-Threatening Behavior, 26,* 181–186.
Parenting enhancement	Responsibility for Children Interview Schedule	LESLIE, L. A., ANDERSON, E. A., AND BRANSON, M. P. 1991. Responsibility for children. *Journal of Family Issues, 12,* 197–210.
Reading for job skills	Ramsay Corporation Job Skills—Office Reading Test	IMPARA, J. C., AND PLAKE, B. S. EDS., 1998. *The thirteenth mental measurements yearbook.* Lincoln: University of Nebraska Press.

completed products must be tracked accurately; and criminal justice agencies similarly keep detailed records. Many of such records are in computer databases already (see, Miller, 2005). The outcomes of programs that are planned to improve health, decrease crime, raise productivity or quality, or increase skills among school children can often be traced in records kept by the organization sponsoring the evaluation. Because most information is kept for the purposes of working with individuals, summarizing information on a program level can provide insights not previously available.

PREPARING SPECIAL SURVEYS

Surveys are used so widely in educational, psychological, and policy settings that we present a brief overview of the principles of survey design.

Format of a Survey

The format of a survey is an important factor in gaining the cooperation of respondents, analyzing the responses, and interpreting the findings. If a survey is to be self-administered, the layout must be attractive, uncluttered, and easy to use. For many evaluations, a structured answer approach format is preferable to using free response (or open-ended) questions because analysis of narrative answers is very time consuming. When the structured approach is adopted, it is still possible to produce a very cluttered survey if the questions have many different answer options. For example, mixing "Yes/No" questions, attitude statements with which respondents are to agree or disagree, and questions about frequency of past behaviors creates difficulties for respondents because they must repeatedly readjust to the response format as they move from item to item. The more difficulty a respondent has answering, the less likely the survey will be completed. The greater the proportion of items that can be answered using one format, the better. Learning how to phrase a variety of questions in ways that permit them to be answered using the same answer format becomes easier with experience. The effort put into making the survey easy to use also helps evaluators when they seek to interpret and present the findings. The mean responses to items with the same answer format can be placed into a single table, thus making comparisons among items easy.

At times the purpose of the evaluation is less well defined and questions with narrative answers are needed. When the range of reactions to a program is not known or when having the respondents' own words might be of value, surveys with open-ended questions are often useful. Patton (1980) used both a structured answer format and open-ended questions when evaluating a performance appraisal system in an educational setting. Readers of Patton's report had access to both the statistical summary of the survey and the personal, often impassioned, free responses. McKillip, Moirs, and Cervenka (1992) showed that some forms of open-ended questions were more useful than others. The most useful information for program improvement was obtained from items that elicited specific comments, such as: "Name one thing you liked and one thing you did not like about [the program]." These open-ended, but directed, questions were more helpful than simply asking for comments. Evaluators planning an evaluation that makes extensive use of open-ended questions should consult materials on developing coding schemes for narrative material (e.g., Glaser and Strauss, 1967; Strauss and Corbin, 1998; Weitzman and Miles, 1995).

Preparing Survey Items

There are a number of useful guidelines for preparing survey items. The most important principle is: Remember who is expected to respond to the items. A statement that is clear to an evaluator might not be clear to someone reading it from a very different vantage point. Questions that have the best chance of being understood are written clearly, simply, and concisely. Such statements cannot be prepared in one sitting; they must be written, scrutinized, criticized, rewritten, pretested, and rewritten. Items written one week often do not seem acceptable the following week. Keep in mind that unless one is testing a skill, all respondents are to be able to answer the questions. If the first draft cannot be improved, then the evaluation team has not learned to evaluate its own work.

There are several characteristics of clear survey items. The items should avoid negatives because negatively worded sentences take more effort to read and are misunderstood more frequently than positively worded items. Double negatives are especially difficult to understand. Well-written items use short, common words. Good survey items focus on one issue; an item such as "My physical therapist is polite and competent" combines two issues. In this case it is possible to interpret a positive answer but not possible to interpret a negative answer. What should the director of the unit do if many people respond negatively—have a workshop on charm or one on the latest physical therapy techniques? Finally, survey items should be grammatically correct.

Several practices can help detect survey items that need improving. First, the statements should be read aloud. Awkward phrasing is often easier to detect when read aloud than when reviewed silently. Second, imagine someone reading the item who dislikes you and may be looking for a reason to criticize your work. (No kidding, this will really help you to detect problems with any of your written material.) Third, have a colleague read the draft items. Fourth, think through how to interpret each possible answer to each item. As mentioned above, sometimes one answer can be interpreted but another cannot. Fifth, if ambiguities remain, they probably will be detected if the revised draft is administered as an interview with several people from the population to be sampled. Ask them to paraphrase each question; if they can, the question may well be clear.

Once survey items are prepared, they must be arranged into an order that is easy to use and appears logical to the respondent. The first questions should refer to interesting issues and not be threatening. The goal is to entice the potential respondent into beginning the survey. Later, questions dealing with socially controversial issues can be included. It is crucial to remember that people like to be consistent; consequently, the first answers may affect how later items are answered. If this is a severe problem, consider making two different forms of the survey so that order can be examined. The demographic items (such as age, gender, or occupation) are best placed last since these are least likely to interest respondents. During an interview, however, demographic items should be addressed first in order to build rapport (Babbie, 2003). In all cases, the use to which the information is to be put should be explained.

Instructions and Pretests

The instructions accompanying a survey need to be clear since no interviewer is available to clear up difficulties. It is best to underestimate the skills of respondents and give more instructions and examples than might be necessary. Once the survey and instructions are prepared, it cannot be assumed that potential respondents will interpret instructions and items just as the evaluator intended. The best practice is to administer the survey to a small sample of people to learn how they understand the instructions and the items. It is likely that the survey will need to be revised once more.

Summary and Preview

The use of measures of different variables from multiple sources of information is one of the core qualities of valid and useful evaluations. When choosing measures of variables, evaluators use the criteria for good measurement instruments to evaluate the specific approaches being considered. Is something important being measured? Is the approach sensitive to small changes? Does the measure seem valid, reliable, and cost effective? Could the measure itself create changes in the variable being measured? In choosing variables and information sources, evaluators seek data sources that are not subject to similar limitations; instead, evaluators seek variables that complement each other.

The selection of appropriate criteria for evaluation studies and the use of good ways to measure criteria are marks not only of competent evaluators, but also of ethically sound work. As social scientists whose findings can have practical impacts on others, evaluators face a greater number of ethical dilemmas than those who study only theoretical questions. Chapter 5 deals with some of these ethical issues.

Study Questions

1. Consider a program setting with which you are familiar. You might think of the Financial Affairs Office of your college, a hospital laboratory, or a preschool center. Think of some survey items that the participants would be competent to

answer and some that require specialized training to answer and thus should not be addressed to participants.

2. In that same setting identify the groups who might be surveyed or interviewed to obtain information on the quality of the program. What aspects of the program is each group especially able to provide useful information?

3. Consider the variables and information sources that might reflect the quality of the program you have been considering. Arrange variables in two columns—place variables that would be expected to put the program in a favorable light in one column and variables that would be expected to highlight program problems in the second column. Compare the columns: How do those two sets differ?

4. Think of some evaluation questions that can only be answered using interviews and some that can be answered best by quantitative measures. How do these two sets of questions differ from each other?

5. Suppose that an unethical evaluator wanted to stack the deck to guarantee a favorable evaluation of a program. What types of variables would one use to achieve this? In contrast, suppose that someone wanted to guarantee an unfavorable evaluation: What types of variables would one choose to do that?

Additional Resource

FOWLER, F. J., JR. 1998. Design and evaluation of survey questions. In *Handbook of applied social research methods*, eds. L. Bickman and D. J. Rog. Thousand Oaks, CA: Sage.

> This chapter provides a very readable description of the development of surveys with many good and bad illustrative items. Many stakeholders who request evaluations seem to believe that anyone can write survey questions. The problem is that the findings from poorly prepared surveys are seldom interpretable.

Ethics in Program Evaluation

5

E valuators often find themselves in ethical dilemmas that are seldom experienced by social scientists engaged in basic research. Although the following scenarios are hypothetical, experienced evaluators can identify with the problems described below.

A project that cannot be done well. Evelyn Marshall works for a social science firm, Evaluation, Inc. The firm's staff is interested in winning a contract to evaluate an early parole program initiated by a state legislature. The central question to be answered is whether early parole leads to better outcomes (e.g., fewer re-arrests) after release from prison relative to the outcomes of prisoners who served a greater portion of their sentences. The wording of the request for proposals is clear: The legislature wants an evaluation that examines whether the program is causally related to a lowered arrest rate after release, and the evaluation is needed within six months. Marshall also learns that the parole board will not randomly assign prisoners to receive early paroles and that there are legal reasons why random assignment would be impossible. Under these constraints Marshall knows that she does not have enough time to test the effectiveness of the program. Should she and her colleagues prepare a proposal even though they know that it is impossible to do what the legislators want? NO.

Advocacy versus evaluation. Morris Franklin completed an evaluation of the Central Community Mental Health Center outreach program for

[Handwritten notes at bottom: No random assignm t! / Early paroles are better people / better people = less chance for rearrest]

high school students whose poor school performance is thought to be related to drug abuse. As typically occurs, Franklin found evidence that supports the program's effectiveness (all stakeholders like the program), evidence that does not support the program (grades of the participants did not go up), and some ambivalent evidence that could be interpreted as favorable or unfavorable depending on one's point of view (program students hold more part-time jobs than those not in the program). Franklin's report was received favorably by the center's director. Meetings were scheduled to consider the possibility of adding a tutoring phase to the program to help improve the participants' grades. Evaluator Franklin felt that he had done a good job. Later that week, however, the director asked him to write a proposal to the school board for funding that would permit an extension of the program to other high schools in the area. When Franklin mentioned the negative findings, the director told him to focus on the positive findings; "I want an upbeat proposal," he said. Would it be unethical to write the proposal but not mention the known weaknesses of the program that the evaluation detected? *No!*

STANDARDS FOR THE PRACTICE OF EVALUATION

The need for ethical standards in research has prompted a number of organizations to develop statements defining ethical principles to guide the work of research teams (e.g., American Educational Research Association, 1994; American Psychological Association, 1992; American Sociological Association, 1989). Because the findings of program evaluations may be applied soon after evaluations are completed, evaluators face many more situations calling for ethical choices than do basic researchers, and many of these choices are different from those faced by laboratory scientists. Consequently, several statements of principles have been prepared specifically for the practice of program evaluation (Joint Committee on Standards for Educational Evaluation, 1994; Rossi, 1982). Table 5.1 includes the ethical principles adopted in 2004 by the American Evaluation Association ("Guiding Principles for Evaluators," 2004).

This chapter includes material based on the statements of ethical conduct in research, as well as descriptions of good program evaluation practices. The reason for combining these two issues lies in the authors' belief that ethics in evaluation means more than respect for research subjects and honesty with money and data. We believe that evaluators have the responsibility to provide clear, useful, and accurate evaluation information to the stakeholders with whom they work. Furthermore, evaluators seek to work in ways that have the potential to improve services to people. Ethics are more complicated for evaluators working in settings designed to help people than for social scientists working on issues with little immediate relevance to organizations because errors in basic research are not likely to harm people. The route from a basic research study to a service is long; along this route are many opportunities to

TABLE 5.1   Ethical Principles Adopted by the American Evaluation Association

1. Systematic Inquiry: Evaluators conduct systematic, data-based inquiries.
2. Competence: Evaluators provide competent performance to stakeholders.
3. Integrity/Honesty: Evaluators display honesty and integrity in their own behavior, and attempt to ensure the honesty and integrity of the entire evaluation process.
4. Respect for People: Evaluators respect the security, dignity, and self-worth of the respondents, program participants, clients, and other evaluation stakeholders.
5. Responsibilities for General and Public Welfare: Evaluators articulate and take into account the diversity of general and public interests and values that may be related to the evaluation.

Note: Each principle was followed by several subpoints. The statement was ratified by the membership of the American Evaluation Association, July 2004.
Source: www.eval.org/Guiding%20Principles.htm, retrieved May 16, 2005.

identify and discard errors. In contrast, poorly done evaluations have affected the provision of services to people, disrupted the staffs of service organizations, and encouraged the use of harmful, novel medical treatments. For these reasons, we view ethics in evaluation as relating to all stages of an evaluation—from initial planning through the presentation of the results to interested parties. Morris Franklin learned that there may be crucial ethical dilemmas even after the evaluation has been completed. Our discussion divides ethical issues into five categories: treating people ethically, recognizing role conflicts, serving the needs of possible users of the evaluation, using valid methods, and avoiding negative side effects of evaluations. *Hard to do.*

ETHICAL ISSUES INVOLVED IN THE TREATMENT OF PEOPLE

The first responsibility of an evaluator, as it is with the basic researcher, is to protect people from harm. Since harm can be done to people in a variety of ways, concerned evaluators guard against harm to all people associated with a program. *This is a little far fetched!*

Compensating for Ineffective, Novel Treatments

Often the first issue evaluators face concerns whether any harm can come to someone receiving the program that is being evaluated. Although medical, educational, and social service programs are offered with the purpose of helping those who participate, sometimes programs have either no impact, or a negative impact. A controversial evaluation was reported by Sobell and Sobell (1978), who designed a program for alcoholics based on behavior principles that theoretically should have permitted participants to drink at moderate levels after treatment. The principles underlying this program contradict the traditional assumption that alcoholics cannot drink without a high risk of again becoming dependent on alcohol (Burtle, 1979; McIntyre, 1993). It is ethical to conduct an evaluation of such a project; however, evaluators working with treatments that differ from accepted practices should be sure that if a new treatment fails, the program participants receive adequate additional services so that they will not be harmed by the program being evaluated. Pendery, Maltzman, and West (1982) argued that Sobell and Sobell did not follow the participants long enough to learn whether controlled drinking was effective for the participants. Indeed, hospital records showed that many participants were back in the hospital within weeks or months of discharge from the controlled drinking program. Published reports of the evaluation had implied that the new approach to treatment was a viable alternative to the traditional treatment that emphasizes abstinence.

Obtaining Informed Consent

Another way to protect people is to obtain prior agreement from program participants who are to take part in the evaluation. This is especially important when evaluators plan an evaluation that includes random assignment of program participants to different forms of treatment or to a control group not receiving the treatment. When people are asked for their agreement, it is important that their consent be informed—that is, they must understand the request before giving consent. Informed consent means that potential participants themselves make the decision about whether to participate, and that sufficient information about the program be provided to enable them to weigh all alternatives. If a person is misled or not given enough information about the risks involved, then informed consent has not been obtained, even if a person has signed an agreement to participate. Unfortunately at times consent forms have been written in a style that researchers understand rather than in a style that potential program participants can understand (Gray, Cooke, and Tannenbaum, 1978).

Attempting to provide enough information to enable people to give informed consent can create an additional ethical dilemma for an evaluator. Revealing too much information about a new form of service can create expectations on the part of the participants or demoralize those not selected for the new program (Cook and Campbell, 1979). When informed consent procedures have the potential to change the behaviors of the people in the evaluation, then the validity of the evaluation can be threatened. There is no clear way to resolve such a conflict. One approach, included in the American Psychological Association's ethical principles, is to consider the potential harm to the participants. For example, Mexican-American women applying for family planning services were randomly assigned to a treatment group (oral contraceptives) or to a control group (placebo, look-alike pills) without their knowledge (Bok, 1974). The high cost to the control group—10 pregnancies—argues that these women should have been given complete information about this study. Clearly the

Chapter 5 *Fake Birth Control pills ?! ARE U SERIOUS !*

women sought family planning services; if the experimental service had not been available, the women may have altered their behavior or obtained services elsewhere. Such gross violations of ethical principles in research and evaluation are far less frequent in recent years than they were in the past.

Maintaining Confidentiality

unless you get informed consent!

Information gathered during an evaluation is to be treated with the utmost care so that the privacy of program participants or managers not be invaded. The confidentiality of information can be protected in a number of ways. Identifying data with a person's name is not always necessary. If matching pretests and posttests is necessary, researchers can use information that only a particular respondent would recognize, such as the first name and birth date of the respondent's mother. If contacting the respondent later is necessary, the project director alone should keep a master list of the respondents' names and addresses and the code identifying the data. Some evaluators working with very sensitive information have stored the names and codes in a different country. Few evaluators deal with information that sensitive; however, confidentiality once promised must be preserved.

ROLE CONFLICTS FACING EVALUATORS

Evaluators gather information for the purpose of assessing the value of program plans, implementation, or outcomes. Since people serving on the staff of programs earn their living from their work, it should not be surprising that conflicts can occur between evaluators and program staff. The clients served by a program also have a stake in the conclusions of an evaluation; if the program is suspended, they may lose a needed service. The stakeholders of publicly funded programs include government agencies and taxpayers. Although few taxpayers are aware of evaluations or even, for that matter, the programs themselves, taxpayers' interests are served when programs achieve objectives efficiently. In an important sense, many ethical dilemmas arise from conflicts of interest among the stakeholders involved with the program. Ideally, evaluators serve all stakeholders even though evaluators are usually employed by only one stakeholder—most often the organization management. As mentioned in Chapter 2, forming clear ideas of who wants the evaluation conducted and how all the stakeholders could be affected by an evaluation is crucial. The stakeholders can be expected to have different, even conflicting, interests; anticipating these conflicts can spell the difference between a botched evaluation caused by angry disagreements among stakeholders and a carefully balanced, albeit controversial, evaluation.

Identifying the stakeholders of a program is an important ethical task. Imagine an evaluator charged with conducting an evaluation of a new method of sentencing convicted criminals. A state governor proposed and the legislature approved a sentencing process for certain crimes called *Class X crimes*. The legislation was passed because it was widely believed that the sentencing practices of judges were too lenient and varied widely from judge to judge. The legislature took the determination of length of jail sentences for certain crimes out of the hands of judges: A defendant judged guilty of a Class X crime now faced a sentence determined by law. Who were the stakeholders for an evaluation of this law?

First, the state legislators who commissioned the evaluation are stakeholders since they wrote the law that was being evaluated. The governor had an interest in the outcome of the study because he proposed the law and would want all evaluations of his work to be favorable in order to enhance his chances of reelection. Those state legislators who voted for the law likewise would have wanted a favorable finding. In contrast, some legislators who opposed the law may have preferred to see their position vindicated by a finding that the law did not have the intended effect. All citizens who look to the courts to help in preventing dangerous individuals from committing additional crimes had an interest in this project. Judges, too, had a stake since their day-to-day behavior was being studied. Prison officials needed to be aware of the evaluation findings, especially with respect to the possible influence of the new sentencing procedures on their facilities. Police officers also would have been interested to learn how the new sentencing law had been implemented. Defense lawyers, defendants, and the state attorney's office would also have had stakes in the outcome of the evaluation because their strategies might depend on how sentences were determined. Clearly, many groups care about the findings of program evaluations.

Evaluators should try to minimize potential conflicts among the stakeholders before the evaluation begins. Evaluators would be subject to less pressure if they could negotiate agreements on such issues as: Who will have access to the findings? What information is to be used? How would different patterns of findings be interpreted? If the study begins without settling these questions, the probability that different groups can manipulate the evaluation to suit their own purposes increases. At times, suspicions and disputes about ownership of information have made it impossible to conduct a credible evaluation. Individuals who do not want an evaluation conducted benefit from such a result; all others, however, lose.

Public conflicts among stakeholders complicate the work of evaluators; moreover, less visible conflicts also exist. Some writers argue from a social justice ethical point of view (see Rawls, 2000) that evaluators should examine the program assumptions and outcomes in order to learn if justice is served by the program and how it is administered. Evaluators try to detect when programs lead to undesirable outcomes for some stakeholders that might be overlooked if the means of measures of outcomes are examined without considering the range of outcomes (Ericson, 1990).

RECOGNIZING THE NEEDS OF DIFFERENT STAKEHOLDERS

The stakeholder concept was introduced to highlight the potential role conflicts for evaluators. Considering the needs of different stakeholders is also important for making an evaluation as useful as possible for all those who may use or be influenced by an evaluation (Datta, 2000). Figure 5.1 illustrates how stakeholders' views can lead to different conclusions, even when interpreting the same information. Focusing on the needs of one stakeholder group can easily lead to narrow and misleading conclusions (McGarrell and Sabath, 1994).

Program Managers Are Concerned with Efficiency

Those who are responsible for managing an organization are concerned about the efficiency of its operations. For-profit firms must produce goods and services in an efficient manner; otherwise, competing firms will win a greater proportion of the market. In time, inefficient firms go out of business or are bought by more efficient ones. Nonprofit human service agencies do not operate on the same principles as private firms; however, effective managers seek to provide the most service possible within limited agency budgets. In a manager's judgment, the most important aspect of an evaluation may frequently be information on the efficiency of the program. Chapter 12 covers the cost-effectiveness questions so important to managers.

FIGURE 5.1   An illustration of how stakeholders' values can conflict.
                   (*Source*: Brotman, 1983)

Success or Boondoggle? It Depends on How You Look at It

Differences in the views of various stakeholders are illustrated in the controversy over workfare programs, which require applicants to hold part-time, temporary jobs. The idea is that welfare recipients should do some work for the assistance they receive. While they continue to look for steady work, they spend a week or two a month in public or nonprofit organizations doing jobs that would not have been done by regular employees.

Some critics say the program is shortsighted, that the people do not learn real work skills, and that the state does not adequately supervise these temporary "employees." Other critics say workfare merely requires welfare applicants to sing for their supper, making welfare programs punitive. A public aid official counters by saying that some workfare participants need workfare to learn that holding a job requires coming to work, staying all day, not hitting anyone, and bathing before they leave for work. Nonprofit service organizations report that the day-care, janitorial, and food service assistance they get through workfare has improved their services to other poor people.

An evaluator would be hard pressed to gather data that would be acceptable to all stakeholders, because there are fundamental value conflicts that data will not resolve.

Staff Members Seek Assistance in Service Delivery

The needs of the staff are best served if the evaluation can provide practical guidance, improving the effectiveness with which they serve clients, students, patients, or customers. An evaluation of the flow of information through a large division of a firm may reveal inefficiencies. If the staff is provided with viable alternatives to the current procedures, they may be well served by an evaluation. An evaluation of teaching effectiveness in a college can help identify the areas in which new faculty members have the most difficulty and, thus, lead department chairs and college deans to develop preventive actions to assist new faculty members before serious problems fester (Angelo and Cross, 1993). An evaluation of a medical residency program can estimate not only the proportions of unnecessary medical tests ordered by medical residents, but the reasons for such errors in judgment. In this way education programs can be improved and residents can serve their future patients more effectively (Posavac, 1995).

Evaluators also know that an evaluation is a good vehicle for recognizing the good work of staff members. Evaluations that focus on shortcomings to the exclusion of providing positive feedback are seldom as useful as more balanced ones.

Clients Want Effective and Appropriate Services

Evaluators must also consider the program participants. The people for whom a service is designed frequently have no voice in the planning and implementation of either programs or evaluations. Upon reflection, this oversight seems almost bizarre: The group most affected by programs is the least consulted. However, participants are not unified, they seldom have spokespersons, and they do not hire evaluators. Among the ways evaluators can fulfill their responsibilities to participants is to compare the participants' needs with the service offered, to help the staff and manager better understand those needs, and to structure recommendations around both needs and strengths. It is not unknown for recommendations to be made without understanding the needs of the target population. The interests of the manager and staff have sometimes taken precedence over those of the participants. It should be noted that there is no reason to assume that program participants—students, patients, or trainees—know fully what they need, but that does not mean that their views can be ignored.

Another aspect of the stake participants have in an evaluation is their interest in continuing to receive service during an evaluation. Conducting an evaluation without causing some disruption in normal service is usually impossible; however, ethical concerns require that service disruption be minimized.

Community Members Want Cost-Effective Programs

Most service agencies receive some of their financial support from local community residents through taxes and contributions, or indirectly through reductions in property taxes often enjoyed by nonprofit organizations.

In some ways the local community is in a position similar to that of the people served: The community is dispersed and does not hire evaluators. Human service agencies often receive further support from national or state bodies, charitable organizations, and foundations. These groups certainly have a stake in the success of the programs they support. Frequently government offices and foundations commission evaluations of programs receiving their support. In these instances their interests are probably well protected. Ethically planned internal evaluations also reflect the interests of the groups that supply the financial backing for the service agencies.

THE VALIDITY OF EVALUATIONS

After potential harm to participants is minimized, possible role conflicts explored, and stakeholder needs identified, evaluators can turn to ethical issues associated with the validity of an evaluation project. In the authors' view, conducting evaluations that are not appropriate to the purposes for which they were commissioned is just as unethical as, for example, not protecting the confidentiality of information obtained from participants. The following sections cover the ethical ramifications of four of the most frequently found threats to the validity of evaluations.

Valid Measurement Instruments

Evaluators in educational and mental health settings frequently use standardized, published tests when measuring the expected outcomes of programs being evaluated. The most well-developed tests are standardized achievement tests designed to estimate a child's progress in school. Because these tests are so well developed, there is a temptation to use them even when they may not be appropriate to measure the outcomes of a program. In other words, one cannot simply ask if a measurement tool is valid because validity varies depending on the setting and the specific program participants. Choosing an inappropriate way to measure a hypothesized outcome can obscure the effects of a program (Lipsey, Crosse, Dunkle, Pollard, and Stobart, 1985; Lipsey, 1990) or, even worse, lead to a misleading conclusion. For example, in an evaluation of a course on ecology, a standard achievement subtest on science that included questions on hygiene, biology, and earth science was used as an outcome variable (Joint Committee on Standards for Educational Evaluation, 1994). This subtest was not appropriate for measuring the achievement of the students in the innovative ecology course. The evaluation's negative findings did not reflect the actual outcomes of the program.

Failing to notice the differences between the specific content of the test and the material covered in the course was a critical failure. It is unlikely that any standardized test can measure the achievement in an ecology course because few such courses were taught in high schools until recently; the evaluator should have recognized that. The school district would have been better off had the evaluation not been conducted at all; the program was saddled with a negative evaluation that—although not valid—had to be explained by program supporters.

Skilled Data Collectors

It is likely that people with little training can competently administer a standardized test; however, many evaluations use information collected through personal interviews. Interviewing is not an easy job. Good interviewers possess interpersonal skills and common sense that will permit them to obtain the information needed while maintaining the goodwill of the person interviewed. It requires a degree of maturity and a respect for truth to be able to record and report attitudes at variance with one's own. Rice (1929) found that two interviewers of destitute men were reporting very different answers to an interview question concerning why these men found themselves in their homeless condition. One interviewer reported that many men attributed their problems to alcohol; the other reported that many said they were victims of an unjust society. The fact that the first interviewer favored prohibition while the second was a Marxist suggests that the interviewers' reports were influenced by their own social views.

Skill in gaining the cooperation of people is also required of good interviewers. Guba and Lincoln (1981) note that interviewers need to exercise polite persistence as they seek to speak with potential interviewees. Carey (1974) interviewed terminally ill patients as part of an evaluation of hospital care for dying patients. It is difficult to conduct such interviews without appearing to be more concerned about data than the personal tragedies of the patients and their families. Children present a very different challenge. Interviewing children in a compensatory education program designed to improve self-confidence, study habits, and social skills would require patience and skill to gain the cooperation of the children. An interviewer without experience in working with children may learn very little about their feelings and attitudes because children do not respond to social expectations as adults do. Indeed, if young children do not feel respected, they might not say anything at all!

Appropriate Research Design

One theme of this book is that the research design must fit the needs of those who might utilize the information sought. As later chapters illustrate, different needs require more or less scientific rigor. However, once an information need has been articulated, conducting the evaluation would be unethical if it is known at the outset that the planned evaluation cannot answer the questions that the sponsors asked. One would hope that this would be unusual; however, Vojtecky and Schmitz (1986) concluded that few evaluations conducted on health and safety training programs provided accurate information on program outcomes. This seems related to the dilemma faced by Evelyn Marshall, as outlined at the beginning of this chapter; it is unlikely that she can conduct an evaluation that answers the questions the state legislature has specified.

At this point Marshall has at least three alternatives: (1) go ahead with the project and use her skills to make it seem as though the completed evaluation answered the questions originally posed, (2) decline to conduct the evaluation and hope that she can find an alternative contract to keep herself productively employed, or (3) negotiate about the actual questions to be addressed by the evaluation. The first alternative is unethical and the second is risky for Marshall; however, the third may well prove productive. Frequently sponsors of evaluations are unskilled in research methods and do not know when they have given an evaluator an impossible assignment. It may be that the legislature does not really need an evaluation that relates changes in parole procedures to later parolee behaviors. What is needed may be only a careful documentation of the actual implementation of the new law. If negotiations reveal that implementation is the primary issue, Marshall can conduct the evaluation; in fact, she can do a better job than she would have been able to if she had to devote effort trying to convince others that she was able to answer the original questions.

Adequate Descriptions of Program and Procedures

A basic characteristic of science is its public nature. Science is to be conducted so that others can evaluate the procedures used and repeat the research. In this way, errors in research can be detected. Frequently evaluations are not described in sufficient detail to permit others to understand either the program or the evaluation procedures. Patton (1980) illustrated the advantage of describing the implementation of a program as a part of a program evaluation. He found that the evaluators of a program to help young low-income mothers learn parenting and financial management skills concluded that the program was ineffective when, in fact, the program had not been implemented. If the evaluators had observed and described implementation, they would have learned that the planned program had not been put in place. A large proportion of evaluations have not addressed implementation issues (Lipsey et al., 1985; Shadish, 2002; Summerfelt, 2003).

Besides describing the program, the evaluation procedures should be presented in enough detail so that others can understand how the evaluator obtained and analyzed information. As will be mentioned later, all interested parties do not want to know all details of the evaluation procedure. However, such detailed reports should be available to people who are considering implementing the program elsewhere or who want to compare evaluations of similar programs from different settings. If it is impossible to compare evaluations because they are inadequately reported, one might wonder if the report writers were clear in their own minds about what was done.

AVOIDING POSSIBLE NEGATIVE SIDE EFFECTS OF EVALUATION PROCEDURES

The ethical issues in this section are less central to the conduct of basic research; however, in an applied research arena these questions can take on immense significance both for evaluators and for stakeholders affected by the evaluation study.

Can Someone Be Hurt by Inaccurate Findings?

Inaccurate findings can show either falsely positive findings—erroneously suggesting that the program is effective—or falsely negative findings—erroneously suggesting that the program is not effective. When such false conclusions are due to random statistical variation, the first false finding is called a *Type I error*, and the second is termed a *Type II error*. There is clear evidence medical research sometimes provides support for treatments that are later found to be of marginal or no value (Ioannidis, 2005); the original evaluations seemed positive due to Type I errors. Such false conclusions can also be made when insufficient attention is paid to the design of an evaluation. Without careful thought, evaluators can focus on the wrong variables or use too short a time span to show either positive or negative effects. At other times an evaluator's enthusiasm for a program may lead to falsely optimistic conclusions.

The possibly misleading work on alcoholism treatment by Sobell and Sobell (1978) was discussed earlier in the light of the follow-up study done by Pendery, Maltzman, and West (1982). It is possible that the treatment of alcoholics at other institutions may have been redesigned when therapists read of the apparently favorable results the Sobells claimed for the controlled drinking therapy. Basic researchers are cautioned to care for the safety and welfare of the people actually studied in an experiment. In addition, evaluators need to think about how program planners might use an evaluation of a program. Inadvertently encouraging the use of a harmful program due to insufficient care in conducting an evaluation is an ethical problem with which basic researchers need rarely be concerned; however, it is often an important issue for evaluators.

In contrast to falsely favorable evaluations, falsely negative evaluations can also harm people by encouraging the elimination of beneficial services. Lazar (1981) described one overlooked aspect of Head Start, a summer preschool program for children from low-income families. According to Lazar, Head Start made its strongest contribution to the future school achievement of the children not by what it taught, but by the way it involved mothers in the education of their children. Showing mothers how to work with their children

[handwritten: Contradictory in its use of cited works]

and introducing them to a school system encouraged them to develop a level of involvement with the education of their children often not found among lower income families. Evaluations that focused only on the intellectual growth of the children during the eight-week program were too narrow. The falsely negative conclusions could have harmed other children if Head Start programs had been eliminated. Comprehensive evaluations of preschool programs such as Head Start have shown them to raise the skills of the children (Darlington, Royce, Snipper, Murray, and Lazar, 1980; *Head Start Impact Study*, 2005), in contrast to the methodologically flawed initial study (Cicarelli, Cooper, and Granger, 1969).

[handwritten: What is head steert in 1969?]

Consider Statistical Type II Errors

Type II errors, being unable to conclude statistically that a program is effective when it is, in fact, effective, can occur because the sample of program participants involved in the evaluation was small or just happened to be atypical, and when the measures of outcome were poor. Whenever measurements are made on a sample of people rather than on the whole population, and whenever measurement instruments are not perfectly reliable, random variation can produce Type II errors. Evaluators can seldom test whole populations, and the information sources available to evaluators are never perfectly reliable. Basic researchers worry about Type II errors because conducting research that yields inaccurate conclusions is a waste of time. However, Type II errors in a basic research study typically cause no harm to others. Evaluators, on the other hand, have an additional worry about random statistical errors: They do not want to conclude falsely that a valued program is ineffective. Thus, evaluators are much more concerned about Type II errors than are basic researchers (Lipsey et al., 1985; Sackett and Mullen, 1993; Schneider and Darcy, 1984).

Unfortunately, evaluators work in situations that make Type II errors very likely. In an attempt to reduce the demands made on program participants providing information, short surveys may be used and the number of variables may be limited. To reduce the disruption of services, only a few participants may be tested. A study of the effects of oat bran on cholesterol levels involved only 20 healthy participants (Swain, Rouse, Curley, and Sacks, 1990). It should not have been surprising that no effect was found; follow-up evaluations showed that the conclusion of the initial evaluation was a Type II error (see Ripsin, Keenen, Van Horn et al., 1992). After reviewing 122 published program evaluations, Lipsey et al. (1985) concluded that the research designs of a large proportion of evaluations were too weak to detect even a moderately sized effect, not to mention a small effect. The extent of the use of weak designs in medical research was decried by Freiman, Chalmers, Smith, and Kuebler (1978). In basic research the probability of making Type II errors, are 5 to 15 times the probability of making Type I errors (Rosnow and Rosenthal, 1989). Two ways to reduce

Type II errors are to use large samples and outcome measures with high reliability (Lipsey, 1990).

Pay Attention to Unplanned Effects

Ethical evaluators are careful to examine the programs as implemented, not just as designed. One aspect of this issue is the low level of actual implementation of programs, as discussed earlier. A second aspect of this issue involves possible negative side effects of a program. Just as physicians are concerned about side effects of medications, evaluators work most effectively when they are alert to unexpected negative effects of a program. For example, welfare procedures may demean recipients, prison regulations may cause dependency leading to more difficulty in making decisions after release, and an arbitrary method of introducing safer working conditions may alienate employees. Such outcomes, of course, are not found in the goals of the programs as planned. Because program planners and managers might not even anticipate the possibility of negative outcomes, evaluators can make useful contributions if they detect important negative side effects of programs.

Chapman and Risley (1974) described a program in which children were paid to pick up litter. The program developers did not expect the children to bring in bags of household garbage from their homes: The program staff refused to pay for these bags. The children then threw the household garbage into nearby yards, certainly an unwanted side effect. The program was revised so that payment was made not for bags full of litter but for cleaning up specific yards. Recognizing a negative side effect led to a better program. Bingham and Scherer (2001) reported that a sexual harassment educational program given without prior announcement at regularly scheduled university department meetings had an adverse effect on male participants. Table 5.2 includes some additional negative side effects from policies with desirable goals. Sieber (1981) and Howard (1994) describe at length negative side effects from policies and laws that added to the very problems that they were supposed to alleviate and created new problems.

Analyze Implicit Values Held by the Evaluator

Conflicts between the role of the program advocate and the role of evaluator have already been mentioned. Other unexamined values may be hidden in statistical analyses. Ball and Bogartz (1970) examined the overall mean achievement of children watching "Sesame Street" and concluded that the series was successful in achieving some of its goals. Cook, Appleton, Conner, Shaffer, Tamkin, and Webber (1975), however, divided the child viewers on the basis of socioeconomic background and discovered a positive correlation between improvements in cognitive skills and income level: The gap between the children of lower and upper income groups actually increased. Although "Sesame Street" was designed particularly to appeal to children of families

TABLE 5.2 Serious Negative Side Effects Unexpected by the Program Developers

DESIRABLE GOAL	PROGRAM	NEGATIVE SIDE EFFECT
Reduce auto pollution	Pollution control devices	Reduced gas mileage
Save energy	Burn waste sawmill material for heat	Loss of nutrients that could have been returned to the soil
Improve food production	Use fertilizers and farm machinery	Poor farmers in poor nations who could not afford costs sold farms and became unemployed city dwellers
Raise quality of public school teachers	Test public school teacher competence	Insulted good teachers; implied that meeting the minimum standard defined good teaching

with lower incomes, it appeared more effective with the children of more well-to-do families. In other words, even though the program had a positive impact, it did not provide the special help for disadvantaged children that was a fundamental goal of the program. Without a creative reanalysis of the evaluation, this important—but subtle—finding would have been overlooked. Some writers argue that when program benefits are uneven, the less privileged group should benefit more (Bunda, 1983). What is important for evaluators to recognize is that merely examining overall effects implies endorsement of the utilitarian ethics of Jeremy Bentham, who argued that the most ethical outcome would lead to the "greatest happiness for the greatest number" (see Waller, 2005). Bentham ignored disparities among the people (see, for example, Veatch, 1975). It is always best to deal with ethical issues in an explicit manner.

INSTITUTIONAL REVIEW BOARDS AND PROGRAM EVALUATION

Students beginning a project for a program evaluation class frequently ask whether they need approval from their university's Institutional Review Board (IRB) before beginning. IRBs are demanded by federal law to ensure that medical and behavioral research studies are conducted ethically and research subjects are protected from harm. Colleges, universities, hospitals, and other agencies sponsoring research are required to have a committee which examines research plans to be sure that subjects are treated in compliance with ethical standards. Do evaluators need to seek the approval of IRBs? There is disagreement among evaluators about this. Newman and Brown (1996) "strongly advise" evaluators to obtain IRB approval. Surely no harm will be done to an organization if IRB approval is sought. However, requiring IRB approval for program evaluation would lead to rather odd limitations on the activities of program managers. MacQueen and Buehler (2004) raise these points in the context of the evaluation of public health interventions.

Imagine an arts and sciences college that began special, low-enrollment sections for first-year students. Suppose that these sections, called "freshman seminars," are supposed to (a) encourage interaction among class members, and (b) orient students to college life while still covering the essentials in the existing courses (that is, in psychology, history, political science, etc.). The college curriculum committee, the dean, and the admissions office would be interested in knowing whether students noticed a difference between freshman seminars and other courses and whether they found the experience valuable. Does the dean need IRB approval to evaluate the implementation of and the reaction to freshman seminars? It would seem strange to say that the dean cannot evaluate part of the curriculum for which he/she is responsible. Furthermore, it would seem strange to say that the dean could evaluate these courses, but that someone working in the dean's stead would need approval by a committee.

Suppose a student in a program evaluation course has the opportunity to complete a class project for a manager of a human resources department in a nearby company. It would seem odd for the student to need IRB approval in order to complete a project that the manager wants done and, in fact, supervises. IRB regulations were not designed to control these situations. IRBs are not charged with supervising how managers evaluate activities in their own agencies. Instead, IRBs are charged with supervising *research*, especially research done with publication in mind. Many IRBs have concluded that evaluations such as those just described do not fall under their purview and, thus, those IRBs would not seek to examine proposals to carry out such evaluations. Reports of these evaluations are not going to be presented beyond the organizations sponsoring the activities being evaluated. Not requiring IRB approval does not mean that one can be reckless or careless about how program evaluations are carried out. The dean and the HR manager keep student and employee records confidential as part of their normal work. All people acting in the stead of managers are expected to follow such practices as well. If you find yourself employed as a planner or evaluator, be sure you know the policy of your organization. If no one has thought of the issue before, we do not recommend that you seek to add to the bureaucracy of the organization.

The situation changes if a faculty member or college student is *not* acting as the program manager's agent. Suppose that a student approaches a program director requesting to carry out a program evaluation for a master's thesis.

Although the project may be a program evaluation, the project looks a lot more like research instead of an aspect of responsible program management. In such a case, we recommend seeking IRB approval prior to gathering data.

Last, exercise common sense: evaluating a sex education curriculum for a middle school is much more sensitive than evaluating a new scheduling procedure for college students. Evaluators of programs in socially controversial areas (such as drug rehabilitation or sex education) would be wise to consult with someone familiar with evaluations in such areas even if there is no IRB in the agency sponsoring the program.

ETHICAL PROBLEMS EVALUATORS REPORT

The following two explorations into the ethical problems in evaluation practice provide some clues about the ethical problems most likely to be met. Newman and Brown (1992) asked evaluators about the most frequent and most serious problems they have observed, whereas Morris and Cohn (1993) asked evaluators about the ethical challenges they have faced themselves. The five most serious violations of good evaluation practice concerned changing the evaluation focus after examining the data, promising confidentiality when it could not be guaranteed, making decisions about the evaluation without consulting the clients, carrying out an evaluation without sufficient training, and making it easy for partisan groups to delete references to embarrassing program weaknesses from reports (Newman and Brown, 1992). The challenges evaluators themselves have met (Morris and Cohn, 1993) are similar to some of the issues identified by Newman and Brown. The most serious and most frequent ethical problem evaluators reported to Morris and Cohn was the difficulty in presenting findings clearly, completely, and fairly. This problem was selected by 59 percent of the evaluators surveyed—the next most frequent problem was selected by only 28 percent of the respondents. The source of the difficulty in presenting complete and accurate reports was said to be largely due to evaluators being "pressured" by stakeholders to alter the presentation of findings. At times, evaluators themselves have been reluctant to present all the information, but this was thought to occur only half as often. The challenge is to get the stakeholders to recognize program weaknesses in a spirit of problem solving rather than denial. Evaluators need to acknowledge that program improvement is a gradual process because the skills of staff cannot be enhanced quickly and funding decisions are seldom made by the people managing the program. Furthermore, evaluators need to recognize that if we want clients to accept critical comments constructively, clients need to feel respected. We, too, have experienced pressure to alter reports, but we also know that an insensitive presentation of critical comments does not serve the ultimate goal of evaluators—to facilitate the improvement of human services.

Summary and Preview

The major ethical issues involved in conducting evaluation studies fall under five topics: the protection of people studied, the danger of role conflicts, meeting the varying needs of different stakeholder groups, avoiding threats to the validity of the evaluation, and staying alert to negative side effects that may be related to the program or the evaluation itself. The applied and political nature of the settings in which program evaluations are conducted create more ethical dilemmas for program evaluators than are experienced by basic researchers. Although these conflicts and limitations require evaluators to exercise considerable care in carrying out evaluations, these issues also make the role of the evaluator vital and exciting.

This chapter completes the general, introductory section of this text. We now move into specific tasks of the evaluator. Measuring needs for programs and developing methods to monitor programs are essential tasks in themselves, but they also help clarify the conceptual development of programs. These aspects of program evaluations are addressed in the next two chapters.

Study Questions

1. Analyze the different views of stakeholders who would be involved with the development of a teacher evaluation procedure in a college or university. Be sure that you do not assume that all students have the same interests or that all faculty members would react to such evaluations in the same ways.

2. Contrast the problems that Type I and Type II errors create in basic research versus those in program evaluation, with special regard to ethical considerations.

3. Some evaluators do not mention all negative or unfavorable findings in official evaluation reports, but do bring such issues to the attention of program managers during private meetings. What are reasons favoring such a practice? What problems might this practice create?

4. Suppose you have been asked to develop a report on the wishes of employees of a nonunionized company concerning benefits. After a day of interviewing you bump into an employee whom you do not know as you are leaving the plant. He tells you that the company's general manager has told the employees to hide their true feelings and thus mislead you into thinking that they are quite happy with the way things are. Because employees do not want to rock the boat, he says that everyone is going along with that idea. The employee hurriedly walked off. If he is telling the truth, what ethical problems does that give you? What should you do next?

5. Imagine how to deal with pressure to violate confidentiality.

   a. It is not unknown (although not common) for evaluators to be asked to identify individuals who made certain statements. Consider how to keep this problem from ever coming up. *Consent forms*

   b. Suppose someone alleges that someone else in the organization is engaged in criminal behavior? It could be misappropriation of funds. What ethical duties would you have to the accused, to the accuser, and to the organization sponsoring the evaluation and the program?

Additional Resource

JOINT COMMITTEE ON STANDARDS FOR EDUCATIONAL EVALUATION. 1994. *The program evaluation standards: How to assess evaluations of educational programs.* Rev. ed. Thousand Oaks, CA: Sage.

Although these standards refer to "educational evaluation" it is not hard to generalize the principles to any evaluation. The standards assume the broad approach to evaluation espoused in this chapter; an ethical concern to treat people fairly and justly and to complete evaluations in ways that maximize their usefulness to stakeholders. The standards are presented in four categories: Utility, Feasibility, Propriety, and Accuracy. The discussions of all of the standards are accompanied by case studies of how things can go wrong and what actions would have been better.

The Assessment
of Need

$$\boxed{6}$$

Human services and educational programs are developed to serve
people in need and to facilitate positive development. Congress
appropriates funds for federal nutrition agencies, small towns sponsor volunteer fire departments, and school districts build and staff schools
because communities have decided that needs of people will be unmet
without such agencies and services. How do we decide that there is a need
to be met through community action? Who decides? What information can
be gathered to demonstrate the level of community need? Perhaps the
wants of a population must be changed so that it recognizes its own *needs*
(Weiss, 2002). How does an evaluator work with planners who select programs to be offered?

Perceptions of need are greatly influenced by local and national media.
When a series of reports on local crime is presented on TV news, people
begin to feel less safe even if they experience no direct problems themselves
(Heath and Petraitis, 1986). Groups that attract the attention of media often
create the sense that their concerns are more important than those of others
(Morgan, Fischhoff, Bostrom, Lave, and Atman, 1992; Slovic, 1993).
Although opinions formed by media feed into political judgments about what
is needed and what should be funded, planning committees usually seek
more quantified, representative information on which to base their work.
When we analyze the way people use the term need, we discover that people
mean many different things when they say that they need something. In this

chapter, we first develop a definition of need so that evaluators remember to check on how the term is being used. Next, we review the most widely used methods of studying needs for material goods and human services without ignoring a community's strengths. If it is likely that an evaluator will be called upon to evaluate a program still being developed, internal evaluators might seek to be part of the planning committee. Being involved in the planning effort permits evaluators to help the planners formulate clear program goals and impact models.

DEFINITIONS OF NEED

Many analyses of need do not include a definition of need. When evaluators and program staff talk about assessments of need, they usually refer to measuring a discrepancy between what is and what should be. Roth (1990) pointed out that there are at least five discrepancies that people could have in mind when they speak of needs. There might be a discrepancy between the actual state and (a) an ideal, (b) a norm, (c) a minimum, (d) a desired state, or (e) an expected state. In social service settings, it is probably safe to assume that discrepancies from ideals are seldom being discussed. But sometimes discrepancies from a norm are used to define a need as occurs when school children of normal aptitude read below their grade levels. This approach, however, leads one to conclude that people do not have needs when they enjoy an actual state that equals or exceeds the norm, minimum, or expected states (Scriven and Roth, 1990). This would lead to the odd conclusion that Americans drinking a glass of orange juice each morning do not need vitamin C because they have enough; a discrepancy definition, if used alone, is not helpful. Most assuredly, people do need vitamin C because without any we would, in time, become ill.

It is likely that many evaluators have been able to conduct needs assessments without a clear definition of need because program planners possess an implicit understanding of what is meant; nevertheless, it seems wise to adopt an explicit definition. Scriven and Roth's definition has merit: Need refers to something (X) that people must have to be in a satisfactory state. Without X they would be in an unsatisfactory state; with X they achieve but do not exceed a satisfactory state. For example, people need access to a health care worker when they accidentally cut themselves severely enough to require stitches. McKillip (1987, 1998) describes a difficulty with this definition. While we can all agree that someone needs stitches, we draw different conclusions about needs as we move from community to community. Most people in the world live in situations in which a bachelor's degree is not needed. However, in nations with knowledge-focused economies a college education is very important and, indeed, needed to hold a large proportion of jobs. A teenager may want a cell phone that can transmit images, music, and text to gain status and convenience, but not having one would hardly make his life unsatisfactory. However, a real estate executive may need such a cell phone for client services because without it, she may lose enough business to place her in the unsatisfactory state of unemployment. In other words, a need cannot be defined without regard to the social context in which a person or group lives and works. Consequently, McKillip (1998) concluded that the decision that an unmet need merits a programmatic response is the result of "... *a value judgment* [not an objective assessment] that some *group* has a *problem* that can be *solved*" (p. 263). Note also that McKillip points out that only problems that we think we can solve are treated as unmet needs.

Lurking beneath some of the confusion about the definition of need is the distinction between things people need on a regular basis (such as oxygen or vitamin C) versus things needed only once (such as a high school diploma). Another confusion occurs among those community resources whose use is fairly predictable (such as elementary schools) versus those whose use may be predictable for a whole community, but whose use cannot be predicted on an individual basis (such as a trauma center). Individuals may believe that they will never need a trauma center (and most people will be right); however, the community at large may need a trauma center.

When estimating the need for any type of program, distinguishing between the incidence and the prevalence of a problem is helpful. Incidence refers to the number of people experiencing a problem during some time period; prevalence refers to the number of people who have the problem at a given time. For example, the incidence of the common cold is high: Most people contract at least one cold each year; children are especially susceptible. However, most people usually recover quickly, so the prevalence at any one time is low. The distinction is important: A response to a problem will be different depending on whether the problem is viewed as widespread but temporary, or less widespread but long lasting. For example, attempts to help unemployed people will differ depending on whether it is believed that the unemployed to be served are merely between jobs or are likely to be out of work for a long time.

Note that the definition of need does not rely on people knowing that they have a particular need. People may be unaware of a need (an iron deficiency), deny a need (alcoholics usually deny a need for rehabilitation), or misidentify a need (some adolescents desire drugs when they need social skills). Of course, people often know when they need assistance with housing, education, health care, or employment. There is no one procedure or one source of data that provides clear information on needs.

SOURCES OF INFORMATION FOR THE ASSESSMENT OF NEED

The major sources of need-relevant information include objective data about the social and economic conditions of a community, facts and opinions that the residents themselves provide, and the conclusions of experts who know the community well. Before heading out with surveys in hand, evaluators should address several preliminary issues. First, who are the people whose unmet needs are being studied? Second, what are the resources currently available to these people?

Describing the Current Situation

Population to be studied. The people to be studied should be identified before gathering any data. The population might be the residents of a state, the pupils of a school district, or the employees of a factory or business. Instead of defining the population as all members of a geographical area or organization, evaluators might narrow their definition to unemployed men, home-bound elderly, unmarried pregnant teenagers, or women employees. Some public agencies may be limited in whom they may serve. Private organizations such as hospitals and businesses may have fewer limitations and thus more difficulty in identifying the people they wish to serve with a new clinic or new product. A university opening a branch campus would want to know how many of its current students live in the area of the new campus, how many area students will graduate from high school during the next decade, and how many people in the area are currently enrolled in continuing education programs. Some information describing the population would be easy and inexpensive to obtain; other information, hard and costly. The needs assessment report might show that part of the relevant group has great unmet needs, whereas other subgroups require no additional attention. Learning how the people seek to meet unmet needs would be important.

An evaluator can contribute to the planning process by being concerned with specificity. It is one thing to talk about the need for services to juveniles in trouble with the law and quite another to know the number and percentage of community male adolescents aged 16 to 19 arrested each year. Saying "The community's elderly residents lack easy access to social opportunities" is less informative than reporting "2,200 residents over age 75 have no access to public transportation and that half of them would require transportation in order to participate in services offered to them if the services were housed in the town hall."

Current resources in the community. Critics of social programs fault some well-intentioned planners for ignoring the strengths of communities and residents when developing programs (Fine and Vanderslice, 1992). Indeed, the concept of needs assessment has been criticized for a myopic focus on problems without regard for how existing resources could be strengthened (McKnight, 1995). Social program planners might take a hint from businesses: It would be unwise to locate a new store or restaurant in a community without noting the location of established businesses. Thus a careful cataloging of current programs, employers, health care facilities, churches, schools, and community organizations should be included in a needs assessment.

The cooperation of such organizations can make programs more successful in reaching people in need, and the integration of existing services and organizations can lead to more comprehensive opportunities for eligible residents.

Social Indicators of Need

Communities needing additional social services probably display many dysfunctional characteristics. Trying to measure the degree of dysfunction—or its converse, well-being—is difficult. One approach is to track variables, such as crime and school dropout rates, that are symptoms of social problems (Felson, 1993). Just as symptoms of physical illness can lead physicians to diagnose an illness, social indicators can suggest the underlying social problems that should be addressed (Carley, 1981; Ferriss, 1988). When a social problem is alleviated (as occurred with the advent of Medicare), social indicators should show a lower degree of social distress and dysfunction.

Where are social indicators found? A national census provides one objective approach to measuring the extent of need using social indicators. U.S. census information is divided into census tracts and enumeration districts, which are smaller than tracts (see, for example, www.census.gov). The Internet resources provided by the U.S. Census Bureau make census information widely accessible; however, a printed version is available (*Statistical abstract of the United States*, 2004–2005). Obtaining summary data for communities of interest permits evaluators and planners to examine many variables that could indicate unmet needs. Since the census information may be divided by race, gender, and age, it is possible to pinpoint areas of greatest need. Furthermore, comparing the community under study with patterns for the whole region, state, or nation makes it easier to detect differences that reveal needs.

Social indicators are also available in crime reports from the FBI (Uniform Crime Reports, see www.FBI.gov/ucr/ucr.htm) and from the Bureau of Justice Statistics (www.ojp.usdoj.gov/bjs/). States as well as the Department of Labor track rates of employment and unemployment. The Gross Domestic Product and the Consumer Price Index are social indicators that reveal the level of economic activity and rate of inflation. Other social indicators come from private sources. SAT scores from the Educational Testing Service reveal something about the state of American high schools. Many organizations founded to support social and health causes compile and publicize indicators such as campaign contributions to politicians by organizations, the level of citizen confidence in the president, or the number of hazardous waste dumps in each state. We are awash in social indicators. One should begin looking for sources of appropriate social indicators using Internet searches on the topic of interest. Evaluators working with local agencies may not find the information they need for the specific community in which they are working. However, locally gathered information when contrasted with regional and national data can provide a powerful argument that there are local problems that might be solved or at least relieved by new or refined programs.

It is important to remember that indicators of problems do not reveal how those problems can be solved. Planners need a theory connecting the indicator to an unmet need as well as one connecting a possible intervention to the hoped-for outcome. With physical health, a high temperature indicates a problem. However, the problem causing the temperature is not obvious. Without a valid theory connecting elevated temperatures with a specific illness, ineffective remedies may be used. Recall that during American Colonial times, a flushed face and high temperature were thought to indicate the presence of too much blood. That invalid theory led physicians to bleed people.

Using social indicators to identify community problems and to shape programs requires knowing the relationship between the indirect measures of the problem and the underlying social, educational, or economic malady. Gaining such knowledge is certainly not easy. What malady underlies the decline in SAT scores? Some say TV watching, a passive entertainment that diverts attention away from reading; others, the loss of parents who take an interest in school work; and still others, unimaginative teachers. The alleged maladies suggest different remedies. Even if we agreed on the malady, sometimes several different responses are still suggested. If many teachers are not teaching well, perhaps teacher salaries should be raised to attract more competent people, perhaps we need to test teachers, or perhaps teacher certification requirements are keeping out people with wide experiences who may become excellent teachers, but who lack the traditional credentials.

Do limitations on the use of social indicators mean that they cannot be used? No, but the limitations do mean that social indicators cannot be used as the only source of information about the needs of a community. Social indicators are like physical symptoms; they can tell us that problems exist and where they are most pressing. They cannot tell us what the fundamental causes of problems are or what society should do about them. Other sources of information can assist evaluators and planners to be more specific about the causes of the underlying problems and the options for alleviating them.

It is important to note that social indicators can be corrupted. De Neufville (1975) reported that information showing that the rate of unemployment in urban centers in the United States was reaching 20 to 25 percent was suppressed by some government agencies. Other nations have experienced great problems when local governments were forced or at least strongly encouraged to produce favorable reports indicating economic progress. Fraudulent social indicators are ultimately discredited, but often not until policies have been affected. Information is increasingly difficult to control as suggested by our references to Internet resources; however, as with all data, evaluators do well if they carefully assess the credibility of social indicators before using them. With the wide variety of information available on the Internet, it may become harder to purposefully distort social indicators in developed, knowledge-intensive countries than in the recent past when access to information was more easily controlled. Unfortunately, false reports spread rapidly as well.

Community Surveys of Need

A straightforward way to estimate community needs is simply to ask people about their needs. The residents of a community have opinions about the development of human services and about the particular services needed. Their opinions can be part of the information used in planning. If a service is relevant to all residents, the community should be surveyed systematically to obtain a representative sample of the opinions of the residents. Obtaining a truly representative sample is extremely difficult and thus expensive. A possible compromise is to use intact groups that are likely to be fairly representative of the community. Such a strategy would not be as expensive because intact groups completing a survey do not require much time from a survey administrator. Public schools and church groups are organizations that attract participants from wide sectors of a community. Depending on the nature of the program being planned, special groups of likely users could be sought. Thus, an interviewer gathering ideas about the needs of the elderly might use more detailed questions when a household including elderly people is found.

A survey to assess needs is often used to estimate the magnitude of need and the acceptability of particular approaches to meeting needs. Preparing a survey requires much care. Because completed surveys look simple, few people realize how much effort is required to write clearly, avoid leading questions, and obtain the information desired (Schwarz and Oyserman, 2001). When assessing needs it is easy to write questions that encourage respondents to endorse plans; one could list various services and ask if the services "should be available." If we were asked if our hometown should have agencies able to provide counseling for residents having a personal or family crisis at any time of the day or night, we might answer "yes." If we were asked whether a manufacturer should add safety features to appliances to keep people from getting hurt even when they misuse the appliance, we might answer "yes" again. Although such hypothetical questions appear to get right to the heart of the matter, they are inadequate in at least three ways. First, the questions do not deal with unmet needs, but with possible solutions to problems. As mentioned in Chapter 2, planners often fall into the trap of dealing with potential solutions before fully understanding the problem being addressed. It would be best to include questions on residents' opinions about the extent of community problems and about their own problems. Figure 6.1 includes several questions dealing with employment. Second, asking whether a service "should be available" would be a leading question. Attitude measurement research has shown that people tend to agree more readily than disagree with questions (Babbie, 2003); this bias is called *acquiescence*. To avoid writing leading questions, it is helpful to use questions that require responses other than agreement or disagreement. Asking people for examples of problems or to compare

FIGURE 6.1   Section of a community needs assessment survey. (Adapted from Warheit, Bell, and Schwab, 1977)

40.	What do you consider your main job or occupation?

_____

_____

(describe by title and kind of work)

___ Don't know
___ Not answered

41. Are you presently employed?

___ Yes, full time *(> 29 hrs.)*
___ Yes, part time
___ No
___ Don't know
___ Not answered
___ Not applicable

41.A. *If yes,* For whom do you work?

_____

_____

(Organization or type of industry)

___ Self-employed
___ Don't know
___ Not answered
___ Not applicable

41.B. *If yes,* How many hours a week are you employed? *(include all jobs)*

___ ___ hrs./week
___ Don't know
___ Not answered
___ Not applicable

42. *If employed less than full time, ask:* Are you working less than full time because of any of the following:

	YES	NO	DK	N/AN	N/AP
Retired due to age	1	2	3	4	5
Physical injury or illness	1	2	3	4	5
Mental illness or disability	1	2	3	4	5
Fired or laid off	1	2	3	4	5
Going to school	1	2	3	4	5
Have children at home	1	2	3	4	5
Pregnancy	1	2	3	4	5
Consider self homemaker	1	2	3	4	5
Unable to find suitable work	1	2	3	4	5
Not looking for work	1	2	3	4	5
Others (please list)	1	2	3	4	5

_____

_____

the relative extent of two different problems might be useful approaches. Third, the hypothetical questions suggested earlier fail to mention costs of providing the services and fail to acknowledge that providing one service means that another cannot be provided. When respondents are asked what they would pay to support such services or additional safeguards, they are less enthusiastic (see Viscusi, 1992); however, research has shown that answers to questions about willingness to pay for services may be misleading (S. S. Posavac, 1998).

Services Already Available

People with unmet needs often seek assistance from a variety of sources that provide services related to what they believe they need, or they travel far to obtain services, or they do without the care that could benefit them. Evaluators can contrast the extent of need estimated with the level of services currently available in a community. Furthermore, a thorough analysis of the services available assures planners that new services would not be duplicating the work of existing agencies.

A planning group exploring the need for additional mental health services should identify all agencies, public and private, that provide at least some therapy or support for people with mental health or substance abuse problems. Thus, clinics, hospitals, courts, Alcoholics Anonymous chapters, school drug-abuse counselors, public health visiting nurses, church-based counseling centers, physicians and psychiatrists, and social workers should be considered in the effort to learn about the people being treated in some way for emotional problems.

Planners may be required to work directly with agency files in order to develop a demographic description of clients. When this is necessary, absolute guarantees of confidentiality must be made and kept. When contacting such agencies for estimates of caseloads, it would be helpful to ask for leads to additional providers of care. Developing estimates of the number of people using services is particularly difficult when services are provided informally, as child care often is.

Information concerning people needing care, but not getting it, would be very hard to obtain since few in community agencies would be aware of such people. One way to estimate the numbers of such people is to examine agency reports of individuals who sought assistance but did not receive it because they did not meet qualification requirements, could not afford the fees, or had problems that did not fit into the services provided by the agency. Love (1986) illustrated another way to include unserved people in a needs assessment. Love used case studies of troubled teenagers to show how the structure of the welfare and mental health services in metropolitan Toronto made it impossible for an adolescent to get help even though his alcoholic father had thrown him out of his home. The unstable and, at times, aggressive 17-year-old had several recent addresses in different communities and needed several different services. It was unclear where he should have sought help, and only a few agencies could assist him with his multiple problems. Although several compelling cases do not show the extent of unfilled needs, case studies illustrate vividly that service reorganization or expansion may be needed to meet certain types of needs.

Key Informants

Key informants are people who know a community well and could be expected to know what needs are going unmet. Finding such people is not easy, however. One way to start is to meet with professionals whose work brings them into contact with people who may have unmet needs to be served by the program being considered. In addition, people active in the community, such as clergy, politicians, or YMCA leaders, can be approached for information. All key informants can be asked for recommendations of people who might also have information. A sample formed using such recommendations is called a "snowball sample" (Babbie, 2003). Guidance counselors in schools might have some good ideas for needed changes in vocational school curricula and they might be able to recommend human resource directors in local businesses who would have valuable information on strengths and weaknesses of recent high school graduates. For health issues, physicians, clergy, clinic managers, school nurses, and social workers would all be important. Although surveys can be mailed to such people, a far better level of cooperation can be obtained if they are interviewed personally.

Key informants are sought because they have the closest contact with residents in need; however, this close contact is also the source of their most glaring weakness. Since people in need are memorable and since key informants may see a great number of such people daily, the numbers of people in need are often overestimated. Kahneman and Tversky (1974) called this tendency the "availability" bias because the person making the estimate can easily recall individuals who fit the category. Consequently, psychologists are likely to overestimate the number of people needing counseling and remedial reading teachers are likely to think that a greater number of people need their services than in fact do.

A related problem with key informants is that their expertise may lead them to view a problem in ways that are quite different from how others view the problem. Give a child a hammer, and the child begins to act as though everything needs to be hammered upon. Teachers view education as the answer to social problems, lawyers view legal services as a primary unmet need, trucking company executives are not likely to view railroads as a solution to shipping needs. Having expertise in a particular form of service makes it likely that informants would readily think of ways of meeting unmet needs that are related to their expertise. A premature focus on any one alternative, call it B, leads to overestimating the likelihood that B is the correct one to relieve unmet needs (see Sanbonmatsu, Posavac, and Stasney, 1997).

Focus Groups and Open Forums

There are alternatives to conducting needs assessment surveys of representative samples of community residents. These alternatives have the additional advantage of encouraging residents to share their views about community needs with each other. Two approaches that are used are focus groups and open forums.

Focus groups. Marketing research firms use small informal groups to discuss new products and ideas for new products (Malhotra, 2004). Although the kinds of questions addressed to focus groups are similar to the open-ended questions used in interviews, a discussion among seven to ten group members prompts participants to reflect more thoughtfully about the reasons for their opinions than they would if interviewed alone. The focus group leader tries to remain in the background to encourage a relaxed atmosphere and to foster sharing of opinions among members. Mitra (1994) pointed out, however, that leaders must be sure participants keep on the topic. Focus groups usually consist of people who are similar to each other in age, income level, and education. Since the goal is to foster a free exchange of opinions, great differences among members could intimidate some members who might limit their own participation. Although similar to each other, the members of a focus group do not know each other prior to the meeting and, most likely, will not see each other afterwards. Some incentive for attendance is usually given since invited participants must travel to the meeting location and spend, perhaps, two hours in the discussions.

Focus groups can be used in any phase of an evaluation; however, they serve particularly well in learning about the reactions to potential services or changes in current services of community agencies or private organizations. Krueger and Casey (2000) described using focus groups to discover why agricultural extension classes were drawing fewer and fewer enrollments among farmers in Minnesota even though a written survey suggested that farmers were interested in such classes. It could have been assumed that financial troubles were responsible, but focus groups told a different story. Farmers said that they were interested and that they could afford the tuition; however, they wanted to be sure that the instructors were knowledgeable and that the material was applicable to their farms. In addition, it was learned that personal invitations would be better than the printed flyers that had been the standard way of announcing the classes. After changes had been implemented, attendance increased markedly.

Although expected participants in a program may not be aware of all details related to a new service, it helps if their views are taken into consideration as plans develop. One use of focus groups is to test reactions to specific proposals in order to reduce the number of programs that are underutilized. An English department faculty member developed a series of workshops for non-English faculty members in her college to show how they could help students to improve their writing. She obtained funds from the dean, but failed to assess whether faculty would attend the workshops. At the first workshop there were more graduate student program evaluators present than faculty participants. If a focus group of faculty members had been presented with the plans, she might have learned that few faculty members were interested in attending a workshop to learn how to help students write more effectively.

The questions addressed to focus groups tend to be open-ended questions. Figure 6.2 includes some questions that could have been used in focus groups of rural business people. Plans were being made to develop an assistance program for small rural businesses as part of a state-funded project to encourage rural economic development. Extension classes for owners and managers of rural businesses were being considered, but before such classes could be developed, colleges needed to identify the information needs of business owners. These questions were designed to reveal those needs.

Open forums. An open forum is another method based on group interaction. Unlike focus groups that are selected on the basis of some common characteristics, participants of an open forum are a self-selected group. Often a governmental agency will announce the date of a community meeting to consider some planning issue. In many cases there are legal requirements to have such meetings. Those who learn of the meeting and choose to attend can

FIGURE 6.2 Focus group questions to learn about the information need of owners of rural businesses. Note that discussion among the members occurs after each question. (Adapted from Krueger, 1994)

1. Over the past few weeks, did you have an experience in your business that caused you to seek information? Describe that experience and tell us where you went for the information.
2. Over the past year, think of times in which you needed help in managing your business; jot down those situations.
3. We have a list of topics suggested by some other owners and managers for programs to help them in their businesses. Look over this list and compare it to yours. Please report which items are the most important to you. (When a topic is suggested, the leader can ask the next question.)
4. What makes the area of [topic] important to you? (After such a question is discussed, others will have suggestions that will also be discussed.)
5. A topic that was mentioned by several people was [topic]. Where would you go to learn something about it?
6. People get information in different forms; how would you prefer to get the information? (The leader is to probe to clarify answers such as: in-person contact, phone calls, newsletters, meetings, workshops, classes.)
7. What makes a provider of business information credible? How do you know when you can trust the information you get?

participate. McKillip (1998) recommends that participants' comments be limited to perhaps three minutes and that detailed procedural rules be presented clearly and repeatedly.

The advantages of open forums include the unrestricted access to anyone who wishes to participate, the very low cost, and the possibility that good ideas may be offered. One major disadvantage is that self-selected groups are not representative of a community because many people cannot or will not attend such meetings. Once when a small town held an open meeting to discuss how to spend a small federal grant, only one resident attended; he urged the development of a children's park along a railroad right-of-way, a location the planners viewed as dangerous. A less obvious disadvantage is the possibility that public discussions may raise expectations that something can and will be done to meet the needs discussed. It is also possible that assertive individuals with personal grievances can turn the meetings into gripe sessions producing little information on the needs of a community (Mitra, 1994).

Users of focus groups or open forums need to be cautious in drawing conclusions from the views of specific individuals. The needs of individuals can be quite compelling to casual viewers of TV news programs; in fact, even people trained as researchers have been known to put aside the findings of carefully conducted research and adopt conclusions based on the experiences of one or two articulate individuals. Rook (1987) describes how case studies can influence attitudes and health-related behaviors more powerfully than more valid, but abstract, information.

INADEQUATE ASSESSMENT OF NEED

The reason to assess needs is to improve the quality of program planning. Without understanding needs, program objectives cannot be developed; when objectives are not specified well, the program cannot be evaluated. When needs and the context of needs are not assessed accurately, programs and services cannot be as efficient or effective as possible. Furthermore, providing programs designed to meet needs that are already being met is not a good way to spend resources. The most common problems are: Sometimes needs are not measured, the context is not understood, the type of implementation required is not considered, and the denial of need is not considered.

Failing to Examine Need

It might seem a truism to say that program designers should be sure that proposed programs are planned on the basis of the needs of the people to whom the services are directed. We wish it would be unnecessary to make this point, but sometimes programs are implemented without careful attention to unmet needs. College administrators were concerned about the high attrition rate of freshmen who withdrew from college even though they were in good academic standing. As tentative ideas about possible program changes were being considered, it became apparent that the focus was on the desire to retain students, not on meeting the needs of the students who withdrew. Administrators had only speculated about the students' unmet needs and how program changes might prompt more students to reenroll for the sophomore year. Perhaps the attrition rate was being caused by personal and family situations that the college could not influence, or perhaps the students developed interests in fields not included in the departments of the college. Attempts to lower the attrition rate of such students are bound to fail because no retention program could meet such students' needs.

Another example of failure to examine need occurred in 1993 when it was proposed that the U.S. federal government provide free immunization vaccines for all children under 18. This was proposed because it was believed that cost was a barrier to immunization. However when poor children—the least immunized group—are covered by Medicaid, immunizations are free already. According to the General Accounting Office (Chan, 1994, 1995), the reasons some poor children go without immunizations include parental disinterest and physician lack of initiative in immunizing children when they visit for other reasons. The planned, and nearly implemented, program would not have led to higher immunization rates because need had not been assessed properly.

Failing to Examine the Context of Need

It is quite possible to have an accurate understanding of a community's need, but to fail to assess the community's capacity to support the program or the cultural context in which a program would be implemented (McKnight, 1995). One of the tragedies of the relationship between the developed nations and the undeveloped nations during the last several decades is the repeated failure of foreign aid initiatives to reflect the economic and cultural context of the nations being aided. Many well-intentioned efforts have been misdirected. At best, such efforts do no harm beyond wasting resources; at times, such efforts have left many in the recipient nations in worse conditions (Devarajan, Dollar, and Holmgren, 2000). In the area of health care, a basic problem is assuming that the residents of developing nations need advanced medical services. Unfortunately, developing nations cannot support advanced technologies, and the foreign aid available can provide this type of care to only a small minority of the population. Inappropriate programs have weakened some indigenous health care systems that had provided useful care for people, but were not at the level of medical care available in developed nations (Illich, 1976; Manoff, 1985).

Bringing foreign nationals to European or North American medical schools for training means that such people will become accustomed to technology-intensive medical practices. Partially as a result of this training, some physicians have returned to their home countries to practice in city hospitals serving only the rich; in recent years 90 percent of the medical resources of Nigeria have been spent in cities where only a minority of the population lives (Manoff, 1985). This happens while many rural children go without immunizations that are inexpensive. Boone (1994) asserted that foreign aid "most likely supports the consumption of the richest people" (p. 69).

A more favorable outcome occurred when planners examined treatment for severe diarrhea, which can lead to the death of children in poor areas if the fluids and nutrients lost are not replaced. Such fluids can be replaced using intravenous feeding; however, the cost would be staggering for an undeveloped nation. Premixed packs of salt, sugars, and other ingredients were developed to make it easier to prepare a drink for affected children. Widespread introduction of such premixed packages, although costing only a fraction of intravenous methods, would have been unfortunate because the packs were still too expensive to supply everyone in need and their use would imply that the people could not take care of themselves. Manoff (1985) reported that planners calculated that 750 million packs would have been needed in 1990. A better approach was to use locally available ingredients in recipes that could be taught to residents. Health care programs that provide medically appropriate skills are far more effective than ones that meet the needs of a few but foster feelings of helplessness among many others.

Failing to Relate Need to Implementation Plans

Sometimes a program is prepared on the basis of a reasonable understanding of unmet needs, but the implementation makes it difficult for people to participate. Food stamps are designed to assist poor families to purchase food at reduced costs; it is a compassionate response to nutrition needs. Unfortunately, through local indifference and target group ignorance only 20 percent of those eligible for food stamps were using them in the early years of the program. An advertising campaign in New Mexico tripled the number of eligible people using food stamps in six months (Manoff, 1985). In 1997 only half of eligible households participated in the food stamp program (Castner and Cody, 1999). Winett (1995) argues that many health promotion programs fail to consider all aspects of effective marketing.

Failing to Deal with Ignorance of Need

If a group in need does not recognize the need, a program must include an educational effort (Cagle and Banks, 1986; Conner, Jacobi, Altman, and Aslanian, 1985). People screening for and treating high blood pressure deal daily with patients who do not recognize a need for care. When the condition first develops, elevated blood pressure seldom produces noticeable symptoms; in addition, medication can have undesirable side effects (Testa, Anderson, Nackley, and Hollenberg, 1993). Because patients expect to feel better, not worse, after taking medications, many reject the treatment. A rejected treatment means program failure, even though the medication is effective in reducing the likelihood of strokes and other cardiovascular diseases.

Some people believe that when it comes to good health practices and the availability of educational opportunities, society fulfills its responsibility by simply providing the facts. They argue that publicly funded service providers are under no obligation to persuade anyone to take advantage of the programs. In contrast, social marketing techniques (Weinreich, 1999) are used to foster the adoption of more adaptive health behaviors, wise use of government services, and the maintenance of safer environments. Social marketing is needed, Manoff (1985) argued, not only to provide basic education, but to strengthen motivation. Such efforts are needed to counter the extensive advertising that encourages the use of products that can harm health, such as very sweet and high-fat foods, cigarettes, and alcohol (Winett, 1995).

USING NEEDS ASSESSMENTS IN PROGRAM PLANNING

Once the level of need has been assessed for a particular population, then program planning may begin. Planners seek to develop a service or intervention to help the population achieve or approach a satisfactory state. The probability of developing a successful program increases markedly when the important stakeholder groups are involved in the planning and cooperate in selecting both the services to be offered and the mechanisms for delivering them. Stakeholders can be involved through formal representation on committees or in focus groups responding to developing plans.

After outcome goals have been specified, the next step is to consider the intermediate goals that need to be achieved on the way to achieving outcome goals. Intermediate goals could include, for example, accomplishments, behaviors, attitudes, or levels of knowledge. In order to specify intermediate goals that would indicate how much the target population is being helped, planners must describe the program theory. Unfortunately, as mentioned in Chapter 2, planners sometimes develop programs without asking what must happen to the program participants before they can reach the outcomes hoped for; in other words, an impact model needs to be developed as the program is planned.

After developing an impact model, the planning group can specify what actions the agency must take to implement the program. The resources that need to be considered include the knowledge and skill of the staff, the physical resources, financial resources, advertising, and outreach efforts. Since planners cannot operate with blank-check assumptions, the projected resources required are compared with the financial support that would be available. If the resources are not sufficient, the planners have several options. One temptation is to leave the goals intact while reducing the intensity of the program and hope for the best. If the planning had been sound and if the conceptual basis of the plans is valid, such a decision is a prescription for failure (Rivlin, 1990). To fail in the complex task of helping people change is not a disgrace, but to continue to plan a program that planners suspect cannot work well because it is too weak is a waste of valuable resources and fosters cynicism about social programs. More useful alternatives include reducing the number of people to be served, narrowing the focus of the service, or even changing the plans to meet a different need, one that requires fewer resources.

Although this presentation seems straightforward and linear, the planning committee will frequently check back to verify that they are faithful to the mission of the organization that will sponsor the program. In fact, while developing intermediate goals, planners might discover that some of the outcome goals were unrealistic. What does not change is the need to work in a generally backward direction during the planning process, beginning with what is to be accomplished and ending with a plan to achieve those goals (see Egan, 1988a, 1988b; Egan and Cowan, 1979). If there are no clear goals, rational planning cannot occur. Surprisingly often, people in agencies and organizations sense a need, but do not measure it carefully or even explore it in a qualitative manner (Mathison, 1994). Sometimes they then watch helplessly as the program fails to have an observable impact on the population in need. Altschuld and Witkin (2000) discuss how evaluators can help in translating a needs assessment into a program, but the actual planning is not a primary responsibility of evaluators.

Summary and Preview

The importance of assessing needs before beginning to plan programs cannot be overstated. The definition of need emphasized that we are trying to learn what people need in order to be in a satisfactory state, in their social context. Although we tend to know a lot about our own needs, we often do not fully understand what it takes to satisfy our own needs, as illustrated by marginal understanding of objective nutritional needs. Since educational, psychological, and social needs are so terribly complex, it would not be surprising to learn that these needs are not fully understood either. Consequently, it is wise to seek information on needs from a variety of sources. Community surveys, agencies currently serving people, social indicators, focus groups, and expert informants are sources of information on needs. Once needs are clear, planning may begin. Planning has the best chance of success if the conceptual basis of the program is developed and used to set the outcome and intermediate goals.

After programs are in place, evaluators continue to contribute since programs must be monitored to guarantee their integrity. Furthermore, information gathered by monitoring serves to show what aspects of a program should be adjusted. Chapter 7 includes an introduction to management information systems and their use in program evaluation.

Study Questions

1. Examine the daily newspapers for articles on social services or consumer products that show how a careful analysis of need for a human service or a new product was affected by an analysis of need. Note that if the example concerns a consumer product, the definition of unmet need in this chapter may not be appropriate; in such cases, manufacturers are usually dealing with meeting wishes or preferences, not serving unmet needs.

2. Look for examples of agencies or producers who failed because they did not conduct an appropriate needs assessment before offering a service or bringing a product to the marketplace. What kind of information might the organization have sought to avoid the error?

3. Many colleges sponsor a learning assistance program for students who do less well in their classes than they want to. Sketch a plan to do an assessment of needs for such a program. Assume that there is a program already, but the college dean wants to know how well the services match the needs and whether services should be expanded. Consider the information you want and the sources as well as the methodology to use in gathering the information.

4. Under what conditions would an assessment of needs be threatening to an organization?

5. Suppose that one was asked to develop an assessment of needs for alcoholism treatment for a large city. The question is whether facilities are located in the best places and where the city should devote more resources when funds are available. Assume that several indicators are combined into one index of showing problems with alcohol. This index could be the total of alcohol sales per capita, police reports of alcohol-related domestic disputes, juvenile court records of underage drinking, etc. Suppose further that all the funds devoted to alcoholism treatment were known and added up. Last, imagine the index of need and the total of treatment funds are available for each one of the city's wards. How might these two variables be used to learn which wards are underserved?

Additional Resource

WITKIN, B. R., AND ALTSCHULD, J. W. 1995. *Planning and conducting needs assessments: A practical guide*, rev. ed. Thousand Oaks, CA: Sage.

> The authors take the reader through every step required to identify and estimate the extent of the unmet needs of groups. They discuss the methods described in this chapter and additional ones in considerable detail. Approaches to using needs assessments in program planning are illustrated as well. The treatment is definitely hands-on with numerous examples of needs assessments. In all stages of the project they endorse the close collaboration with stakeholders and focus readers on the people to be served by the program, which is the approach we follow.

Monitoring the Operation of Programs

Program monitoring "is the least acknowledged but probably most practiced category of evaluation" (ERS Standards Committee, 1982, p. 10). The most fundamental form of program evaluation is an examination of the program itself—its activities, the population it serves, how it functions, and the condition of its participants. Program monitoring includes an assessment of the resources devoted to the program and whether this effort is directed as planned. It is a serious mistake to plan an evaluation that focuses only on the long-term results, ignoring its activities. Careful program monitoring yields "impressive results" (Lipsey et al., 1985).

Monitoring is a basic activity of any organization. Businesses monitor their performance by counting receipts at the end of every day and by performing inventories of stock. Human service managers monitor their activities in some ways similar to those used by for-profit businesses. However, education, health care, criminal justice, and welfare agencies are designed to change the people served in some way, not simply please them, a critical difference (Weiss, 2002). Consequently, the end products of human services—well-functioning people—cannot be measured as reliably, validly, or easily as store inventories or account balances. The place to begin is to ask whether a program has been implemented as planned. If well-designed advertisements encouraging seat belt use are not published or broadcast, there is no reason to evaluate the impact of the material. If drug abusers do not attend a drug rehabilitation program, then there is no need to ask whether the program reduced drug abuse.

Managers need basic information to facilitate their planning and decision making, to anticipate problems, and to justify continued support for the program. If it is discovered that the people receiving the services of a program have needs that are quite different from the needs the program was planned to meet, the program must be altered. An increase in the participant drop out rate would suggest problems. Without a program monitoring system, managers might be slow in noticing the problem until it is severe and difficult to correct. The techniques described in this chapter apply to programs expected to remain in place. A limited, inexpensive program would not merit the attention required to develop a management information system as described in this chapter. However, many programs such as a college counseling center, a community mental health center, and a local consortium of organizations for serving the needs of homeless people, are expected to continue to offer services indefinitely; these organizations need convenient access to data describing the service.

Evaluators (for example, Carey and Lloyd, 1995; Mowbray, Cohen, and Bybee, 1993) have shown the value of monitoring the process of providing a product or service, not just evaluating the final outcome. A management information system provides information showing that the program is operating as planned. Keeping track of operations is similar to following progress during an automobile trip as we watch for route markers and familiar landmarks. While planning a trip, most drivers take note of intermediate locations in order to monitor their progress and to be sure they stay on the correct route. We don't simply plan a trip, aim the car, drive for four hours, and ask: "Are we there?" The last point is so obvious that it is hard to understand why so many service providers, program planners, and evaluators fail to apply this principle to program evaluation. All too often an evaluation plan includes only an assessment of success in achieving the ultimate outcome, not the services actually provided or the intermediate steps needed to reach the desired outcome.

MONITORING PROGRAMS AS A MEANS OF EVALUATING PROGRAMS

Some of the information that evaluators summarize for program staff are fairly straightforward descriptions of the clients served and services provided. At times, managers and staff seem to believe that such information is unnecessary because they think that they have an accurate and complete understanding of the service they provide. However, it is common knowledge among evaluators that managers and staff often hold opinions that are incorrect. Without counting and summarizing, counseling agency staff greatly overestimated the median number of treatment sessions clients came to (Posavac and Hartung, 1977), and nurses overestimated the variety of illnesses of the patients they cared for (Carey, 1979). Solberg et al. (1997) described the need for better information systems in medical care commenting ". . . most of the defects in the current process of care for patients with diabetes or other chronic diseases are the result of an inconsistent, disorganized approach *that is the natural result* of relying almost entirely on the memories of individual clinicians" (p. 586, italics in original). When information systems have been implemented, improvements in care have resulted (Williams, Schmaltz, Morton, Koss, and Loeb, 2005). Because it is so easy to be misled by our impressions, a summary of the client population and services provided would be an appropriate first step in an evaluation.

A description of clients and services can be done once as a snapshot of the agency or as a regular activity in order to track the agency over time. Managers of smaller and newer programs may benefit from summaries of information in the records; this process is time-consuming and sensitive because files contain far more material than would be needed to describe the agency's clients and the services provided. In larger agencies, an ongoing information system would be needed because a hand retrieval of information would not be feasible. Larger programs usually need reports for accrediting and regulatory agencies, each with its unique information requirements. A procedure to gather information and summarize it periodically is called a management information system. Some writers view the development of management information systems as an activity crucial to the survival of service organizations (Freel and Epstein, 1993). Wargo (see Evaluator Profile 6) describes the importance of information systems for evaluators.

Beyond these fundamental needs for information on services provided and people served, services to people can be improved with better access to

---

EVALUATOR PROFILE 6

Michael J. Wargo: Management Information Systems and Program Evaluation

After conducting program evaluations in consulting firms, Dr. Wargo conducted evaluations of federal government-sponsored volunteer organizations such as the Peace Corps and VISTA. He organized the evaluation unit of the Food and Nutrition Service of the U.S. Department of Agriculture. He earned a Ph.D. in experimental psychology (Tufts University).

Dr. Wargo was asked about the use of management information systems (MIS's) in program evaluation. Dr. Wargo responded: ". . . (E)valuators are going to become more dependent on MIS's. It's just too costly to collect new data for every evaluation. Evaluators should use their skills to help design MIS's that are useful for evaluation purposes as well as for program management."

He continued, "Five to ten years from now most of the information evaluators use will be information collected for other purposes. It's too costly to collect information the way we have in the past, and it takes too long."

Adapted from Hendricks, M. 1986. A conversation with Michael Wargo. *Evaluation Practice*, 7(6), 23–36.

information. Spath (2000) reported that because 10 billion pages of patient records were being produced each year; complicated—yet accessible—information systems were needed if hospitals and physicians wished to track patient care. This chapter is an introduction focused on smaller agencies that do not require information systems as complicated as those needed by hospitals.

WHAT TO SUMMARIZE WITH INFORMATION SYSTEMS

Evaluators are often asked to develop information systems to assist a specific agency or program. Because each agency is unique, each information system includes a unique collection of variables. The issues described in this section must be adapted to the needs of the people served, the kind of services offered, and the institution offering the program.

Relevant Information

The information gathered must be central to the purpose and mission of the program. The appropriate information can help set staff levels, satisfy accreditation criteria, plan for space needs, and monitor quality. Effective evaluators gather only information that is important, not information that might be interesting. Because every piece of information recorded increases the costs of data collection and analysis, evaluators guard against including information that is not of use to the agency.

Actual State of Program

A second point is that an information system must describe the actual state of the current program. Evaluators are careful to distinguish between the program as described and the program as administered. Many programs that look very good on paper fail because staff did not or could not follow the design or procedure as planned. Reporters for the *Chicago Tribune* (Stein and Recktenwald, 1990) visited city parks during periods when activities were officially scheduled, only to find field houses locked or abandoned. If the reporters had limited their study to the official activity schedules, they would have assumed that the programs were being offered. There is no excuse for an evaluator to permit written plans, no matter how official, to substitute for on-site observations.

The information necessary to describe the services rendered include (1) the type of services offered by the program (such as job training, group therapy, immunizations), (2) the extensiveness of the program (such as hours of training or therapy, skills to be learned, facilities), (3) the number of people participating in the service, especially the proportion of people completing education or therapeutic programs, and (4) indicators of quality. To be useful the system must permit convenient retrieval and summarization of information.

Program Participants

If a program is well planned, the population to be served would have been specified carefully and the program tailored to meet the needs of that group. An information system should document the identity and the needs of the people using the service and compare these findings to the program mission. In other words, the fit between the program and the needs of those using it should be examined. If the fit is not close, changes in the program can be considered. If the agency had not defined the group to be served, a description of the people using the agency may be especially enlightening.

Program participants are routinely described by gender and age. The choice of additional information depends on the specific nature of the program. Such information may include where the people live, the major problems for which they are seeking assistance, the source of referral, and ethnic background. In some settings the barriers to obtaining services might be important to know. Transportation difficulties, childcare needs, and length of time spent on the waiting list might be useful in describing a program and suggesting improvements.

Providers of Services

The information system should include a description of who gives the services. In some settings, less-well-trained people work under someone else; a casual examination of the program might imply that the supervisor was the provider. For example, a licensed psychiatrist may sign insurance forms, but employ social workers who provide therapy. It may be important to understand the program to know who actually works with the participants. Staff may be underqualified or overqualified. An evaluation of a project staffed by volunteer lawyers to help ex-convicts readjust to community life showed mixed results because the released prisoners looked to the volunteers for legal aid, not for general readjustment help. Thus, the skills of the volunteers impeded the achievement of program goals (Berman, 1978).

PROGRAM RECORDS AND INFORMATION SYSTEMS

Monitoring using an information system is more efficient when evaluators help to choose the information gathered by the agency to describe participants and services delivered. When appropriate information is gathered consistently, the types of reports illustrated in this chapter can be prepared without great cost.

Problems with Agency Records

It is impossible to monitor a program that does not keep adequate records (Vroom, Colombo, and Nahan, 1994). However, it is no secret that the records of many human services are often abysmally incomplete. Lurigio and

Swartz (1994) described the difficulties they had as they tried to work with the inadequate records of jail-based drug treatment programs. Records are often in poor condition because record keeping is dull and does take time. Individuals attracted to human services often have more to do than they have time for and view keeping records as time taken from clients, students, or patients. In the very short run, that view may be correct. Furthermore, records may well have been less important in the recent past when impressionistic evaluations of success and effort were sufficient in many settings. However, impressionistic evaluations no longer satisfy the requirements of regulatory and accrediting agencies. We need better ways to maintain and summarize agency records.

Increasing the Usefulness of Records

Methods of summarizing information must be developed to increase the usefulness of files because information that cannot be summarized is not helpful to evaluators or program stakeholders. Retrieving material from client folders is a time-consuming task. Furthermore, it is a sensitive task because the privacy of participants must be protected. It is more efficient to develop an information system that permits the regular summary of participant descriptors, services provided, and quality indicators without manually searching through files that often contain personal material important to the participant and staff but irrelevant to an evaluation.

It is necessary for the program director and other information users to develop a list of essential variables useful in managing and evaluating the program. A point repeatedly stressed in this book is that information is gathered only when it is useful. If there are legal requirements to obtain certain information, or if decisions are to be made on the basis of information, then it should be gathered. If material could reveal suspected negative side effects, it should be included as well. The challenge to information system developers is to summarize such information in helpful ways. Managers need relevant and useful information, not just more information (Ackoff, 1986).

How Records Can Be Used to Monitor Programs

The best way to gather and store information is with a relational database program. A database is a collection of information. A database program permits one to choose the variables of interest and then summarize the information it contains. Information in a database can be numerical or verbal. Imagine a table with names of program participants down the left side and columns for identification numbers, addresses, ages, etc. A *relational* database is a *set* of tables that are related and linked to each other by common variables; these links permit great flexibility and efficiency in entering and retrieving information. Each table contains information on a critical aspect of the program that is essential in managing the services provided. An illustration is in order.

Agencies record keeping!
already successful!

Imagine a counseling center; let's call it New Hope. The critical aspects of New Hope include:

- Clients: clients' names, addresses, source of payment, etc.
- Staff members: names, category, supervisor, etc.
- Services: type of service given to a specific client by a certain staff member on a particular day for a certain charge, etc.
- Appointments: client, staff, date, etc.
- Bills: client, amount billed, payment received, etc.

Each of these critical aspects of New Hope forms a table. See Figure 7.1. For example, each client forms one row in the Client Table. Everything that is crucial for the center to know about a client is listed in this table. Figure 7.2 on page 138 is an illustration of part of a Client Table. Note that social security numbers ought not to be used as identification numbers. The Appointment Table includes one line for every appointment made by clients with any staff member. The client's name (or ID number) is entered, but nothing else about the client is entered because the Appointment Table is linked with the Client Table that already contains information about clients. Linked variables are indicated in Figure 7.1. All of the information in the Client Table would be available if needed to organize information included in the Services Table. This linking is what gives a relational database its power. All of the information in the entire database, that is, in any of the tables, is available to answer questions about the services of the center.

FIGURE 7.1   An outline of a relational database for a counseling center. Each client forms an entry (a row) in the Client Table, each appointment forms a row in the Appointment Table, and so forth. The common elements in the tables permit the tables to be linked without needing to duplicate information from table to table.

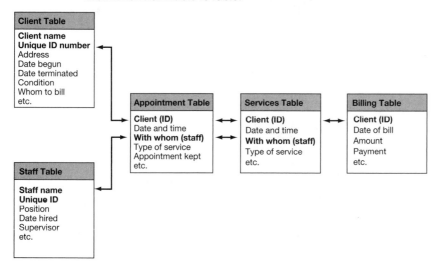

FIGURE 7.2 The Client Table of a relational database includes information about clients needed to provide services and respond to regulatory agency requests for information about clients. There would be a great deal more information included in such a table than is illustrated here.

Name	ID	Street Address	City	Zip	Age	Date Began Services	Date Ended Services	Bill to Whom	Address	Etc.
Sarah	445	61 Downer	Nelson	67523	34	6/25/2005	7/21/2006	Sarah	61 Downer	
Mary	556	87 Maple	Union	67539	29	7/29/2005	Active	Mary	87 Maple	
Jim	667	992 Center	Union	67539	16	8/2/2005	Active	William	922 Center	
Frank	882	32 Grove	Union	67540	43	8/2/2005	Active	Frank	32 Grove	
Jenny	981	87 Hazel	Junction	67533	53	8/7/2005	Active	Jenny	87 Hazel	

etc.

Evaluators who are asked to develop an information system for an agency have several tasks. First, they must understand the services the agency provides. Second, they will need to understand the *essential* aspects of the agency. For a small counseling center, the five aspects listed above and in Figure 7.1 seem critical and perhaps sufficient. This relational database is simple because all clients of New Hope are really in one program, counseling. In contrast, imagine a training center for the residents of a town. Perhaps some are in the literacy program, others in the parent support program, others in job training, etc. The database for such a complicated center would require more tables so that all of the services can be represented efficiently; however, there would still be just one database for the center. After coming to understand the center and the critical aspects of its services, the specific pieces of information needed for each table must be defined. The type of program, the needs of the clients, and reporting requirements will dictate what should be gathered. Figure 7.3 includes some possible variables that might be relevant for clients of New Hope. An evaluator will work closely with the administration of the agency, but would be wise to contact similar agencies to learn about their information systems. And, as mentioned before, some searching on the Internet will provide leads on more suggestions.

The information provided by a new client completing the form in Figure 7.3 would be entered into the Client Table. When a client's address or other information changes, the information would be updated. A report could be generated each month showing the number of new clients to New Hope. A table like Figure 7.4 would summarize the new clients for a month. In addition, a graph could be prepared giving the number of new clients per month across the most recent 12-month period. Examining trends across a span of months gives a view of caseload trends. After the center was open for some time, it would be helpful to examine the problems which new clients report each quarter. Because the number of new clients in a month with any specific problem can be low, it might not be useful to examine specific problems each month— random variation would hide any trends. However, carefully examining quarterly information would permit the manager to spot changes in the problems clients bring. Changes in client characteristics would be relevant when staff members are replaced or added. Depending on the problems presented, counselors with particular qualifications might be sought.

As clients receive service, information is added to the Services Table. Each staff member would complete an Encounter Form after providing any type of service. Figure 7.5 is an example of what such a form could contain. A receptionist could provide such forms each day with the client's name and ID entered. The staff member would complete the form after the appointment and return it to the receptionist for entry into the Services Table. If a new appointment had been scheduled, the receptionist would enter that into the Appointments Table as well. The therapist would probably keep written notes separate from the database record; however, the value of a database is that written comments can be entered into the Services Table just as the client's address

FIGURE 7.3   An application form for potential clients of an outpatient counseling center.

Welcome to New Hope Center for Effective Living

Please complete this form and return it to the receptionist in the envelope provided. The information you give us is *confidential and will be carefully secured.*

Name _____

Address _____

Zip _____   Telephone _____

Marital Status: (Circle one)
      Never married   Married now   Widowed   Divorced/Annulled   Separated

Sex: Female   Male   Couple application

Age: _____   Age of spouse if married now: _____

Who referred you to the center? (Circle one)
      Myself, friend, family   Hospital   Another agency: _____
      Another client   Physician   Other: _____
      Clergy   Psychiatrist

What problem(s) has prompted you to consider counseling at this center?

      _____

      _____

What form of counseling are you most interested in at this time? (Circle one)
      Individual   Family   Marital   Group

Who lives in your immediate family?
      Adults (List names and give their relationship to you.) _____

      _____

      Children (List names and give ages.) _____

      _____

Have you previously received counseling from some other agency or counselor?
      Yes   No

If "Yes" and if you do enter therapy with a counselor from the center, may we contact this person or agency about you?
      No   Yes (Give name of counselor.) _____

            Please sign _____ Date: _____

Where are you employed? _____

Please give the name and address of any insurance company that will meet part of your expenses at the center.

Name   Address   Ident. No.

_____   _____   _____

FIGURE 7.4   An illustrative monthly report describing new clients to a counseling center.

NEW CLIENTS FOR MAY 2006

MARITAL STATUS, GENDER AND AGE	FEMALE	MALE
NEVER MARRIED	28	12
MARRIED NOW	48	15
WIDOWED	3	0
DIVORCED, ANNULLED	15	3
SEPARATED	4	0
TOTAL	98	30
AGE (MEAN) - YRS	34	27

SOURCES OF REFERRAL	N	%
SELF, FRIEND, FAMILY	27	21
ANOTHER CLIENT	5	4
CLERGY	67	52
HOSPITAL	15	12
PSYCHIATRIST	2	2
OTHER SOURCE	11	9
TOTAL	127	100%

PROBLEM CODE (MORE THAT ONE MAY APPLY)	N	%
MARITAL PROBLEMS	42	33
INDIVIDUAL ADJUSTMENT ISSUES	104	81
PROBLEMS AT WORK	30	23
PROBLEMS AT SCHOOL	8	6
PROBLEMS WITH CHILDREN	62	48
ALCOHOL, DRUG USE	28	22
NON-ORGANIC PHYSICAL SYMPTOMS	16	12

SERVICE SOUGHT	N	%
INDIVIDUAL THERAPY	77	60
FAMILY THERAPY	13	10
MARITAL THERAPY	29	23
GROUP THERAPY	5	4
NOT SURE	4	3

NUMBER (%) HAVING PREVIOUS PSYCHOTHERAPY 45 (35%)

NUMBER (%) EMPLOYED 92 (72%)

was entered in the Client Table. The example in Figure 7.5 includes only space for a short rating of the client's condition. Depending on the type of services provided the kinds of ratings or the extent of information would vary.

Note that the client's ID is sufficient to link the Services Table to the Client Table. The staff ID would permit linking service information to the Staff

FIGURE 7.5   Illustrative Encounter Form that would be completed after every service provided at New Hope. The information on this form would be entered into the Services Table and the Appointments Table if another appointment had been made.

Table. This linking permits presenting any information about services separately for any groups of clients defined by demographic information that was entered into the Client Table. For example, Figure 7.6 is an illustrative report of the clients who ended their contact with New Hope during May 2005. The breakdown by age was chosen for illustrative purposes; any variables in the Client Table could have been used. Information about the amount and type of service received, mean functional status at the beginning and at the end of the therapy, amount of charges, number of referrals, and the type of termination could be summarized and related to the demographic information previously obtained. Using just the information in Figure 7.6, the manager and staff can learn that about one-quarter of the clients apparently reject the service offered. This conclusion can be drawn because 24 percent of the clients accept only two or fewer counseling sessions and 29 percent cease attending without discussing their withdrawal with their therapists. A director would probably seek to lower these percentages. This illustrative report suggests some hypotheses about how to approach such a goal. The lower part of the report shows that older clients rejected therapy more frequently than younger clients did.

FIGURE 7.6 A report on the clients terminated during one month, including characteristics of services rendered to these clients.

REPORT OF TERMINATED CLIENTS IN MAY 2005

CASES TERMINATED: 84

RATINGS OF FUNCTIONAL STATUS

LEVEL		CLIENTS AT EACH FUNCTIONAL LEVEL WHEN THERAPY BEGAN	AT TERMINATION
DYSFUNCTIONAL:	1	0 (0%)	0 (0%)
DYSFUNCTIONAL:	2	0 (0%)	1 (1%)
DYSFUNCTIONAL:	3	2 (2%)	0 (0%)
DYSFUNCTIONAL:	4	25 (30%)	3 (4%)
FUNCTIONAL:	5	41 (49%)	2 (2%)
FUNCTIONAL:	6	8 (10%)	7 (8%)
FUNCTIONAL:	7	6 (7%)	4 (5%)
FUNCTIONAL:	8	2 (2%)	21 (25%)
FUNCTIONAL:	9	0 (0%)	46 (55%)
MEAN FUNCTIONAL STATUS		5.00	8.05

TYPE OF TERMINATION AND AGE OF CLIENT

	UNDER 29	30 AND OVER	ALL
MUTUAL CONSENT	25 (76%)	32 (63%)	57 (68%)
CLIENT DECISION	6 (18%)	18 (35%)	24 (29%)
THERAPIST DECISION	2 (6%)	1 (2%)	3 (4%)
ALL	33 (100%)	51 (100%)	84 (100%)

UNITS OF SERVICE AND AGE OF CLIENT

	UNDER 29	30 AND OVER	ALL
2 OR LESS	5 (15%)	15 (29%)	20 (24%)
3 TO 6	7 (21%)	7 (14%)	14 (17%)
7 TO 15	14 (42%)	22 (43%)	36 (43%)
16 TO 30	6 (18%)	7 (14%)	13 (15%)
OVER 30	1 (3%)	0 (0%)	1 (1%)
ALL	33 (100%)	51 (100%)	84 (100%)

Reporting Information Separately for Each Therapist

A report can also be prepared for each therapist. Such reports would permit therapists to compare their clients with those of other therapists. People working in human services seldom have specific information that compares their work to that of their colleagues. However, the value of feedback has repeatedly been demonstrated. Dennis, Soderstrom, Koncinski, and Cavanaugh (1990) reviewed a number of approaches to reducing energy use using feedback to consumers. Often feedback relating to the behaviors of peers is effective, a principle that Tierney, Miller, and McDonald (1990) used to reduce the number of unnecessary medical diagnostic tests. The authors provided each medical resident with a summary of his/her own use of tests in contrast with the use of tests by the other residents.

A report format that could provide information for individual therapists is given in Figure 7.7. The hypothetical report describes the therapist's caseload and the amount of service rendered during the past month. Note that therapist Helper has some problems. He had a higher proportion of clients drop out during the previous month than the other therapists at the center. Of greater importance, those who quit had received less service than was given to other clients before termination. This therapist also has a relatively large number of inactive clients, that is, clients who have not sought service for 90 days or more. The report politely requests that therapist Helper either terminate these clients formally or find out whether they are interested in continued therapy. Last, the report includes a table that summarizes the functional status ratings of Helper's clients who formally ended their contact with the center during the previous month. Note that only Helper and his supervisor see this version of the report. Other therapists would receive similar reports that included the same averages for the center plus their own information.

When problems are identified, remedies can be planned. Helper should approach his supervisor with the problem he is having with losing clients prematurely. Everyone has a string of bad luck once in a while. It is important not to treat variation as a problem when it is simply the result of random effects (see Carey and Lloyd, 1995). If Helper's record does not improve and he continues to lose a relatively large number of clients after only one or two sessions, he should seek some assistance. Perhaps he has become judgmental; or perhaps he is not giving new clients enough hope for improvement. Ideally, noting undesirable practices early in a therapist's career permits improvements in the therapist's techniques before these practices are deeply ingrained. Challenging feedback is often not welcomed, but it is to Helper's advantage to make changes before hearsay and rumor define his work as poor (House, 1976). Feedback on treatment activities was a cost-effective method of improving services to state hospital patients (Prue, Krapfl, Noah, Cannon, and Maley, 1980).

Developing Information Systems for Agencies

Database programs have been around for decades; however, in recent years the programs have become much easier to use. An evaluator new to database development cannot expect to have a database in place over a weekend, but the use of programs such as Microsoft's Access (Prague, Irwin, and Reardon, 2004) can

FIGURE 7.7 An illustrative format for feedback to individual therapists.

REPORT FOR THERAPIST HELPER

	HELPER	OTHER THERAPISTS
TOTAL CASE LOAD ON JUNE 1, 2005	64	433
ACTIVE CASES	49 (76%)	364 (84%)
INACTIVE CASES	15 (24%)	69 (16%)
(NOT SERVED IN 90 DAYS OR MORE)		

THE NAMES OF YOUR INACTIVE CLIENTS ARE:

ARCHIBALD, L.	NORRIS, M. M.
BEST, B.	OVERMAN, S.
BOULDER, M. M.	PAKOWSKI, M. M.
ERNEST, G.	RASMUSSEN, P.
GRAND, K.	THOMAS, A.
HANSEN, M. M.	TRAVERSE, P.
MORRISON, S.	WILSON, G.
NARWELL, B.	

PLEASE FILE A TERMINATION NOTICE OR A REFERRAL NOTICE, OR HAVE AN APPOINTMENT WITH EACH OF THESE INACTIVE CLIENTS BY JULY 31, 2005.

	HELPER	OTHER THERAPISTS
TERMINATED CASES IN MAY		
TERMINATED BY MUTUAL CONSENT	10 (48%)	47 (75%)
TERMINATED BY CLIENT DECISION	9 (43%)	15 (24%)
TERMINATED BY THERAPIST	2 (10%)	1 (1%)
NUMBER OF THERAPY SESSIONS WITH CLIENTS TERMINATED IN MAY 2002 (MEDIAN)	4.0	7.5

RATINGS OF THE FUNCTIONAL STATUS OF TERMINATED CLIENTS WERE:

		CLIENTS AT EACH FUNCTIONAL LEVEL	
LEVEL		HELPER	OTHER THERAPISTS
DYSFUNCTIONAL:	1	0 (0%)	0 (0%)
DYSFUNCTIONAL:	2	0 (0%)	1 (1%)
DYSFUNCTIONAL:	3	0 (0%)	0 (0%)
DYSFUNCTIONAL:	4	2 (10%)	1 (1%)
FUNCTIONAL:	5	1 (5%)	1 (1%)
FUNCTIONAL:	6	1 (5%)	6 (10%)
FUNCTIONAL:	7	2 (10%)	2 (3%)
FUNCTIONAL:	8	4 (20%)	17 (27%)
FUNCTIONAL:	9	11 (52%)	35 (56%)

be learned without training in programming. A major project for a large, complex organization would be best handled in consultation with an experienced database developer. Perhaps there are ready-to-use programs prepared for the type of organization needing to implement an information system. Evaluators would be in a good position to work with the stakeholders to learn what is needed and then to serve as liaisons between a software expert and the service providers. At this point we want to reassure you that one can develop modest database systems for agencies like New Hope without expensive consultants; but you do have to allot some time to the effort and might want to consider attending a workshop as you begin.

Threatening Uses of Information Systems

An information system that can produce Figure 7.7 can also produce tables comparing therapists with each other. Although the performance records of professional athletes are compared in sports pages every day, most people do not have their work closely compared to that of others, especially not in a quantitative manner. In Figure 7.8 the monthly reports of all therapists have been summarized in a way that permits such comparisons. Comparisons can be made among people who do the same tasks, but it would not be possible to compare the work of an outreach worker who tries to recruit drug addicts to seek care with the work of a therapist helping people quit smoking, even though both may work for the same mental health center. However, it could be possible to compare the income generated for the agency by each staff person even though different roles are played by various staff members. In a college faculty members could be compared in terms of how much tuition the courses they teach bring in. We are not recommending this simple-minded analysis because courses for which the same tuition is charged differ in how hard they are to teach. Our point is that once information is in a database, many different analyses can be done, some of which would be threatening to staff.

Reports similar to Figure 7.8 would be available only to the manager of the center. This table permits caseloads, the numbers of inactive clients, and the therapists' ratings of functional status to be compared. Those therapists losing a disproportional number of clients prematurely can be quickly spotted. Note how therapist Helper's record compares with the others. He has the largest proportion of inactive clients and loses more than anyone else before three counseling sessions. However, Helper rates his clients as functioning better than all other therapists (except Nelson) rate their clients. There are at least two interpretations of this contrast. One, Helper has been assigned clients who do not really need counseling. He correctly recognizes them as functioning well and does not provide unnecessary services. Two, Helper's counseling is not seen as helpful by clients. Although they drop out, Helper rates their functioning as "good" to justify his high rate of client loss. The first interpretation is tenable if the pattern does not continue. However, if clients are assigned to

FIGURE 7.8 A report permitting the center director to spot problems and to suggest ways to improve services given.

| | CURRENT CASES AS OF JUNE 1, 2005 | | | | | | TERMINATED CASES IN MAY 2005 | | | |
| | ACTIVE CASES | | | INACTIVE CASES | | | | | | |
THERAPIST	N	% OF CENTER CASES	FUNCTIONAL STATUS (MEAN)	N	% OF CENTER CASES	FUNCTIONAL STATUS (MEAN)	N	FUNCTIONAL STATUS % ABOVE 7	% SEEN FEWER THAN 3 TIMES	MEDIAN NUMBER OF VISITS
ABRAMS	39	11	6.5	4	7	6.3	6	100	33	6
COULDER	29	8	7.2	0	0	DNA	9	89	22	7
GREGORY	43	12	6.8	9	15	5.9	4	75	25	8
HELPER	49	13	6.7	15	25	6.7	21	71	48	4
MATTHEWS	28	8	6.5	1	2	6.0	6	50	17	9
NELSON	29	8	7.0	6	10	7.2	6	80	0	6
NICOLET	36	10	6.6	8	13	6.2	5	75	12	6
PETROVICH	38	10	6.2	10	17	5.9	8	80	0	7
RUDOV	19	5	7.1	1	2	5.0	5	100	0	9
VINCENT	35	10	6.5	4	7	6.3	4	80	20	7
WILLIAMS	20	5	5.9	2	3	6.5	10	100	17	8
ALL	365	100	6.6	60	100	5.4	6 / 84	80	24	7

147

whichever therapist has an opening and the pattern continues, the second interpretation appears more likely. If the information system included a follow-up client satisfaction survey of former clients, it might be easier to distinguish between these alternative interpretations. A negative evaluation does not mean that Helper should be dismissed. It may mean that Helper should have some in-service training; perhaps his approach to setting the stage for counseling is not appropriate to the population utilizing this center. Such possibilities should be explored. If a problem is found and resolved, Helper will be a better counselor and his clients will be better served. Freel and Epstein (1993) reported that an information system in a residential treatment agency identified staff who required training targeted on specific skills.

Even though there will be objections to monitoring as presented in Figure 7.8, there are important reasons to prepare such materials. We believe that accurate information is better than informal impressions of unknown validity. In counseling and educational settings, often just one person has contact with the participants for an extended period of time. Monitoring a program in such situations requires examining the work of individuals to a greater degree than when a service is provided by a team, when personal contact is minimal, or when improvement is more objective. A center director who has the material in Figure 7.8 can take the initiative in helping therapists improve their skills. The interpretation of differences among staff members must be made carefully. Evaluators and managers need to remember that half of the staff will always be below average; the manager should watch for outliers, those therapists who are markedly and consistently below average.

Figure 7.8 should be supplemented with an accounting of time spent on various activities. For example, if Rudov and Williams are devoting much time to community outreach efforts, to administration, or to leading in-service training sessions, their low caseloads are readily understandable. Categories of activities could include therapy, administration, training, and community outreach. One approach incorporating this added piece of information would be to create an additional table, perhaps a Quarterly Time Allocation Table. Such a table would include columns for the activities, the three-month period involved, and the hours per week commitment for each staff member. Consequently, it would be possible to show that a staff member seeing few clients per week has been assigned to agency administration or community outreach. The point of this example is simply to illustrate the power of a relational database program to reflect the details of the agency in which it is used.

AVOIDING COMMON PROBLEMS IN IMPLEMENTING AN INFORMATION SYSTEM

Introducing an information system into a facility is a major effort; there are a number of possible pitfalls in the process.

Guard Against the Misuse of the Information

As with all information, a report comparing individuals with each other can be misused. Critics fear that providing summaries of information usually hidden in files allows such data to be used in a vindictive manner; however, most evaluators believe that providing more information reduces the opportunities for directors to behave autocratically. Most unfair managers restrict information, just as despotic rulers control the media in the nations they rule. Nevertheless, it is crucial to remove fear from an evaluation system. When people fear that information will be used against them, they are motivated to hide their errors (Campbell, 1987; Deming, 1986; Edmondson, 1996; Hilkevitch, 2000) and to avoid asking for assistance. Managers must also guard against the possibility that acceptable variations in style will appear as deficiencies. Some therapists may encourage clients to leave therapy sooner than others do. They may do this because of theoretical convictions, not because of inadequate therapeutic skills. In Figure 7.8 we sought to avoid this confusion by reporting separately the number of clients quitting after only one or two counseling sessions. Even therapists who plan on short-term therapy expect to retain clients beyond two sessions. A related danger is the temptation to use the system in a misguided attempt to monitor staff work at such a detailed level that staff members simply report fictitious information.

Avoid Setting Arbitrary Standards

It is critical to avoid setting arbitrary standards for the staff to meet. The indexes developed using information systems can indeed reflect quality services, but they reflect only some aspects of the service. If pay and promotions of staff are based on these partial views of quality, staff will find ways to meet the standards at the expense of other aspects of their work. Primary and secondary school teachers have learned how to structure lessons to raise standardized test scores that are thought to represent the outcomes of effective schools and college teachers know that assigning higher grades increases the teaching ratings made by students (Gillmore and Greenwald, 1999). Campbell warned that focusing on a particular variable would increase the probability that it would become invalid, indeed corrupted (see, Shadish, Cook, and Leviton, 1991, p. 141). Management information is used most effectively when combined with detailed measures of quality.

Avoid Serving the Needs of Only One Group

People filling different roles in an organization have different informational needs because their responsibilities differ (Freel and Epstein, 1993; Kapp and Grasso, 1993). The needs of the accounting department differ from those of the billing department, which in turn contrast with those of the service delivery staff. By working closely with only one or two such groups, evaluators run the risk of providing information useful only to some groups. If that happens, the information system would be seen as irrelevant by those whose needs remain unmet by the system; such people will resist providing information for the system, thus reducing its usefulness (Binner, 1993).

Avoid Duplicating Records

Human service staff will not cooperate happily with an information system that duplicates information already reported and stored elsewhere. It is undesirable to simply impose an information system as an addition to existing recording procedures; integrating the information required by the old system with the automation of the new system is preferable. Staff members may question the accuracy of the new system. Because staff can seldom describe the population they serve in quantitative terms, they will sometimes be surprised at the summaries from a management information system. As the validity of the system is demonstrated, staff may come to appreciate the added knowledge provided by an information system.

Avoid Adding to the Work of the Staff

Savaya (1998) described the development of an integrated information system in an agency providing family and marriage counseling. Although the staff members were consulted in development of the system and were given training in its use, they were expected to complete assessment forms on their own time. Furthermore, the counseling staff was expected to change the way they assessed the success of their clients. The limited cooperation of the staff made it impossible to use the information system effectively.

Avoid a Focus on Technology

To develop the most useful system, the users must be involved in its design. The information needed, the manner of summarizing it, the frequency of reports, and other issues should be determined in cooperation with those who are expected to use the information. The evaluator may be enthusiastic about getting the system operating; however, learning what is useful requires patient work with the staff and administrators. Although a completed information system is not chiseled in granite, major changes are expensive and disruptive once the system is operational. Involving users early minimizes the possibility of producing an expensive but underused product.

Summary and Preview

Human service agencies can begin an evaluation with a systematic description of their programs, the amount and type of services provided, and the identity of those receiving the services. Such monitoring permits an agency to account for the funds expended and makes it easier to compare a program as implemented with the original plans. These sorts of comparisons can be invaluable in showing what aspect of a program needs additional effort or why a program never had the impact envisioned. Also, the need to complete accrediting agency and government surveys can be met more easily if monitoring for quality assurance is carried out regularly rather than only after requests for information are made.

Monitoring is a crucial aspect of program evaluation; it is essential to keep track of activities. However, stakeholders want to know how successful programs are in helping participants, students, or patients to achieve the goals of the program. The next chapters focus on methods that evaluators and stakeholders use to examine the degree to which programs achieve goals. Such evaluations would be used with reports from the information system for more complete understanding of the agency.

Study Questions

1. How does program monitoring fit into the schematic diagram of the function of program evaluation given in Figure 1.1?

2. Explain how monitoring relates to formative and summative evaluations.

3. People sometimes object to an evaluation of effort on the grounds that monitoring activities does not focus directly on the quality of the services provided. Why does this criticism not negate the reasons for monitoring the activities making up the program?

4. Suppose that you managed a telephone sales office. Twenty people make telephone calls to teachers who use educational DVDs. If these potential buyers are interested in previewing a DVD, they are given a code to permit them to preview it online for seven days to decide whether their school would buy it. How would you develop a monitoring system to keep track of what your employees are doing? How would you measure their success? What type of indexes of success would be important?

5. What types of program evaluation questions can be answered using an information system? What are some questions that an information system cannot answer?

Additional Resource

GRASSO, A. J., AND EPSTEIN, I., EDS. 1993. *Information systems in child, youth, and family agencies: Planning, implementation, and service enhancement.* New York: The Haworth Press.

This book is now dated in terms of software, but the issues discussed are common to agencies planning on developing an information system for their services. The authors described the design, implementation, and evaluation of a computerized management information, program evaluation, and clinical decision-making system designed specifically for social service settings integrating information technology and social work practice. This book can highlight the issues to be faced even though the software now available is much easier to use.

Qualitative Evaluation Methods

Each model of program evaluation presented in Chapter 2 has its advantages and disadvantages. One of the major advantages of qualitative methods (or the naturalistic model) is its flexibility and appropriate use in innovative and novel settings. When stakeholders want information quickly or want to understand a complex program with ill-defined (even conflicting) objectives, highly structured approaches to program evaluation may not be appropriate. Imagine that a new president of a private college has become concerned about the proportion of first year students who, although in good academic standing, do not register for the sophomore year. The president responds to this problem by proposing the development of curriculum changes, additional enhancements in available student activities, dormitory reorganizations, enhanced access to computer terminals, and other steps to improve the experiences of first year students. It is hoped that such measures would lead more first year students to identify with the college, continue their education there rather than transferring, and, in time, become alumni who participate in fund-raising campaigns.

After a period of planning and negotiation among the president's office, student life administrators, a skeptical faculty, admissions, and student organizations, plans are made and the program is implemented. The stakeholders would want timely information to help them make adjustments to these innovations. Some aspects probably need to be strengthened and others perhaps should be dropped. Since a lot of effort and funds are devoted to the program, it should be evaluated. But how?

The program will be evaluated. Without an informed evaluation, cynical stakeholders will find evidence for failure, whereas others will find evidence for success; the question is how to evaluate it fairly and in a way that provides useful information for the stakeholders. The president's office should have a central administrator keeping track of the activities sponsored by the innovation, but more is needed because stakeholders want to know more than a management information system can provide. Qualitative evaluators would supplement the numerical summaries from the relational database with direct observations of activities associated with the program, discussions with participants and staff, and examinations of program materials and artifacts. Often this approach is called *qualitative evaluation* to distinguish it from quantitative measurement.

The term *qualitative data* is used in several ways. Some people think of questionnaire items referring to ratings of impressions or subjective reactions as qualitative data; this is not how the term is used here. Such ratings are numerical and are treated as quantitative data. Others think of the characteristics of people (e.g., college major, on-campus vs. off-campus residence, religious affiliation, etc.) as qualitative variables. Other researchers use detailed coding of field notes or of unstructured conversations, and counts of artifacts as the data for evaluations. Again, the observations have been transformed into quantitative variables. Instead, qualitative evaluation is used here to refer to procedures that yield nonnumerical information that helps evaluators to understand the program or the participants' relation to the program, to interpret quantitative information, or to recognize the unique aspects of different program settings (Strauss and Corbin, 1998).

The first section of this chapter emphasizes data collection approaches particularly central to qualitative evaluation; however, nearly all methodologists (Reichardt and Rallis, 1994) urge that qualitative methods be used together with quantitative evaluation methods as will be illustrated toward the end of the chapter.

EVALUATION SETTINGS BEST SERVED BY QUALITATIVE EVALUATIONS

The emphasis of this text is on evaluation methods that can be best used with programs having identifiable objectives that can be specified and measured quantitatively. Evaluators have been encouraged to develop methods to quantify the degree to which objectives have been achieved. Furthermore, the assumption has been made that with enough care evaluators could discover whether the influence of the program did or did not cause changes in the participants. Given reasonable care in participant selection, it was further assumed that successful programs would probably be effective if implemented at another location.

Experienced evaluators often find that they are asked to conduct evaluations when these assumptions cannot be met and indeed need not be. In order to develop support for a program, innovators may make their goals intentionally vague (Cook, Leviton, and Shadish, 1985). Vague goals permit different stakeholders to read their own goals in the program's objectives. Thoughtlessly following the suggestions in Chapter 5 would lead an evaluator to decline to conduct evaluations of such programs. However, evaluation is possible in such settings. Before getting into specific methods, consider some other settings in which quantitative approaches might be very hard to use.

Admission to Graduate Studies

Applications procedures vary somewhat among graduate programs; however, the vast majority require similar items: an undergraduate transcript, standardized test score reports (such as the GRE), several letters of recommendation, a writing sample, and a statement of purpose. If one wanted to evaluate a graduate admissions procedure, limiting the evaluation to quantitative methods is probably unwise; here are three reasons why it would be unwise.

It is seldom clear how admissions committees integrate the information they examine. Faculty members disagree among themselves about the importance of different parts of the application materials, some depending primarily on admission tests, others grades, and others letters from faculty whom they know.

Although most faculty members can identify a good graduate student when they see one, it is very hard to select applicants who will develop into good students. Undergraduate programs are quite different from graduate programs; merely amassing sufficient credits in a proper mix of courses is not defined as successful graduate work. Consequently, successful undergraduate work does not guarantee good graduate work. Grades have a very limited range in graduate school and make poor criteria by which to judge success. Furthermore, not all graduate students who complete their programs are considered successes by the faculty.

Third, graduate school performance is multidimensional, requiring ambition, creativity, a good memory, endurance, independence, and intelligence. Some students cannot develop the self-initiation needed; others are worried about future job prospects. Since some faculty do a much better job of mentoring than others do, one could wonder whether attrition indicates student failure or faculty failure.

Dissatisfaction with a Library Collection

Suppose that a community public library began to receive complaints about the books and other material that had been added to the collection, and that the number of these complaints increased a few months before a vote on a referendum to raise funds to remodel the library. Library board members wanted to respond to the complaints to reduce objections to the referendum. After some debate, suppose that the board decided to evaluate the acquisitions department.

An evaluator would discover that a library acquisitions department has complex and potentially conflicting goals. Should the library seek to get the most critically acclaimed books or should the bulk of the collection match the intellectual level of the community? How much of the budget should be spent on meeting the needs of school children? Is the library being asked to meet school needs that the school district should meet?

There are also conflicts among goals of stakeholders. Some groups have been complaining of the moral tone of many novels purchased recently. Junior and senior high school children want the library to have multiple copies of frequently used reference materials and they have been asking for access to more computer-based online resources. On the other hand, residents of a local retirement community have picketed the library and board meetings over the unwillingness of the acquisitions department to buy more than a token number of large-print books. And then there was a bitter letter from the music society attacking the board because rock and rap CDs have been purchased in response to requests from young patrons. "Do we satisfy anyone?" the board members asked each other.

Evaluating a Political Campaign

Imagine a politician running for a state-level office who is dissatisfied with the voters' reactions to his campaign. Not surprisingly, he would not turn to a professional program evaluator for an experiment. A political campaign is a diffuse, complicated endeavor. Although the ultimate goal of a political campaign is very objective and quantitative, votes cast is not a useful index of campaign effectiveness if one wants to improve the campaign. An approach is needed that can provide recommendations that can be put to use quickly.

The problem faced by this politician is similar to many other situations in which policy must be evaluated before the ultimate outcome index is available. Major, expensive evaluations have been criticized because it took too long for the results to become available; when the evaluation was completed, it was no longer relevant to the information needs of the policy makers. When, for example, an evaluation of a welfare reform plan (called the "negative income tax") was completed, Congress and the White House were no longer in a mood to even consider the innovative plan, regardless of the findings of the evaluation (Cook et al., 1985; Haveman and Watts, 1976).

These four hypothetical evaluation problems—a strengthened freshman year program, graduate admissions, library acquisition, and a political campaign—are presented to illustrate situations that need evaluation approaches quite unlike monitoring with an information system or the research designs to be presented in following chapters. Crucial characteristics of these situations requiring qualitative evaluations include: (1) a longer cycle between program input and outcome than is expected for classroom lessons, medical treatment, or job training; (2) global success indexes that are based on the whole program rather than on measures of individuals such as medical tests or ratings of improvement; (3) a need for results in a short time; (4) multiple stakeholders perhaps with conflicting values; (5) a request for suggestions for improvement rather than just an evaluation of outcome; and (6) a concern that the social setting of the program or the program itself is unlike those found elsewhere. Most qualitative evaluations are conducted in settings with at least some of these characteristics.

Although this chapter highlights qualitative methods, issues that require qualitative approaches have been mentioned throughout this text. Working with stakeholders to understand what information is most important to them is part of the qualitative approach to program evaluation. In previous chapters, the importance of verifying that a program has been implemented was stressed. Since it is impossible to know what will go wrong ahead of time, qualitative observations are important in the evaluation of implementation and in the detection of side effects.

GATHERING QUALITATIVE INFORMATION

Before we examine observation and interview techniques, the central importance of the evaluator in making qualitative observations must be stressed.

The Central Importance of the Observer

The single most distinctive aspect of qualitative research is the personal involvement of the evaluator in the process of gathering data. In other forms of evaluation, measurement procedures are designed to dissociate an evaluator from data collection. This is attempted by using written measures of the achievement of goals or objective data such as income level or productivity. The criteria of program success are defined before the evaluation begins and measured with little involvement of the evaluation team except to verify that the data are coming in as planned. When this degree of data collection automation is achieved, a form of objectivity is gained. Proponents of qualitative program evaluation, however, would argue that something is lost as well.

What is lost is the evaluator's opportunity to understand the program from the inside rather than standing aloof on the outside (Fetterman, 1998). The opportunity to respond to the information as it is gathered is also lost. In a real sense, the qualitative evaluator is viewed as the measurement instrument. Qualitative evaluators are intimately involved in data collection so that they can react to the observations made. Such reactions may involve adjusting the focus of the evaluation. For example, it may become evident early in the process of observation that the staff's expectations are incorrect or that the program sponsor's goals are different from the goals of the program participants. An inflexible evaluation plan based on a misconception yields useless information.

Some evaluators object to qualitative evaluations for fear that evaluations will become very subjective. The loss of the credibility of the evaluation process would be disastrous for evaluators who have striven to demonstrate that evaluations can be used in improving organizations. Qualitative evaluation can be rigorous (Shaw, 1999); however, rigor means something different from what is needed for basic research. Alexander (1986) stressed that although qualitative evaluators recognize the difficulty, even the impossibility, of finding one correct view of a program, this does not mean that all interpretations are equally legitimate; it is not true that anything goes.

How does one decide when a conclusion based on qualitative information is credible? Consider the tests of the validity of conclusions that are used in daily life. In a mystery story, readers can correctly conclude that "the butler murdered the nanny" by integrating evidence from different sources into a credible, persuasive story. Even when an eyewitness is not available, a defendant can be convicted when caught in a web of evidence. Many court decisions stand on qualitative syntheses of a great number of observations. The tests of validity of court decisions are similar to the tests of the validity of qualitative evaluations. Such tests involve corroborating conclusions with evidence from multiple, independent sources; developing a sense of the correctness of the conclusions; and confirming the conclusions with people who know the program.

Observational Methods

Nonparticipant observers. Since the goal of qualitative evaluation is to understand the program, procedure, or policy being studied, it is essential for the evaluator personally to observe the entity being evaluated. Nonparticipant observation means that observers are present in the program setting, but they serve no role in the administration or the delivery of the service. As nonparticipant observers Bussigel and Filling (1985) observed the teaching strategy of a family practice residency program as they evaluated the quality of instruction. They discovered that relatively little teaching actually occurred and that although the residents claimed that they valued the discussions of psychosocial issues led by psychologists, most either skipped those sessions or slept through them.

Qualitative evaluators seek to develop an understanding of how a program operates; they do not seek to answer predefined questions. It is impossible to specify beforehand the details that reveal how the program operates and that end up being important guides to understanding it. If it were possible to list all the things one would be looking for, qualitative evaluation would not be necessary; a checklist could be developed and a clerical assistant could be sent to make the observations. The evaluator must make the observations in order to detect what is important and discover how the details fit into the overall understanding of the program. Avoiding mental blinders and remaining open to many possible interpretations are the important contributions of qualitative evaluations.

Using nonparticipant observers to gather information is practical when evaluators can be sure that their presence would not change the social system of the program. The presence of observers can lead the program staff to act in guarded ways in an effort to control the impressions of the evaluator. Observers can also make staff members nervous and lower their effectiveness, as we have done when staff members had not been informed that their presentations were going to be observed. When observations become part of normal operating procedures, staff members become surprisingly relaxed to the point of doing things in the presence of nonparticipant observers that could have resulted in suspension if observed by a supervisor (Licht, 1979). Nonparticipant observations would be most feasible in settings that are relatively public, such as schools, libraries, businesses, and even graduate school admissions committee meetings.

Participant observation. When the services of a program are too private to permit a nonparticipant observer to be present or when the staff members are so defensive that they would not be able to carry out their duties, it may be necessary to use a participant observer. A participant observer has a legitimate role in the program. An assistant in an emergency room would know detailed information about emergency room practices. Serving as a secretary in a personnel office or as a dispatcher in a local police station could yield rich data about the effectiveness and the problems of the service being evaluated.

Using participant observation without the consent of the program staff would be unethical and incompatible with our philosophy of evaluation. Approaching evaluation without the agreement of the people whose work is being evaluated violates the spirit of mutual trust that is important in effectively functioning agencies. A better approach would be to explain clearly the part the participant observer plays in the evaluation. Cooperation often can be obtained when evaluation is described as a way to learn about and represent the program to those who do not understand how services are delivered and what problems staff members face. Clearly there are less expensive ways to police a program and one does not need to go to the trouble of conducting an evaluation if service improvement was not the goal of the evaluation. If staff members understand that, cooperation may be obtained.

A variant of participant observation involves a pseudoparticipant going through the system. Sometimes the experiences of pseudoparticipants are indeed used in a summative fashion to gauge the quality of normal treatment. Some stores assign staff to act as though they are customers in their own and competitors' stores in order to assess the quality of services provided (see Stucker, 2004). The therapy and medication practices of mental hospitals were evaluated by Rosenhan (1973) by having people feign mental illness to gain admission to mental hospitals. Once admitted, the pseudopatients reported that the symptoms ceased and they simply participated in ward activities. Rosenhan and his qualitative evaluators were able to provide a chilling critique of the way patients were treated by the psychiatric and nursing staffs of the hospitals. These observations implied that the slow improvement shown by psychiatric patients may be attributed partially to the impersonal manner in which they were treated by the staff.

Examining traces. Traces refer to a wide variety of tangible items associated with living. Archeologists examine traces of societies that have disappeared. Running a program also produces many traces. Records mentioned in Chapter 4 are one form of trace, but there are numerous traces produced by any program. In schools, traces include graded homework, teacher lesson plans, tests, litter in hallways, graffiti on walls, student club minutes, student newspapers and yearbooks, athletic trophies, and damage to desks and lockers. When evaluating a community development program, evaluators might examine discarded appliances and furniture in yards or vacant lots, litter in yards and alleys, abandoned cars, as well as carefully maintained yards, flower beds, families in parks, and newly established small businesses. Pictures taken before and after the intervention might be used in evaluations.

Physical traces add a dimension to an evaluation that is hard to gain in other ways. Someone conducting an evaluation of a school program would gain considerable understanding of the school and community by systematically examining the traces suggested above. This understanding could not be gained without the personal presence of members of the evaluation team. Although evaluators may well think about the traces that might be observed, qualitative evaluators do not begin making observations with a prepared list of items to look for; whatever is important will be discovered through the observations.

The meaning of any one physical trace is nearly impossible to understand. It is the accumulation of evidence from many traces that leads to a conclusion. Furthermore, tentative interpretations are compared with information obtained through interviews and observations of behaviors. By seeking various forms of information from different sources, evaluators seek to draw conclusions that are collaborated in several ways. Qualitative evaluators borrowed the idea of triangulation from surveyors to describe this process. By triangulation qualitative evaluators mean that they use different approaches to learning about the program.

Case Study 2 illustrates an evaluation that used a qualitative approach. Note that Fetterman (1991) used both nonparticipant and participant observations and examined traces as well.

CASE STUDY 2
Using Qualitative Methods in an Evaluation of a University Library

Libraries are essential to the life of a university. Although many people use a library's services, few understand what it takes to make it possible for users to find the books, journals, and microfilms on the shelves. Fetterman (1991) was asked to evaluate a troubled university library. One can ask how many books there are, how long it takes to process an interlibrary loan, or how many departments are involved in approving a new journal subscription. But however important these overall indices of activities may be, they would not tell evaluators why the staff of a library experiences morale problems and why there is frequent turnover among managers. Fetterman spent six weeks as a participant observer in the library; as he worked in acquisitions and cataloging, he interviewed staff members daily and ate lunch with them. This exposure permitted him to learn about the library from the inside. He could not have learned about the problems from surveys, counts of activities, or casual examinations of procedures.

First, he developed a sense of the various stages of getting a book on the shelves. He discovered that management had paid insufficient attention to coordinating these tasks. The different units had their own data management systems used to keep track of acquisitions, but the systems were not coordinated and could not be effectively aggregated to keep track of the whole library. Only by watching people use the systems did Fetterman discover this lack of coordination and its effects on the staff. He discovered the depth of dissatisfaction as he was told about difficulties between catalogers and management and about formal grievance complaints against management that individuals had won. He discovered the marked contrast between what he called "sweatshop" working conditions for catalogers and the plush working conditions of librarians who worked with faculty and students. Overall he learned that the library operation had fostered a number of subcultures that did not appreciate the overall mission of the library.

His recommendations centered on helping the library to develop a unified mission that all members shared. Concretely this meant, for example, a unified information system that would flexibly serve the needs of all and coordinate library information. It also meant that attention needed to be paid to the working conditions of the production staff who prepare materials for shelves and catalogs. Only by close and extended observations was Fetterman able to detect the fundamental problems and make suggestions for improvements.

Comment: This case study is an example of a needs assessment when the needs are not well defined because no one seemed to have an understanding of the overall system. Without understanding problems from all perspectives, it is impossible to develop effective ways to correct problems.

Interviewing to Obtain Qualitative Information

Qualitative interviewing is different from simply administering a written survey orally. A structured survey given orally remains a structured survey. Qualitative evaluators use open-ended, unstructured questions in order to learn detailed information about programs. Interviewers want the respondents to use their own words, thought patterns, and values when answering the questions (Patton, 1980).

Preparing for the interview. Before conducting interviews, evaluators make sure that the interviewee understands the purpose of the interview and has consented to be interviewed. There is no point in trying to mislead the individual as to the purpose of the interview. Such unethical behavior may well create controversy and discredit the evaluation when reports are presented. It is a good idea to confirm the appointment for an interview a day or two beforehand. Interviewers should be on time, even early. One will have better rapport if interviewers dress according to the norms of the organization. One need not dress in a designer suit to interview a business executive, but do not show up wearing a baseball cap.

Developing rapport. Interviewees usually are guarded as interviews begin. A personal relationship is needed to establish rapport and trust between the interviewer and respondent. Rapport can be fostered by asking some orientation questions and showing accepting, friendly reactions to the answers. Starting out asking, "How did you become a librarian?" gives a librarian a chance to talk and relax.

Asking questions. One of the most crucial points in qualitative interviews is to avoid using questions that can be answered "Yes" or "No." Patton (1986) provided several sets of questions that could produce useful information only if the interviewee spontaneously expanded upon answers to the actual questions. Figure 8.1 was inspired by Patton's suggestions. As the questions in the figure show, qualitative interviewers use questions that encourage the respondent to talk and elaborate. The best questions begin with phrases such as "What is it like when. . .?" "How would you describe the employees at. . .?" "Please tell me how. . .?" or "What are people like who. . .?" Someone can refuse to answer questions completely or may provide misleading answers; however, the format of such questions encourages the informant to provide answers revealing important information.

Probing for more information. Sometimes an interviewer senses that there is something more to be said, or the interviewee has not understood the point of the question. Conducting qualitative interviews gives evaluators the opportunity to tailor the interview to the respondent. The purpose of probes is to gain more information. One behavior that will encourage respondents to answer more fully is easy: Interviewers often nod their heads as the respondents speak. This sign of encouragement can often be seen during televised interviews as a journalist keeps nodding while a news maker talks. An interviewer is seeking information; consequently, it is important that the interviewer show a nonjudgmental orientation to everyone. One nods to encourage the speaker whether the interviewer actually agrees or disagrees with what is being said. A generic probe is silence. Instead of bringing up a new question when the respondent has stopped talking, the interviewer can simply remain quiet while looking at the respondent. Being quiet for five seconds has a surprisingly strong impact.

FIGURE 8.1 Two possible sets of questions for a director of an Applied Social Psychology graduate program. The contrasts between the two columns are the important points of this figure. Do note, however, that the qualitative interviewer would not have an inflexible set of questions ready to use. One would have the issues clearly in mind, but the actual questions asked would develop as the interview progressed.

Questions Not Likely to Elicit Useful Information from an Interviewee	Open-Ended Interview Questions That Will Encourage the Interviewee to Provide Information
Is this a social psychology graduate program?	What is the name of this graduate program?
Are you the director?	What is your role in this program?
Is the emphasis on applications of social psychology?	Please characterize the emphasis of the program.
Do the students enter the program with interests in applications?	What are the interests of the applicants to the program?
Do the courses have an applied orientation?	How do the courses relate to the emphasis of the program?
Do the students like the applied orientation?	How do the students react to the applied orientation?
Are the theses and dissertations related to the theme?	How do the theses and dissertations fit into the program's theme?
Do the students seek teaching positions after graduation?	What type of positions do the graduates seek?
Do the graduates get good positions?	How do graduates use the skills learned from the program?

Clearly either approach can be overdone and become artificial. More active probes are also used. The interviewer can probe by simply asking, "Can you tell me more about. . .?" Interviewers may want to check on an interpretation of what was said by asking, "Let's see, if I understand you, you said that. . .If that is correct, can you tell me what happens next?" It is critical to avoid using directive or leading probes. An interviewer who interprets a tone of voice as anger would be using a directive probe if the follow-up question is, "Why does that make you angry?" A nondirective probe would be, "How do you feel when you think about. . .?" In this way the interviewer has responded to the appearance of emotion and can learn about it without running the risk of labeling it incorrectly.

Recording answers. Lincoln and Guba (1985) review the advantages of recording the interview versus taking notes. Although it would be good to have complete records that a tape recording would provide, they recommend using handwritten notes because writing is less threatening, taking notes keeps the interviewer involved, technical problems with equipment can be avoided, interviewers can write their own thoughts down, and written notes are easier to work with than tapes. For large-scale studies, computer programs are available to organize the verbal material (Weitzman and Miles, 1995) and relational database programs might be used as well (Prague, Irwin, and Reardon, 2004). Some interviewers record comments directly into laptop computers, but this can be awkward for both the interviewer and interviewee. Increasingly voice recognition software is becoming capable of converting spoken language into text files (for example, ViaVoice, 2002).

Ending the qualitative interview. A structured interview ends with the last prepared question. In contrast, a qualitative interview could go on and on. When the scheduled appointment is nearly over, when the participants are fatigued, or when the information being discussed has become redundant, it is time to quit. It is best for interviewers to summarize the major points that have been made by saying, for example, "Here is how I understand your views. You have said that you enjoyed teaching the special freshman course, but that you received very little information from the department chair or the dean about how these courses were supposed to differ from regular sections of the same course. You said that you found that frustrating—is that correct?" The advantages of summarizing include getting a chance to verify interpretations before leaving and permitting respondents to expand on some point. Finally, interviewers thank respondents for their attention and thoughtful answers. One might ask if it would be possible to check back later for clarification if necessary.

CARRYING OUT NATURALISTIC EVALUATIONS

Although naturalistic evaluations require more involvement and creativity on the part of the evaluator than do traditional evaluation methods using surveys and checklists, the essential plan of a qualitative evaluation is quite similar to how people go about learning anything. We present the plan of an evaluation in phases; however, we have erred if readers view these phases as a step-by-step recipe. The phases overlap and later phases provide feedback that could lead an evaluator to revise initial conclusions. Nevertheless, different activities predominate at different times during an evaluation.

Phase One: Making Unrestricted Observations

Qualitative evaluations begin with observations of the most crucial program events, activities, written materials, and settings. Qualitative evaluators do not seek to observe a random selection of activities or people. Often they seek out those who know more than others and can provide more information on how things work in that setting. Although there are no restrictions on the observations and interviews, evaluators try to direct the information-gathering process toward important elements of the program. Observations, impressions, and interviews are recorded in field notes. Van Sant (1989) remarked that erroneous conclusions are likely when qualitative evaluations are based on samples of settings, people, or conditions that happen to be convenient or that are determined by program managers. Qualitative evaluators should have unrestricted access and should gather information from all aspects of the program or agency.

Phase Two: Integrating Impressions

The second phase, which actually begins with the first observations or interviews, is to integrate the impressions that are formed during this unrestricted observation period. From these impressions evaluators develop some specific ideas about how the program is run, how services are provided, how participants understand the purpose of the agency, and so forth. Then further observations and interviews are conducted in order to check on the accuracy of these impressions and to "fill in the holes" (Caudle, 1994). With this additional qualitative information, evaluators refine their initial impressions. When additional observations no longer change the impressions, the major part of the information-gathering phase is completed.

Phase Three: Sharing Interpretations

As impressions are formed, qualitative evaluators share their views with stakeholders and other evaluators. The qualitative approach has been misunderstood by some critics as subjectivity running wild. Describing tentative impressions to others who know the program and have a stake in it or who understand qualitative evaluation methodology is a way to obtain feedback so that impressions do not simply reflect the prejudgments of an evaluator. People familiar with the program can provide additional information to correct misunderstandings. Experienced, but uninvolved, evaluators can challenge interpretations that are not adequately supported. Evaluator Profile 7 contains the comments of two evaluators who have audited qualitative field notes.

Phase Four: Preparing Reports

Once checks with stakeholders and colleagues verify the accuracy of the impressions that have been formed, an evaluator is able to present the descriptions of the program and to draw evaluative conclusions about the program. Reports are usually lengthy. One of the central goals of qualitative evaluations is to provide detailed descriptions of programs through the eyes of the stakeholders along with the insights of the evaluator. The job of the evaluator is to integrate the views of many stakeholders so that everyone understands the program better than before. Although the reports contain details to communicate an understanding of the program, stakeholders who need information promptly can be given shorter, more focused reports.

EVALUATOR PROFILE 7

**Elizabeth Whitmore and Marilyn L. Ray: The Credibility
of Qualitative Evaluation Work**

When this material was presented, Elizabeth Whitmore was Assistant Professor of Social Work at Dalhousie University, Nova Scotia. She earned her doctoral degree in Human Service Studies from Cornell University. Marilyn Ray was Director of Policy and Program Planning and Evaluation at the Finger Lakes Law and Social Policy Institute in Ithaca, NY. She also earned her doctoral degree in Human Service Studies at Cornell.

Among their professional activities, Whitmore and Ray study the trustworthiness of qualitative research and evaluation. To do this they have conducted audits of the data of several qualitative evaluations. In one audit they demonstrated "the importance of making sure that interview logs contained data, not just summaries or personal impressions of the interviews." In another audit they reported: "Although (the) evaluation design decisions made intuitive sense, the dependability of the study could not be assessed adequately because the specific logic and rationale behind design decisions had not been recorded anywhere. Such a record is essential for establishing that a qualitative evaluation is indeed more than subjective opinion based on intuition. . . . (T)his finding reinforces the importance and usefulness of comprehensive reflexive logs not only for the individual study but for enhancing the credibility of qualitative studies in general."

Source: Whitmore, E., and Ray, M. L. 1989. Qualitative evaluation audits: Continuation of the discussion. *Evaluation Review, 13*, 78–90.

The report is not presented as a definitive evaluation of the program since additional information can come to light later, conditions may change, and the membership of the stakeholder groups may change. The findings of qualitative evaluations can be applied in other locations to the extent that other settings are similar to the one evaluated. Since qualitative evaluators are sensitive to the many specific factors that can affect program success, generalizing findings to other settings is done only with extreme care.

Are Qualitative Evaluations Subjective?

It would not be surprising if many readers reacted to this presentation with skepticism; it just seems very subjective. Two comments are offered in response. First, some years ago the first author was discussing research methods with a more experienced social psychologist. The conversation concerned the focus of this chapter—traditional quantitative research procedures versus qualitative personal observations. When asked, "If you wanted to learn about a group you knew nothing about, would you go there and live among them or would you send surveys and questionnaires?" the more senior professor responded, "Go and live there." Although we both would have preferred direct involvement as the mode for personal learning, at that time neither of us was bold enough to supplement the quantitative techniques we used with qualitative observations. Qualitative methods permit the development of understandings that cannot be obtained with predefined surveys and checklists. When evaluators understand programs very thoroughly, their evaluations can contain reasonable recommendations that are likely to be used. Stufflebeam (2001) suggests that the way to counter concerns about subjectivity is to use standards of good program evaluation (see Chapter 5) to evaluate the evaluation.

The second response to the concern about the subjectivity of qualitative evaluations centers on the question of how objective other evaluation approaches are. Subjectivity is not observed in the scoring of surveys or in the analyses of program records. However, qualitative evaluators are quick to argue that the choice of variables to assess and decisions about what is important to control and what does not need to be controlled can also affect the findings of evaluations (Guba and Lincoln, 1989; Smith, 1994). Although the ways prejudgments can affect evaluations are different for quantitative and qualitative evaluations, evaluators must be equally wary of unexamined assumptions regardless of the form of evaluation (Reichardt and Rallis, 1994). Let the methodologist who has no shortcomings cast the first stone.

COORDINATING QUALITATIVE AND QUANTITATIVE METHODS

For most evaluators, the question is not whether to use qualitative methods *or* quantitative methods; the question is how to use the methods so that they complement each other in the best ways possible (see Campbell, 1987; Cook and Reichardt, 1979; Maxwell, 1985; Reichardt and Rallis, 1994; Rossman and Wilson, 1985; Silverman, Ricci, and Gunter, 1990). Depending on the evaluation questions to be answered, the relative emphasis on each approach varies. Light and Pillemer (1984) write: "The pursuit of good science should transcend personal preferences for numbers or narrative" (p. 143).

The Substance of the Evaluation

Although a political campaign requires primarily a qualitative evaluation and rapid feedback, the candidate would probably also like a careful accounting of the allotment of campaign funds and a quantitative analysis of opinion polls. The effectiveness of an experimental medication requires primarily quantitative measures indicating improved health and long-term follow-up of patients' mortality and an enumeration of side effects. However, medical research is improved when the focus on length of life is complemented with an examination of the quality of life (McSweeny and Creer, 1995). Rossi (1994) points out that he would use primarily surveys for a program offered in many schools across the nation, but he would use more qualitative methods for a program offered by a few local schools.

Getting Insights from the Most Successful Participants

The success case method was mentioned in Chapter 2. If the participants in a job training program wanted to learn how to make the best use of the program, they might learn from those who have completed the program and obtained a stable job. If the staff of such a program wanted insights in how to improve the program, they too might gain some ideas from those who have done well. Of course, it is true that some participants do well after a program for reasons that have nothing to do with their experiences in the program. A qualitative evaluator looking for successful participants would be sensitive to participants who perhaps did not really need the program. But among those who appear to be typical participants when they started, there are some who have done particularly well. Those former participants might well help staff to learn which activities are less helpful and which are more helpful. They can also tell the staff how they used the skills they were learning. How did they go beyond the activities defining the program? Although the staff has resources that the participants do not have, staff members cannot completely put themselves into the shoes of the participants. Only a qualitative evaluation approach can aspire to gaining insights using such an approach because the critical variables and insights cannot be anticipated and, therefore, cannot be discovered using a survey (see Brinkerhoff, 2003). Note that the strength of such an approach does not focus on the outcomes of the typical, or average, participant as so many evaluation methods do. This is not to say that average results are not important; they are. But creative ideas are seldom suggested by a focus on average outcomes.

Changing Emphases as Understanding Expands

In addition to combining methods in a single evaluation, it is quite possible for an evaluation planned as a solely quantitative evaluation to be enriched by adding a qualitative component when unexpected, negative side effects are discovered. Often evaluators are slow to notice side effects because unexpected effects, good or bad, cannot be anticipated. Evaluation procedures also change when observations cannot be made as planned. In order to make any interpretations of the data it may be necessary to utilize a more qualitative approach.

In a similar fashion, a qualitative evaluation can become more quantitative as the evaluation questions become focused and clear. Once qualitative impressions are well developed, it might be possible to form hypotheses about the expected pattern of some quantitative measures of program outcome. In this way, qualitative evaluators can strengthen some aspects of their conclusions.

The Evaluation Questions

Evaluations have been classified as evaluations of need, process, outcome, and efficiency. Certain questions are more likely to require an emphasis on qualitative methods, whereas others will require quantitative methods. It is not possible to compare program costs with outcomes when using only qualitative information. However, most evaluations have multiple purposes. Implementation must occur before one can expect outcomes to be observed. Evaluation of implementation can be quantitative: How many sessions? How many participants? What proportion of the participants met the official eligibility criteria? But it is also important to know: How healthy are the interactions between staff and participants? How do participant families make decisions to participate? Fry and Miller (1975) showed that an innovative, cooperative public-private effort to assist alcoholics was so badly flawed in conception and implementation that it resulted in acrimonious interpersonal staff relationships that, in turn, led to decreased help for alcoholics, not improved care. In the areas of social and health services, such issues are very important in deciding how to improve programs. Since so many evaluation questions are complex, it seems quite reasonable to expect that those involving both qualitative and quantitative approaches would be better than evaluations limited to one or the other (Datta, 1994).

Cost of Evaluation

Rossi (1994) described the difficulties of mounting a qualitative evaluation of a major program with sites throughout the country. Sending observers to the sites or recruiting and training individuals would be difficult and indeed quite expensive compared to sending surveys to and obtaining records from the sites. Barzansky, Berner, and Beckman (1985) report that the cost of a qualitative evaluation created some problems for them. The expense is compounded by the open nature of qualitative evaluation. Someone commissioning a qualitative evaluation must trust that the work will produce useful information even before the evaluators know what observations will be made or how the observations will be used in reports (Lincoln and Guba, 1985). Costs can be contained better and estimated more accurately if qualitative methods are combined with quantitative methods and used to verify particular issues such as an appropriate assessment of needs or the credible implementation of the program.

PHILOSOPHICAL ASSUMPTIONS

Some proponents of qualitative evaluation methods view the use of qualitative research procedures as flowing from a view of knowledge that is distinctly different from that held by evaluators who make use of quantitative approaches (Guba and Lincoln, 1989; Lincoln, 1990b). At the most extreme, these writers adopt a constructivist philosophy that seems to hold that reality is a function of social agreements rather than something outside of people that can be studied scientifically (see Hedrick, 1994). Guba and Lincoln (1989) asserted that "there is no reality except that created by people" (p. 13). On the other hand, they have also said, ". . . there are external constraints that limit what can be agreed upon" (Lincoln and Guba, 1985, p. 85). Most observers feel that in practice even the most partisan supporters of qualitative-only evaluations don't limit themselves in ways that one might expect on the basis of the subjectivist philosophy they affirm in their more abstract writings (see Datta, 1994).

There is a second theme subject to less confusion that sets the most avid qualitative evaluators apart from the mainstream evaluation community. For most evaluators the purpose of evaluation is to improve the delivery of services to people in need by studying the implementation and impact of programs. Lincoln and Guba (1985) assert that quantitative evaluations are planned and managed in ways that bar some stakeholders from participating in the evaluation. Instead, they argue that evaluations should be consciously directed toward empowering the most disadvantaged groups in society. They call this "authentic evaluation." A number of observers imply that empowering all stakeholders is not possible in many evaluations (Greene, 1987; Mark and Shotland, 1987). It may be that Lincoln and Guba are urging evaluators to do more than they are commissioned to do and indeed can do.

As demonstrated by the evaluators whom Reichardt and Rallis (1994) recruited for their edited volume, there is a long and productive record of qualitative methods being used along with quantitative methods by evaluators who do not accept the philosophical assumptions held by some advocates of qualitative evaluation methodologies (see Denzin and Lincoln, 2000; Guba and Lincoln, 1989). Shadish (1995) has shown that the philosophical underpinnings sometimes presented for qualitative evaluation methods are "at best a distraction, and are at worst downright harmful" to efforts to resolve the debate over how to use qualitative methods in program evaluation.

Summary and Preview

There are settings in which evaluators cannot use the research methods based on the social science model. Some complex programs requiring an evaluation in a fairly short time cannot be approached using only quantitative methods. At times, direct observations are required to understand the program fully. Furthermore, recommendations for program improvement are most likely to be applicable when evaluators have a good understanding of the program and its stakeholders, especially the successful participants. Qualitative methods (talking, watching, and drawing conclusions) appear simple, but are quite complicated as evaluators seek to integrate the information they gather. Nevertheless, the use of qualitative methods in conjunction with quantitative methods strengthens program evaluation.

When the objectives of programs can be specified and when an impact model has been developed, one can use the traditional research methods that have been developed in the social sciences. It is to such forms of program evaluation methodology to which we now turn.

Study Questions

1. Most college course evaluation forms are largely made up of survey items with five- or six-point rating scales. Here are some items taken from one form:
   a. The goals of the course were clearly expressed at the beginning of the term.
   b. The course helped me to develop intellectual skills, such as critical thinking or problem solving.

   Suggest some rephrasing that a qualitative evaluator might use in an *interview* to learn about these same issues.

2. Look back to Chapter 7. Develop some suggestions of how qualitative methods could supplement and clarify the meaning of the summaries of the quantitative material the evaluators gathered. Note the early terminators in Figure 7.6. What interview questions could a qualitative evaluator address that would be very difficult to handle using a written survey?

3. Many observers worry that internal evaluators are under pressure—sometimes overt, sometimes subtle—to produce favorable evaluations. Discuss how such pressures might affect qualitative evaluators.

4. Think back to the program described on the first page of this book. How would an evaluator use qualitative evaluation techniques to gather information on the effectiveness of a sexual assault prevention program offered by a college counseling center?

5. Suppose that a six-month parent education program was developed at an urban university and successfully implemented with mothers who gave birth at a public hospital. When the same program was offered to families qualifying for public aid in several rural areas, young mothers seldom returned for even the second or third session. Use the ideas in this chapter to develop some approaches to learn why the program was so thoroughly rejected in the second setting.

Additional Resource

SHAW, I. F. 1999. *Qualitative evaluation.* Thousand Oaks, CA: Sage.

> Shaw provides a thorough overview of qualitative evaluation methods. He displays a well-balanced approach even toward evaluation methods that he feels typically fail to provide sufficient information to be truly useful. He treats qualitative methods as requiring intense long-term contact with the program, a holistic overview of the culture and context of the program, close attention to particulars, an insider's view, interpretation, little or no standardized instruments, and a coherent account of the program. Shaw argues for rigor in evaluation methods, but goes further than the writers of this text in endorsing advocacy evaluation and seeking out "the data most likely to support programs that can benefit the dispossessed" (p. 194). It seems to us that whether we use qualitative or quantitative methods, rigor is required to *learn* whether a program in fact does (rather than just promises to) benefit the dispossessed; evaluators are not to pick and choose among the data. This is a highly recommended work for anyone who wants to gain a thoughtful perspective on qualitative evaluation.

Single-Group, Nonexperimental Outcome Evaluations

hird grade, a class for diabetic senior citizens, and a parenting skills workshop are programs that begin and end at specific times, are directed to a group of people with similar needs, and are planned to impart similar benefits to all participants. The most common approach to evaluation in such settings is to examine how well participants perform after the program is over. This chapter presents the value as well as the weaknesses of such simple evaluations. The following chapters illustrate how these basic approaches are augmented to improve the validity of interpretations. The reader should develop a sense of how the introduction of each level of control increases the power of the evaluation to demonstrate that experiences in the program helped the program participants to achieve program objectives. The methods in this and the next two chapters are more similar to common research designs than approaches to evaluation discussed so far.

SINGLE-GROUP EVALUATION DESIGNS

Observe Only After the Program

When teachers, nurses, administrators, or judges inquire into the success of programs, they frequently use the simplest form of outcome evaluation because they want to know how the participants are faring after a service has been provided. Do members of a job-training group have jobs three months after receiving job skills training? How many of the people who attended a smoking cessation clinic are in fact not smoking one month after completing the program? The first step in deciding if a program is useful is to learn if the participants finish the program with a level of achievement that matches the program's goals. All that is needed is a set of systematic observations of participants at some specified time after completion of a program. Note that such an approach to evaluation does not even show that the participants changed during a program.

Observe Before and After the Program

The pretest-posttest design is used when stakeholders want to know whether the participants improved while being served by a program. For example, students should read better after a year of reading instruction, and cholesterol levels should be lower after patients have been treated for an appropriate period of time. Experience in the program might have caused the improvement; however, information gathered from such a design does not permit such an interpretation because there are many alternative interpretations that remain viable even when a comparison between a posttest and pretest reveals that change occurred. These alternative interpretations have been called "threats to internal validity" by Campbell and Stanley (1963); these threats will be discussed later in this chapter.

This text is based on the assumption that an evaluation should be designed around the questions to be answered and the complexity of the program. Evaluation is not basic research; evaluators do not assume that an evaluation must be designed to answer the same type of questions that basic research studies would address. When programs are relatively inexpensive, not harmful to participants, and fairly standard, rigorous evaluations are not needed (Smith, 1981). It is important, however, for evaluators to recognize when a more ambitious design is needed.

In some situations the evaluation plan cannot be any more complex than either of these two designs. The Government Performance and Results Act (GRPA) of 1993 was passed to shift the focus of government decision making and accountability away from a simply listing the activities that are undertaken by a government agency—such as grants made or inspectors employed—to a focus on the results of those activities, such as gains in employability, safety, responsiveness, or program quality. Under the Act, agencies are to develop multiyear plans, analyze the extent of the achievement of the goals, and report annually. Although GRPA was initially a requirement for federal agencies, many states in the United States have adopted similar laws (Aristigueta, 1999). The results of the activities of government agencies are evaluated by examining what was achieved. There is no possibility of, for example, comparing scientific activity related to the National Science Foundation (NSF) with the level of activity in the absence of the NSF. Similarly there is no possibility that Social Security payments would be suspended for a year to measure the level of poverty among the elderly without Social Security. Our point is that the only way such national programs can be evaluated is through an examination of key variables after programs have been implemented. As you think about the limitations of such approaches to evaluation, bear in mind that the evaluations of many large-scale governmental programs are, at best, posttest only and pretest-posttest designs.

USES OF SINGLE-GROUP, DESCRIPTIVE DESIGNS

Did the Participants Meet a Criterion?

Sackett and Mullen (1993) point out that in many job training settings there are objective, specific skills that trainees must attain in order to do a job successfully; in such settings a posttest-only evaluation is satisfactory. A number of writers suggest that measures of mental health can reveal when treated people are indistinguishable from people without diagnosed emotional problems (Jacobsen and Truax, 1991). The effectiveness of a law can be measured using a posttest-only design. DiFranza and Brown (1992) examined the effectiveness of a cigarette industry program that purported to reduce illegal cigarette sales to children. Seven months after the beginning of the program, only 4.5 percent of retailers were participating in the cigarette industry program, and of those who participated, 86 percent were willing to sell cigarettes to buyers between the ages of 13 and 16 who asked for them. It is unnecessary to conduct a sophisticated evaluation when a program is ignored by more than 95 percent of the target population and is ineffective even among participants.

Did the Participants Improve?

An important concern is whether the participants changed in the direction that the program was planned to encourage. Do rehabilitation patients speak and walk better after taking part in a rehabilitation program? Case Study 3 describes how a pretest-posttest design was used to evaluate a small program to teach first graders about skin cancer prevention. Certainly improvement is a fundamental objective of programs; however, discovering that change occurred during a program should not be confused with believing that the same change would not have occurred without the program. Some stakeholders appear to believe that a statistically significant difference between a pretest and a posttest provides evidence that the program caused the improvement. A statistically significant finding can only show that the change was unlikely to reflect only sampling error, not reveal causality as explained next.

CASE STUDY 3

A Pretest-Posttest Design to Evaluate a Peer-Based Program to Prevent Skin Cancer

---

A pretest-posttest design was used by Fork, Wagner, and Wagner (1992) to evaluate a peer-based educational intervention designed to make first graders more aware of the dangers of overexposure to the sun. Seven third through fifth graders learned about skin cancer prevention and then prepared presentations designed to teach skin protection to first graders. Both the first graders and the older students were pretested about their knowledge of protection from the sun.

The first graders watched the skits and then were paired off with older student pairs and asked to complete a "sun buster" coloring book. One week after the presentations, both groups of students were tested again. Both the first graders and the older students showed improvement in their knowledge of how to protect themselves from the sun. The matched-group *t* test was used to analyze the findings for each group. The authors felt that the older students enjoyed becoming teachers and the first graders appeared to watch the skits enthusiastically.

Comment: There are uncontrolled threats to the validity of this modest program evaluation; however, they did not seem fatal to the conclusions. The children matured little over the week, and it was unlikely that they were exposed to a similar message elsewhere. The outcome variable was objective information, not attitudes, so it is not possible for the meaning of the instrument to change. The pretest could indeed have sensitized the children to the message. This means that one should consider the pretest to be part of the program.

Did the Participants Improve Enough?

If the improvement from pretest to posttest is statistically significant, evaluators face another issue: Did participants improve *enough* to demonstrate a real effect in their daily lives? Singh, Greer, and Hammond (1977) found that the outcome of a classroom program about civic responsibility was an increase of 3 points on a 92-point attitude test. The authors concluded that the amount of change, although statistically significant, was not large enough to have a practical impact on the children's lives. Some clinical psychologists also advocate research on assessing meaningful change for clients (see Ankuta and Abeles, 1993).

There are a number of ways to assess whether participants changed enough. No approach is definitive; all approaches require thoughtful reflections. Two approaches will be discussed: (1) when an outcome variable itself is meaningful (e.g., successfully holding a job), and (2) when the outcome variable serves as a proxy for a variable that is too difficult or expensive to measure (e.g., improved attitudes about holding a job and improved skill in filling out a job application form rather than actual success on a job).

Outcomes that have meaning in themselves. Imagine a smoking cessation program. Since people buy cigarettes in 20-cigarette packs, smokers can report fairly accurately how much they smoke per day. And they can report if they have quit. Quitting would yield the most benefit, but reductions in rate of smoking are also valuable. A meaningful index of the outcome of a smoking cessation program would be the difference between the number of cigarettes smoked per day before the program minus the number after the program.

$$\text{Reduction} = N_{preprogram} - N_{postprogram}$$

where N is the number of cigarettes smoked per day. After such an index is calculated for each participant, the mean among all participants could be found. A second index would be the percentage of participants who are no longer smoking after the program. Comparing the reductions occurring during a smoking cessation program with the reductions of other similar programs would permit one to learn if a program being evaluated produced a reasonable outcome.

Fitness programs would also permit reporting program outcomes in meaningful units. Increases in maximum weight one can lift, reductions in time needed to complete a lap around a track, and lowered heart rate while doing some specified activity are three meaningful indexes of the results of a fitness program. To decide whether the change was valuable requires comparisons to other fitness programs or comparisons to norms for heart rate appropriate to the age of the participant.

Outcomes that are measured using proxy variables. It is often the case that evaluators cannot measure what is really the desired goal of the program. College faculty want to train educated people, but we settle on calculating a grade point average or using a score on a standard test. Counseling programs are planned to encourage participants to develop into well-adjusted people, but we settle on learning whether former participants score lower on tests of anxiety, stress, or depression. Such variables serve as proxies for the real thing. Because such variables could be measured with a variety of tests that vary in the number of items that they contain, neither a single score nor the mean score for a group of participants can tell us anything about the value of the program. We can, however, standardize the difference between the preprogram and the postprogram means to find a standardized effect size. Once standardized, we can compare the effect size of the program being evaluated to the results of other programs. If the program is designed to reduce a behavior, the standard formula for effect size is:

$$g = \frac{M_{preprogram} - M_{postprogram}}{s}$$

In words, the difference between the mean prior to participating in the program and the mean after the program divided by the standard deviation of the variable measured (e.g., anxiety) is the effect size (see Posavac, 1998; Zechmeister and Posavac, 2003). Here is an example. A counseling program was designed to reduce test anxiety among first year students; assume these means:

$$M_{preprogram} = 37.4$$

$$M_{postprogram} = 31.8$$

If the standard deviation was 6.4, the effect size would be:

$$g = (37.4 - 31.8)/6.4 = 0.88$$

Effect sizes are calculated so that a desired effect of the program produces a positive effect size. If an increase in the value of an outcome variable reflects a desired result, then the numerator of the effect size formula would be reversed.

Two questions should come to mind. First, where did s come from? The assumption is made that the standard deviations of the pretest and the posttest are the same except for random variation. In other words, the particular test-anxious people observed will be somewhat different from each other and any person's score will differ slightly depending on how the questions are interpreted on a given day. You may recall that the assumption of equal standard deviations is also made when using t tests and analyses of variance. So, the best information we would have in this case would be to use a value half way between the standard deviation of the pretest and that of the posttest. Suppose that the standard deviation of the pretest was 7.1 and the standard deviation of the posttest was 5.7; the mean of these two numbers is 6.4.

The second question should be: Is 0.88 good or bad? To decide, an evaluator needs to know the effect psychotherapy has for treating test anxiety. There might be some reports on that. If an evaluator finds some, the effect size can be calculated for each one to gain some perspective on the findings of the program being evaluated. In the absence of such information, evaluators can examine summaries of many evaluations. Lipsey and Wilson (1993) summarized more than 300 reviews of evaluations in different areas. They found that the median effect size was 0.44 with the 20th percentile being 0.24 and the 80th percentile being 0.68. In the context of these norms, an effect size of 0.88 would be evaluated as a large one.

The third question—one that might not have come to mind yet—is this: Is it valid if I make my judgments using Lipsey and Wilson's benchmarks? Well, not necessarily. You must retain your common sense. If a workshop was offered to teach how to use Access (the database program mentioned in Chapter 7), a pretest might show just about zero skill in using Access, but a posttest might show a sizeable increase. In this context, we would expect a very large effect size because most participants started at just about zero skill. In contrast, imagine a new medication for people who have had a heart attack that reduces mortality by just 1 percent among people 45 to 60 years old. A 1 percent increase in skill using Access would not be a good finding, but a 1 percent reduction in death rate due to a heart attack among middle age people is a good finding.

We would like to tell you exactly how to interpret an effect size; we cannot. However, finding an effect size does permit one to compare change across similar programs which have used similar, if not identical, measures of outcome. That is something we could not do if we did not use the effect size formula.

Program evaluators who want their work to have an impact on agencies need to be sensitive to the issue of meaningful change, not just statistically significant change. Determining what constitutes a meaningful change is a task for evaluators to address with program stakeholders. Interpretations are more valid when additional information is available: with detailed knowledge of the program, the participants, alternative programs, and the costs of the alternatives, it becomes possible to define meaningful change. Improvements over the posttest only and pretest-posttest approaches are discussed in Chapters 10 and 11. Techniques to relate costs to outcomes are discussed in Chapter 12.

Relating Change to Service Intensity and Participant Characteristics

In educational and training programs one sign of an effective program is that participants who receive more service change more than those who receive less. The more primary school grades that students complete, the better their reading skills. However, eating more food is related to better health only up to a point; then it leads to problems. The most healthy have found their optimal levels. For the most part, services offered to the poor provide less than the optimal level, although some argue that this is a complex issue (McKnight, 1995). Although correlating service received with outcome may be interpreted in different ways, it can be very useful in certain situations. For example, an important study in the history of medical research followed just this strategy. In 1835 Pierre Louis (Eisenberg, 1977) reported on his comparisons of the amount of blood drawn from patients with their progress in recovering from pneumonia (then called inflammation). Early nineteenth-century medical theory led to the expectation that the more blood drawn, the better the treatment and the more likely a recovery. Louis measured the volume of blood drawn from patients then followed their condition. He found that their condition after treatment was not related to the volume of blood removed. This finding was an important influence on the medical practice of the time and contributed to the eventual discrediting of bloodletting as a form of medical treatment. Louis was unable to conclude anything about the cause or proper treatment of pneumonia, but he did identify a useless treatment.

Another reason to do an evaluation even if it is unable to identify the cause of a change is to search for characteristics of the participants that might be related to achieving program goals. Do men experience better outcomes than women? Do members of minority groups complete a program as frequently as majority-group clients? These questions can be explored, tentatively to be sure, using a simple research design. If policy-relevant relationships are found between outcome and a characteristic of participants, then that variable would be involved in any future evaluations. The finding may even have an immediate impact if a program appears to have a good effect on some segments of the target population but little effect on other segments.

Although it is quite easy to discuss the value of relating personal and service characteristics to success in a program, the statistical method of correlating improvement with other variables is often misunderstood. The most intuitive approach is to subtract pretest scores from posttest scores, call the differences improvement, and correlate the improvement with any other variables of interest. This seemingly obvious method is not endorsed by methodologists. Change scores—the differences between pretests and posttests—should not be used because they are based on questionable statistical assumptions (Nunnally, 1975). Furthermore, the complex methods suggested to deal with change scores are hard to explain to clients and other stakeholders and are controversial, even among experts. Yet because the lengths of some services, such as psychotherapy, are not standardized and because people receive differing amounts of service, it is of interest to relate outcome to the amount of service received. Fortunately, when evaluators are interested in relating change to a characteristic of the program participants or amount of service, there is a valid technique available.

The best way to work with outcome and participant characteristics is to use advanced structural equation modeling (see Raykov, 1999), methods beyond the scope of this text and the resources of most internal evaluators. However, there are some analyses of change that will inform stakeholders. A valid way to relate change to the amount of service received or to some characteristic of the program participants involves *partial correlation*, not raw change scores (Judd and Kenny, 1981). Partial correlation may sound complicated but it is not. First, think about the problem. Those participants who finish the program at good levels are probably those who started at better levels relative to the other participants. For example, students who do well in course X are likely to have higher GPAs prior to the first day of class. The relationship is not perfect, but we think most students expect to find the principle to be true in general. Second, it would not be surprising to find that those with the higher pretest scores turn out to have participated in a program more regularly than those with lower pretests. In college, it is generally true that students with higher GPAs attend class more regularly than those with lower GPAs. In other words, if these principles are correct, we usually expect to find positive correlations among pretest scores, posttest scores, and participation levels. If we want to learn whether degree of participation predicts better outcomes, we need to control statistically for the differences in the pretest scores, otherwise the correlation between participation and outcome would be large just because both variables correlate with the pretest score. We can control for pretest differences by using a partial correlation between the posttest scores and participation, holding pretest scores constant.

Figure 9.1 includes hypothetical data for 26 participants in a 20-session job-training program. Imagine that the evaluator wanted to learn how closely attendance was related to improvement in skill level of the trainees. Partial correlation, in effect, statistically removes the effect of pretest differences among program participants on the correlation of the posttest and the level of participation. Few evaluators would calculate correlation or partial correlation coefficients using hand calculators; most will use a computer. To do a partial correlation, we specify which variables we would like to correlate (in this

FIGURE 9.1   Hypothetical data illustrating how change in skill level can be correlated with amount of service using a partial correlation in order to adjust for differences in level of skill prior to the beginning of the program.

Program Participant	Skill Level		Training Sessions
	Before	After	
1	24	26	18
2	23	29	18
3	19	26	20
4	18	27	16
5	20	19	17
6	24	31	19
7	25	22	15
8	24	25	15
9	21	22	17
10	14	16	12
11	21	30	18
12	14	26	17
13	18	22	17
14	16	15	17
15	23	26	17
16	14	13	13
17	23	26	16
18	19	29	16
19	17	28	15
20	16	27	17
21	14	15	17
22	22	21	18
23	25	26	17
24	23	19	16
25	21	27	17
26	22	29	18

case the posttest score with the level of participation) and the variable that is to be controlled (in this case the pretest score). For the data in Figure 9.1, the partial correlation is 0.40, indicating a fairly strong relationship between improvement in skill level and number of sessions attended. Training sessions seem valuable in skill level development; the better performance of those who came most frequently is not due to the fact that those who came more frequently started at a higher level.

We concluded that the partial correlation was "fairly strong" on the basis of the values of correlations that are found in the social science research literature. Cohen (1987) found that 0.10 is small, 0.30 is moderate, and 0.50 can be considered large. As mentioned above, these values are guides that need to be adjusted for the context in which the evaluator is working.

It is crucial to note that this internal analysis is appropriate only when there are fairly sizable differences among trainees in class attendance and stakeholders want to learn how important attendance is. If all trainees had come to 19 or 20 sessions, thus reducing the range of attendance, the partial correlation is likely to be low, as correlations usually are when the range of one variable is small (Brown, 1984). In that case, it might appear that attendance did not matter that much. However, the proper interpretation would be that it does not matter much whether trainees attend either 19 or 20 sessions; the low partial correlation would not have indicated that 12 sessions would be just as helpful as 20.

Although a positive partial correlation between outcome and level of participation in a program supports the value of the program, it does not eliminate all nonprogram alternative interpretations that might explain why participants improved. The reasons for caution in concluding that a program caused improvements are described in the balance of this chapter.

THREATS TO INTERNAL VALIDITY

Regardless of whether an evaluation shows that participants improved or did not improve, it is important to consider several plausible explanations for the findings. We neither want to claim a program is effective or ineffective if some nonprogram influence was responsible for the findings. The phrase "internal validity" refers to the degree of certainty the evaluator may have concluding that a program caused participants to improve. Many evaluations use these single-group designs. Knowing why these designs fail internal validity criteria permits evaluators to assess the validity of evaluation designs.

Actual but Nonprogram-Related Changes in the Participants

Two threats to internal validity refer to real changes that occur in participants due to influences that are not part of the program.

Maturation. Maturation refers to natural changes in people due solely to the passage of time. Children can perform more complex tasks as they get older; people get increasingly tired as they go without sleep; and there are predictable patterns to the development of adults. If an evaluation uses outcome variables that can be expected to change merely with the passage of time between a pretest and a posttest, maturation could be a plausible explanation. In other words, the evaluator may well have found that real changes have occurred during the course of the program; however, the reason for the changes could be that the program lasted six months and thus the participants are six months older and more experienced—not that the participants gained anything from the program. Sometimes people get better over time (e.g., most people with back pain experience improvement with time even without treatment) and sometimes people get worse over time (e.g., as children get older a greater proportion experiment with smoking and drugs). When using a single-group design, an improvement such as seen with back pain can make a program look valuable over time, but a behavior like drug experimentation can make a prevention program look bad as time goes by.

Finding that maturation has occurred does not mean that it is the only explanation for the changes that were observed. Nor do plausible, alternative hypotheses mean that the program had no effect. Interpretations would be easier if the evaluator could learn how much of the change was due to maturation and how much was due to the program. Using the one-group pretest-posttest design, this separation cannot be made. Methods to estimate the change due to maturation involve testing other groups of participants or potential participants as well as testing at a greater number of time periods, as explained in the next chapter.

History. History refers to events occurring between the pretest and the posttest that affect the participants. For example, an economic recession may make even the most well-designed program to help people find jobs look like a dud. On the other hand, an economic recovery would make a poorly run program look like a winner. These concurrent national economic changes are plausible alternative interpretations of any changes found among the participants of job training programs.

Some of the same approaches used to account for maturational effects can help isolate historical effects: Test additional groups and test at additional times as described in the following chapter. However, history is less predictable than maturation. Unexpected national events that affect the outcome criteria can occur at any time or may not occur at all during a given evaluation. In addition, Cook and Campbell (1979) pointed out that history need not refer only to events affecting all participants; when something unusual happens in a particular program group, this effect is called *local history*. Events such as an argument among staff members, a particularly unusual individual in a therapy group, or a local community disaster cannot be accounted for by any evaluation design except for designs that are replicated in a number of different locations.

Apparent Changes Dependent on Who Was Observed

Three threats to internal validity must be considered when participants are not a random or representative sample of the people who might benefit.

Selection. Participation in many human service programs is voluntary. Self-selected people are different from the typical members of the target population. In the posttest-only form of evaluation, the process of self-selection may mean that the participants were relatively well off when they began the program. The fact that the posttest detects a desirable state reveals nothing about the effectiveness of the program. College teachers most likely to join faculty development programs are "good teachers who want to be better" (Centra, 1977). After a faculty development program, most of these teachers will continue to be good teachers. Their competence tells us nothing about the quality of the program—these teachers were better than the typical teacher from the beginning. Observations of their achievements before the program permit evaluators to estimate the unwanted effects of self-selection.

Attrition. People differ in whether they will begin a program and they differ in whether they will complete a program they began. The posttest-only design is inadequate when participants leave before completing the program. Students drop courses they do not like, clients quit therapy when they learn that personal growth is hard, and medical patients sometimes die. The longer it takes to carry out an evaluation, the more attrition is likely to occur (Keating and Hirst, 1986).

The level of achievement observed at the end of a program may indicate how well the program functioned, how good the people were who chose to participate, or how motivated the people were who stayed until the end. As a general rule, those who stay are more prepared for the program than are those who drop out. Failing students are more likely to drop a course than are those earning B's and A's. Patients who die were probably among the least likely to have benefitted from a treatment program. Without a pretest, evaluators cannot accurately gauge the effectiveness of a program. A director of a small drug-abuse program remarked informally that his program had a 90 percent success rate. Upon inquiry, however, it was learned that only approximately 10 percent of those beginning remain for the full program. Having success with 9 out of the 100 who begin a program is markedly different from having a 90 percent success rate.

As with selection, the pretest-posttest design handles participant attrition fairly well. By pretesting, evaluators know who dropped out and how they differed from those who remained. The pretest-posttest design enables evaluators to know when preprogram achievement and participant dropout are not plausible explanations for the level of outcome observed at the end of the program.

Regression. The threat of regression toward the mean is one of the hardest to understand. However, as with basic statistics, many people already have an intuitive understanding of regression toward the mean even though they may not apply it consistently.

People can be misled by the effects of regression (Kahneman and Tversky, 1974). If you think carefully about the following example, you will understand what regression means and why its effects usually go undetected. It is said that after a particularly good landing, aviation trainers do not compliment the trainee, because when such a compliment is given, the next landing is usually done less well. On the other hand, the trainers severely reprimand the trainee after a poor landing in order to elicit a better landing on the next try. It is clear empirically that complimented exceptionally good landings are often followed by less good ones, and reprimanded bad landings are often followed by better ones. However, let us see why the compliments and the reprimands may have nothing to do with the quality of the next landing.

Imagine learning a complex task. Initially, quality of performance fluctuates—sometimes better, sometimes worse. What goes into the better performances? At least two things: the skill achieved and chance. Pilot trainees know that they should touch the plane down with the nose up, but they do not at first sense the precise moment to lower the wing flaps and, at the same time, adjust the elevators to obtain the proper touchdown angle (Caidin, 1960). Sometimes they make adjustments a little too soon and sometimes a little too late. Because these errors are due partially to chance, the likelihood of a trainee doing everything at the precise instant two times in a row is low. Therefore, for trainees the probability is low for two consecutive good landings—or two consecutive bad ones. In other words, a trainer should not expect two consecutive good landings by a novice regardless of what is said or not said.

The effects of regression toward the mean can be further illustrated with a silly but instructive example. Choose 20 pennies and flip each one six times, recording the number of heads for each penny. Select the pennies that produced the most "excessive" heads—five or six heads can be considered excessive. Reprimand those pennies for producing too many heads. Then flip just those pennies six times again and see if the reprimand worked. If the penny yields fewer heads than it did during the first set, the penny is now behaving in the way it was urged to behave. On the average, the reprimand will appear to have been effective 98 percent of the time if a penny originally produced six out of six heads, and 89 percent of the time if the first result had been five out of six heads. The binomial distribution permits the calculation of these percentages (McClave, Benson, and Sincich, 2005).

In summary, regression to the mean warns that whenever a performance level is extreme, the next performance is likely to be less extreme. This principle applies to landing airplanes and flipping pennies as well as to emotional adjustment. If people who currently are the most depressed are followed for three months, it is likely that they will be less depressed as a group. This does not mean that they will be at a healthy level of adjustment. Most likely, they will still be more depressed than the general public. However, some of the transient random events that caused the worst depression will have passed, and as a group they will be less depressed than before—with or without therapy.

Is regression a threat to the internal validity of the pretest-posttest evaluation design? Not necessarily, but it often is. If all the members of some intact group are tested before and after a program, then regression is not a problem for evaluations using this design. For example, if all children in a school are given a special reading curriculum, regression will not be a threat to internal validity. However, if only the children reading at the lowest levels on the pretest use the special curriculum, regression will be a threat to the interpretation of the pretest-posttest change. Children score low on a test not only due to poor reading skills, but also due to such random things as poor guessing, breaking a pencil point, having a cold, misunderstanding the instructions, worrying about an ill sister, or planning recess games. A day, a week, or a semester later during a second test, these events will not be experienced by exactly the same children. Generally, these retest scores will be higher than those from the first test for the children who previously scored the worst. This does not mean that all poor-scoring children will improve; it does mean that their average will go up. For the children who scored the best, their average will come down.

Regression is often a plausible alternative hypothesis for pretest-posttest change when service programs are aimed at those people who are especially in need of help. Remedial programs are not prepared for everyone, but for those who have fallen behind: reading poorly, earning low wages, or feeling emotional distress. Sometimes a screening test to select people for a program is also used as the pretest in an evaluation plan. For example, students scoring the most poorly on a reading test are placed in a reading improvement program, and a second administration of the same test or a parallel form is compared with the pretest scores. This is a poor practice; regression is a very plausible explanation for at least part of the improvement. On the other hand, if poor readers or troubled clients get worse when regression effects should have led to improvement, then the evaluation can be interpreted. The correct interpretation is that the program is ineffective.

Changes Related to Methods of Obtaining Observations

Two additional plausible hypotheses, testing and instrumentation, are generated by the evaluators themselves and by their observation methods.

Testing. The effect of testing refers to changes in behavior due to the observation technique. The results of two administrations of an observation tool may differ simply because respondents have become more familiar with the tool. Ability test scores increase reliably on the second administration for people initially unfamiliar with a test (Murphy and Davidshofer, 2005). People interviewing for jobs gain from the experience and can present themselves better on subsequent interviews.

A second aspect of testing effects is called reactivity. People behave differently when they know they are being observed. This concept was discussed in Chapter 4; however, it is worth recalling. Clients, patients, prisoners, and schoolchildren will be affected when they know someone is recording their behaviors, opinions, or feelings. Observation techniques vary in how reactive they are.

The pretest-posttest design is clearly weak in the control of testing effects. If participants were unfamiliar with observation procedures, scores might change on the second test. The direction of change that should be expected due to repeated testing does not seem clear except for ability and achievement tests, on which improvement is expected.

Instrumentation. Instrumentation refers to the use of measurement procedures themselves. Most college instructors know that they are not totally consistent when grading essay examinations. Standards can change as the instructor becomes familiar with how the students answered a question. The standard may become higher or lower. If measures that are not highly objective are used with a pretest-posttest design, it would be wise not to score the pretest until after the posttest is administered. Then the tests can be shuffled together and scored by someone who does not know which are pretests and which are posttests.

If the measures require observations that must be made before and after the program, the examiners may become more skilled as they gain experience. Thus, the posttests may go much more smoothly than the pretests. If so, a change in instrumentation becomes a viable alternative to concluding that the program had an effect. In such situations, examiners who are highly experienced before the pretest is administered are the most effective.

Effects of Interactions of These Threats

In addition to these seven threats to internal validity, interpretations can be confused by the joint influence of two threats. This could occur if parents seek special educational opportunities for their children (an example of self-selection) because their children are developing more rapidly compared with the children of parents who do not seek special educational opportunities for their children (an example of different rates of maturation). This effect is called a *selection-by-maturation interaction.*

Internal Validity Threats Are Double-Edged Swords

When examining a comparison between means, it is important to consider whether an apparently positive effect could have been caused by a threat to internal validity increasing the difference between the pretest and the posttest. Although attention is usually focused on these threats masquerading as program effects, it is also quite possible for one of these threats to hide a program effect. Therefore, the lack of a program effect, when the samples are large and the measures reliable, could be due to an ineffective program or an uncontrolled threat to internal validity serving to reduce the difference between pre- and posttest. Examples include an economic downturn, participants being tired at the posttest, the most successful participants being unavailable for the posttest, initially good-scoring participants regressing toward the mean, and more sensitive observation procedures detecting dysfunction that was missed by a less sensitive pretest.

In the next chapter several design enhancements will be presented as ways to eliminate plausible explanations of change that are not related to the program. Only when such explanations are implausible can good outcomes be attributed unambiguously to the program. Likewise, good experimental control would provide better understanding of apparent program failure.

CONSTRUCT VALIDITY IN PRETEST-POSTTEST DESIGNS

Construct validity refers the concept (or construct) that a variable actually measures. When evaluators use participant self-report measures in pretest-posttest designs, it is necessary to examine whether the program might lead to changes in how participants label their own problems and strengths. Veterans suffering from post-trauma stress reported that a program was very helpful, but described themselves as functioning less well and experiencing more symptoms than they did before completing the program (Spiro, Shalev, Solomon, and Kotler, 1989). Was the program harmful? It appeared that the program led them to a more accurate recognition of their problems and a greater willingness to acknowledge them. The program was helpful, not harmful. Evaluators have distinguished different kinds of change; to differentiate among them we call them *alpha, beta,* and *gamma* (Arvey and Cole, 1989; Millsap and Hartog, 1988).

An *alpha* change is a real change in the behavior of interest. The cause of the change is a question of internal validity, as discussed above. *Beta* changes occur when respondents change their understanding of the meaning of the scale. For example, exposure to a really good golfer may lead a person to rate her own skills less favorably than when playing only with friends. People with better insight into what level of skill is possible may see themselves as functioning less well than they did when they completed a pretest; this change appears numerically as a loss, but the change may indicate a more accurate self-appraisal. *Gamma* change refers to differences between the pretest and the posttest that are due to a reconceptualization of the meaning of the variable being measured. For example, a high school teacher might not see his physical symptoms as resulting from stress; once he does, his ratings of his own stress level may change because his understanding of the meaning of his symptoms has changed. Data taken from records may also be subject to these artifacts when official definitions change over time. Variables that can be measured objectively would not be subject to *beta* and *gamma* change. When a variable could mean different things to different participants or different stakeholders, we say that the variable lacks construct validity.

For evaluations requiring a pretest that includes self-reported behaviors, attitudes, or intentions, Aiken and West (1990) suggest several strategies to minimize these threats to construct validity, including (1) distinguishing information gathered to evaluate programs from that needed to make treatment decisions, (2) leading respondents to expect that what they report will be validated in some way, (3) using interviewers who are experienced with both the program being evaluated and the problems that the respondents have, (4) providing explicit reference groups for respondents to compare themselves with (e.g., "How do your leadership skills compare with other managers in your division?" rather than "Rate your leadership skills from 1 [poor] to 10 [excellent]"), and (5) using behavioral anchors rather than evaluative terms (e.g., "I am so depressed that I cannot accomplish anything" rather than "Very depressed"). Retrospective pretests are better than tests given before the program begins because after experiencing the program, participants have a better understanding of their behaviors (Evans, Stanley, Coman, and Sinnott, 1992; Robinson and Doueck, 1994; Spiro et al., 1989).

OVERINTERPRETING THE RESULTS OF SINGLE-GROUP DESIGNS

When evaluators use a simple design, there may be a temptation to seek to compensate for the design's weaknesses by measuring many variables. When this happens, the chances of a Type I statistical error increase. People not trained in research methods seldom appreciate the high probability that patterns of relationships will be observed among some variables just through sampling error. Many people grossly underestimate the probability of random coincidences, but instead think that causal connections have been observed (Paulos, 1988). Type I errors refer to statistically significant differences between pretests and posttests even when the program is ineffective. Type I errors occur for exactly the same reason that flipping 20 coins six times each will appear to identify some coins with a tendency to produce a surprisingly high proportion of heads. We can recognize that random variation was responsible simply by repeating the set of six flips. Unfortunately, when performing evaluations, new observations cannot be obtained as easily as flipping coins several additional times.

A second reason why Type I errors are not discovered is related to hindsight bias. Hindsight bias is the tendency to believe we could have anticipated something *after* we are aware of what in fact happened (Bryant and Guilbault, 2002). In program evaluation it describes the tendency to make sense of most any set of data after having examined it. Once a puzzled graduate student (actually, the first author of this text) presented a professor with findings that seemed markedly at variance with the professor's research. The professor examined the columns of correlations and quickly interpreted the findings in a way that coincided nicely with the previous studies. In order to do that he developed novel, elaborate interpretations that had not been part of the original theory. A week later the student discovered that the computer program had malfunctioned and the initial results had been mislabeled. An alternate program produced results that were quite compatible with the professor's work. When faced with a page full of means for different measures or with a page of correlations, creative people can make sense of them—even when the variables are mislabeled!

These problems, ignoring the possibility of Type I errors and falling prey to hindsight bias, are most likely to affect interpretations when many variables have been measured and when research is not carefully controlled. Evaluators often have access to many demographic variables and can extract many process and outcome variables from agency records. Without a clear impact model indicating how the program processes are expected to work, it is easy to succumb to the temptation to correlate everything with everything. Then, evaluators or their clients may force interpretations onto the results. Novel findings are best treated as very tentative, especially if they appear in the context of a large number of analyses that were not suggested by the theory underlying the program. All evaluation designs can be overinterpreted, not just single-group designs; however, the tendency seems more likely whenever the design is basically a descriptive design with very little, if any, experimental control.

USEFULNESS OF SINGLE-GROUP DESIGNS AS INITIAL APPROACHES TO PROGRAM EVALUATION

When there are previously specified desirable levels for the outcome variables, and when the participants do not drop out during the program, the pretest-posttest design may be sufficient to document the program's success. However, even when standards are not available, the reader should not gain the impression that these approaches do not have any other legitimate uses. These single-group designs are less intrusive and less expensive and require far less effort to complete than more ambitious methods. Thus, these designs can serve important functions in an evaluator's toolbox as first steps in planning a more rigorous program evaluation. When standards are not available, the purposes of single-group evaluations include: (1) assessing the likely usefulness of a more rigorous evaluation, (2) searching for promising variables related to success in the program, and (3) preparing an agency for more controlled evaluations in the future.

Assessing the Usefulness of Further Evaluations

Before embarking on a rigorous evaluation that controls for many plausible alternative interpretations, a single-group design would serve to show whether there is any improvement to explain (Patton, 1989). If no participants get jobs for which they were trained, it is likely that no further study is needed. The objectives were not achieved. No statistical analysis is needed. If the rehabili-tation program participants finished at desirable levels of function, a pretest-posttest design might show that they improved while in the program. This finding may well satisfy some of the stakeholders. Moreover, finding reliable improvements might justify a more complex evaluation. A simple design was a first step in learning whether the use of a phone helped pretrial defendants to raise bond. Showing that 22 percent of the defendants who used a phone (that was available on a temporary basis) did raise bail suggested that a more rigorous evaluation could be worth the expense (Lenihan, 1977). Had only 2 or 3 percent been successful, the possible effect would have been very small, and no further study would have been done.

Correlating Improvement with Other Variables

The use of the pretest-posttest design and partial correlations permits relating improvement to the amount of service and to characteristics of the partici-pants. Finding a sizable standard deviation for an outcome variable suggests that outcomes for different subgroups of participants could be quite different. It may be that a program planned for a very needy population primarily bene-fits people who are relatively well-off. Thus, the favorable mean outcome could be due to relatively competent people choosing to participate in the pro-gram. If so, further evaluation efforts may be unnecessary until the program is changed. On the other hand, a favorable outcome at the end of a program may really indicate a general improvement for many participants. Perhaps the improvement is due to the impact of the program; further work would be merited.

Preparing the Facility for Further Evaluation

A third reason for conducting an evaluation using only the participants is to help the staff accept the idea of evaluation. As described in earlier chapters, service providers—from paraprofessional counselors to teachers to physi-cians—are beginning to recognize that their work can and will be evaluated, even though the quality of service is hard to quantify. If evaluators begin their work with less threatening approaches, they have better chances of leading service providers to see the usefulness of evaluation and to value the contribu-tions of evaluators.

The methods described in this chapter are among the least threatening. There is no possibility of learning that another program achieves the same level of success at a lower cost. When staff and managers fear that another pro-gram is more efficient, the resulting anxiety can lead to hostility and limited cooperation with the evaluator. Just this type of reaction occurred during an internal evaluation of a hospital program. The program director initiated the evaluation and showed remarkable openness to evaluation, making com-ments such as, "Maybe we don't help people as much as we think we do—we should know that" and "If a patient is institutionalized after leaving here, we have failed." However, when the evaluators proposed increasing the internal validity of the evaluation by gathering observations from a neighboring hospital without an equivalent program, the director seemed to change his position. Such a comparison could conceivably have shown that similarly diagnosed patients without a program did as well as those in the expensive program. Then he said that the additional data were unnecessary since the value of this type of program was well known and fully documented. The expanded study went on because no controlled studies could be found supporting the value of such programs, a situation that is surprisingly familiar to those who carefully search for support for some widely accepted practices in medicine (see, for example, Eddy, 1990). The director mellowed when it became clear that the neighboring hospital had very few patients with the appropriate diagnoses and thus no information could be forthcoming that would question the effectiveness of his program. Cooperation and cordial relations returned.

Rational use of resources requires that ultimately such comparative studies be done. But they should not be done in a way that leaves a staff demoralized—perhaps the evaluators in the case above were too assertive in seeking additional observations. Internal evaluators who try to insist on methodologically rigorous evaluations may find that they lose their influence with the staff. Beginning in a nonthreatening way permits evaluators to gain the confidence of staff members and managers. This strategy is not meant to imply that rigor is unnecessary; however, using less rigorous evaluations at first can be useful in earning the trust of the staff.

Summary and Preview

This chapter emphasized two major points. First, a sympathetic understanding of the needs of the users of an evaluation may indicate that a simple research design serves quite well to meet the information needs at a particular time. Second, single-group designs cannot answer many questions that are critical to stakeholders because many interpretations of findings remain plausible. These plausible interpretations are called threats to internal validity.

The next chapter contains several approaches to clarify the interpretation of outcome evaluations. These procedures require making additional observations of (1) the program group, (2) non-program groups, or (3) variables not expected to be affected by the program.

Study Questions

1. Not many years ago, when a child had frequent bouts of sore throat and earache, family doctors recommended removing the child's tonsils. Typically, the child's health improved afterwards. Parents and physicians attributed the improved health to the operation: What threats to internal validity were ignored?

2. Some 50 elementary schoolchildren witnessed a brutal murder on their way to school in a suburb of a large city. The school officials worked with a social worker, a school psychologist, and others in an attempt to help the children deal with their emotions, to avoid long-term ill effects, and to help parents with their children. A year after the tragedy, there appeared to be no serious aftereffects. What assumptions are necessary to claim that these efforts were useful?

3. Politicians are notorious for attributing any improvements in governmental and economic affairs to their own efforts and any deterioration to the policies of others. What threats to internal validity are most likely to make such interpretations invalid?

4. Why can a smoking cessation clinic be evaluated using a one-group design?

5. Prepare some examples of pretest-posttest evaluations that would appear favorable because of threats to internal validity. Also, prepare some hypothetical examples of evaluations that would appear ineffective because of threats to internal validity.

Additional Resource

SHADISH, W. R., COOK, T. D., and CAMPBELL, D. T. 2002. *Experimental and quasi-experimental design for generalized causal inference.* Boston: Houghton Mifflin.

> This text is the standard research design resource for program evaluators. It is the successor of the classic work by Campbell and Stanley (1963) and the more recent standard by Cook and Campbell (1979). The first two authors are very highly respected methodologists whose writings are relevant to program evaluation. Shadish has been the president of the American Evaluation Association and has published widely on program evaluation. Cook is, perhaps, the most eminent living social research methodologist. The late Donald Campbell has been associated with more innovations in social research methods than anyone has tried to count. Threats to internal validity are discussed in detail in Chapter 2 and other chapters.

Quasi-Experimental
Approaches to
Outcome Evaluation

V ery simple research designs can answer some important questions for
stakeholders. However, Chapter 9 stressed that those designs seldom
permit evaluators to identify the cause of changes in program participants in an unambiguous fashion. Whenever program administrators or
government officials commission evaluators to discover whether programs
cause such changes, evaluations of greater complexity must be conducted.
In order to show that something causes something else, it is necessary
to demonstrate (1) that the cause precedes the supposed effect in time;
(2) that the cause covaries with the effect, i.e., the more of the cause, the
more of the effect; and (3) that no viable explanation of the effect can be
found except for the hypothesized cause. It is easy to satisfy the first criterion,
and the second is not that difficult to test either. Both can be demonstrated
using the methods described in Chapter 9. The third, however, is much more
difficult and is the focus of the present and the following chapters.

In this chapter several research designs are presented that possess
greater internal validity than the simple designs already described. The
validity of outcome evaluations seeking to test causal hypotheses can be
increased by (1) observing the participants at additional times before and
after the program; (2) observing additional natural groups of people who
have not experienced the program; and (3) using a variety of variables,
some expected to be affected by the program and others not expected to
be affected. Designs using these methods were called quasi-experiments by

Campbell and Stanley (1963); although these methods do not achieve the air-tight control of true experiments, quasi-experiments control for many biases and can thus yield highly interpretable evaluations—if carefully planned and applied in appropriate settings.

MAKING NUMEROUS OBSERVATIONS

Making numerous observations across time can help resolve two related problems. First, we need to be able to distinguish (1) random changes from time period to time period from (2) a systematic change that reflects actual changes in the variable being measured. All program variables show variation over time. For example, the number of crimes on a given day or week is not a constant, nor is it a uniformly decreasing or increasing value. Although there are some predictable influences on the number of crimes committed (for example, cold weather inhibits violent crime, warmer weather seems to encourage it; see Anderson, 2001), there seem to be no systematic causes of most changes in the day-to-day rate. Nevertheless, commentators in popular media often talk as though such causes were well known and effective remedies well understood.

A few days after several thousand police officers were temporarily laid off in New York City, there were two days in which an abnormally high number of murders occurred: nine on July 8 and eight on July 9 (Egelhof, 1975). These two high-crime days were contrasted with the average across the year—four per day. Egelhof implied that if it had not been for the layoffs, the high number of murders would not have occurred. Should anyone have tried to explain the high rate on these two days? Was it due to the layoffs of police officers? There are a number of reasons why the reporter's conclusions were unfounded. Because we know that warm weather is associated with high levels of violent crime, it was wrong to compare an average for all the days in the year with data from the middle of summer. If the mean number of murders was available for July in New York City, we also need to know the standard deviation in order to reflect the day-to-day variation. To decide whether these two days were unusual, one could use the mean for days in July along with the standard deviation to find a range of values that would include, say, 90 percent of July days. Such a range is called a confidence interval and can be approximated by adding 1.67 times the standard deviation to the mean and subtracting that value from the mean.[1] Without information on day-to-day variation, one cannot know whether there is anything that needs to be explained.

---

[1] The value of +1.67 can be found from a standard normal table; it is the value of z that divides the highest 5 percent of the normal curve from the rest of the distribution; a −1.67 similarly divides the lowest 5 percent from the rest of the distribution. Consequently, what is left is the middle 90 percent.

A related procedure called *statistical process control* is used in manufacturing (Wheeler and Chambers, 1992) and increasingly in human services (Carey and Lloyd, 1995; Spiring, 1994) to identify when a particular observation is sufficiently different from the general pattern to merit attention.

For the moment, let's assume that the murder rates on July 8 and 9 were unusual. Was the newspaper reporter correct in attributing the cause of these additional murders to the reduction in the size of the police force? The first criterion necessary for a causal conclusion was met: The police were laid off before the murders. However, it is not known if murder rate covaries with size of police force, and alternative interpretations were not considered. Without information on normal day-to-day variation and the weather, it is impossible to draw even the most tentative conclusions about the effect, if any, of the reduction in number of police officers on murder rate. Ignoring random variation and threats to internal validity can lead to quite erroneous interpretations of the causal connection between two events.

Campbell (1969) illustrated the possibility of an inaccurate interpretation due to limited information when he explored the effects of an automobile speed crackdown in Connecticut. In 1955 there were approximately 14.2 automobile accident fatalities per 100,000 residents. This was a record rate and was especially high compared to the previous year. The governor initiated a crackdown on speeding during the following year and the fatality rate dropped to about 12.2 per 100,000. Could the governor justifiably claim that the measures he ordered were responsible for the reduction in fatalities? Before reading on, readers might stop for a moment to develop an answer to that question.

The way to decide if the governor could take credit for the drop requires information that would permit rejecting interpretations of the drop other than the police crackdown. Data on the fatalities in the years before and after the crackdown year are needed. The number of fatalities before 1955 may show that fatalities per year were systematically rising in response to the number of vehicles on Connecticut roads and the number of miles driven per vehicle. Because accidents usually increase when the number of vehicles increases (holding everything else constant), a steady increase in fatalities, while undesirable, may be unavoidable in this situation. A program to reduce fatalities would be up against strong forces and could be expected to yield limited results.

A second alternative would be to consider 1955 a very unusual year. Perhaps a few very tragic but fortunately rare multifatality accidents occurred. Or perhaps especially bad weather occurred during holiday periods when many drivers were on the road. Because consecutive years with unusual weather patterns are unlikely, a remedy for the high fatality rate is likely to appear to succeed, regardless of how well or poorly conceived. The drop would then be due to regression to the mean, not to any remedy attempted.

The fatality rates for the years before and after the Connecticut speeding crackdown were reported by Campbell (1969) and are given in Figure 10.1.

FIGURE 10.1   Automobile accident fatality rate per 100,000 residents for Connecticut by year, before and after the beginning of a crackdown on speeding drivers. (Adapted from D. T. Campbell 1969. Reforms as experiments. *American Psychologist, 24,* 419. Copyright © 1969 by the American Psychological Association. Reprinted with permission.)

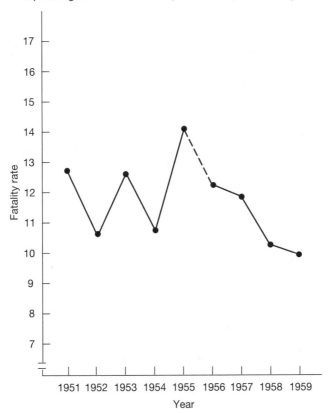

The 1955 rate does appear to be a discrepant value, even though the fluctuations from year to year were large. For now, note that examining accident rates over a number of time periods permits a much more informed conclusion than merely examining the rates just before and just after the introduction of a program to correct a problem. This example is discussed in more detail later in this chapter.

A time series was also used by McKillip (1991) to examine the effect of an HIV (AIDS) testing law in Illinois, which required couples to take an HIV test before being granted a marriage license. By examining the number of marriage licenses granted per month for 116 months, McKillip learned that the law was associated with an abrupt 14 percent drop in the number of marriage licenses obtained in Illinois. Adjacent states, without similar laws, experienced a corresponding increase in marriage licenses, but other Midwestern states not adjacent to Illinois showed no change in the number of marriages. It appeared clear that a sizable portion of Illinois couples were obtaining licenses in adjacent states to avoid going to the trouble of being tested.

TIME-SERIES DESIGNS

In recent years considerable attention has been given to the use of information across many time intervals. The approaches have come to be called *time-series analyses*. Both economists and behavioral therapists use time-series designs. Economists have used information over many time periods, seeking to learn the effects of policy changes on such variables as income level, industrial output, and employment. On a very different scale, behavioral researchers utilize objective measurements of single individuals over many time periods, during which various therapeutic interventions are begun and stopped. The strategy of obtaining base-line measurements before an intervention and documenting both change and the maintenance of change has been adopted by program evaluators.

The data used by economists and behavior analysts are more similar to each other than might be supposed if one only considered the focus of their work. Whether referring to a country or a single child, the researcher obtains one value or makes one observation for each variable during each time interval studied. For example, for economists there is only one GNP and one inflation rate for each time period. For behavior analysts there is only one index of a specific abnormal behavior per time period. Thus, writers can refer to single-subject research in both cases.

Time-series designs applied to program evaluation received encouragement from the work of Campbell and Stanley (1963). Collecting data over many time periods is a way of meeting some of the internal validity challenges described in the previous chapter. Because maturation effects can be traced during the time periods before and after the intervention, the likelihood of confusing a program's effect with maturation effects is greatly reduced when using a time-series design rather than a pretest-posttest design. Similarly, the effects of history will be more easily detected using a time-series design than when an evaluation is performed using observations at only one or two time periods. By relating changes in dependent variables to historical events, it is possible, at least at a qualitative level, to distinguish the effects of the program from the impact of other influences.

A time-series approach to program evaluation minimally includes the following characteristics: (1) a single unit is defined, and (2) measurements are made (3) over a number of time intervals, (4) that precede and follow some controlled or natural intervention (Knapp, 1977). In the language of experimental design, the unit observed (person, group, or nation) serves as its own control. Program evaluators, unlike economists, use time-series designs almost exclusively when a definite intervention has occurred at a specific time. The design is often called an *interrupted time series* (Cook and Campbell, 1979) and the evaluator's job is to learn whether the interruption—that is, the introduction of a program—had an impact.

Patterns of Outcomes Over Time Periods

There are a number of possible patterns observable in graphs of a program's outcome plotted over time periods. Figure 10.2 illustrates some of these possibilities. The axes in each part of the figure are the same: Time intervals are plotted on the horizontal axis and the magnitude of the outcome variable is plotted on the vertical axis. Panel A, illustrates no effect of the intervention; there appears to be no out-of-the-ordinary change in the observations after the program. In contrast, Panel B illustrates what is usually the most hoped-for finding in an interrupted time-series analysis. The graph shows a marked increase from a fairly stable level before the intervention, and the criterion remains fairly stable afterwards. This result may be expected from an effective training program that increased the skills of employees or from the introduction of laborsaving devices. Clearly, the design can be used when the intervention is designed to decrease the value of variables (such as accident rates and failure rates) as well as to increase them.

FIGURE 10.2   Some illustrative possible patterns of a measure of program success plotted over time. Time of the program or intervention is indicated by the dashed vertical line.

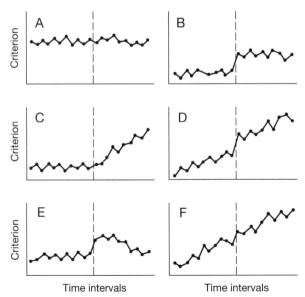

Panels C through F all show some increase after the intervention, but their interpretations are much less clear. Panel C shows an increase in slope after the intervention. The variable being measured began to increase over time after the intervention; however, there was no immediate impact as in Panel B. An influence such as literacy training or improved nutrition, whose impact is diffuse and cumulative, might produce a pattern of findings as in Panel C if economic well-being were the outcome variable. In Panel D there is an increase apparently due to the intervention superimposed on a general increasing trend.

In Panel E there appears to be an effect due to the intervention; however, it seems temporary. Many new programs are introduced with much publicity, and deeply involved staff members believe in the value of the program and work hard to make it effective. However, once the program is part of the regular procedure and the enthusiasm of the staff has diminished, the outcome variable returns to its former levels. In other cases the novelty of a program might lead to temporary effects. Schnelle et al. (1978) showed that a helicopter patrol lowered crime in a high-crime neighborhood, but they wondered whether the effect would hold up if the experiment were to be continued beyond the initial trial period. It is possible that although the novelty of the helicopter patrol served to frighten potential thieves and thus to lower crime for a short period, the airborne patrol's inherent effectiveness might not be strong.

A possible pitfall for an evaluator could exist when a pattern such as that illustrated in Panel F is found. Here a steady increase over time is observed. A naive approach to the analysis would be to contrast the mean of the time periods before the intervention with the mean of the time periods after. These means will be markedly different, but it does not help in understanding the effect of the intervention.

Analysis of Time-Series Designs

A discussion of rigorous analyses of interrupted time-series data is beyond the scope of this text. The methods commonly accepted are described by Reichardt and Mark (1998). The *Trends* procedure of SPSS (*SPSS Trends 13.0*, 2004) can handle interrupted time-series analyses. However, some simpler approaches to analyzing a time series may be completed with relative ease.

When the intervention can be implemented and then removed. Some interventions can be begun and then temporarily suspended. After establishing a baseline, behavior therapists introduce an intervention that is supposed to reduce the frequency of a problem behavior. Suppose that the intervention is effective: The problem behavior decreases. After several observation periods, the intervention is removed. If the rate of maladaptive behavior increases, it appears that the intervention had an effect—the change was not due to just maturation or history. If the intervention is reintroduced and maladaptive behavior decreases again, it is quite safe to conclude that the intervention is effective. This approach is a standard ABAB design used by therapists (for example, Horton, 1987) and organizational psychologists (for example, McCarthy, 1978).

When the intervention cannot be removed, but the effect is large. In other situations, interventions cannot be removed; however, if the effect is large, the impact of the intervention might still be obvious. The medical education research literature shows that resident physicians—physicians receiving their specialization training in hospitals—order more diagnostic laboratory tests for patients than do licensed, experienced physicians (Rich, Gifford, Luxenberg, and Dowd, 1990). To learn whether this general finding held for a particular hospital, we plotted the number of laboratory tests per month beginning four years before a major expansion of residency programs and two years afterwards. Because neither the hospital's size nor its occupancy rate (percentage of occupied beds) changed systematically during that six-year period, the influence of those historical effects was ignored. One striking observation was the increase in the number of laboratory tests during years before the residents began to provide care for patients: There was an average of approximately 500 additional tests each month. However, the increase that occurred between the last month before the program was expanded and the first month of the expanded residency program was more than 10,000 tests. Because a steady monthly increase resumed after this big jump—that is, the graph resembled Panel D in Figure 10.2—we felt safe in attributing the increase to the test-ordering practices of residents who were then ordering the bulk of the tests. These data could have been analyzed using sophisticated methods. Instead, the plots were simply smoothed for the 48 months prior to the increase in the number of residents and, *separately*, for the 24 months after the increase in residents. Figure 10.3 shows the jump at the point when residents began. The smoothed lines in the figure are called *Lowess lines* and can be made in SPSS after having a scatterplot made from the data. It is important to remember that smoothing is done in two steps: first, for the 48-month trend before the residents began and, second, for the 24-month trend after they began. The impact of the residents is hard to ignore in the figure. (Indeed, the program director instituted procedures to reduce the use of tests by residents; the effect of these procedures are reflected in the last 12 months in the figure.) Because the effect was so large, the interpretation seemed clear. If the effect had been smaller, removing and later reintroducing the intervention would have made the interpretation compelling. But since a community hospital does not change into a teaching hospital without great effort, this organizational change was not going to be removed. Similarly, laws are not going to be removed and reinstated in order to be sure that they had the desired effect.

A time-series graph can be smoothed without using a computer. One way is by replacing data points with the median of three adjacent points

FIGURE 10.3   Number of laboratory tests before and after medical residents began
to provide care to patients of the hospital. A Lowess line was found for
the 48 months prior to the beginning of the residency program and
for the 24 months after the program began. Note the jump between
the 48th and 49th months.

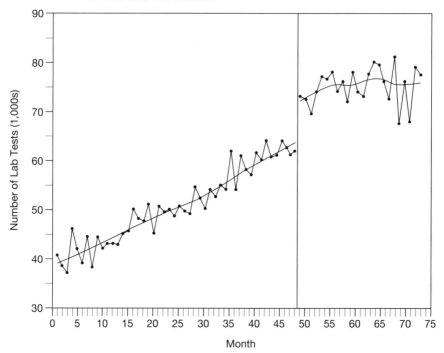

(Marsh, 1988; Tukey, 1977). Suppose that the following observations were
made for a 15-month period: 30, 22, 40, 17, 35, 25, 32, (Intervention), 45, 23,
55, 42, 47, 35, 52, and 43. First, plot these values the way the time-series results
were plotted in Figure 10.2. Then plot the medians. The median of 30, 22,
and 40, the first three points, is 30; this value is plotted for the second month.
Then the median of 22, 40, and 17 (i.e., 22) is plotted for the third month.
Continue through the entire series. By the way, you probably won't get the
point if you don't actually do this! When you are finished, you will see that the
graph has been smoothed and the effect of the intervention can be clearly
seen. This technique is useful when the intervention is expected to have a
lasting change or when a change is permanent (as was the introduction of resident physicians in the hospital), but the measure of the outcome shows large
random fluctuations from time interval to time interval. Smoothing procedures are not applicable when the intervention has only a short-lived effect
such as occurred when a private, midwestern university won the NCAA

basketball championship and enjoyed a spurt in freshman enrollment only in the following year, not in the years thereafter.

When smoothing techniques are described the first time, some listeners object saying that the data are being changed. Smoothing a graph is no different from finding the mean of a set of numbers in order to identify the general pattern. We seldom list our raw data in reports; instead we report means and standard deviations. A smoothed graph can reveal a pattern in a graph better than a graph of the raw data can just as a mean reveals a typical value better than a list of original data points.

OBSERVING OTHER GROUPS

Nonequivalent Control Group Designs

The simple time-series design increases the interpretability of an evaluation by extending the periods of observations over time. Another approach is to increase the number of groups observed. If the pretest-posttest design could be duplicated with another group that did not receive the program, a potentially strong research design would result. As long as the groups are comparable, nearly all the internal validity tests are satisfied by this design, called the *nonequivalent control group design*. Nonequivalent control groups may also be called *comparison groups*.

A larger improvement between pretest and posttest is expected for the program group than for the comparison group, as illustrated in Figure 10.4. A statistical tool to analyze such data is the two groups by two time periods analysis

FIGURE 10.4   Hypothetical results of a nonequivalent control (comparison) group design.

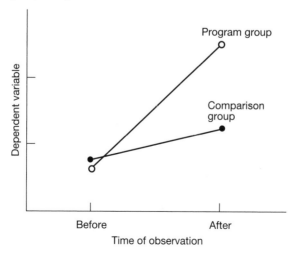

of variance, with repeated measurements over time periods (Kirk, 1982). Other statisticians call this a *mixed design*. If the program is successful and the group means follow the pattern in Figure 10.4, the analysis of variance would reveal a significant interaction between group and testing period. Other statistical analyses could also be used: Reichardt (1979) showed how to use analysis of covariance using pretests scores to control for initial differences among program participants. However, he also showed that depending on the pattern of the group means, this approach to analysis can bias the results in different directions. His discussion is beyond the level we can review in this text. However, the use of analysis of covariance with experiments is discussed in the following chapter. It is important to realize that the different approaches are available; none is always correct. Before beginning a statistical analysis it is always wise to inspect the data carefully. Ideally, we would want to find that the standard deviations associated with the means in Figure 10.4 are similar. Furthermore, the figure shows that the means before the program were nearly equal; if the pretest means are quite different, analyses of nonequivalent control group designs may be misleading.

Note the positive features of this design. Including the comparison group permits the isolation of the effects of the program from the effects of several plausible interpretations of change. Because the comparison group would have been tested at the same times as the program group, both groups have had the same amount of time to mature. Historical forces have presumably affected the groups equally. Because both groups would have been tested twice, testing effects should be equivalent. Finally, the rates of participant loss between pretest and posttest can be examined to be sure that they are similar. Nonequivalent control groups are especially useful when part of an organization is exposed to the program while other parts are not. Since selection to the program is not in the hands of the participants, and since the participants' level of need does not determine eligibility, the comparability of the groups is quite good. Unfortunately, as will be shown later, these favorable conditions are not often met. As mentioned in Chapter 9, the possibility that the meaning of the dependent variable has been affected by the program must be considered; if that is likely, a comparison between pretest and posttest would not be valid.

Problems in Selecting Comparison Groups

Comparison groups are chosen according to the evaluation questions to be studied. A no-treatment group would be used when one seeks to learn if the program has any effect. However, a no-treatment group would not be appropriate if stakeholders want to compare different ways of offering a service. In that case, different programs would be compared. If there is a suspicion that attention alone could affect an outcome, then the comparison group would be a placebo group, that is, a group that experiences a program not expected to affect the outcome variable.

The major weakness in all nonequivalent control group designs is the difficulty of finding a comparison group sufficiently similar to the treatment group to permit drawing valid interpretations. For example, it is possible that those who choose to be in a program may be maturing faster than those in the comparison group. Parents who seek out special programs for their children may also be devoting more attention to their children at home than are parents who do not seek out special programs. Another problem arises if program participants are chosen because of extreme scores on the pretest, and the comparison group is selected from those with less extreme scores. If so, as mentioned in Chapter 9, the results may be distorted by regression effects.

Evaluators seeking a solution to the problem of pretest differences between the program and comparison groups have matched people in the program group with those in the comparison group. People are chosen to form a comparison group because they resemble the program participants on income level, objective test score, rated adjustment, locality of residence, or other criteria. While matching is often used to select comparison groups, there are situations when it would be wrong. The widely cited initial negative evaluations of Head Start (Cicarelli et al., 1969) were criticized for the way matching was carried out (Campbell and Erlebacher, 1970). Head Start was designed for disadvantaged preschool children most lacking in school-relevant skills and attitudes. In addition, nutritional and medical goals were involved (Zigler and Muenchow, 1992).

When Head Start was initially evaluated, it was already widely accepted and offered in many communities (Datta, 1976); therefore, the program could not be withheld from any group of children. The evaluation utilized a posttest-only design with national samples of children, some in Head Start and some not. Those not in Head Start were matched with Head Start children. The evaluation compared standard test scores of Head Start children in first, second, and third grades with the scores of similar non-Head Start children; it concluded that Head Start was largely a failure. Critics attacked the methodology on a number of grounds; however, the focus of the present discussion is on regression effects that likely led to the conclusions of the Head Start evaluation.

The population of children available for the non-Head Start comparison group was less disadvantaged than the children in Head Start, so the children selected as matches could not be equivalent to the Head Start children. In order to find children qualifying for Head Start who had cognitive achievement scores similar to those of children not qualifying, either or both of the following points had to have been true: (1) the comparison group was selected from among the less able children not qualified for Head Start; or (2) the treatment group was selected from among the more able children who attended Head Start. To understand the effects of regression toward the mean in this invalid form of matching, it is important to understand why the previous sentence is true. Once a group is selected on the basis of need for a national program, no other group is just like the people in the program. There are no good comparison groups. However, on some variables (for example, family income, school grades, test scores) there will be overlap among those who qualify and those who do not. Who will overlap? The people in the "needy" groups who overlap with the "not needy" group must be among the relatively better-off among the "needy" people. Those in the "not needy" group who overlap with the "needy" children must be among the least well-off among the "not needy" group (Crano and Brewer, 1986).

Consider the following example. Suppose a teacher wanted to provide a special spelling program for all the second graders. If the teacher wanted a comparison group, she could find some third graders who scored as low as the second graders. Are these groups equivalent? Probably not. These third graders could only be found among the lower portion of the third grade, a population that, in general, is more skilled than the second grade treatment group. What will happen upon retesting the groups? Because no spelling test is perfectly reliable, the low-scoring third graders in the comparison group will look as though they improved, not only because they learned some new words but also because they are regressing toward the mean of third graders. This regression will make the second graders' improvement due to the program appear relatively smaller than it may actually have been.

In other words, the groups of children have different influences raising their scores. The program children will probably show improvement because the *new* program has affected them and because they matured a bit. The comparison children will improve because of exposure to the *regular* spelling classes, added maturity, and regression. The initial Head Start evaluation was biased in the same way as this hypothetical teacher's evaluation would be (Campbell and Erlebacher, 1970). Because human service programs typically produce small improvements, the size of the regression effects might even exceed the program's effect. In fact, Campbell and Erlebacher argued that regression effects made compensatory education look harmful when, in fact, the programs may have had small positive influences. The moral is clear: The nonequivalent control group design is especially sensitive to regression effects when groups are systematically different on some dimensions. Because a systematic preprogram difference between treatment and comparison groups is likely to be found in compensatory education evaluations, the nonequivalent control group design can be applied only with caution.

The emphasis on regression to the mean should not imply that this is the only weakness of nonequivalent control group designs. Regression was stressed because some stakeholders may believe that selecting certain participants for inclusion in the evaluation can compensate for the effects of preexisting differences between the pretest scores of the groups. There are many other reasons why existing groups may differ from each other. One might compare neighboring classrooms in an attempt to learn if a novel teaching method used in one classroom is more effective. Although the children in the two classrooms seem equivalent, it might be learned later that the teacher in the comparison (i.e., nontreatment) classroom had been using methods that are similar to those used in the program. Or, when patients of two physicians are used in an evaluation of a patient education brochure, it may turn out that the physician handing out the brochure has systematically encouraged her patients to read about their illnesses and treatments. Thus, her patients are more likely to read such material than are the patients of other physicians. This preexisting difference between patient groups may make the patient education program appear more effective than would have been the case if a different physician had been asked to distribute the material.

In sum, although differences in groups at the pretest can lead to over- or underestimates of the effects of programs, the nonequivalent comparison group design is quite powerful and useful when similar groups are available to form treatment and comparison groups. Case Study 4 is a large nonequivalent control group program evaluation; in spite of the large scope of this project, some nagging concerns remained about uncontrolled threats to internal validity after it was completed.

CASE STUDY 4
Nonequivalent Control Groups Used to Evaluate an Employee Incentive Plan

Petty, Singleton, and Connell (1992) examined an employee incentive program in a utility company. The objectives were to increase productivity, decrease costs, and improve employee morale. The incentive system provided financial rewards for employees if group goals were met. By involving employees in the design of the incentive system it was expected that employees would like the system. The program group consisted of one company division (n = 618) that volunteered for the evaluation; the comparison group was selected by the management as the company division that was most like the program group (n = 587). The outcome variables included the costs of running each division during the year-long evaluation, the productivity of each division based on five existing company indexes, and employee attitude tests to assess morale and reactions to the incentive plan.

The program group (1) performed better on expenditures (i.e., it spent less than had been budgeted, whereas the comparison group spent more), (2) achieved higher productivity compared both to goals and to a baseline from the previous year on nine out of ten variables, but (3) did not show better morale relative to the comparison group. Overall, 72 percent of the employees said that they wanted to continue working under the incentive plan, the company balance sheet benefitted, and customers had lower costs.

(continued)

CASE STUDY 4
continued

   Unfortunately, even though 72 percent of the employees wanted to continue the plan, it was discontinued because union members and managers of other divisions reacted negatively to the plan. The evaluators speculated that management had failed to involve stakeholders adequately during the trial year.

Comment: An issue that the evaluators did not discuss was how the budget savings were obtained. It may well be that jobs were done more efficiently, but it is also possible that some expenditures were deferred. Any organization can achieve significant savings over the short run by deferring maintenance, but it will incur additional costs later. The authors did mention that the program group had selected itself for the evaluation—the effect of self-selection was impossible to assess in this evaluation. Furthermore, the managers and employees in the comparison group knew about the evaluation; informal information suggested that there was some effort to outperform the program division. This evaluation illustrates some of the difficulties experienced when evaluating innovations in operating organizations and using nonequivalent control groups. Attempts to control for these effects would have required a considerably greater effort than the current evaluation, which involved 1,205 employees, $707,567 in bonuses, and at least an 18-month data collection period. The only way to control for all the plausible alternative explanations would require examining budget expenditures over several years rather than just one year, including additional company divisions with variations of the program, and working more intimately with employee and management stakeholders. Evaluation is not for the faint of heart.

REGRESSION-DISCONTINUITY DESIGN

There is one situation in which a comparison between nonequivalent groups can be made in a manner that is much more powerful than the methods presented so far. When eligibility for a service is based on a continuous variable, such as income, achievement, or level of disability, it may be possible to use the regression-discontinuity design (Trochim, 1984, 1986). Suppose, for example, that 300 students are tested for reading achievement in the fall. Those scoring the lowest are defined as those most in need of extra assistance. If the program has facilities for 100 students, it seems reasonable and fair to take the 100 with the lowest scores into the program. This strategy is simply a special case of the nonequivalent control group design; however, unlike other ways of choosing a comparison group, the evaluator has a quantitative measure of how the two groups were formed.

   If all 300 are retested at the end of the school year, what would be expected? Note that we would not expect the 100 to outperform the 200 regular class students. If the program were effective, we would instead expect that the treated children would have gained more than they would have had they stayed in their regular classrooms. The regression discontinuity design enables the evaluator to measure such effects.

FIGURE 10.5   The relationship between pretest and posttest scores when people scoring 3 or below are eligible for special assistance to improve posttest performance. The graph on the left illustrates the case when the assistance was not effective; the graph on the right illustrates how the data would appear if the program enabled the eligible people to perform 2 points better than they would have without special assistance.

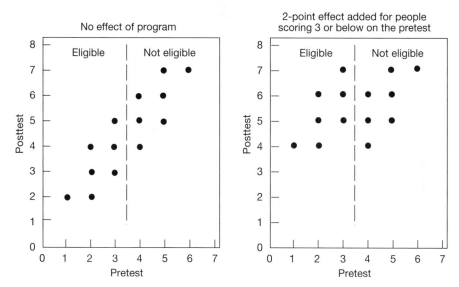

Figure 10.5 illustrates the key concepts. The scatterplot on the left shows how we would expect a pretest and a posttest to be related; there is a strong, linear, positive correlation. The pretest and posttest, do not have to be identical; they simply have to measure the same construct—reading skills, mastery of chemistry, parenting skills. If those who are low on the pretest received an effective program that added two points to what the participants would have had on the posttest, the scatterplot would look like the plot on the right side of Figure 10.5. To measure the effect of the program requires the use of multiple regression as explained in Box 10.1. The scatterplots in the box show why evaluators need statistical analyses. Without the regression analysis, it would have been impossible to notice the sizable effect of the program. The regression analysis does detect it and plotting the regression line displays the discontinuity very clearly. If the special program were equivalent to the regular class, one would expect a smooth relationship between pretest and posttest. If the program were actually (heaven forbid!) worse than the regular classes, we would expect program students to score lower than expected on the basis of the pretest. In such a situation the discontinuity would be the reverse of that in Figure 10.5 and Box 10.1.

BOX 10.1: How to Do and Interpret a Regression Discontinuity Analysis

----

If you have studied multiple regression, carrying out a simple regression discontinuity analysis is very easy. First, one needs pretest and posttest information on a group of people. Only the people on the low (or high) end of the pretest are exposed to the program. We must have two observations for all the people regardless of their scores. Suppose that students with less than 60 percent on pretest, a placement test, were eligible for remedial help prior to taking a regular course. To evaluate the effectiveness of the remediation, we can use a regression discontinuity design. The posttest, the final in the regular course, is the dependent variable (the variable to be predicted). The placement test is one independent variable, X_1, and getting remedial help or not is the second independent variable, X_2. The value of X_2 for the 100 students getting help is 2; the value of X_2 for the 200 students not getting help is 1.

We have every reason to expect that the placement test will be a strong predictor of the final in the course. If the remediation was helpful in improving scores on the final, then X_2 will also be a strong predictor of final also.

The figure below (left side) shows a scatterplot in which program participation led to improved posttest scores. The regression line is shown in the figure; the program effect creates the discontinuity seen in the sudden drop at the dividing line between the eligible scores (60 or lower) and those not eligible (above 60). The regression equation supports the conclusion that participation in the program led to higher scores on the final.

$$\text{Final} = 21.25 + 0.57 \times (\text{Placement test score}) + 7.67\, X_2$$
$$\text{where } X_2 \text{ equals 1 for those not eligible and 2 for those eligible.}$$

The relationship of being in the program (or not) with Test Two was statistically significant ($t(297) = 4.027$, $p < 0.0005$). The effect of the program was +7.67 points. The effect size of the program is

$$g = t\sqrt{(1/n_1 + 1/n_2)} = 4.037\sqrt{(1/100 + 1/200)} = 0.493$$

This effect size indicates that the remediation produced a moderately large effect according to the findings of Lipsey and Wilson (1993) mentioned in Chapter 9.

Additional details on using regression discontinuity analyses in more complex situations are given by Trochim (1984, 1990) and his colleagues (Reichardt, Trochim, and Cappelleri, 1995). Although the examples of regression discontinuity designs are usually presented in the context of compensatory programs for those who are in danger of falling behind, they are equally relevant to evaluate programs for the gifted and talented (Marsh, 1998). Note the scatterplot on the right below. This is the same scatterplot as on the left, but without the regression line. It is not easy to detect the effect of remediation without the help of a regression discontinuity analysis.

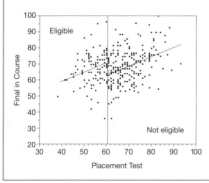
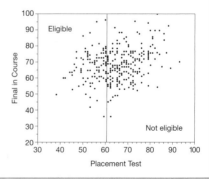

OBSERVING OTHER DEPENDENT VARIABLES

At this point the methods described in Chapter 9 have been expanded to include observations of the program participants at many times and to include observations of groups other than the program participants. It is possible to increase the validity of interpretations by observing additional dependent variables that are not expected to be changed by the program, or, at most, changed only marginally; this design has been called the *control construct design* (McKillip, 1992; McKillip and Baldwin, 1990).

The added dependent measures must be similar to the major dependent variable without being strongly influenced by the program. If the children do read better after a special program, it might be expected that they would do better on a social sciences test than they did before the reading program; consequently, a social sciences test would not be a good control construct measure for a reading program. However, a test of mathematical skills requiring only minimal reading levels might be an excellent additional dependent variable. Patients in a health education program concentrating on avoiding heart disease should show increased knowledge about heart functioning, cholesterol, and related topics. They would not be expected to show greater knowledge of osteoporosis. When it is possible to find additional dependent measures that (1) would be affected by the same threats to internal validity as the outcome measure, but (2) would not be affected by the program, this design is a powerful one. This design was used in evaluating the Medicaid-required second opinion on surgical procedures by comparing the percentage reductions for ten procedures requiring a second opinion with the reductions for nine procedures not requiring second opinions (Tyson, 1985). McKillip, Lockhart, Eckert, and Phillips (1985) evaluated the effects of a media-based alcohol education campaign on a university campus using control constructs that were alcohol-related, but were not the subject of the campaign. This paper has been condensed and rewritten in the format recommended for evaluation reports and included in the Appendix of this text.

COMBINING DESIGNS TO INCREASE INTERNAL VALIDITY

Time-Series and Nonequivalent Control Groups

The most interpretable quasi-experimental designs are those that combine the approaches described above. If a group similar to the program participants can be observed, the simple interrupted time-series design is strengthened considerably. The effect of the Connecticut speeding crackdown was much easier to isolate by examining the fatality rates of four neighboring states. Figure 10.6 contrasts the means of these four states' fatality rates with that of Connecticut. As can be seen in the figure, there seemed to be a general downward trend in all five states; however, Connecticut's 1957–1959 rates

FIGURE 10.6   Automobile accident fatality rate per 100,000 residents for Connecticut and for comparable states. (Adapted from D. T. Campbell 1969. Reforms as experiments. *American Psychologist, 24,* 419. Copyright © 1969 by the American Psychological Association. Reprinted with permission.)

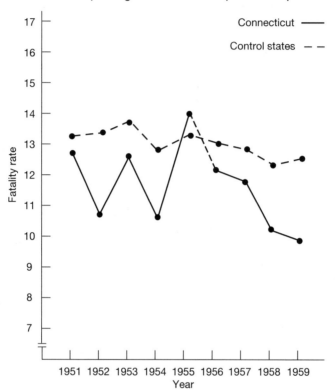

were increasingly lower than those of the neighboring states. Although regression toward the mean is a plausible interpretation of the drop from 1955 to 1956, the continued favorable trend is hard to explain if the crackdown, which was kept in force during the following years, did not have an effect. Riecken and Boruch (1974) argue that tests of statistical significance are less important than a qualitative understanding of the various threats to the validity of causal conclusions about the impact of an intervention.

A key to drawing valid interpretations from observations lies in being able to repeat the observations. If a finding can be replicated, one can be more sure of conclusions than if conditions make replication impossible. The time-series design with a comparison group that receives the same program as the treatment group but at a later time provides additional safeguards against validity threats. Figure 10.7 illustrates the most interpretable pattern from such an evaluation.

FIGURE 10.7   Hypothetical results of an interrupted time-series design with switching replications.

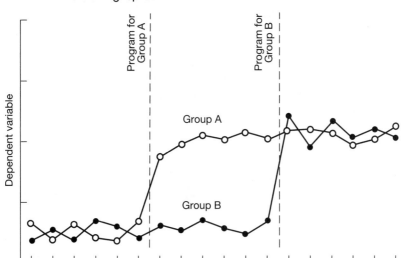

The design is called an *interrupted time series with switching replications* (Cook and Campbell, 1979). If the observations fit the pattern in the figure, little in the way of statistical analysis needs to be done. The project by McKillip et al. (1985) on which the example evaluation report (see the Appendix) is based shows how this design can be used to track the impact of a media-based educational campaign.

Selective Control Design

By understanding the context of a program, evaluators may be able to identify the threats to internal validity that are most likely to affect an evaluation. Evaluators may then choose comparison groups to control for specific threats to internal validity so that the most plausible alternative interpretations are eliminated. When the appropriate nonequivalent control groups are available, the selective control design can be a powerful approach (Cordray, 1986).

Here is a simple example of planning an evaluation based on a selective control design. The dean of a college of arts and sciences requested an evaluation of a junior year abroad program offered by the college. The report was needed for a board of trustees meeting to occur in six weeks. Clearly, there was no opportunity for a time-series design. (As we mentioned earlier, it is not uncommon for evaluators to work under a deadline.) The evaluation was planned around the obvious comparison—college seniors who had studied abroad the previous year versus seniors who had remained at the parent campus. In making this comparison, self-selection cannot be ignored as a threat to internal validity. Students who study abroad for a year are different from those who remain at home. One could estimate the preexisting differences between these two groups by testing individuals before they went abroad, but a pretest-posttest design was impossible due to the short time allotted for the study. Because the decision to study abroad requires much planning, students sign up early for the program. By comparing seniors who have been abroad with sophomores arranging to go abroad, the self-selection threat could be controlled, because both groups have selected themselves into the program. However, now a second threat to internal validity becomes a problem: Sophomores are less mature than seniors. Two years of age may not be that critical for middle-aged and elderly people, but two years may make quite a difference for an evaluation of a program for college students. By adding one more group, sophomores who did not intend to study abroad, the major threats to the internal validity of this evaluation were controlled.

The design is summarized in Figure 10.8. If self-selection were related to high scores on dependent measures, one would expect the groups in the upper row to have higher scores. If maturation led to higher scores, those in the right-hand column should have higher scores. If the program, junior year abroad, had an impact, then the upper right-hand group, the self-selected seniors who studied abroad, should have especially high scores as illustrated. If students studying abroad developed as hoped, an interaction would have been found in a 2 by 2 analysis of variance. Unfortunately, the sophomores planning to go abroad could not be surveyed in time for the trustees' meeting; consequently, the means in the figure are hypothetical.

FIGURE 10.8   Hypothetical mean scores on a measure of international understanding (high numbers indicating more international understanding) for the students in the junior year abroad evaluation. A program effect is indicated by these means.

		Maturation Level	
		Sophomores	Seniors
	Students who will study or have studied abroad	50	65 (Treatment group)
Self-Selection			
	Students who have not studied or do not plan to study abroad	40	45

A more complicated selective control design was described by Lawler and Hackman (1969). They wished to evaluate the success of having custodians design their own incentive plan to reduce absenteeism. The authors believed that an incentive plan would work best if the employees designed it themselves. Since it was impossible to have different incentive plans for employees working together, the program was tested using intact, existing work groups, and non-equivalent control groups were used in the evaluation. Three work teams making up the program group developed their plans in consultation with the program planners/evaluators. The first non-program comparison group had an incentive plan similar to that developed by the program group, but it was imposed on them by management. Including this group enabled the evaluators to distinguish between the effect of an *employee-designed* incentive plan and the incentive itself. A second comparison group simply met with the program planners to talk about work and absenteeism. This group was necessary to show that any reduction in absenteeism would have been due to the incentive plan rather than a positive reaction to getting attention from management. Finally, a comparison group with no incentive and no discussion was added.

The data were analyzed using a time-series technique because (1) the rate of absenteeism may change slowly, and (2) absenteeism is recorded daily whether or not there is a program. Comparing the level of absenteeism for the 12 weeks before the intervention with the level 12 weeks afterwards showed that the participant employees improved from 12 percent absent to 6 percent absent, whereas the rates for the other groups did not change. Note that without each of the three nonequivalent control groups (as in the junior year abroad program), some alternative interpretations would have remained plausible. The comparison groups were selected to counter specific, plausible interpretations of a reduction in the absenteeism of the program group.

The design did not deal with some threats to internal validity because they were not plausible in this setting. For example, instrumentation refers to possible changes in measures of outcome because the observer becomes more vigilant or experienced during the course of an evaluation. Because job absenteeism is a critical variable in work settings, the development of a program is unlikely to lead to any changes in the measurement of absenteeism. Similarly, testing was ignored because attendance is always recorded in job settings whether there is a special program or not. Thus, an evaluator need not worry about whether the evaluation led to increased employee monitoring that in turn affected the employees' behaviors rather than the program.

Summary and Preview

The use of quasi-experimental designs in program evaluation is widespread. These approaches often minimize disruption yet permit gathering sufficient information to isolate the probable effects of innovative programs. However, the use of quasi-experimental designs cannot be mechanical; evaluators need to consider which specific threats to internal validity must be accounted for in each evaluation. Anticipating these threats can cause headaches for evaluators: There is no standard approach to planning quasi-experimental evaluations. Sometimes the preferred statistical methods to use with these designs are controversial.

When conditions permit a controlled experimental evaluation, evaluators often take the opportunity so that they can control most threats to internal validity. When an intervention is expensive, affects many people, or might lead to serious side effects, it is desirable to conduct a controlled study. Chapter 11 describes the value and some of the limitations of evaluating programs with experiments.

Study Questions

1. Explain which threats to internal validity are not covered by an evaluation of a parole program in which male parolees who are tested before and after the program are compared to a sample of men living in the same neighborhoods as the parolees.

2. Assume that reading levels in a school district had been steadily declining over a period of years and that a new reading program was implemented to counter the trend. After two years, reading levels declined again, but the superintendent announced that the reading program was a success because reading levels would have declined even more without the program. What would be necessary to evaluate the validity of such an interpretation?

3. Suppose that a new treatment were offered to patients of a group medical practice in an upper-middle-class suburb. As a comparison group, similarly aged patients with the same diagnoses were found in a county hospital providing free (Medicaid) coverage to poor families. Evaluate this nonequivalent control group evaluation design.

4. A problem with quasi-experimental evaluations is that often a particular set of results can be interpreted, but a different set cannot. For example, assume that a service to a disadvantaged group is supposed to lead to higher scores on some variable (see question 3). If the postprogram level of this disadvantaged group is higher than that observed in a middle-class comparison group, the interpretation of the evaluation is relatively easy. However, if the postprogram level of the initially disadvantaged group improves, but is still lower than that of the middle-class comparison group, then there are a number of possible interpretations. Explain these statements.

5. If you did not plot and smooth the time series given in this chapter, do so now and carry out the smoothing process.

Additional Resource

SHADISH, W. R., COOK, T. D., and CAMPBELL, D. T. 2002. *Experimental and quasi-experimental design for generalized causal inference.* Boston: Houghton Mifflin.

This text is the standard research design resource for the program evaluators. It is the successor of the classic work by Campbell and Stanley (1963) and the more recent standard by Cook and Campbell (1979). In the new work, Chapters 4 through 7 provide more details on the quasi-experimental designs described in this chapter.

Using Experiments to Evaluate Programs

E ven after carefully designed quasi-experimental evaluations are completed, concerns linger that some effect other than the program
caused the change in the participants or masked a real program effect.
A way to minimize these concerns is to adopt an evaluation design strategy
that best controls for threats to internal validity. The easiest way to do this is
to use an experiment based on observations of people randomly assigned
to participate in the program or to some alternative control experience.
This chapter reviews the need for experimentation as a tool in program
evaluation, describes the most opportune times to implement an experiment, and makes practical suggestions for dealing with the problems of
conducting experimental research in organizational settings.

EXPERIMENTS IN PROGRAM EVALUATION

Benefits of Experiments

In the previous chapter, we described quasi-experimental designs that can
be used when it would be unethical to assign people to experience or not
experience a program or when organizational conditions are such that random assignment is not practical. In such settings evaluators utilize existing
intact groups; however, such groups develop for reasons other than the
need for an unambiguously interpreted evaluation. Consequently, it is very
likely that the groups will not be equivalent before a program begins.

Several ways have been used to make the groups more comparable—matching, finding similar groups, or using statistical adjustments. In some situations these approaches serve fairly well, but often nothing suffices to control the threats to internal validity fully. In Case Study 4, Petty et al. (1992) remained concerned that the program group that had volunteered for the evaluation of the incentive plan was different from the comparison group. Treatments for a chronic illness that exhibits cyclical patterns cannot be studied validly without forming equivalent groups randomly (Deniston and Rosenstock, 1973). Selecting matches from existing groups creates statistical pitfalls for the unwary evaluator (Cook and Campbell, 1979). Although the selective control design has much to recommend it as a quasi-experimental approach, considerable foresight is required to anticipate which internal validity threats must be controlled in each specific evaluation setting. Experiments avoid these problems.

Experimental Designs

The simplest experimental design involves randomly assigning people either to one or more program groups or to a control group and then contrasting the scores of the people in the groups on outcome posttests. If the groups are formed randomly, there is no need for pretests because the groups cannot have been systematically different before the experiment began (Boruch, 1998). Consider some of the threats to internal validity that an experiment controls: (1) the groups cannot differ in rate or level of maturation, (2) people cannot select themselves into one or the other group, (3) although *individuals* begin with different severity levels, the *groups* do not begin the experiment at different levels on the outcome variable, (4) all people experience the same amount of testing, and (5) all groups represent the same population so the groups cannot be regressing toward different means. In other words, if everything goes right, the posttest means can be validly contrasted using standard statistical techniques. Having more than two groups simply means that analyses of variance will be required instead of t tests. Analysis of variance (ANOVA) is briefly described in Box 11.1 along with a refinement we will mention soon.

If possible, it is always advisable to measure program participants prior to the beginning of a program. If people have been randomly assigned to groups, the means of the groups will not be systematically different before the program begins. Having a pretest measurement that is correlated with the outcome variable permits the use of analysis of covariance (ANCOVA), a statistical test much less subject to Type II errors than is an independent groups t test or ANOVA. ANCOVA is also briefly described in Box 11.1.

Using pretests provides evaluators with another advantage: they can help in describing findings to stakeholders. If it is possible to measure the variable that will be used as the outcome both before and after the program, one can describe the change during participation in the program as improvement; many stakeholders will value such information. There is another advantage to

BOX 11.1: Analysis of Variance and Analysis of Covariance

Analysis of variance (ANOVA) refers to a statistical test in which three or more groups are observed—perhaps an innovative community reinforcement program (CRP) group, a traditional program (TP) group, and a waiting list control (WLC) group. If participants are randomly assigned to one of these three groups, the means of outcome measures taken from the three groups can be validly compared. An ANOVA leads to an F ratio indicating whether differences among the group means are large enough to reject the belief that the groups are equivalent (i.e., the null hypothesis). For example, marijuana users seeking treatment were randomly assigned to a relapse prevention program, an individualized assessment and advice program, or a waiting list control condition. Suppose that four months after treatment the evaluators found the following means and standard errors of the means for the three groups for a measure indicating marijuana addiction problems.

Program Group	Mean	Standard Deviation	Standard Error of Mean
CRP ($n = 33$)	43.22	15.67	2.73
TP ($n = 32$)	47.91	19.65	3.47
WLC ($n = 33$)	48.34	20.33	3.54

Suppose that an ANOVA does not show that the means differed to a statistically significant degree. Does this mean that the CRP was unsuccessful? It might have been, but evaluators would note that the treated CRP participants were better off than TP participants and that both groups of treated people were better off than those in the wait-list group. The ANOVA procedure compares the differences in the means with the difference one should expect between the groups on the basis of the standard errors of the groups. Standard errors indicate the uncertainty of our estimates of the means due to random sampling error. If we could control for the random variance in the outcome variable, we might discover that there were indeed statistically significant differences among the three means. This is where analysis of covariance (ANCOVA) may help us.

When there is a pretest of some sort that assesses the severity of problems created by marijuana use among all the participants, we may be able to reduce the size of the standard errors. In simple terms, ANCOVA permits us to predict the clients' level of problems after the program on the basis of their levels of problems before the program began. Even if people are helped, if they had relatively more severe problems before the program, they are still likely to have relatively more problems than other participants at the end of the program. ANCOVA allows us to control for these preexisting differences among the participants and makes it less likely that we could miss a true program effect.

To use ANCOVA one simply specifies that the premeasure is the "covariate" when using a computer program. ANCOVA is misused if one believes that it can control for differences between the groups such as we would expect to find if marijuana users had chosen which program to participate in. In other words, ANCOVA cannot compensate for biases due to uncontrolled threats to internal validity. If there has been random assignment to groups and the evaluator has a preprogram measure that is correlated with the outcome measure, ANCOVA is a valuable statistical tool to reduce Type II error.

using pretests when one can be sure that their use does not create a problem by sensitizing participants to the outcome measure (a threat to internal validity—testing). Adding pretests to the basic experimental design assures evaluators that if problems were to develop in the implementation of randomization, some analytic options are still available (Flay and Best, 1982). Unfortunately, everything does not always go right. At worst the data can be treated as a pretest-posttest nonequivalent control group design.

Another refinement in forming program groups randomly is to place similar people into "blocks." Perhaps people might be blocked (i.e., grouped) on the basis of age, skill level, severity of disease, or previous experience in similar programs. Then people are assigned randomly to program groups from all blocks (Dennis, 1994). The advantages of this refinement include having the option of analyzing the data to examine the relationship of the variable used to block the people. It may be that older participants are more strongly affected by a program than younger participants.

OBJECTIONS TO EXPERIMENTATION

Although experiments have clear advantages in making evaluations interpretable, many people object to experimentation in service settings. It is important for evaluators to be familiar with the most common objections, lest they encounter them for the first time while they are planning an evaluation or, even worse, after random assignment to a program has already begun.

Don't Experiment on Me!

People are not eager to participate in an experiment perhaps partially because experimentation has sometimes been associated with the "mad scientist" of science fiction. Moreover, the popular media do not use the word *experiment* in the careful way experimental design textbooks do. Consequently, it is not surprising when people not trained in social science methods equate experiments to evaluate the effects of social programs or medical treatments with a covert plan to administer dangerous drugs to unsuspecting people or with an undisciplined attempt to learn about behavior. Evaluators planning an experiment will be careful to treat the question of experimentation with great respect. The advantages of experiments should be stressed and the fact that the innovative program has been carefully planned by competent personnel should be made clear to possible volunteers and committees overseeing the research.

We Already Know What Is Best

Experiments are sometimes carried out on treatments that many professionals believe do not require evaluation. Particularly tragic are ineffective medical interventions that have negative side effects. Noncontrolled studies had led physicians and nurses to believe that pure oxygen increased the survival rate for premature infants; however, at first, it was not known that using pure oxygen could also leave the infant blind. Once this terrible side effect was suspected, it became important to learn whether it was necessary to use pure oxygen with premature infants. During research on the value of oxygen, some nurses who thought they knew best switched the oxygen on at night in order to be sure that the babies in the regular air group got some pure oxygen. Once controlled research was complete, it was learned that the administration of pure oxygen was indeed responsible for abnormal growth in the developing retinas of infants. Only later was it learned that air with a higher concentration of oxygen (but not pure oxygen) could be administered to increase the survival rate of premature infants, yet with little chance of hurting the development of their retinas (Silverman, 1977). Inadequate evaluations of the effects of drugs administered to coronary patients to stabilize irregular heart beats resulted in the premature deaths of tens of thousands of patients between 1985 and 1989 (Moore, 1995; see also Hine, Laird, Hewitt, and Chalmers, 1989). Eddy and Billings (1988) report that the quality of medical evidence is not as high as commonly believed.

I Know What Is Best for My Client

Some service providers are convinced that they know what is best for specific clients, students, or patients. Consequently, they are not eager to commit themselves to follow the treatment dictated by a random assignment procedure. Similarly, people are hesitant to become involved in experimental evaluations of services because they believe that human service providers can choose the service that is best for meeting their needs. The fact of the matter is that the reasons for the choice of treatments provided to many people are quite unknown. Different counselors follow different theories of psychotherapy, physicians do not follow set treatment protocols (Eddy, 1990), different cities and states set up different welfare policies, and judges do not assign identical sentences to people convicted of the same crimes. Although there may be quite valid reasons for choosing different treatments, an individual provider does not make the same choices even when faced with clients with the same problems and different caregivers are not consistent with each other (Dawes, 1994).

It takes considerable tact to explain to service providers that their beliefs may not be always valid. Providing examples of noncontrolled evaluations that were later invalidated by controlled studies may help providers see the possibility of misperceptions and the advantages of unambiguous documentation of service effectiveness. Earlier we mentioned the idea that society would benefit by treating new human service programs as if they were experiments—treating failures as an indication of our incomplete understanding of people and organizations, not as an indication of low motivation or incompetence of service providers (Campbell, 1969; Deming, 1986). Unfortunately, some human service providers act as though a negative evaluation indicates that they are at fault rather than their theories or techniques; therefore, they develop rationalizations whenever particular individuals do not seem to benefit from a service. By explaining away all failures, program personnel miss the opportunity for growth that could occur if they improve their practices on the basis of feedback. At these times evaluators feel the full force of the conflict between their skeptical role toward service programs and the providers' confidence in the effectiveness of the services they give.

Experiments Are Just Too Much Trouble

Anyone who has conducted an evaluation in an organization knows that a commitment of time and effort is needed. Experiments in nonlaboratory settings require a lot of nurturing to plan, implement, and monitor (Boruch, 1997; Dennis, 1994). Evaluators should not agree to conduct an experimental evaluation if they do not have access to the resources needed to carry it through properly; however, it may take only a little additional effort to carry out an experimental evaluation compared to a noncontrolled study. Sometimes particular organizational arrangements provide opportunities to conduct an experimental evaluation. Carey (1979) was able to conduct an evaluation of alternative approaches to hospital nursing because different forms of nursing were implemented on the two general medical floors of a hospital. On one floor nurses followed the widely used team approach in which different nurses take specific responsibilities for many patients (e.g., administer medications), while on the other floor nurses followed the primary nursing model in which a single nurse is responsible for all of the care needed by four patients. Since patients were assigned to rooms by the admissions center on the basis of bed availability, not diagnosis or physician preference, random groups of patients were formed. In this case, conducting an experiment did not add any burden to the hospital beyond the effort of data collection. A similar approach developed by the Cleveland MetroHealth Center was based on four parallel medical care provider firms working in the center. Patients were randomly assigned to the firms (Neuhauser, 1991). Contemplated changes were evaluated in one or two of the firms before the successful changes were implemented in the entire health care center.

What is often overlooked in considering the cost of an experimental evaluation is the cost of *not* doing an experiment. Several examples were suggested above of situations in which medical care that was believed to be beneficial actually harmed patients. Reviews of research on several medical treatments that at one time had widespread support revealed that they had never been evaluated adequately. Gilbert, Light, and Mosteller (1975) comment that the alternative to experimenting on people is "fooling around" with people. Seldom do service providers inform their patients, clients, or trainees that the service or care offered has not been fully evaluated, even though that is often true (see Eddy and Billings, 1988; Dawes, 1994).

THE MOST DESIRABLE TIMES TO CONDUCT EXPERIMENTS

A theme of this text is that evaluation should be built into the daily operation of all organizations. Usually such evaluation practices will not be experiments but rather the administrative-monitoring and performance-monitoring approaches described in Chapters 7 and 9. We agree with Lipsey et al. (1985) that the experimental model is not the all-purpose program evaluation methodology. There are, however, circumstances that are best served by an understanding of cause and effect relationships that can be best studied with experiments.

When a New Program Is Introduced

When a program is new, there are several conditions likely to increase the interest of staff and management in an experimental evaluation. First, when people are randomly assigned to receive the current form of service in order to form a control group, it is hard to argue that they are being treated unfairly. However, when people believe deeply in a new program or feel desperate for an effective service, they may still raise the issue of fairness; this occurred when some new treatments for AIDS were studied (Palca, 1990).

Second, a new program may take some time to implement, thus providing time for an evaluation. In large organizations, many new programs go into effect in phases; evaluators can use such delays to conduct evaluations. The implementation of training, the delivery of new equipment, or a reorganization seldom take place in all divisions of a company at one time. It might be possible to schedule the locations of the introductions randomly. Then, as the program is begun in different divisions or locations, several groups will be receiving the program at the same time, but in different locations. Ideally, the variables that are expected to change will change as the program is implemented. If similar impacts are observed at different times, history, maturation, and regression toward the mean are not plausible alternate explanations for change. In order for administrators to schedule implementation in ways that permit an evaluation, evaluators must have input into the planning committee and administrators must value information on the effectiveness of their decisions.

Third, when there is a need to document the program's success, experimentation may be desired. This documentation may be for internal or external purposes. In the case of demonstration projects funded by grants, funding agencies want evidence that the program might work elsewhere. A fourth reason why new programs are more likely to be evaluated is because there may be less anxiety over the possibility of failure as compared to a program that became widely accepted before being rigorously evaluated. Regardless of the type of organization, evaluators working with new programs need to encourage a spirit of exploration among the staff because even well-planned innovations often do not work as well as hoped (Dial, 1994; Light and Pillemer, 1984).

When Stakes Are High

When a program is expensive, when large numbers of people are involved, or when the behaviors to be changed are important, controlling all possible threats to internal validity is desirable. Welfare policies, the organization of school districts, safety regulations for automobiles, and efficient provision of medical care are issues that have a great impact on many people. Proponents of programs to relieve the effects of social problems or to reduce the risk of injury or disease advocate many new services or policies. Since no society can carry out all that might be done, selecting the best use of funds is wise. As discussions of policy failure and negative side effects of programs show, resources have been wasted when support was given for policies that had not been shown to be effective and efficient or that may even have had the reverse of the impact desired (see Howard, 1994; Sieber, 1981).

Sometimes when the stakes are high, proponents want to avoid taking the time for experimental evaluation because there are people clearly in need who may benefit even though the intervention has not been evaluated. Evaluators know that sometimes such enthusiasm is misdirected; however, it is important to encourage evaluation without appearing to be a cynical naysayer. One way to carry out an evaluation in such a context is to examine the criteria used to determine need. If there are people whose levels of need fall between those without needs and those clearly in need, perhaps an experiment can be conducted with those people (Crano and Brewer, 1986). This method of forming experimental groups was used to assign first year students with marginal writing skills into either regular English sections or into remedial English sections (Aiken, West, Schwalm, Carroll, and Hsiung, 1998). Neither those clearly ready for college work nor those with definitely deficient skills were used in the experiment.

When There Is Controversy About Program Effectiveness

No reader of this book would be surprised to be told that stakeholders often disagree about whether a program is likely to be effective or even what defines effectiveness. Recall the controversy over workfare programs highlighted in Figure 5.1. In medical care, physicians disagree with each other over whether they should train medical students in the development of good interpersonal skills. Although patients are more satisfied with physicians who show that they have carefully listened to them, some physicians argue that interpersonal skills cannot be taught. Case Study 5 describes a controlled experiment in which medical students were randomly assigned to a training program in communication skills or to a control group.

When Policy Change Is Desired

Program evaluations based on experimental methods are sometimes implemented when there is widespread dissatisfaction with current policies, but no consensus on what changes to make. A desire to change welfare policies accompanied by uncertainty about how alternative policies would affect people led to ambitious evaluations of experimental income maintenance programs (Kershaw, 1972). The need to prevent, or at least to reduce, the rate of school failure of disadvantaged rural and urban children led to a series of

CASE STUDY 5
Teaching Doctors Communication Skills: An Evaluation
with Random Assignment and Pretests

After being trained in medical diagnostic techniques, many physicians come to focus on pathophysiological complaints, failing to recognize the social and psychological aspects of the patient's life. Although the training leads to diagnostic skill, physicians seem to get worse at relating to patients as their training progresses. Evans, Stanley, Coman, and Sinnott (1992) evaluated the effectiveness of a communication skills program that involved lectures and guided practice of skills. A 20-minute diagnostic interview with a patient was videotaped for each of 60 medical students who were then randomly assigned to the communication program or to take additional medical histories of patients for a period of time equivalent to the program. After the lecture portion of the program, both groups were videotaped again. After the workshop practice portion, both groups were videotaped a third time. The two posttest assessments were not available for two program students and three control students.

The video tapes were rated independently by two evaluators who did not know whether the tapes were from program or control medical students or whether the tapes were pretests or posttests. Using a previously developed system of assessing the skills of medical students in taking a medical history, evaluators made 16 ratings ranging from setting the patient at ease through how to close interviews effectively. The program group and the control group were contrasted using analyses of variance, which showed that the communication skills of the trained students were better than the control students after the lectures; their means exceeded the means of the controls on 14 of the 16 variables. After the complete program, the scores of the program students again exceeded those of the control students; the means of the program students exceeded the means of the controls on 15 of the 16 variables. The pretests permitted evaluators to use a more powerful repeated measures design; with groups of only 28 and 27 it was necessary to have as much statistical power as possible. The evaluation showed that medical students can learn to practice improved communication skills.

Comment: The evaluators did not speculate on whether these improvements would carry over to the students' future work when they were not being observed; this would be a question of external validity, not a question of whether one can correctly interpret the differences between program and control groups. Note that the evaluators reported attrition among the members of their groups; the rate of attrition was low.

experiments with Head Start, a preschool program aimed at improving cognitive skills, health, and nutrition (Datta, 1976).

When Demand Is High

An experimental evaluation is clearly justified when more people want a program or a service than can be helped in existing facilities (Dennis, 1994). To increase demand, the program should be publicized as part of the evaluation effort (Cook and Shadish, 1994). Unfortunately, such additional publicity could have an effect on those not selected for the program group. The control group may not act as they would have had they not heard about the program. Additional threats to internal validity created when a control group knows about the program are described near the end of this chapter.

Randomized, controlled experiments became more common in the 1990s, especially in the areas of community health promotion and labor economics (Cook and Shadish, 1994). The U.S. Department of Education has endorsed experimental evaluations (2003). Furthermore, evaluators conducting large scale, policy-relevant national evaluations are doing fewer quasi-experiments and more controlled experiments. Internal evaluators will probably carry out experiments primarily when the situation is especially propitious, as was the case with the team versus primary nursing example above.

GETTING THE MOST OUT OF AN EXPERIMENTAL DESIGN

So far this chapter has emphasized that experiments have some clear advantages over other approaches to outcome evaluation and can be implemented in a variety of situations. Experiments have sometimes been begun without sufficient planning. Once begun, experiments have a way of breaking down without careful nurturing. And, sometimes the analyses of information obtained from an experimental evaluation have been misinterpreted. To complete an experiment successfully, evaluators guard the evaluation's integrity in a number of ways (Dennis, 1994; Rezmovic, Cook, and Dobson, 1981).

Take Precautions Before Data Collection

Work closely with stakeholders. Evaluators who work closely with stakeholders are more likely to be able to preserve an experimental design than those who assume that the agreement by an agency director is all that is needed to guarantee that evaluation procedures will be followed (Dennis, 1994). As mentioned in earlier chapters, keeping staff informed, having staff respond to proposed procedures, providing feedback, and being sensitive to the work of the agency are efforts that will reward evaluators with greater cooperation. In addition to these activities, which apply to all evaluation plans, the attrition rate of an experiment's participants is a major concern. If people decline to participate after learning to which group they have been assigned or after spending time to provide data needed for the evaluation, one loses the equivalence of the groups that had been achieved through random assignment.

Minimize attrition. One way to reduce attrition is to postpone random assignment until the pretest data have been collected and some attrition has already occurred. The advantage of this strategy is that only relatively committed and responsible participants become part of the experiment because they can be expected to provide the information needed for the outcome variables. This approach to reducing attrition will produce an internally valid evaluation; however, the findings can no longer be applied to the entire population the program is designed to meet. In other words, such an evaluation has limited external validity; one cannot know the degree to which its findings can be generalized to an entire population. Riecken and Boruch (1974) criticized an evaluation of welfare reform because when the information requirements were explained to participants, only a small proportion of eligible people agreed to participate. On the other hand, if a treatment is very controversial, a negative evaluation using only the participants who are the most likely to remain in the program may make an important contribution. Fuller and colleagues (1986) studied the effectiveness of disulfiram as a treatment for alcoholism using only those alcoholics thought most likely to benefit—612 of the 6,626 who requested treatment. When the evaluation revealed that disulfiram provided little advantage even to this select experimental group, the value of the new treatment was severely challenged.

Other approaches to minimizing attrition include offering incentives for completing the program and outcome measures on schedule, obtaining the names and addresses of relatives of participants who would know where to locate participants who move before providing data, devoting time and effort to seek out participants, and being persistent in following up missing participants (Cook and Shadish, 1994; Shadish, 2002). Including some variables for which there will be no attrition, such as information from agency records (Dennis, 1994) is a good precaution.

Plan a statistically powerful experiment. Stakeholders, government oversight offices, and foundations expect statistical analyses of evaluations. When planning an experiment, one needs to choose a size of sample that permits appropriate statistical analyses. The choice of sample size need not be a guessing game (Shadish, 2002). First, as mentioned earlier, it is necessary to learn how much improvement would justify the expense of the program. This is a hard decision for program staff and managers. However, once the outcome measures have been selected, evaluators can work with stakeholders asking, "What is the smallest difference in scores between participants and nonparticipants that would be enough for you to believe the program was a success?" To help in this discussion, evaluators might present the findings of other evaluations of similar programs and use the findings of the review prepared by Lipsey and Wilson (1993) to provide a context. After stakeholders agree, one can use the standard deviation of the measure to calculate the minimum effect size they are saying would justify the program. Suppose that it is agreed that a reduction of 10 points on a standard depression checklist would be acceptable. If the checklist has a standard deviation of 22 among moderately depressed people, the effect size that is desired is: 10/22, or 0.46. This value is about equal to the effect size from the typical program studied by Lipsey and Wilson.

With the effect size in hand, one can use power tables (see Cohen, 1987; Lipsey, 1990) to find the sample size needed to have a good chance of finding a statistically significant difference *if* the outcomes match or exceed the minimum effect size said to justify the program. We have not reproduced power tables here, but we want to provide a little perspective on the decision. If a design used includes only posttests on a program group and a non-program group, the analysis will be an independent groups t test. To have a 50 percent chance of detecting an effect size of 0.46, one needs approximately 27 people in each group using a one-tailed test of the null hypothesis (using p of 0.05 or less as the criterion of statistical significance). In other words, if 54 people are available for the experimental evaluation and if the participants change almost a half of a standard deviation on the outcome criterion, sampling error will lead to only half of similar evaluations being statistically significant. Perhaps the stakeholders want a better chance. The sample size needed for an 80 percent chance to detect an effect size of 0.46 is 60 in a group, or 120 people altogether. The biggest challenge in this process is to know what size of effect makes the program worthwhile. Staff members frequently expect bigger differences than are indeed found in evaluations of similar programs.

Keep Track of Randomization While the Experiment Is in Progress

Once the experiment has begun, evaluators remain in close contact with the agency sponsoring the program to check that the randomization procedure is being carried out and that the program is implemented as planned. Furthermore, there are additional threats to internal validity that can develop after an experiment has begun.

Diffusion or imitation of the program can occur when people in control groups learn about the program and, in effect, administer it to themselves. In an evaluation of Students Against Drunk Driving (SADD), students at one of the schools included in the non-SADD control group spontaneously formed a SADD chapter during the course of the two-year evaluation (Klitzner, Gruenewald, Bamberger, and Rossiter, 1994).

Attempts to compensate the control group occur when staff seek to give special services to the people in the control group in order to make up for their not receiving the program. The efforts by nurses to give premature infants pure oxygen even though they were assigned to the regular air group were mentioned above (Silverman, 1977). In other evaluations, staff have provided additional attention to control groups. Attempts to compensate the controls have the effect of reducing the differences between treatment and control groups—thus making the program look less effective; in an extreme situation, compensation of controls could discredit a program that would have proved worthwhile if the experimental evaluation had not been tampered with.

Some control groups have felt a *rivalry with experimental groups*. Such a rivalry was mentioned in the evaluation of the employee incentive plan described in Case Study 3.

Resentful demoralization can occur when controls come to believe that the members of the experimental group have an advantage over them and, as a result, the people in the control group reduce the effort they might have expended had they not become aware of the program. This can easily occur when a job training program is offered to some unemployed people. People without the program could feel that in a tight job market those with the program experience will get the available jobs; consequently, controls may believe that it is not worth the effort to look for work. When a control group feels demoralized, its members may expend little effort to resolve their own problems; this reaction would contribute to making the program seem more effective than it really is.

Another issue of concern to evaluators trying to maintain an experiment is the possibility of an unplanned event occurring exclusively to either the control or treatment group that affects outcomes. Cook and Campbell (1979) call these events *local history*. For example, in an evaluation of group therapy particularly good interpersonal chemistry may make a group especially successful regardless of the approach to group therapy being evaluated. In contrast, some unique interpersonal conflicts among group members might make the same therapy seem ineffective or even destructive. The way to minimize the effect of local history is to provide the program and assess its effectiveness in many small groups (or even to individuals if appropriate), not just to one or two large groups. If small groups are isolated from each other, the possibility of imitation of the program, compensation for the controls, rivalry with the program group, and resentful demoralization affecting the evaluation may well be reduced as well.

A review of these threats reveals a general concern of evaluators who are studying outcomes. Quantified outcome data do not reveal very much about the day-to-day functioning of the program. Thus, outcome evaluations are most effective when they are supplemented by program monitoring (as described in Chapter 7) to estimate the degree to which the program has been implemented. Furthermore, evaluators often include observations of the program in order to develop an understanding of the quality of the interaction between staff and participants, the degree to which the program fits the needs of the participants, and how the program fits into the overall organization sponsoring the program or the community in which the program is offered. Such issues are addressed by using qualitative methods in conjunction with quantitative outcome evaluation methods.

Analyze the Data Reflectively

There is a great deal of misunderstanding about statistical hypothesis testing (see Nickerson, 2000). Many undergraduate and some graduate students pass their statistics courses believing that when a t test (or other test of statistical significance) is not statistically significant, they have evidence that the groups are the same or at least any differences between them are so small as to be trivial. As shown above if sample sizes are small there is a very good chance that an effective program will not lead to a statistically significant result. When evaluation designs with little statistical power are planned and analyzed, it is wrong to conclude that there has been program failure. Regardless of whether the null can be rejected or not, the best statistical information to report is the 90 percent confidence interval. We suggest the 90 percent rather than the 95 percent confidence interval because in program evaluation we usually hypothesize that the participants will be better off than the non-program group. Such a hypothesis leads to a one-tailed test. Let's imagine that the depression checklist was used with only 24 people in each group and the evaluation found a difference between the means of the two groups of 9.4 points. If the pooled standard deviation had been 22, the 90 percent confidence interval would be

$$(M_t - M_c) \pm t \times \text{ (standard error of a difference}$$
$$\text{between two means) } =$$
$$(M_t - M_c) \pm t \times (S_{pooled}) \times \sqrt{(1/n_t + 1/n_c)} =$$
$$9.4 \pm 1.68 \times 22\sqrt{(2/24)} = 9.4 \pm 10.67 =$$
$$-1.37 \text{ to } 20.07$$

Perhaps it would help to rewrite the confidence interval graphically:

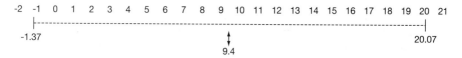

What does this confidence interval tell us? It tells us that the difference is not statistically significant because the low end of the confidence interval extends below 0.0. It does *not* tell us that the program failed to make an improvement; there is no more reason to believe that the true difference is less than 0.0 than to believe that the true difference is more than 18.7 (that is, 20.07 minus 1.37) points. What can an evaluator say? When faced with a finding that is not statistically significant, evaluators should say this:

1. A difference of 9.4 points was found; this difference is less than the 10.0 points that was deemed the minimum to justify the expense of the program.
2. The *t* was not statistically significant; this will disappoint our funding agency.
3. The confidence interval indicates that with our small samples, the difference between the groups could be trivial or it could far exceed the minimum needed to justify the service.
4. An effect size of 0.43 (that is, $g = 9.4/22$) was found; this effect size is not very much smaller than the minimum believed necessary.

In summary, we must remain cautious. The evaluation showed there is a chance that this program is sufficiently effective; however, the samples were small and the difference found was not as large as needed to provide a good chance to detect even the minimum difference needed. We should continue to monitor this program.

These points may sound like weasel words, but they are accurate statistically. And, they do not label a program as ineffective when there is a greater than 50 percent chance of a Type II statistical error (see Abelson, 1995; E. J. Posavac, 1998). If an evaluator were told, "We wanted 10 points, but we also don't want to drop a program that is effective unless we are really sure that it is not," given these results, we would recommend continuing the program, but also continuing the evaluation.

Summary and Preview

Whenever program evaluations are designed to learn whether or not a human service program caused any change in the people served, an experimental evaluation design should be considered. It should not, however, be forced on a program or facility that does not support the requirements of experimental research. When completed, program evaluations based on experimental research designs are easier to interpret and to analyze than are the less well controlled evaluations described in Chapter 10. However, even the most carefully designed evaluations are not interpretable if they are not carried out as planned. Evaluators recognize that many human service professionals do not fully understand the advantages of the experimental approach and could in all innocence reduce the validity of an experimental evaluation by providing extra care for the control group. As with all forms of evaluation, someone needs to monitor the way people are assigned to groups, how the data are collected, and how the program is implemented.

Few program outcomes are worthwhile regardless of costs, and many socially desirable objectives can be approached in more than one way. Consequently, costs are frequently related to program outcomes using cost-benefit and cost-effectiveness procedures, which are described in Chapter 12.

Study Questions

1. List the advantages and disadvantages of experimental and quasi-experimental designs in program evaluation. You might use parallel columns so that when you are finished, you have a concise way to compare these two approaches. This effort could help you on a test.

2. Using language that can be understood by someone without training in statistics and research methods, explain the advantages of experimentation, including the random assignment to groups. Imagine you are addressing elementary school teachers, nurses, or police officers. The adequacy of your answer depends both on technical accuracy and audience accessibility.

3. Suppose that after an experiment has been described (as in question 2), someone asks: "If the new program is worth the time and effort to study it, someone must think it is worthwhile. And if the staff believes that the new program is good, how can you justify not just letting everyone benefit from the program? Having a control group is unjust. And it takes too much time." How would you respond?

4. Austin decided to carry out a program evaluation of a drug rehabilitation program for women on probation using an experimental design. He asked probation officers to randomly assign women from their caseload to the program or to a control group. The program lasted 15 weeks with three meetings per week. After the program was over, the participants were referred to a less intense follow-up program. Austin prepared rating forms for the probation officers to use at the end of the 15-week program to rate the success of the women for whom they were responsible. They were to use the forms to rate the degree to which the program participants and the control women were following a drug-free life, developing a stable lifestyle, and avoiding further legal problems. Austin planned to use these ratings as his outcome variables to compare the condition of those in the program with those in the control group. Austin followed some procedures that were almost guaranteed to make his findings uninterpretable. List problems with his procedure and what he might have done differently to produce a more credible evaluation.

5. Marjorie was a new evaluator in a clinic setting. She was not yet clear on her role. She learned that several short courses on pregnancy and baby care were offered to expectant mothers. Only 40 percent of eligible mothers attended. Because these programs had never been evaluated, Marjorie proposed an evaluation to the Clinic Medical Director. Marjorie suggested that those women indicating interest in the courses be randomly assigned to the courses or some alternative such as a workshop on family budgeting. She proposed using a checklist of problems that the new mothers experienced after their babies were born as an outcome assessment. If the courses are valuable, she said that those who completed the courses should experience fewer problems.

There are many problems with this proposal. First, list the ethical and design problems. Second, suggest something in connection with these classes that Marjorie might evaluate.

Additional Resource

SHADISH, W. R., COOK, T. D., AND CAMPBELL, D. T. 2002. *Experimental and quasi-experimental design for generalized causal inference.* Boston: Houghton Mifflin.

This is the same resource recommended for the previous chapter. Chapters 8, 9, and 10 are devoted to randomized experiments. Chapters 11, 12, and 13 concern the central issue for evaluators who find themselves called on to show whether a program shown to be effective can be applied in settings other than the one in which the evaluation was carried out.

Analyses of Costs and Outcomes

Programs have not been adequately evaluated if costs have not been considered. Even an evaluation controlling for all the threats to internal validity and finding statistically and substantively significant improvements in program participants can be a negative evaluation if the costs necessary to achieve those improvements exceed what society is willing to pay or exceed the costs of alternative approaches that can resolve the same problems. Recommendations for program development that are not accompanied by cost estimates are, according to Demone and Harshbarger (1973), simply statements of philosophy and should not be taken seriously. Being able to relate program outcomes to costs is becoming increasingly important to evaluators who want their findings to be used in agency decisions. Concerns over the efficiency of human services have become very widespread (Fals-Stewart, Klostermann, and Yates, 2005; Hatry, Newcomer, and Wholey, 1994). Unfortunately, service providers and evaluators seldom have training in cost accounting, and those who work in nonprofit organizations are remarkably naive about the costs of providing services (see King, 1994; Yates, 1994). If you eavesdrop on almost any discussion about higher education budgets among college faculty members, you will discover that many faculty members do not know how colleges fund their activities.

Cost analyses, however, are not a novel among business managers. The local hardware store manager counts receipts every evening and periodically records costs. By converting transactions into dollars, managers can compare costs (salaries, inventory, and buildings) with cash receipts. A comparison of these figures tells managers whether they are making or losing money. Of course, bookkeeping is not that simple; however, the principle is straightforward and the unit of analysis, dollars, is widely accepted. In human service settings the principles are less clear, and the benefits are usually hard to convert into dollars.

Cost projections and program objectives are used in choosing among possible programs before anything is implemented. Program planners seek to propose services that will justify the investment of funds. After a program has been offered, evaluators assess the quality of the program's implementation and impact relating that information to the funds expended using the methods described in this chapter.

COST ANALYSES AND BUDGETS

Placing costs into categories helps evaluators recognize what is needed to support a program.

Types of Costs

Variable versus fixed costs. There are costs that must be borne simply to open an agency's doors to the first client. If car mechanics are to be trained, the cost of facilities and tools must be covered before even one person enrolls. Such costs will be the same whether one or twenty people are trained. On the other hand, there are costs that vary depending on the level of program activity. The costs of supplies and maintenance will increase with additional students. Universities have high fixed costs due to large physical plants and tenured faculties. Adding a few more undergraduates adds very little to variable costs; even a 5 or 10 percent increase in enrollment does not increase the university's expenses very much due to the fixed costs. On the other hand, falling enrollments and large fixed costs are very hard on university budgets.

Incremental versus sunk costs. Incremental costs are those that must be covered day by day in order for a program to provide a service—staff salaries or repairs, for example. Sunk costs are those that have been expended already. The difference between the original cost of a car and its current value is a sunk cost. The reason to make this distinction lies in the difficulty that people have in understanding that sunk costs should not determine future behavior; incremental costs should. Two years after the U.S. Postal Service installed a billion-dollar package sorting system, the GAO recommended that the system be scrapped (*Chicago Tribune*, 1990). The costs of maintaining it—incremental costs—were more expensive than the alternate ways of sorting packages. The original cost of the equipment was simply irrelevant to the decision about the future because incremental costs were going to exceed the benefits that would be obtained by continuing to use the system. People find it very difficult to "cut their losses" but in some circumstances the losses will simply continue in the future. Choosing to abandon a failed policy or expensive, but inadequate, equipment are often difficult decisions to make, even when not doing so would mean that losses will continue to increase as time goes by (Brockner et al., 1984).

Recurring versus nonrecurring costs. As the name suggests, recurring costs are those that are due at regular intervals, such as salaries, rents, and utilities. Equipment or buildings that are expected to last a number of years before wearing out are nonrecurring costs.

Hidden versus obvious costs. This distinction is presented just to highlight the point that some costs are easily recognized, but others easy to overlook, especially when service is expanded. For example, a plan for a building addition always includes the cost of the new structure. But there have been times when planners forgot to consider furniture or custodial expenses. When a program expands its staff, not only must additional salaries be added to the budget, but fringe benefits and liability insurance costs must be taken into account as well.

Direct versus indirect costs. Another way to divide costs is to consider those that are associated with providing services and those that support the agency that makes it possible to provide services. The salary and fringe benefits of a social worker make up the direct cost of providing service to a specific client. However, in order to provide that service, the agency must be managed, receptionists must make appointments, telephones must be available, and buildings must be cleaned. All of these expenses (and more) are incurred if the agency is to remain operational. Often indirect costs are called *overhead*. When estimating the costs of providing a program, planners must consider both direct and indirect costs.

Opportunity costs. A mistake often made by people considering adopting a program is to ignore the necessity of making choices among alternative uses of funds and effort. By adopting program A, it is impossible to adopt a different one. What cannot be done is called an *opportunity cost*—a lost opportunity, if you will. The most costly factor in attending college is not the tuition—the most costly factor is the income students cannot earn while attending college. As mentioned earlier, most college graduates more than make up for the cost of tuition and the foregone wages in time. However, in other settings the selection of one program makes it impossible for an agency to serve another purpose. There are usually many promising activities that cannot be supported within a budget even though all of them are needed and contribute to meeting the mission of the agency. Whenever money is spent to relieve one need, it cannot be used to relieve some other need, an opportunity cost. In debates about support for programs, many proponents of particular activities tend to ignore the programs that cannot be supported if the programs being recommended are supported.

An Example Budget

Figure 12.1 gives the budget of a small Special Opportunity Program for underprepared college students. The proposal writers assumed that a small furnished office could be found in an existing building. The writers did not include maintenance, custodial services, or insurance costs because these would be the same regardless of what program the university decided to support and house in the space. University administrators would have those estimates if needed. The budget covers the particular costs that would be associated with this program. University administrators would decide whether this program helps fulfill the mission of the university better than some other activity that might be housed in that space.

The Necessity of Examining Costs

Public and private agencies cannot ignore costs. Since funds are limited, choices are always being made. A rural Arkansas county instituted services for elderly residents to improve the quality of their lives and to provide services

FIGURE 12.1 Proposed first year budget for a Special Opportunity Program to serve 35 college students.

Salaries (Employees)	
Director (half-time)	$30,000
Secretary-Office Manager (half-time)	$16,000
Fringe benefits (17.5% of employee salaries)	$ 8,050
Student Assistance Stipends	
3 Advanced Tutors (graduate student teaching assistants)	$34,500
3 Basic Tutors (work-study undergraduate students)	$ 3,300
(Assumes University contribution of 45%; state contribution of 55%)	
Total Compensation	$91,850
Office Support	
Supplies	$ 3,000
Computer and Printer	$ 3,000
File cabinets	$ 900
Copying and Printing	$ 1,700
Phone	$ 1,500
Total Office Support	$10,100
Program Total	$101,950

that would postpone admissions to nursing homes (Schneider, Chapman, and Voth, 1985). The evaluators discovered that although most elderly residents thought that having the services was a good idea, only 12 percent came to the center once or more often per week. Depending on the accounting assumptions adopted, the cost to run the center *per user* per year was 58 to 71 percent of the cost of educating one school child for nine months. While those who used the services benefitted, this center seemed to cost more than the value of the services provided.

Although the Arkansas senior center cost analysis was part of an evaluation of an operational program, planners also try to project costs of policies and programs before implementation. Unfortunately, many guesses are grossly in error. Sometimes the program does not attract as many users as guessed and sometimes far more people seek a service. In 1973, Congress passed a bill to pay for kidney dialysis through Medicare for people suffering kidney failure and unable to obtain a kidney transplant. When the bill was approved, the costs were estimated to be in the low millions. However, by 1978 the costs were $1 billion, which was half of the entire budget for the National Institute of Health. The federal government paid $2.4 billion for dialysis in 1987 (Colburn, 1987), more than $6 billion in 1992 (Dor, Held, and Pauly, 1992), $9.74 billion in 1995 (Schreuder, 1998). The total cost to Medicare for kidney failure is expected to reach $28 billion in 2010 (*Baseline Report*, 2001). These services extend the lives of people. We are not suggesting that this is a bad way to spend federal funds; our point is simply this—it is hard to provide an accurate estimate of future costs for a program. These levels of costs were not expected and made it impossible to deal with other pressing health concerns. Not meeting other needs is an opportunity cost that raises important ethical questions (see Moskop, 1987).

COMPARING OUTCOMES TO COSTS

Determining costs is one part of the job—although not always easy, it is the easier part. The more complex task is estimating the benefits of a program. Benefits occur when goals are achieved. Surgeons prevent premature deaths when they remove diseased appendixes. Because their patients lead productive lives afterward, there are considerable benefits to this and many surgical procedures. A commission to reduce the number of government forms was reported to have saved 350 times as much money as the cost of the commission (Abelson, 1977). Increased earnings is a benefit of college completion (Gross and Scott, 1990). It was estimated that benefits accrue to the friends and family members of participants in drug use prevention programs (Caulkins, Rydell, Everingham, Chiesa, and Bushway, 1999). French (2000) found favorable returns for alcoholism treatment services.

Another way to compare costs and benefits is by first calculating how much money one would have in the bank if the cost of the program were saved rather than spent on the program. Imagine the amount available if a student saved the money that could have been earned instead of attending college (less living expenses) plus the cost of tuition, books, and fees. Assume that this money is invested. Using the research literature on the wages of different occupations, an economist can contrast the average lifetime wages of college graduates with those of workers who completed high school only. As noted above, a person who began working immediately after high school would have a sizable account by the time a college graduate began a full-time job; however, the college graduate would be earning more per year. Would the employed high school graduate remain ahead? It is possible (using techniques not covered in this book) to calculate the rate of interest that the high school graduate would need to get on the amount saved (by not attending college) so that the investment would equal the benefit of attending college. It turned out that over a 30-year career a high school graduate would need to find a source giving 34 percent per year on the investment in order for it to make financial sense to go to work right after high school in the 1970s (Sussna and Heinemann, 1972). Since few investments can match that rate of growth, such analyses mean that financial benefits of college graduation exceed its costs. Similar analyses show different percentages, but lead to the same conclusion—college is worth more than the cost (Sanchez and Laanan, 1997; for a similar European-based study, see Hartog, 1999). However, it might not be worth the *extra* cost to attend to an elite university rather than a good one (Kahn, 2000).

The Essence of Cost–Benefit Analysis

An evaluation of a helicopter police patrol conducted by Schnelle et al. (1978) illustrates the essence of cost–benefit analyses. In the neighborhood studied, most burglaries occurred in daylight hours and were perpetrated by local youths. Because a police officer in a helicopter can repeatedly observe large areas, it was thought that an airborne patrol might prevent crime. Schnelle Kirchner, Uselton, and McNees (1977) showed that a helicopter patrol reduced neighborhood crime. The burglary rate during the 9 a.m. to 5 p.m. shift was the variable of interest. There was a mean of 1.02 burglaries per day committed during the periods of regular automobile patrol, whereas there were only 0.33 burglaries per day when the helicopter patrol supplemented the ground patrols; however, such a patrol raised costs. It is reasonable to ask if the reduced number of burglaries justified the extra costs.

Because the helicopter, pilot, and hanger were already part of the police department, these costs were not considered. Presumably the helicopter would be redeployed in an emergency. Note that while the program did make use of an otherwise wasted resource, the cost–benefit analysis would have been greatly changed if the police department had wanted the helicopter

FIGURE 12.2 The calculation of the benefit-to-cost ratio of the helicopter patrol.

	Total	Per Day
Cost of the program (24 days)	$3,032	$126
Cost of the burglaries during no-helicopter patrol periods (55 days)	$27,171	$494
Cost of burglaries during helicopter patrol periods (24 days)*	$3,853	$161
Benefits (for 24-day program)	$8,004	$333
Benefit/cost ratio	————	$333/$126 = 2.6

*The burglary cost figures were not supplied by Schnelle et al. (1978); however, these costs could be approximated from their report.
Note: These costs and benefits are not corrected for inflation because a ratio is taken; changes would cancel out leaving the ratio unchanged.

elsewhere and the stakeholders wanted to maintain this helicopter patrol. The costs of additional fuel and maintenance were included. These costs were compared to the benefits defined as the value of the goods not stolen. Figure 12.2 summarizes the calculation of the benefit-to-cost ratio. The cost of the helicopter was easy to calculate. The cost of the burglaries was estimated from insurance company material. The fact that the benefit-to-cost ratio was 2.6 indicates that the program was worthwhile: The value of the goods not stolen exceeded the cost of the patrol.

Several costs and benefits were not considered. Residents' feelings of security may have increased (a benefit), but irritation at the noise may also have increased (a cost) and feelings of privacy may have decreased (another cost). Fewer burglaries meant that there were savings in police and court costs, and police officers may have been able to devote more time to other crime-preventive and investigative work (more benefits). Ignoring these benefits and costs illustrates an important principle for evaluators. Once the essential questions can be answered, evaluators do not seek additional information because measuring or estimating the values of more variables would unnecessarily make the evaluation more costly for the stakeholders. For Schnelle et al. (1978) the essential question could be answered using costs and benefits that were relatively easy to estimate. Therefore, they did not attempt the very difficult task of pricing additional benefits and costs. Since the benefit-to-cost ratio was so large, they effectively showed that the helicopter patrol paid for itself. Such a conclusion is often sufficient for evaluators who are not interested in learning the "real" benefit-to-cost ratio; an evaluator is satisfied with enough information to support a practical decision. If there were some alternative activity for which the helicopter could have been used, a more complete analysis of costs and benefits would have been required.

Schnelle et al. were able to ignore costs and benefits that would have been very difficult to estimate; however, such estimates must be used in many cost–benefit analyses. Rajkumar and French (1997) examined efforts to estimate the intangible costs (e.g. increased pain, suffering, fear) of the crimes committed by people using drugs. Because drug use prevention programs reduce criminal activity, such reductions should be included in the outcomes of drug use interventions. Doing so would show that drug use prevention programs produce benefits that clearly exceed the programs' costs. The Army Corps of Engineers has routinely used the estimated recreational value of water projects to help justify construction costs. To calculate the benefit-to-cost ratio of a safety program that reduces on-the-job injuries, it is necessary to estimate the dollar value of the extended working lives of employees. If a job-training program permits some participants to leave welfare, benefits may be estimated from wages earned. But what is the dollar value of better mental health? Of reduced anxiety among cancer patients? Of a 5 percent gain on a standardized reading achievement test for sixth graders? Of increased art and music appreciation? Clearly these outcomes are valued, but how much they are worth is subject to disagreement.

Military planning provides an even more striking example of the limitations of cost–benefit analysis. How are the benefits of a bomb calculated? Bombs destroy. Benefits, if there are any, accrue if a war is won or averted. However, the net outcome of a war is negative, not positive, even for the victor. Instead of calculating benefit-to-cost ratios, one can ask how effective the bomb is in fulfilling its purpose. Cost-effectiveness analysis was developed to use in situations in which the dollar values of benefits are very difficult to quantify and, yet, a choice among alternatives must be made.

The Essence of Cost-Effectiveness Analysis

A bomb could be rated in terms of the size of the hole it makes in cubic yards divided by the cost of the bomb. There is no way to decide if the cubic yards per dollar figure is good or bad until it is compared to a cubic yards-to-dollar ratio of a second bomb. By comparing the two ratios, military planners can choose the bomb with the bigger bang per buck. This same approach can be utilized in human service agencies whenever improvement can be quantified. If two or more programs effect an improvement of the same behavior or reduce the frequency of the same problem, the effectiveness per dollar can be found for each program, thus permitting the more cost-effective program to be identified. Suppose that several programs designed to help alcoholics to abstain from the consumption of alcohol were to be evaluated. Effectiveness could be measured by the percentage of participants abstaining for 12 months. For each program the effectiveness to cost formula would be:

Effectiveness to cost ratio = (percent abstaining)/cost

The program with the highest ratio is the most cost effective. To avoid needing to present many decimal places, one could give cost in thousands of dollars rather than in dollars.[1]

Cost-effectiveness analyses are important in measuring the productivity of businesses. Day (1981) described how a plant in Ohio routinely calculated three indexes to help in monitoring its production of titanium. First, pounds of titanium produced were divided by the number of employees; second, pounds of titanium were divided by the total assets of the plant; and, third, since energy use is high in producing titanium, pounds of titanium were divided by the BTUs needed in production. The second index is the traditional measure of cost-effectiveness—output divided by costs; however, the other two help managers identify the aspect of the plant's operation that was responsible for good or poor efficiency. Comparisons were made to past efficiency levels to detect problems and to trace the impact of new procedures or better equipment. This example is far afield from what readers of this text expect to be asked to do, but the example is used because it illustrates how evaluators can adapt cost-effectiveness analyses to the needs, measures of outcome, and costs of the agency in which they are working.

Peterson (1986) described three approaches to using cost-effectiveness analyses in planning and managing an agency. First, if a *set amount of money* is made available to alleviate a need, an analysis can be done to learn which way of spending the funds is expected to achieve the best outcome for the funds available. For example, suppose the goal was to reduce highway fatalities. This goal could be met by spending the specified funds on more police patrols, on an educational program to increase seat belt use, or on construction to eliminate some dangerous turns on rural highways. The approach that promised the best return would be chosen. Second, the costs of achieving *a specified outcome* can be compared for various possible approaches to a problem. A school district wishing to raise average daily attendance rates from 87 to 92 percent could consider developing a lottery for which students get one ticket for each week of perfect attendance, initiating an automated telephone system informing parents when their child is absent, or redesigning the vocational curriculum. Third, if one is required to use *a specified type of program* to address a problem, the cost-effectiveness of different intensities of single type of program might be found. A city council might, for example, ask to what degree coronary deaths would be reduced by spending 2, 4, or 6 million dollars on paramedics and intensive care ambulances.

---

[1] Sometimes the reciprocal is used, that is, cost divided by effectiveness. In that case, the most cost-effective program is the one with lowest ratio. It makes no difference how the ratio is calculated; it is important to know which version was used.

When Outcomes Cannot Be Put into the Same Units

In the earlier examples, the outcomes of different programs could be placed into the same units—for example, the number of highway of deaths expected to be prevented could be compared for several programs. However, it is not unusual for planners to be asked to choose among programs designed to achieve different objectives, none of which is easy to put into dollars. How is Congress supposed to compare the outcomes of funds supporting space research with outcomes of Medicare services? A college dean cannot agree to support every proposal from faculty members, some of whom want more chemistry faculty, others want a bigger art gallery, yet others think that an American Studies Institute should be funded. And the coach claims that with two more basketball scholarships, the college will become very competitive in women's basketball. Although the cost of these proposals can be estimated, their likely benefits to the college cannot be converted into the same units. Cost-utility analysis was developed to aid in making such choices (Levin and McEwan, 2001). In brief, cost-utility analyses require stakeholders to examine and compare the perceived desired outcomes (the subjective utilities) with the costs of these very different proposals. The hypothetical Special Opportunity Program, whose budget was given in Figure 12.1, would be compared to other proposals in subjective terms, not in terms of quantified effectiveness or the dollar values of benefits.

SOME DETAILS OF COST ANALYSES

There are a number of detailed issues to examine when conducting an analysis of costs. Although these points are subordinate to the major conceptual ideas presented above, they can affect the impressions people receive from cost–benefit and cost-effectiveness analysis. There are no standard ways of dealing with these issues.

Units of Analysis Must Reflect the Purpose of the Program

The units of analysis used should be compatible with the goals of the programs compared. Binner (1977, 1991) illustrated how use of two different units can make quite a difference in a cost analysis of inpatient psychiatric care. The most obvious approach might be to calculate the cost per day. If 100 patients are living in a facility and the cost for the year is $7,300,000, then the cost per patient per day would be $200. Is dollars per patient per day a reasonable unit? That question can only be answered in the light of the objectives for institutionalizing a person. If the goal is to aid patients to function in society outside of the institution, cost per patient per day is a misleading unit. Using this unit would encourage the managers and tempt the funders to seek a lower cost per day so that more people could be served. Seeking to house people for the lowest possible cost has been termed warehousing people. On the other hand, if the goal really is to rehabilitate people so that they come to live independently in society, a better unit would be cost per discharged, rehabilitated patient.

Note how the unit chosen affects the conclusion drawn from a cost-effectiveness analysis in the following example. Binner (1977) discussed a state hospital that could house and feed a patient in 1901 for $2.38 per day (in 1974 dollars!). The cost per discharged patient in 1901 was $10,309. Comparing this hospital to 1974 averages, Binner found evidence for a 1300 percent increase as well as evidence for a 50 percent decrease in costs. Binner showed how both figures were true. In 1974 the average cost per patient-day was $30.86 (the 1300 percent increase), but the average cost per alive discharged patient was $5,513 (the 50 percent decrease). Should state legislators have been alarmed over the increase or encouraged by the decrease? If the goal of treatment was to restore patients to the community, legislators should have been encouraged by the decrease. The difference in these figures reflects the increased concern over providing counseling, restoring community contacts, and prescribing medications. Developing these services raises the cost per day, but lowers the cost per discharged patient; patients were more likely to return to the community in 1974 than they were in 1901.

Kane and Kane (1978) made the same point as Binner when they urged that nursing homes for elderly people be evaluated on the basis of the health and mental status of residents. Using costs per resident per day to evaluate the efficiency of nursing homes encourages the erosion of treatment standards and results in limited privacy, superficial medical care, recreational opportunities centered on TV viewing, and artless food preparation.

When thinking about the unit of analysis, you should remember that the impact of a program is not necessarily linear. It would probably be harder for a person to develop new job skills leading to an income increase from $0 (i.e., unemployable) to $15,000 than to improve from $4,000 to $19,000, even though these are numerically identical improvements. Helping an unemployed person to hold a job may require teaching about a job behavior as well as teaching specific job skills and, consequently, would be harder than helping an employed person to improve skills in order to qualify for a better job.

Future Costs and Benefits Are Estimated

A sophisticated cost analysis includes benefits expected to occur in the future. Successful rehabilitation for drug addicts is expected to mean that the individual will become productive and not require additional services in future years (Rajkumar and French, 1997). Improvements in work skills, psychological adjustment, and physical health may well have benefits for the children of people served. The worth of these long-term benefits is, not surprisingly, hard to estimate. Viewing the human service recipient as a member of a family and a community system is a way to become sensitive to possible benefits as a consequence of the program participant making some behavioral change as a direct result of the program. Successful drug rehabilitation should lead to less crime (Gerstein, Johnson, Harwood, Fountain, Suter, and Malloy, 1994) because addicts frequently support their addictions through theft. If crime is reduced, commercial activity may increase since business owners will be more inclined to venture into the locations previously at the mercy of addicts. Also, a lower crime rate would mean that the community could lower the amounts spent on detection, prosecution, and punishment of criminals.

Noneconomists face problems in comparing programs requiring funds and providing benefits at different times in the lives of programs. The funds needed and the benefits available in the future are worth less than the same amount of money and benefits available now. This principle makes sense when you ask yourself whether you would prefer $100 now or in 12 months. Ignoring for the moment our normal preference for instant gratification, it makes economic sense to have the money now because if it were put into a savings account it would be worth more than $100 in 12 months. This observation helps to explain why state lottery prizes spread out over 20 years are not worth the value that is claimed. The present value of the twentieth $50,000 payment of a million-dollar prize is only $10,730 when the prize is announced because that sum invested in an account paying 8 percent per year would be worth $50,000 after 20 years.

Calculating the current value of future benefits is called discounting and can get tricky. The point to remember is that the cost of programs should include what could be obtained by an alternate use of resources. For example, is it worth investing $100 now in order to guarantee receiving a benefit of $200 10 years from now? The answer depends largely on the assumed rate of return for an alternative use of the $100. The amount one could obtain from this alternative use is the opportunity cost. If the rate of return for the alternative use were 3 percent, it would be worth investing the $100 in the program (not in the bank) and waiting for the $200 because $100 invested at 3 percent would be worth only $131 in 10 years; the opportunity cost is less than the benefit. On the other hand, if the rate of return were 8 percent or more, the program would not be worth supporting because an 8 percent return would yield $216 in 10 years; the opportunity cost would exceed the benefit.

In order to handle the possibility of getting different results simply because different assumptions were used, a sensitivity analysis is performed by repeating the analysis with a variety of plausible assumptions (Levin and McEwan, 2001). If the program plan is promising under a range of assumptions, even some that do not favor the program, we can have more confidence in the findings. If different assumptions result in different conclusions, then even greater care must be devoted to the planning process. Critics of the cost–benefit analyses provided by the proponents of large-scale water resource projects have asserted that the rates of interest assumed were unrealistically low (for example, Hanke and Walker, 1974). If low rates are assumed, smaller future benefits from the project seem more desirable than if higher rates of return are assumed; the plans seem to be failing a sensitivity analysis. It is probably obvious that fluctuating inflation rates greatly complicate these analyses.

Who Pays the Costs and Who Reaps the Benefits?

The discussion up to this point has been phrased in terms of whether one should devote resources now to reap a benefit later, implying that the one who bears the costs is also the one who reaps the benefit. However, most programs are sponsored and paid for by people who do not obtain the benefits. The costs of primary education are borne by a community, whereas only the children (and their parents) and the teachers benefit. The other residents of the community at best benefit indirectly; if a community gains a reputation for having good schools that attract and hold residents, the values of homes remain high and good employees are not likely to move away. A tax increase referendum is more likely to pass if residents believe that they benefit at least indirectly by having good schools in their community. Public transportation systems are often criticized by people who are required to support them through taxes but who do not use buses and rapid transit trains.

Yates (1999) points out that the perspective taken will affect the conclusions of cost–benefit analyses. If governmental funds cover program costs, programs that seem worth the cost to individuals may not seem worthwhile from a societal perspective. This point is mentioned in the comment to Case Study 6. Another example of the contrast between the stakeholders who pay versus those who benefit from a policy is seen in the rapid development of outpatient surgery practices. Hospitals came under intense pressure from insurance companies and federal and state governments to lower costs or at least to limit increases. One response to this pressure was to develop outpatient surgical centers. Patients needing minor surgery do not stay in the hospital overnight as they would have 10 or 20 years ago. The cost of providing outpatient surgery is markedly less than surgery and a hospital stay. Family members are expected to take care of the patient after surgery (a cost) but the patient does not benefit from this change in procedure. The savings gained through outpatient surgery go to Medicare, Medicaid, and insurers (Evans and Robinson, 1980). Although it was hoped that society in general would pay lower costs for medical insurance or taxes when the costs of surgery were minimized, evidence suggested that surgeons raised their fees for surgery done outside of hospitals (Millenson, 1987). This negative side effect was not an outcome that planners had in mind when outpatient surgery clinics were encouraged. Do note, however, that outpatient treatment is preferred by patients and that being an outpatient reduces the chances of infections, which is an additional benefit to patients.

CASE STUDY 6
The Value of Providing Smoking Cessation Clinics for Employees on Company Time

An Ohio hospital offered a smoking cessation clinic during working hours; 70 of its employee smokers participated. Six months later 11 program participants reported that they had quit smoking. Weiss, Jurs, Lesage, and Iverson (1984) examined the cost to the hospital to provide the program and the projected benefits to the hospital.

The cost factor was based on the cost of the program and the salaries paid to employees while they attended. Depending on the salary of the employee participants, program costs varied from $1,504 to $2,930 for a class of 20 employees, or from $75 to $147 per employee.

Projected benefits to the hospital were based on lower costs for health and life insurance and lowered absenteeism. Based on published research, these projections were assumed to apply to the hospital sponsoring the program.

The more years an employee was expected to remain with the hospital after quitting, the more savings the hospital would experience. Using employment records, the evaluators projected the mean expected years of future employment at the hospital for male and female employees of various ages and thus calculated the expected savings to the hospital if a person of that age quit smoking.

At this point the evaluators had the cost of the program to the hospital and the projected savings for a quitter, with separate values for four ages for both men and women. By using different research databases, two discount rates, and four ages, the evaluators showed that the benefit to the hospital if one male employee quit smoking ranged from $100 for a 55-year-old to $380 for a 25-year-old.

The evaluators showed that even if just two of the eleven people who said they quit did not relapse, the program would return more to the hospital than the program cost. If just one did not relapse, the program would still have a benefit-to-cost ratio greater than 1.0 as long as the employee who quit was approximately 50 or younger. Under some assumptions, even with older employees the program was projected to return more than it cost. For all ages if only two quit, the program was clearly worth offering. Note that two successes among 70 would be a quite conservative success rate of 2.8 percent; consequently, it seemed safe to believe that offering the program benefitted the hospital.

Comment: It is important to note for whom this evaluation was done—the hospital that employed the participants of the program. The greater the number of employees who quit smoking, the more the hospital would save through reduced insurance costs and increased employee productivity. Some people (well, at least many students taught by the first author) have difficulty recognizing that health-promotion programs are not offered for the purpose of saving money. Instead such programs are offered to improve the quality and to extend the length of life. Everyone will die in the long run and in the process most amass significant medical care costs near the end of life. The authors of this evaluation showed that the program saved money for the employer, but smoking cessation programs don't save total medical care costs over a person's life time (Barendregt, Bonneux, and van der Maas, 1997). This fact does not mean that smoking cessation programs are not to be offered; it means that we need to point to ways other than money saved as the reason to offer them.

Pointing out the contrast between those who pay and those who benefit should not be taken to mean that this discrepancy is unusual. People voluntarily enter into many contracts from which they hope to receive no financial benefits. Home, life, health, and car insurance policies are designed to provide money to those in need after an illness or accident. The costs are borne by many who never have the occasion to use the benefits. The year-to-year benefit is the peace of mind gained by knowing that large expenses would be covered if a misfortune occurs. Most policy holders are satisfied with such assurances and would be delighted never to need to receive a financial benefit from their insurance.

Some critics of cost–benefit and cost-effectiveness analyses argue that the techniques are flawed because they are not sensitive to long-range costs. House and Shull (1988) argue that many analyses of the effects of the use of natural resources do not reflect the cost to future generations. For example, the financial value of forests would lead an owner to clear-cut the forest, sell the logs, and leave the forestland bare (Clark, 1989). The contribution of the forest to soil conservation, oxygen replacement, and ecological variety would not be considered by a single-minded owner because society in general bears those ecological costs, not the owner or the buyer of the wood. These costs are borne by future generations who may suffer if environmental damage leads to a lowered quality of life. This cost–benefit analysis reveals why the market and current prices lead some companies to engage in clear-cutting forests when it seems clear that this is a bad long-term policy for future generations. Cost analyses can highlight issues in a way that is not possible without relating costs and outcomes.

Using Cost–Benefit and Cost-Effectiveness Analyses

If the benefits of a program can be priced in dollars and a cost–benefit analysis can be done, one approach to program selection is to adopt the program with the largest benefit-to-cost ratio. Many decisions involve far more than simply supporting or not supporting a program (Nagel, 1983a). Because government agencies have limited budgets, agency managers are not free to choose a program with the highest benefit-to-cost ratio if the cost exceeds the allotted budget. Instead, managers ideally should seek to obtain the most benefits for the resources available. Given the costs of the various programs and the size of the budgets, the best program to select might not be the most efficient.

If the outcomes of alternative programs are expressed in different units, stakeholders and managers can still use analyses relating costs with outcomes to select which programs to maintain or expand. The crucial technique is to list all possible courses of action and compare them to each other, taking two at a time. For example, suppose that a program to train 3,000 unskilled workers per year to fill maintenance positions could be funded for 10 years for the same costs as a road improvement project that is expected to save five accidental deaths and twenty injuries during the same 10 years. If both outcomes are equally likely (according to past research and evaluations), which course of action should a state legislature choose? This selection can be made without estimating the value of jobs and averted deaths and injuries; however, the selection would reflect the relative importance of the two outcomes for the majority of legislators. Next, a third program could be compared to this selection. Thus, even when cost–benefit and cost-effectiveness analyses cannot be done, relating costs to outcomes illuminates the debate and allows the stakeholders to see options more clearly than they could without such analyses. At a time when limitations on the financial resources of governments and other organizations are crucially important, analyses to help decision makers understand the impact of their choices seem worthwhile.

MAJOR CRITICISMS OF COST ANALYSES

There are a number of criticisms of both cost–benefit and cost-effectiveness analyses. Users of these approaches profit by being aware of these criticisms, which point out limitations of these useful techniques.

The Worth of Psychological Benefits Is Hard to Estimate

As mentioned above, improved mental health is hard enough to price, but what about clean air? Clean streams? An unlittered park? One approach is to study what people are willing to pay to escape environmental deterioration. Another approach is to calculate what must be paid to induce workers to accept employment in dirty, dusty, noisy, or dangerous occupations (Viscusi, 1992) and examining the premiums people are willing to pay for property in more desirable locations (Pearce and Markandya, 1988). These approaches are indirect and may well never prove to be totally satisfactory, but they do provide some guidance.

Placing a Value on Lives Seems Wrong

People are very uncomfortable when asked to consider the idea that dollar values can be placed on lives. Economic analyses based strictly on current or projected earning power place low values on the lives of children because children cannot earn anything until 10 or 15 years in the future. Indeed, discounting future earnings is not the way to learn what value people place on lives (Viscusi, 1992); people do not act as though children are to be valued on the basis of economic potential. Considerable resources are expended on all children, especially sick children. A very ill, premature baby may be hospitalized for months at a cost of tens of thousands of dollars. Similarly, economic analyses fail when applied to the elderly, who are unlikely to hold any jobs and thus would appear to have a negative economic value.

Nevertheless, society does act as though lives have financial values. These values are estimated by examining what additional wages are required to hire people for jobs in which injury or accidental deaths are higher than most jobs and what people are willing to pay to reduce a risk. Elephant handlers receive extra compensation relative to zoo workers taking care of less dangerous animals (Viscusi, 1992). By examining the higher rates of job-related death among elephant handlers, one can work backwards to learn what value has been placed on a life. Here is an easier example of working backwards. The risk of dying in an automobile accident is almost 1 per 100,000,000 miles (National Safety Council, 1999). This means that if you drive 10,000 miles per year, you have a risk of dying in a vehicular accident of 1 out of 100,000,000 divided by 10,000, or 1 out of 10,000 in a year. Of course, you lower your risk by never driving when tired or after drinking, but let's just accept the average for the U.S. population. Suppose you could spend a sum of money and reduce your risk to one-half of the average rate, that is, to lower the risk to 1 out of 20,000. What sum would you pay? Think about it for a second—$50 per year? $100 per year? $200 per year? How much? If you would be willing to pay $200 per year, you are in effect valuing your life at $4 million ($200 divided by the risk you are willing to tolerate, that is, 1/20,000, is $4 million). This illustration is artificial because we are seldom presented with such clear questions; however, we make decisions daily to buy a carbon monoxide or smoke detector or not, to replace a worn extension cord or use it anyway, or to buy a bicycle helmet or do without one and save the $40. In 1992, Viscusi reported that similar decisions by workers revealed that they value a life at between $3 million and $7 million.

Examining policies in terms of the costs to reduce risk can reveal unnoticed assumptions. The National Research Council reported to Congress that requiring seat belts in school buses was estimated to cost $40 million per death averted (Derby, 1989). It does not take too much imagination to think of ways to spend money that would have a better effect on children's health than placing seat belts in school buses. Suggesting alternative uses of such money would not mean that policy makers did not value the lives of children riding buses; it does mean that there are more cost-effective means of reducing accidental deaths of children.

Okrent (1980) cited reports that $10,000 was spent to reduce each accidental death among agricultural workers, but that $20 million was spent to prevent each death among high-rise apartment occupants in Great Britain. No one decided to spend such disparate amounts to protect different types of people, but it is useful to examine the effect of different policies in this way so that people and their governmental representatives can reconsider policies from time to time. If the members of a society are not pleased with the results of policies, then the policies should be changed. The act of learning what are the effects of society's actions does not devalue lives. Estimating dollar amounts can appear to devalue life if the critic assumes that there is an infinite reservoir of funds to protect people from every possible risk. At times some people act that way, especially when they demand others to bear extravagant costs to reduce specific risks. However, public resources are not infinite; choices must be made among a variety of good things. It has been suggested that *less* effective medical treatment be used at times because the most effective requires an exorbitant cost (Kent, Fendrick, and Langa, 2004).

Cost–Benefit and Cost-Effectiveness Analyses Require Many Assumptions

Whenever future costs and benefits are estimated, assumptions and projections must be made. Since there is a great latitude in selecting assumptions and making approximations, it is not surprising that cost–benefit and cost-effectiveness analyses can be used to support predetermined opinions (Joglekar, 1984). Being open about assumptions and giving the reasons behind approximations enables others to assess the validity of the analyses. Furthermore, adopting different assumptions and discount rates permits evaluators to offer a range of conclusions. If such a range still supports the policy, one can have increased confidence in the conclusions. Cummings, Rubin, and Oster (1989) reviewed the literature on the effect of physicians encouraging patients who smoke to quit; they concluded that even if only 1 percent of smokers quit after such discussions, such efforts are more cost-effective than treatments for mild hypertension and some other common preventive medical activities.

Conducting a sensitivity analysis is critical. If the program appears to be cost-effective regardless of the specific estimates made, then the conclusions take on more credibility. If a program can be shown to be cost-effective only when rather tenuous assumptions are made, then the analysis may be greeted with skepticism (Joglekar, 1984). Case Study 6 illustrates the practice of calculating a range of benefits for a program. Readers still uncomfortable with placing dollar amounts on relieving personal suffering or preventing accidental deaths should remember that financial considerations are not the only basis of program selections. But financial issues cannot be ignored.

Summary and Preview

Cost accounting is a necessary aspect of operating an organization in both the public and private sectors. Efficient use of resources requires that costs be categorized as aids to program selection and management of existing programs. If program benefits can be converted into dollars, ratios of benefits to costs can be calculated. If program outcomes cannot be converted into dollars, programs effecting similar outcomes can be compared to learn which program is more efficient. Even when quantitative indices cannot be calculated, stakeholders must be able to examine outcomes in the light of the costs of programs and alternative uses of the funds.

This chapter ends our discussion of evaluation strategies. Experienced evaluators know that the field is an amalgam of quantitative analysis, practical understanding of programs and policies, and skills in working with organizations. These methods and skills produce information for stakeholders; how to report such information and how to encourage the use of information are the final topics in this text.

Study Questions

1. Pretend that you are involved in planning a storefront legal aid program for poor residents. Draw up a budget for the first year. Take educated guesses as to salaries, rent, supplies, and so on. Label each entry as to whether it is a recurring, fixed, hidden, or some other category of cost. Some costs will have more than one label. Group the costs as direct or indirect costs.

2. Compare two reading programs using effectiveness-to-cost ratios. Program A costs $6,000 and results in a one-month reading gain. Program B costs $13,000 and leads to an average gain of a half-month reading achievement. Suppose Program A serves 100 children and Program B serves 300. Which of the two programs is more cost-effective?

3. Compare cost–benefit and cost-effectiveness. Think of the different types of decisions that can be made and the kind of information needed to do the analyses. Summarize your results in two columns.

4. The state of medical technology is such that ill or injured hospital patients can be unable to see, hear, communicate, read, walk, groom, or dress, but yet be considered alive because their hearts are still beating. They may be kept alive through feeding tubes and heart and lung machines. Sometimes extraordinary efforts are made to resuscitate such patients when coronary failures occur. This problem has ethical, legal, and cost considerations. What might a cost-effectiveness analysis suggest about emergency resuscitations for patients who have been kept alive through feeding tubes but with no chance of returning to health or communicating with others? Think about psychological costs and benefits, opportunity costs, and alternative services to other ill patients as you think through your answer.

5. What are the advantages and disadvantages of cost-utility analyses?

Additional Resource

LEVIN, H. M., AND MCEWAN, P. J. 2001. *Cost-effectiveness analysis*, rev. ed. Thousand Oaks, CA: Sage.

> Although the title suggests that this book is only about cost-effectiveness analysis, it covers cost–benefit and cost-utility approaches as well. This is an accessible presentation quite appropriate for program evaluators. The principles used in discounting future benefits and costs are presented. Many of the examples refer to education; however, the principles apply to programs in any area.

13

Evaluation Reports: Interpreting and Communicating Findings

Communication is a multidimensional, interactive process; consequently, to be as effective as possible, evaluation reports must be multidimensional and interactive. While it would be an unusual evaluation without a written summary report, evaluators err if they assume that the end product of an evaluation is a single written report. Without careful consideration of the process of communicating, even well-crafted evaluation reports will not be understood, and, if not understood, the information they contain cannot be utilized. Communication is a complex process; just as we plan controls for threats to internal validity, evaluators need to plan for threats to effective communication.

The first steps in communication were mentioned in Chapter 2. Involving stakeholders in formulating the evaluation questions and planning the evaluation engages stakeholders in the project; it is essential. In large organizations or government agencies in which evaluations are mandated by administrators without consultation with managers or staff, evaluators often seek to work with program staff so that programs are reflected accurately and information is provided that can be used for program improvement. Even if a program director cannot decline to cooperate with the evaluator, the director remains an important stakeholder whose goodwill is helpful. Hegarty and Sporn (1988) described the importance of involving stakeholders in their evaluation work in the U.S. Food and Drug Administration, stressing that effective evaluators avoid appearing to work behind someone's back. Following the suggestions in the first chapters improves the chances of getting started in a positive way.

After initial discussions, a communication plan needs to be developed that reflects the information needs of the stakeholders. This chapter stresses the importance of explicit planning for communication. Next, the principles to guide the preparation of oral and written reports are described. Because few stakeholders are able to draw out implications from tables of numbers, evaluators should make use of graphs as much as possible. Last, sharing drafts to obtain feedback before finishing the final report is suggested.

DEVELOPING A COMMUNICATION PLAN

Explore Stakeholder Information Needs

The first step in developing a communication plan is to prepare a list of the different information needs of the various stakeholders and the times during the evaluation when the evaluators will benefit from feedback from stakeholders. While the stakeholders have information needs, they also provide information. A program evaluator will be more effective if stakeholders can respond to the plans of the evaluators and provide interpretative insights that can come only from those intimately familiar with the program.

Plan Reporting Meetings

It is helpful to schedule the planned meetings with the stakeholders. Figure 13.1 illustrates a communication plan for a hypothetical evaluation of a new developmental skills program at what we will call Sanders College. The program serves students who have been admitted as part of an outreach program for promising but underprepared high school graduates. The purpose of the formative evaluation is to gather information on how well the program operates and meets the needs of the students, and to develop suggestions for improvements. Stakeholders include the students served, the staff, the director of the program, and the college dean. Although somewhat removed, other important stakeholders include the parents of the students and the college administration, which approves the funds for the program. Imagine that the evaluation project was planned during the summer and began with student orientation just before fall classes began. The completed evaluation is needed in time for the staff and dean to make changes in the program in the following academic year.

As Figure 13.1 shows, the evaluators listed the times when different stakeholders would use information and when it would be helpful to get feedback on tentative findings. Meetings are scheduled with the participants, students in the program. Meeting with the participants is often done during program evaluations, but such meetings would have different functions in different types of programs. In a hospital setting, evaluators would probably interview

FIGURE 13.1 An illustrative communication plan for an evaluation of a program to serve the academic needs of underprepared college students.

Stakeholder	Information Needed	Format of the Communication	When Information Will Be Available	Setting
Research team	Progress to date, next step in the project	Team meetings, internal memos	Once every 2 weeks	Team meetings
	How to solve problems in the evaluation meetings	Special meetings	As needed	Team and one-on-one meetings
Program Director	Progress updates	Oral presentations and one-page memos	Once a month	Meetings of the lead evaluator and director
	Final Report of recommendations	Oral presentation and written final report	March 15	Formal meeting
Staff advisory group	Information to be gathered	Oral presentations and discussions	During planning of the evaluation	Group meeting
	Tentative recommendations	Oral presentations and discussions	During the interpretation phase	Group meeting
Student advisory group	Information to be gathered	Oral presentations and discussions	During planning of the evaluation	Group meeting
	Tentative recommendations	Oral presentations and discussions	During the interpretation phase	Group meeting
Dean of the college	Progress updates	Copies of the one-page memos for files	When memos are given to program director	Inter-office mail
	Final Report on the recommendations	Oral presentation and the written Final Report	April 2	Formal meeting

some patients to understand a program being studied, but few hospital patients spend long periods in the hospital and most do not feel well enough to want to meet with evaluators. On the other hand, the participants in the Sanders College program are involved for at least an academic year, thus groups of them would be available for brief meetings. Note that the content of the meetings would be different for the various stakeholder groups because their information needs are not the same. The dean is to be informed through short progress memos, but the director is scheduled to receive more detailed updates.

Set a Communication Schedule

The dates when reports are to be made to the director and the dean are related to the academic calendar. It would be important for the dean to have recommendations to discuss with the director before the planning for the following academic year has begun. By April 2, many incoming students will have been accepted into the following year's program; however, it is not too late to increase or decrease the number of students involved relative to the first year. Also, there is time to change the level of financial support or to plan some changes in the staffing pattern. Many of the reporting dates could be altered as conditions warrant; however, the dates for reporting to the director and the dean are inflexible because they must have time to make plans for the following year.

PERSONAL PRESENTATIONS OF FINDINGS

Evaluators learn quickly that managers are busy and unlikely to spend a great deal of time puzzling over written evaluation reports. Consequently, evaluators prepare reports compatible with the learning style of managers; oral presentations are usually appropriate (Hendricks, 1994). Although the content of these reports is different from written reports, the director and dean should have a written report before the personal presentation. Although they may have paged through the report before the meeting, evaluators do not assume that stakeholders have read reports before the meeting.

Need for Personal Presentations

In spite of our high tech communication systems, people still respond more favorably to person-to-person contact than to other forms of communication. Note in Evaluator Profile 8 how Frechtling said that personal presentations were critical in her work as an evaluator in a large school district. In a real sense the communication of evaluation findings is a form of attitude change intervention (see Posavac, 1992). That is, evaluations are commissioned because people are looking for new ways of approaching a program. Ideas about the program are expected to be affected by the evaluation. Learning

Joy Frechtling: Presenting an Evaluation Report

Joy Frechtling was the Head of the Division of Program Monitoring in the Montgomery County (Maryland) Public Schools. Previously, she had worked with the National Institute of Education. Dr. Frechtling earned a Ph.D. in Developmental Psychology (George Washington University).

A common concern among evaluators is the best way to present results to the stakeholders. She was asked the following questions: "Do you mean that to have an impact there must be a discussion? If there's only a (written) report, can it have an impact?"

Dr. Frechtling replied: "Probably not, because no report is perfect. Unless people take the time to sit down and discuss it, they're not going to act on it. They're not interested. . . . We try to keep them informed. Toward the end, we show them a draft report before it goes to the superintendent or goes public. They have a chance to review or make comments on it. If we can't reach an agreement, they can even write a rejoinder that goes forward at the same time the report does. This involvement also serves another function, because sometimes we find that program changes are made even before the report is issued."

Adapted from Wills, K. 1987. A conversation with Joy Frechtling. *Evaluation Practice*, 8(2), 20–30.

occurs more easily through interpersonal dialogue than through written material (Preskill, 1994). One reason for this is that people pay more attention to a person than to words on a page. Personal presentations are also effective because the presentation can be adjusted for the audience being addressed. Specific questions can be asked and answered. Even facial feedback showing puzzlement, skepticism, or agreement provides evaluators with information that can be used to improve the presentation.

Content of Personal Presentations

A personal presentation usually includes a short review of the background of the evaluation. In the communication plan illustrated in Figure 13.1, the dean is to receive progress reports. Consequently, only a brief reminder of the reasons for the evaluation and an overview of the procedures used are given in oral presentations. Most presentation meetings last between 30 to 60 minutes; the time available should be focused on describing the findings and recommendations and fielding questions. The details of the sampling procedure and data analysis would not be discussed because the decision maker (in this case, the dean) wants to learn about the conclusions. If evaluators have gained the trust of stakeholders, administrators are not going to second-guess the methods used.

FIGURE 13.2   An illustrative chart that might be used as a handout during a personal presentation.

Planning Question 5. Are Elderly Residents Underserved by the Community Mental Health Center?

Rationale   The Center's mission is to provide needed service to all sectors of the community; however, few elderly people make use of the Center.

Core observations
- The percentage of community residents over 65 has increased to 15%; 3% are older than 75.
- Nearly half of residents over 75 live with relatives; in 45% of these families no one is home during the day time except the elderly person.
- Police officers report that they believe that there has been an increase in calls from elderly people or about elderly people having a problem when no one else is available.
- Community services to the elderly are limited to home nursing care for seriously ill elderly who qualify for Medicaid and the Central Library's Seniors & Classics book discussion program.
- Several CMHC's in the northern part of the state have developed a drop-in, informal "day care" service for ambulatory seniors; and an up-to-seven-day respite care service for families with seniors needing to have assistance available at all times. Sliding scale costs are charged for each service.

Recommendation   Plan to increase service to elderly residents by beginning with a drop-in center based on a membership fee. Develop a need assessment to estimate the community response to a respite care service and the fees that would need to be charged.

During personal presentations, visual aids are helpful. Using an overhead projector or computer generated visuals helps to make major points and to keep the attention of the audience on the message. Each visual should focus on one major point. A set of handouts matching the overheads could be distributed (Hendricks, 1994). Figure 13.2 is an example of a possible handout— it does, however, contain too much information for one overhead or screen. Regardless of the technical sophistication of the presentation, it is wise to give listeners something to take with them.

A major misunderstanding, and a devastating experience for evaluators, occurs when stakeholders claim that the findings were already well known and that the evaluation team added nothing to their knowledge about the program. Of course, it is true that an evaluator might work independently from the stakeholders and indeed duplicate existing knowledge. If evaluators work closely with stakeholders as recommended in this text, however, it is more likely that some of the information will be new. Claims that "nothing new has been found" may be an example of hindsight bias (Guilbault, Bryant, Brockway, and Posavac, 2004). Researchers have documented a tendency for people to incorporate new information into what they know, and come to believe that they "knew it all the time." Professionals receiving evaluation reports are also susceptible to this bias. This tendency should not be confused with a conscious attempt to deny threatening evaluations or to avoid working with new ideas; hindsight bias seems quite common and automatic. The challenge to the evaluator is to demonstrate to the stakeholders that the information is new to them while not damaging the interpersonal relationships between the evaluator and the stakeholders.

Some evaluators seek to get stakeholders to state explicitly what they expect the evaluation to show. Since stakeholders may not like to make statements publicly that might prove to be incorrect later, this strategy needs to be handled carefully. We have used the following procedure: (1) provide listeners with a graph that includes the axes, scales, and a title, but no data; (2) suggest that they plot the results that they expect the evaluation to have found; and (3) only then provide the complete graph with all the data. When listeners do this, they can compare their own expectations with the data (this minimizes hindsight bias), yet they do not have to reveal publicly that they were wrong. This has worked well in settings in which unit managers meet to receive feedback on their employees' work attitudes on a variety of scales. Managers are given the scale averages of the whole division, but not those of their own units until after they committed themselves privately to how they think their own employees feel. No one knows how right or wrong any individual manager was; however, each manager can see what information he or she anticipated correctly and what findings are indeed new. Note that this procedure also involves listeners in the feedback process rather than letting them remain passive.

Audience for the Personal Presentations

Along with the dean of Sanders College, others present for the summary report would probably include the program director, the assistant dean directly responsible for the program, the evaluator/presenter, and an assistant to the evaluator. The size of the program influences the size and nature of the audience. When federal programs are described, a much larger number of people would be present compared to the small program at Sanders College. Even with small projects, it is helpful for more than one member of the evaluation team to participate in the presentation. The second member can distribute the handouts, handle visual aids, supply information the presenter may have forgotten, and clarify questions. Since the assistant is not responsible for the presentation, he or she has more time to assess the audience's reaction to the presentation.

Distributing Drafts of Reports

Before the personal presentation to the program director and the dean, a written draft should be available to the director. This version should be called a draft and labeled "Confidential." Although the interpretations and recommendations of possible areas of improvement have been presented in conversations with the staff and students, recommendations are subject to change. After looking over the draft report, the director may be able to suggest additional recommendations or may point out errors. A discussion of the draft is likely to result in changes in the report.

Calling this report a "draft" avoids offending the most senior administrator, who may feel that the final report should come to him or her before being released elsewhere. If any concern is raised, the evaluator can point out that draft reports have been discussed, but that the final report is being presented first to the administrator. After the oral report and with the administrator's approval, the written final report can be made available to others. Organizations vary in how formal they are regarding handling information; among the many reasons to work closely with stakeholders is to develop a good understanding of the assumed communication patterns in the organization sponsoring the program.

CONTENT OF FORMAL WRITTEN EVALUATION REPORTS

The personal presentations to decision makers are the single most important report. However, there are many other channels for reporting program evaluations; this section describes the content of the written report.

Remember the Purposes of the Formal Report

Evaluators are nearly always expected to submit a report describing the overall program evaluation. Even when major stakeholders have been regularly informed about the progress of the evaluation and have participated in the oral briefing, an overall report is necessary. First, it is crucial to provide a written record that the evaluation was carried out. Those who arranged to fund the evaluation may need a tangible report for budget accountability. Second, the written report can answer questions about the findings of the evaluation or about its methodology that may arise later. Third, if administrators make a decision on the basis of the oral briefing, they will want the written report as backup if others question the reasons for a decision. Fourth, since administrators, program staff members, and evaluators take new positions or retire, their memories of the evaluation are lost. The written report remains for others to examine. Write with that in mind: Use dates, not phrases such as "last year"; include the individuals' job titles, not their names; put a date on the cover page. Without a written report some people may propose a new evaluation of a program already studied. It is not unusual for members of planning committees to suggest gathering data on an issue only to learn that a study on the same question was completed a year or two earlier. Even if planners decide that an additional evaluation is needed, access to the written report of a previous study would be very helpful to future evaluators. In some rare instances, stake-holders have asked for an oral report only; it appeared that in those cases the organization did not want anything in their files that might have been relevant to a legal challenge.

Provide an Outline and a Summary

Figure 13.3 is an illustrative report outline; after adding page numbers to this outline, it serves as a table of contents for the report. While most program directors read evaluations of their programs carefully, many administrators read the summaries only. Summaries are not like abstracts that precede many research articles. Unlike journal abstracts, summaries are longer and can stand alone. Abstracts often contain phrases such as "the implications of find-ings are discussed" without mentioning the implications at all. A summary is a short version of the report that includes the recommendations; conclusions are not saved for the discussion section. Summaries are often two pages long although their length varies with the complexity of the evaluation.

When writing reports, some beginning evaluators are hesitant to use sub-headings and instead write page after page providing readers with little assis-tance in sensing the general flow of the report. Readers of evaluations need all the help we can give them. Think about reading this text with only two or three headings in each chapter. Without subheadings, a textbook is hard to follow.

Describe the Context of the Evaluation

An overall written report includes a description of the program setting, the program staff, and the purpose of the evaluation. These topics would be men-tioned only briefly in an oral report because the audience often includes those who requested the evaluation, and they have been kept informed about the project as it was carried out. However, the audience of the written project report is more difficult to anticipate; consequently, it is written for readers who know little about the program or staff and for those who may replace the administrators who commissioned the evaluation.

A description of the program that was evaluated is also important. It is impossible to predict with accuracy how a program will evolve, how funding will change, or how directors will alter it. For future readers to make sense out of the report, the program itself must be described. Some of these descrip-tions can make use of material already prepared by the program and simply placed in an appendix. It may be that some organizations have better records than universities, but it is often surprisingly difficult to find program descrip-tions after several years have passed and the director of a program has left the university.

It is also essential that the purpose of an evaluation be described. Although the vast majority of evaluations are formative (designed to develop ideas for

FIGURE 13.3 Outline of a program evaluation report. Note the use of informative subheadings.

The Implementation of the Physician Residency Program at General Medical Hospital: The Effects on the Culture of the Hospital Have Been Substantial

Summary

The Residency Program

1. The development of General Hospital into a teaching hospital
2. Differences in the provision of medical care between teaching hospitals and community hospitals
3. Concerns that led to the evaluation of the implementation of the Residency Program

Procedure and Methodology

1. Information sources
2. Aspects of hospital culture assessed
3. Interview procedures

Findings

1. Many stakeholders value the challenge and the excitement of a teaching hospital.
   - Reactions of attending physicians
   - Reactions of nurses and other hospital groups providing care to patients
   - Views of residents
2. The technical quality of care may have increased; however, there are fears that interpersonal aspects of care have suffered.
   - Perceptions of technical skills
   - Perceptions of interpersonal aspects of care
       Staff rapport with residents
       Patient rapport with residents
       Care of terminally ill patients
       Coordination of residents with nonmedical hospital personnel
3. There have been major organizational effects of becoming a teaching hospital.
   - A greater number of physicians are employed by the hospital.
   - The outpatient center was begun in order to provide education in outpatient care for residents.
   - Conflicts have occurred among residents of different specializations.
   - Residents order more diagnostic tests than attending physicians thus increasing the cost of treatment.

Conclusion and Implications

Overall comments
Implications

Appendices

A. Resources and references
B. Tables showing growth of residency programs
C. Interview forms
D. Tables of means and standard deviations of interview questions with numerical answers

---

program improvement), it is wise to state the purpose of the evaluation in the report. The precise issues that were to be addressed should be listed. There are major differences between a project to assess the training needs of staff members and a project to evaluate the effectiveness of current training programs, even though the two projects might well measure some of the same variables.

Describe the Program Participants

Reports usually include a description of those who received the services of the program. Demographic information helps others to judge whether the program was particularly suited to the people served and whether the program might be appropriate in other settings. Beyond information such as age, education, and gender, a description of participants might include how the people came to enter the program. It makes a difference whether the people served represent the target population for whom the program was designed or whether they learned about the service and sought it out on their own and are different from the target population. The rate of attrition and the descriptions of those who did not complete the program would be interesting to anyone hoping to improve it. We repeat a point from Chapter 5: Respect the confidentiality of the participants.

Justify the Criteria Selected

Whether the project was a needs assessment or a summative evaluation, certain criteria were selected to indicate unmet needs or program success. Indexes of unmet needs should be related to the problem on which the needs assessment focused; outcome criteria should be described and related to the goals of the program. In a report of an outcome evaluation, this section might be an appropriate place to provide the impact model of the program.

Evaluators are coming to appreciate more fully how weaknesses in observation techniques reduce the statistical power of an evaluation to detect an effect of a program (Lipsey, 1990). Evaluators may want to document that they considered these issues when they planned the evaluation; however, it might be a good idea to place technical material regarding the reliability and validity of measurement tools in an appendix since this material could be difficult for administrators and service delivery staff.

Describe the Data-Gathering Procedures

It is important to describe procedures used to obtain data because the way information is gathered can affect the findings. Poorly trained interviewers extract less information than well-trained ones; the 1990 census is less accurate for describing current unmet needs than the 2000 census; self-report surveys are subjected to more self-interest biases than material gathered from records. It would be good to show that the people responsible for data gathering were independent of the program evaluated.

Provide the Findings

Use graphs. The availability of user-friendly software has reduced the need to have graphs drawn professionally for all but the most complicated and expensive evaluations. Figure 13.4 shows the value of displaying not only the means of groups, but the confidence intervals as well (Cumming and Finch, 2005). The means for the graph (left panel) were taken from Box 11.1. The innovative treatment group (CRP) did do better than the traditional program (TP); however, the mean for TP participants lies within the 95 percent confidence interval of the CRP group. Clearly this would be weak evidence for the value of the innovation. In the right panel, the means and confidence intervals provide a much more favorable outcome. The confidence intervals provide a way to place the differences among the means in a context. The set of findings (on the left) does not provide confidence in the difference observed, but the second set of means (on the right) does permit concluding that the innovation led to a better outcome. Note that the range of possible scores for the outcome measure was given in the vertical axis. This range is a second way to place the findings in a context. In program evaluation, stakeholders want some confidence that program differences have a practical import for participants. Seeing group means in the context of the worst and the best values of the scale helps to interpret the differences found. In basic research, the focus is on finding any difference that would reflect on the theory being tested; in evaluation, it is important to know the level of the outcome, not just relative level. It should be remembered that just because a type of graph can be made by a computer program does not mean that the graph is a good one.

FIGURE 13.4 Illustration of the value of including 95 percent confidence intervals when reporting means of groups.

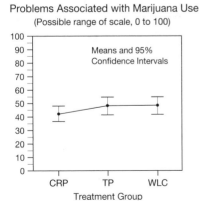

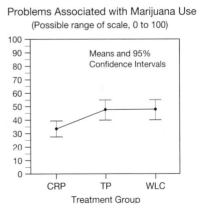

Anticipate misunderstandings. There are a number of interpretation pit-falls for evaluators and readers of evaluations. While program evaluations share these problems with other research methods, the problems may be especially critical to evaluations because evaluations could affect how staff members earn their living. Inaccurate or misleading interpretations of evalua-tion findings can have serious implications. Recognizing the possibility of such misunderstandings encourages evaluators to prepare reports written so as to minimize the possibility of such misuse of findings.

Many audiences, including some well-educated ones, confuse the size of a sample with its representativeness (Nickerson, 2000). Large, self-selected sam-ples responding to a survey are often overvalued, even when a small response rate means that the findings cannot be treated as describing the population of interest. Smaller, carefully sampled representative groups yield more accurate estimates of the population values, but may be criticized unfairly simply on the basis of size.

Although many people can understand the implications of a difference between two means, standard deviation is a very hard concept for people to understand (Carey and Lloyd, 1995). Readers sometimes interpret a statisti-cally significant difference between two group means to indicate that the dis-tributions of the scores of the people in the two groups hardly overlap (Posavac and Sinacore, 1984). The way to avoid misinterpreting differences in means is to graph data. Suppose that a department chair becomes concerned about the difference in the grading practices of the faculty and teaching assis-tants (TAs) in her department. One approach to examining this question would simply be to compare the mean of percentages of A and B course grades assigned by faculty members versus TAs. Suppose that she learns that the mean percentage is 53 percent for faculty and 63 percent for teaching assistants. The difference in the means is statistically significant ($t(116) = 3.723$, $p < 0.0005$). The effect size is 0.70 indicating a large differ-ence relative to the guidelines suggested by the findings of Lipsey and Wilson (1993). Many stakeholders are likely to misinterpret such findings; many would believe that the low probability reveals that most TAs assign higher grades than most faculty members do. This misunderstanding can be avoided if the difference between means is interpreted in the light of variation within groups. Figure 13.5 shows the two distributions of percentage of A or B grades. It is easy to see that the sections show wide variation in the level of grades assigned regardless of the type of teacher. In presenting evaluation findings, anticipating common misinterpretations increases the usefulness of the report. If the dean decided to act on these findings or to seek more infor-mation, the wide variation would be important to understand.

Another common misinterpretation is reacting to the size of the numerical difference between two means or two percentages. Differences cannot be interpreted without concern for the nature of the variable involved. Even small numerical differences might have marked social importance. Most programs,

FIGURE 13.5 Stem-and-leaf plots of the percentage of A and B grades assigned by teaching assistants and faculty members. The stem-and-leaf plots reveal (a) that the percentage of A and B grades is higher among teaching assistants than among faculty members, but (b) that sections taught by both types of teachers show wide variation in the percentage of A and B grades assigned. It is important that stakeholders recognize the variation within both groups and not unreflectively assume that most TAs assign higher grades than most faculty members.

Percentage of A or B Grades for Teaching Assistants and Faculty Members

Teaching Assistants		Faculty Members	
Frequency	Stem & Leaf*	Frequency	Stem & Leaf
0	1	1	1 . 8
0	2	0	1
0	2	1	2 . 9
[>]1	3 . 2	8	3 . 02334555
1	3 . 79	4	3 . 6789
0	4 .	10	4 . 0011122344
2	4 . 78	5	4 . 56778
5	5 . 01234	12	5 . 000111223334
5	5 . 56678	6	6 . 677899
8	6 . 00002344	8	6 . 01123355
16	6 . 5666677777788999	5	5 . 67889
1	7 . 3	6	7 . 003445
4	7 . 5679	2	7 . 69
1	8 . 3	2	8 . 03
2	8 . 6	0	8
1	9 . 1	1	9 . 3

* All of the original data points are in these plots. The *stem* column is the tens digit, and the *leaf* column is the units digits. For example, the first data point for TAs (see the [>]) means that 32% of the grades of one TA were A or B grades. Down further in the TA plot, we can see that 16 TAs assigned A and B grades to 65 through 69% of their students. There were 12 faculty members who assigned A or B grades to 50 through 54% of their students.

even well-implemented ones, produce only small changes in outcomes. Consequently interpretations of group differences are best made in the context of the size of program effects actually observed among many programs (Light and Pillemer, 1984). As mentioned earlier Lipsey and Wilson (1993) gathered nearly 300 summaries of evaluations that involved thousands of individual evaluations. They found many programs produced effect sizes of only 0.25. That value indicates that the mean of the program group was only about a quarter of a standard deviation larger than the mean of the comparison, or wait list group. Even smaller effects have proved important, especially in medical areas when the dependent variable is life or death (Rosenthal, 1990).

Type II errors are overlooked so often (Freiman et al., 1978; Lipsey, 1990; Shadish, 2002) that the issue bears repeating. It may be that the resources provided to the evaluator were insufficient to perform an evaluation with enough statistical sensitivity to detect a socially valuable effect. Even small reductions—one-half of a percent—in drug use and alcohol abuse can have valuable social benefits (Caulkins, Rydell et al., 1999) yet be impossible to detect without huge samples. Although none of us enjoys pointing out that one of our evaluations may not have been designed well enough to detect a socially useful effect, recognizing this possibility is better than writing a report that criticizes a program rather than acknowledging the limitations of the evaluation. Report readers who interpret "$p < 0.05$" as program success, but "$p < 0.07$" as program failure do not understand the high rate of Type II errors (Abelson, 1995).

Use appendices. The description of findings cannot be done thoroughly in an oral report and can become quite lengthy in the written report. Because the audience of evaluation reports is made up of people not schooled in research methods or statistical analyses, details such as tables of means, standard deviations, and probability levels are better placed in an appendix to the report. The value in following this policy is to produce a complete record of the findings for anyone to use who would like to trace the connections between findings and recommendations. Also, evaluators usually want to demonstrate that they did carry out the analyses required to support the interpretations they have made.

Develop Recommendations

Many evaluators have concentrated their efforts in design, data collection, and analysis, developing recommendations nearly as an afterthought. Schedules need to be planned so that there is time to work on understanding what the evaluation means and which recommendations make sense for the program (Weiss, 1988). As the communication plan in Figure 13.1 implied, recommendations are best developed in consultation with the stakeholders. Tentative recommendations can be suggested to stakeholders to learn if the recommendations are reasonable in the light of limitations on the agency. Depending on the relationship between evaluators and program managers, these negotiations would be carried out in different ways. When evaluators have been working at the request of program managers, the recommendations will be heavily influenced by the agency if only because recommendations thought to be inappropriate will not be carried out. Ideally, the evaluation will have provided new insight to the program managers who intend to use the information to improve the agency. Furthermore, the different perspective of the evaluation team may persuade the agency staff to reconsider their understanding of the target population or the outcomes that are thought feasible; however, evaluators have no power to push the agency beyond what it is willing to do. In contrast, when the administration of a facility has ordered that one of the programs it sponsors be evaluated or when a governmental department commissions an inspector general's office to carry out an evaluation of one the programs the department supports, the evaluation team can make recommendations that the program managers may not immediately support. This does not mean that an evaluator works without consulting the program managers; often initial drafts are shared, as previously mentioned. However, if the evaluation team cannot agree with the program management, there is no reason to change the recommendations. Unresolved disagreements can be indicated in the written report by including a statement from the program manager, as is the practice of the Office of Inspector General of the U.S. Department of Health and Human Resources (Office of Inspector General, 1990).

Recommendations need to be kept within the psychological reach of the stakeholders. Recommendations that would require major changes in the organization will simply be rejected. Even if an evaluation suggests that there are major problems with the program's plans, its implementation, or its effectiveness, evaluators have greater chances of influencing the program when the changes recommended are considered feasible to implement. If an evaluation was designed to contribute to program improvement, then it must not be thought of as a way to grade the program. As long as no malfeasance or injustices were discovered, the purpose of an evaluation is to support improvement regardless of how well the program functions.

Evaluators are careful to avoid assuming that they are experts in how programs should be designed and managed. Sometimes stakeholders will not want any recommendations. Perhaps the word "recommendations" can be avoided when evaluators believe that the evaluation points to needed changes or new initiatives, but they want to avoid appearing intrusive. Maybe a term such as "implications" might be softer, permitting the raising of issues without offending management sensitivities.

Formal Reports Should Look Attractive

Written reports are prepared with care both for content and appearance. In applied settings, managers deal regularly with consultants and salespeople who present attractively prepared proposals and descriptions of new products. Evaluators lose credibility if their reports look like term papers; it may not be fair, but it's true.

Evaluators often place the logo of the agency on the cover of the report. One can use a report binder with a clear plastic cover so the cover page of the report shows through. The most inexpensive laser printer produces what to a nonexpert's eye looks like typeset printing. We suggest that colored paper be used for appendixes—choose muted colors, not pink or goldenrod. The use of colored paper serves two purposes: Many people feel that the report is indeed prettier and they are assured that they are not expected to read the whole report—just the white pages.

Provide Progress Reports and Press Releases

Since evaluations take at least several months to complete and since there may be some misgivings about what may be learned through the evaluation, critical stakeholders should be informed about the progress of the project from time to time. Progress reports can be made on a regular schedule (as suggested in Figure 13.1) or at milestones in the evaluation cycle. For example, progress reports might be made when data collection begins and when collection is completed. Progress reports can also be used to thank staff members who cooperated in one or another phase of the evaluation.

When the community is a stakeholder, press releases might be appropriate to report to people outside the agency (Torres, Preskill, and Piontek, 2004; W. K. Kellogg Foundation, 1998). Of course, before an evaluator releases information beyond the agency, it is essential to have an agreement with the appropriate stakeholders. Some private agencies may not permit such publicity; others may crave it. In contrast, reports of some government-sponsored evaluations are assumed to be public documents once the report has been accepted by the director of the evaluation office involved.

Summary and Preview

Communicating the findings of an evaluation cannot be treated as an afterthought; communication should be planned when the evaluation is being planned. Communication is more likely to be carried out if a plan is spelled out explicitly from the start. Evaluators are wise to keep stakeholders apprised of progress, especially if the evaluation takes more than two months to complete. A personal oral presentation of the findings is the best way to present the findings to those who might use the evaluation in making decisions. Evaluators are wise to anticipate misunderstandings and provide appropriate information to avert them. A summary written report documents the details of the evaluation; serves as the official record that the evaluation did take place; and includes details of the procedure, findings, and statistical analyses. In addition, briefer reports and press releases are useful forms of communication with stakeholders.

When evaluators report their findings, they are concerned especially with encouraging the stakeholders to utilize the findings. Although stakeholders are the ones deciding how to use an evaluation, there are some practices that evaluators can follow to increase the probability that good recommendations are followed. These practices are described in the last chapter.

Study Questions

1. How might a communication plan for a qualitative evaluation differ from one for a quantitative evaluation?

2. Suppose that you had conducted an assessment of the needs of student athletes for academic assistance. Think of the variables you might gather. Develop a form that could be used to get stakeholders to make their expectations explicit before receiving the findings of this needs assessment.

3. Find a journal article describing an evaluation. Prepare an outline of an oral presentation of the findings of the evaluation. Prepare an outline of a written report for that evaluation. Note how these outlines differ from the outline of the original journal article.

4. Prepare a summary of the article you have been using. Note how the summary differs from the abstract.

5. List the stakeholder groups who should be part of the feedback process for the report you have been using. What are the differences in the type and detail of the information these groups would want to know about?

Additional Resources

HENRY, G. T., ED. 1997. Creating effective graphs: Solutions for a variety of evaluation data. *New Directions for Evaluation, No. 73.* San Francisco: Jossey-Bass.

> The authors of the chapters in this text discuss and illustrate good graphical presentations for program evaluators. Effective graphs make it impossible for the stakeholders to overlook the critical findings the evaluator wants to call attention to.

TORRES, R. T., PRESKILL, H. S., AND PIONTEK, M. E. 2004. *Evaluation strategies for communicating and reporting: Enhancing learning in organizations,* rev. ed. Thousand Oaks, CA: Sage.

> This volume contains an incredible amount of terrific, practical advice. Beyond advice, however, the authors provide many illustrations of tables, graphics, charts, and handouts. This work shows how far evaluators have come in developing communication strategies that go far beyond what was standard practice not many years ago. The major lesson as emphasized in the current chapter is that effective evaluators plan for communication. While conducting an evaluation it can be very easy to focus on the technical issues of getting, analyzing, and interpreting data forgetting that all that work can only be useful if others understand the findings. This work will help you.

How to Encourage Utilization

Presenting reports in a way that gets attention is but one aspect of encouraging stakeholders to use evaluations. Unfortunately, in many evaluations a report has been the only effort to encourage utilization. This chapter examines obstacles to utilization so that evaluators can recognize them and perhaps deal proactively with them. Evaluators can contribute to an organization if they can assist in developing a learning culture in which stakeholders are willing to consider the implications of the findings of evaluations. Even when the interpretations of evaluations are ambiguous, evaluations often have implications that might not be evident from a superficial examination of the findings.

A number of evaluators have studied how evaluations are used. Here are a few examples. Bigelow and Ciarlo (1975) studied the reaction to evaluations in a large community mental health center with 30 management and supervisory personnel. The authors concluded that managers were disposed to use the information, that evaluations affected their intentions to modify programs, and that evaluations resulted in further exploration of particular management questions. Leviton and Boruch (1983) followed up on 21 federally sponsored evaluations of education policy. They found clear evidence that the evaluations had affected the programs evaluated and the development of new laws. Patton (1986) reported an examination of the effects of health program evaluations; he found that evaluation information became part of the knowledge base and reduced the uncertainty of administrators. After the introduction of a management information system (see Chapter 7) the managers of a large, residential agency for children discovered that some widely-accepted indicators of good service to children did not apply to their agency. As a result of information about the children served, the managers changed some of their practices (Overstreet, Grasso, and Epstein, 1993). We conclude that many evaluations are utilized, but evaluators have to recognize the complex role that agency managers fill and the multiple uses of evaluations (Weiss, 1998).

OBSTACLES TO EFFECTIVE UTILIZATION

The common obstacles to implementing findings from evaluations are discussed first. Evaluators are not always in a position to remove these roadblocks, but if aware of them, evaluators might be able to minimize their effects.

Constraints on Managers

Program managers may not be able to utilize findings from evaluations because there are many influences that restrict their freedom (Sonnichsen, 1994). It may seem to evaluators that decision makers do not pay sufficient attention to evaluation findings and that they do not wish to reexamine policies in view of the information provided. It is just as likely, however, that a manager must satisfy a variety of competing constituencies. Meeting the needs of the diverse stakeholders of a complex agency within a budget requires compromises. At times evaluators have overestimated the freedom administrators have in using new information to make program changes; organizational constraints may make it appear that evaluations have been ignored.

Value Conflicts Among Stakeholders

When stakeholder groups are polarized on an issue, it is likely that evaluation findings will be hard to use. When people hold hardened positions linked to values, evaluation findings may fall on deaf ears or parties may endorse some parts of evaluations while rejecting other parts. A clear example of the effect of polarization was seen in the interpretations of the evaluation of the Federal Gun Control Act of 1968. Zimring (1975) concluded that since his study showed that the impact of the Act was limited given the problems it sought to alleviate, his report could be used both by gun control advocates to argue that stronger controls were needed and by those opposed to controls to argue that the evaluation showed gun control efforts had failed. Sommer (1990) found a similar situation when he conducted a study for a local farmers' market. Between the time he began and the time he finished, the board of directors had changed. Because the philosophy of the new board was quite different from that of the old one, the report was seen as irrelevant.

When stakeholders hold strong views, evaluators are probably helpless to effect much change. When less polarization is found, it may help to seek agreement ahead of time on what would constitute support for certain conclusions. There is no way an evaluator can stop stakeholders from changing their minds once the findings are available; however, discussing evidence in the abstract before information has been gathered may be a way to diffuse some of the effects of strong opinions and encourage people to approach an evaluation with an open mind.

Misapplied Methodology

Evaluators have sometimes tried to accomplish more than their resources permitted. In their review of published evaluations, Lipsey et al. (1985) showed that although many outcome evaluations were planned to investigate the causal effects of a program on an outcome, relatively few were implemented in ways that would have permitted the evaluation to isolate causal relationships. This can occur when too few program participants are observed, when threats to internal validity are not controlled satisfactorily, or when the outcome variables are not measured reliably or validly as mentioned in Chapter 10.

Limits on resources in the context of overly ambitious or vague evaluation requests make valid experimental or quasi-experimental evaluations impossible (see Moskowitz, 1993). Frequently, people untrained in evaluation methods do not appreciate the challenge of conducting valid research in service settings. A program evaluation that cannot be interpreted damages the reputation of the discipline and wastes agency resources. It is important to match the evaluation design to the needs of the agency seeking the evaluation. Seldom is it necessary for an internal evaluator to show that the program caused a change in an outcome variable; seldom is a summative evaluation wanted (Posavac, 1994). Often evaluators can help stakeholders by developing a method to track and verify implementation or by helping the staff to clarify their implicit impact model (Lipsey and Cordray, 2000).

Evaluating a Program at Arm's Length

This text has encouraged evaluators to work closely with stakeholders in planning and implementing program evaluations. This is advisable so that evaluations reflect accurately both the program and its context. Working at a distance without close contact with stakeholders who administer and provide the services will be an obstacle to full utilization when an evaluation is completed. When people are involved with an evaluation, utilization of recommendations to effect program improvement is more likely (Fross, Cracknell, and Samset, 1994; Torres, Preskill, and Piontek, 2004). When an evaluation has been crafted to reflect the staff's information needs, the staff members are going to be more interested in the findings. Stakeholders are far more likely to give recommendations a respectful hearing if they feel the evaluation team understood the population served, the agency housing the program, the program itself, and the staff. Such understanding cannot be gained through meetings with higher administrators and a careful examination of official program descriptions; it can only be gained through time-consuming interactions involving lots of listening to the stakeholders closest to the participants and day-to-day operations.

DEALING WITH MIXED FINDINGS

When some findings of an evaluation support a program and others do not, proponents of a program focus attention on supportive findings while explaining away the negative ones. The problem of dealing with mixed results is accentuated when there is disagreement within the agency over the value of the program or when jobs are involved.

Don't Abdicate Your Responsibility

Evaluators could report the findings and leave the interpretation to the stakeholders—to administrators, staff, or funding agencies. This can be accomplished by omitting interpretations of the findings and drawing no implications from the evaluation. There are times when evaluators are asked to carry out a study and explicitly told not to make recommendations. In such cases, the agency has hired an evaluation team for its research and statistical expertise, not for its possible contribution to organizational development. In such cases, allowing others to decide what the mixed findings mean is quite appropriate.

Usually, however, evaluators can play a meaningful role in program planning and refinement. In addition, program personnel expect evaluators to try to figure out what the mixed findings mean for the program. Evaluators do not act as though the numbers speak for themselves, because indeed they do not. Findings will be interpreted—if not by an evaluator, then by others with definite self-interests (Richmond, 1990). If evaluators refrain from making clear interpretations, they are avoiding responsibility for what they were hired to do. Although service staff are seldom trained to translate evaluation or research findings into policy implications, discussions with them will help evaluators understand the implications of the findings, but it is the responsibility of the evaluators to seek to discover them.

Don't Take the Easy Way Out

There is always a temptation to please the evaluation sponsor. An evaluator working for the agency sponsoring the program might be tempted to place great importance on consumer satisfaction, which is often surprisingly favorable even when more objective outcomes show little program impact. The course ratings of even poor college teachers are usually in the satisfactory range, the vast majority of hospital patients are satisfied with their treatment, and clients typically report being quite satisfied with psychotherapy (Gaston and Sabourin, 1992). Other excuses for not dealing with the unfavorable parts of mixed findings include: (1) noting that the outcome measures were unreliable and thus insufficiently sensitive to detect program effects, (2) questioning the size or representativeness of the sample, and (3) finding reasons why the program may not have been at full strength when evaluated. Since no evaluation is perfect, it does not take that much creativity to find faults with an outcome evaluation that one wants to ignore. These issues should have been dealt with during the planning phase, not during the interpretation phase of an evaluation.

Choosing to emphasize the more favorable findings certainly may be appropriate at times. Perhaps the unfavorable findings concern only the less important objectives or only small portions of the target population. However, stressing the positive and ignoring the negative in order to please the evaluation sponsors, to avoid hurting the feelings of friends, or to remain eligible for continued funding is unethical. When a program or a policy does not show strong positive effects, some other program might be a better use of resources.

Show How to Use the Evaluation to Improve the Program

The best way to deal with mixed results is to emphasize that the purpose of the evaluation was to help managers and staff improve or refine their conceptualization of the program. A number of evaluators suggest that utilization is often viewed simplistically because evaluators have not thought through what might be utilized from an evaluation (Nagel, 1983b; Leviton and Boruch, 1983; Weiss, 1998). It is simply not true that the only utilization of an outcome study is to continue a good program or discontinue an ineffective one. By reflecting on alternatives with the stakeholders, evaluators can develop more sophisticated applications and recommendations.

To reduce worry among managers and staff about less than totally favorable evaluation findings, we have found an analogy from medicine to be helpful. Managers are asked to view evaluators in the same way as physicians view laboratory personnel in hospitals. Physicians are responsible for developing medical care plans to address their patients' illnesses. However, before developing medical care plans, physicians order laboratory tests, X-rays, and other diagnostic procedures. After studying the results of these tests, physicians develop a better understanding of the strengths of their patients and form hypotheses about the causes of their symptoms and the best course of treatment.

After the treatment begins, patients are tested again to evaluate the effectiveness of the medical care. If the results are favorable, physicians conclude that the treatment is effective and treatment continues. If the test results show that the patient is not improving, physicians conclude that the problem is difficult to diagnose or does not respond quickly to treatment. Alternate treatment plans may have to be developed. Follow-up testing could also reveal negative side effects that must be taken into account as the treatment plan is modified. Although a physician may not be pleased with the test results, helping the patient is facilitated by having the test findings. In a similar manner, managers and staff can work with evaluators to examine evaluation findings that will reveal the strengths and weaknesses of a program.

USING EVALUATIONS WHEN AN INNOVATIVE PROGRAM SEEMS NO BETTER THAN OTHER TREATMENTS

When evaluators conclude that treatment and comparison groups do not differ on outcome criteria, they may face challenges in working with stakeholders. But, first, evaluators must be sure of their conclusions. In some cases, there might be a silver lining.

When Can Evaluators Be Sure Groups Do Not Differ?

Evaluators carefully review their own procedures before concluding that a program did not have an effect. In Chapter 11 we mentioned that a naive use of statistics had led evaluators to believe that an evaluation showed no impact when, in fact, the evaluation design and analyses were inadequate to detect valuable changes in program participants (e.g., Julnes and Mohr, 1989; Lipsey, 1990; Meehl, 1990; Yeaton and Sechrest, 1986, 1987).

Although often ignored in practice, it is widely known that a nonsignificant statistical test can be produced by small samples, by marginal implementation, by unreliable measures, or by demanding that only a low probability of a Type I error be tolerated. Before concluding that the treatment group and control group did not differ, it is necessary to analyze each of these problems. In Chapter 11 we mentioned that power tables can be used to inform the choice of sample size to raise the probability of detecting a specified effect size if the program causes it. Thus, the first step is to be sure that the sample sizes were sufficient. In addition, evaluations should include an examination of the degree of implementation. In the early stages of many programs, implementation is marginal and many programs are never fully implemented (Shadish, 2002). Before concluding that a program failed, it would be important to know just what it was that failed. Was it the program as planned, or a program that included only half of the planned components? Third, were the measurement tools sufficient to capture the essence of the program? Fourth, some evaluators seem to believe that credibility is enhanced when they test null hypotheses with the same low probabilities as used in basic laboratory research. Holding to a rigorous barrier to rejecting the null hypothesis means that the chances of missing a program effect will be large. Julnes and Mohr (1989) present three alternative approaches to avoiding Type II errors (that is, missing a program effect). One method is to raise alpha level above 0.05. A higher alpha means the Type I errors will be larger, but Type II errors are smaller. Posavac (1998) shows how to pick an alpha level so that the probabilities of Type I and Type II errors are equal. One may conclude that an innovative program is equivalent to no (or the standard) treatment only after having made a good effort to find a difference (Fitch, 1995). It is important to demonstrate that the probability of a Type II error is very low before saying, "There are no differences between the groups."

Another aspect of making a good effort to find an effect before concluding that a program is just as effective as the control program is to examine the impact model. A useful impact model would have included (1) intermediate outcomes as well as final outcomes and (2) specified characteristics of the participants most likely to benefit from the program. A good effort would have involved testing implications of the impact model. Theoretical and statistical issues are part of a good effort at finding a program effect.

Are Evaluations Valuable Even When No Advantage for the Innovation Is Found?

If a good effort has been made, one may conclude that the evidence strongly suggests that the innovation was not as effective as hoped. Negative findings are disappointing; however, there might be a bright side to finding that a standard treatment was as effective as an innovative program. If the control group received the standard treatment, it might be true that a less expensive program is just as effective as a more expensive one. In criminal justice, a critical outcome variable is recidivism. Waldo and Chiricos (1977) showed that although work-release programs for prisoners did not lead to lower recidivism of convicts as was hoped, work-release did not lead to greater rearrest rates either. Even though work-release did not provide the greater level of rehabilitation that innovators had expected, it was less expensive to permit a prisoner to participate in a work-release program than to simply keep him in a traditional prison. In other words, work-release programs can be supported—not because they are better at rehabilitating prisoners, but because they are cheaper and yield as good (or as bad) results as regular prisons. After the evaluation, work-release programs could still be supported, but for different reasons than suggested initially. Case Study 7 describes an evaluation of another alternative to regular prison sentences with a similar finding.

CASE STUDY 7
Evaluations of the Outcomes of Boot Camp Prisons: The Value of Finding
No Differences Between Program and Comparison Groups

> Frustration with the high recidivism rates of released convicts has led to experiments with alternative approaches to sentencing convicts. At the end of 1989, 14 states had experimented with prisons that had adopted the rigorous physical regimens and austere living conditions of military boot camps. Mackenzie (1990) described and reviewed the impact of these programs in a multisite evaluation conducted for the National Institute of Justice. These programs are funded to provide offenders with a sense of discipline and respect for authority. Those completing the programs qualify for release sooner than those who serve time in regular prisons. Perhaps not surprisingly prisoners seem to prefer the boot camps to standard prisons. At the time of Mackenzie's report, only five states had completed preliminary evaluations. The evaluations were based on comparisons of the recidivism rates of offenders who completed a boot camp program with the recidivism rates of parolees who had not served any of their sentences in boot camp programs. The four states with comparison data provided nine comparisons—the rearrest rates for boot camp prisoners were greater than the rearrest rates for parolees in five of the comparisons and less than the rearrest rates for four comparisons. None of the differences were large and no statistical tests were done. Since the costs of the boot camp programs are less than the costs of keeping the offenders in regular prisons for a longer time, states save money when prisoners participate.
>
> Comment: Boot camps for juvenile offenders were still in the news over a decade after this study. Boot camps are still controversial (Styve, MacKenzie, Gover, and Mitchell, 2000). It seems that most participants prefer them to more traditional types of confinement; however, some observers criticize this approach to punishment.

DEVELOPING A LEARNING CULTURE

Some individuals and organizations appear to defensively reject information and suggestions to initiate different activities. Change for change's sake is not needed in human service organizations; however, willingness to consider new alternatives is needed to assure that high quality work is carried out efficiently (see Argyris, 1985; Argyris, Putnam, and Smith, 1985; Torres, Preskill, and Piontek, 2004).

Work with Stakeholders

The utilization of evaluation findings is more likely if evaluators have worked closely with the staff and managers in planning and carrying out an evaluation and if they continue to work with the stakeholders after an evaluation is officially completed. This approach extends the evaluator's role beyond what had characterized the field in the past. Often evaluators were called upon to gather data, present a report, and move on. While evaluations conducted in such a manner could be useful, the probability of effective application increases if the

EVALUATOR PROFILE 9

Angelina Iturrian: Evaluation in a Faith-Based Organization

Ms. Iturrian is a program evaluator with Lutheran Hour Ministries, which is an auxiliary of the Lutheran Church-Missouri Synod. Her undergraduate work at Southern Illinois University Edwardsville was in psychology and statistics. She also earned a Masters in Public Administration from SIUE.

Ms. Iturrian was asked about the biggest challenges in her position. She said that she was the first person to hold a position as an evaluator in Lutheran Hour Ministries. "In positions I held in the past, people requested evaluations; being the first evaluator here was a very difficult hurdle for me. I had to learn about the different departments and services FIRST so that I could then come up with a plan on how I could then serve THEM. I always drew up proposals that sold the benefits and gave them very clear ideas on what to expect. I took every opportunity I could to be involved with groups and development teams. I didn't wait for invitations; I asked for them. The impact was that I became involved from the very beginning—which meant I had a better picture of the program or service and they also had a better idea of what I could bring to the table."

She continued, "I have to accept that evaluation here is a balancing act between the benefit of rational tools and trust in God's faithfulness. As a faith-based organization, research is certainly not the final answer. However, I can build trust in what evaluation can offer to being good stewards of God's resources. Now, I have plenty of offers to be involved."

Source: Personal communication, July 2001.

evaluator's role includes working with stakeholders while they implement changes. If evaluators continue to gather data and provide feedback about the effectiveness of changes, the cycle of planning, implementing, evaluating, and making program adjustments is completed as suggested in Figure 1.1. This expanded role is not easily filled by external evaluators; however, the roles of internal evaluators often include more intense work with stakeholders. In Evaluator Profile 9, Angelina Iturrian describes how she developed close cooperation with the developmental teams in her organization.

Adopt Developmental Interpretations

The recognition that not every innovation or creative idea will be a success is an essential element of a culture that facilitates effective utilization of evaluation findings. Program directors and staff must feel free to innovate, but they must also be willing to recognize and learn from failures. The willingness to set aside less productive ideas and procedures enables staff to experiment with new approaches to achieve program goals.

When failures are hidden, it is impossible to learn from them. If approaches that failed are unknown, then marginally effective efforts to change organizations go unquestioned and are not improved. A more fruitful approach is to measure competence not only by skill in avoiding errors but by skill in detecting them and acting on the information openly. Edmondson (1996; 2004) showed that the attitude of nursing managers toward nurses who reported "avoidable drug errors" (ADEs) were related to how many were reported. Managers who defined their roles to include coaching and the development of their staff were more likely to be informed of errors. Those who used a punitive management style learned of fewer errors and thus had less opportunity to change procedures to reduce future ADEs. We must learn to reward those who own up to failures and learn from their errors so that changes in programs can be made. Evaluation procedures should not inadvertently encourage hiding errors.

While an atmosphere that respects freedom to fail is essential for an effective use of evaluation findings, it is beyond the power of evaluators to single-handedly create such a culture if it does not exist. In healthy organizations, administrators understand that innovation entails the possibility that even well-designed and fully implemented programs might not work as well as imagined. When a healthy attitude toward innovation exists, evaluators make every effort to encourage it. It is crucial that evaluators avoid implying that evaluation has a punitive role. It is important to keep staff focused on the point of evaluation—data-driven program improvement—not the preparation of summative report cards. When central administrators request an evaluation of a program, it may be useful for evaluators to request an explicit statement from administrators that the purpose of the evaluation is to encourage reflection and further development, not simply to expose failure. Of course, it may well be that the most defensive organizations will not sponsor evaluations in the first place.

Frame Findings in Terms of Improvements

A third element of a productive attitude involves leading staff and managers to expect that evaluations will include some recommendations of new ways to deliver a service or for refinements in the objectives of the program, rather than a stark presentation of good news or bad news (Torres, Preskill, and Piontek, 2004). It is extremely rare that an existing program is terminated or continued solely on the basis of an evaluation. Nevertheless, program managers who are deeply involved with their programs worry about continued agency support. As a result, they often look for one-line summaries of evaluations: Does the evaluation support the program or doesn't it? Might this approach be similar to that of students who check the grade on a paper, but fail to read the professor's comments? Evaluators raise the chances of findings being utilized effectively when they have helped program personnel understand that nearly every evaluation brings both good and bad news, and that the important question is: What directions for program improvement are provided by the evaluation? The goal is to improve and modify programs, not to enshrine or destroy them.

During an evaluation of a physical medicine and rehabilitation unit in a community hospital, the unit team understood from the beginning that the rehabilitation unit was going to remain intact regardless of the outcome of the evaluation. However, administrators were interested in learning how much progress stroke patients were making during their stay in the unit, and also whether those who had improved during the hospitalization continued to improve, or at least maintained their capabilities, after they had returned home. The findings of the evaluation showed that during the hospitalization, stroke patients improved their physical skills (walking, eating, dressing) more than their cognitive skills (speaking, remembering). The evaluation also showed that the majority of patients who made progress during hospitalization maintained their improvement after returning home. This information helped the rehabilitation teams consider whether a follow-up program geared to patients who did not maintain their improvement was needed.

Treat Findings as Tentative Indicators, Not Final Answers

Treating evaluation findings as tentative indicators will contribute to maintaining a learning culture. It would be convenient if one evaluation could provide the definitive word on an issue; however, those who expect a final conclusion from an evaluation are bound to be disappointed (Figueredo, 1993; Shadish, 1993). One reason for treating findings as tentative is that specific agency conditions can lead to a program working well in one location or with people having particular needs but not in another agency or with another population. Program effectiveness is dependent on specific aspects of social settings and the staff involved. Although we evaluate programs and develop avenues for pursuing improvements, we cannot expect to generalize about other settings or about what would happen if conditions changed markedly in the current setting. Our findings can be treated as hypotheses about what works best.

Recognize Service Providers' Needs

Evaluators have often focused on research methods and provided valid information without understanding the needs of service providers. One way to avoid this problem is for evaluators to assume multiple roles within an agency (Goering and Wasylenki, 1993). Many people who study evaluation and later carry out evaluations in agencies have been trained primarily as service delivery professionals. Those people may have an advantage in being able to conduct evaluations that are carefully targeted to the information needs of service providers and are more likely to be utilized. Besides having a good understanding of the details of agency services, evaluators who provide services themselves have more credibility with other service providers than methodology-focused evaluators have (Champney, 1993). Of course, a close identification with service providers might limit the likelihood of such evaluators

EVALUATOR PROFILE 10

Chris Burns Perkins: From Primate Research to Program Evaluation

Chris Burns Perkins works in Charlotte, NC, as an independent management consultant to behavioral health care organizations. She earned her master's in Anthropology (Yale University) and worked in primate research for 10 years. While teaching at a junior college, she was asked to help develop a program evaluation system in a drug and alcohol rehabilitation center. (She reports that in both primate research and addictions treatment evaluation the fundamental task is the same—measure changes in behavior objectively over time.) Later, after accepting a full-time position in evaluation, she supplemented her undergraduate psychology major with course work in addictions therapy and studied regulatory standards for addictions treatment.

She points out that she is more effective as an evaluator because she understands both research and treatment. "This allows me," she says, "to suggest changes to programs that aren't getting results. Importantly, changes to programs and to the ways they are evaluated must also meet current regulatory standards. . . "

She went on to mention that her biggest challenge ". . . is convincing administrators at drug and alcohol treatment centers to allocate time for post-discharge follow-up surveys. These surveys determine whether or not treatment helped the client use less alcohol or drugs. Follow-up takes time. . . But without follow-up information, the counselors and administrators have no idea how effective their treatment programs are; they are just shooting in the dark."

Personal communication, August 2001.

maintaining the necessary openness to the need for change. The best evaluators work closely with stakeholders and learn their professional language so to recognize their needs and, ultimately, increase the utilization of findings, but yet maintain an objective posture toward the program. In Evaluator Profile 10, Chris Burns Perkins illustrates the value of understanding the service providers' perspective and describes the importance of encouraging a learning culture.

Keep Evaluation Findings on the Agency's Agenda

Sonnichsen (2000) argues that utilization is more extensive when evaluators keep reminding managers and program planners about the findings of an evaluation. It may seem that once an evaluation report has been made, the information presented will be utilized soon or not at all. In fact, often there are times when evaluation information is immediately relevant and times when it is not. Unfortunately, as time passes, it would not be surprising to discover that an evaluation had been forgotten several months later when an occasion arose in which the findings could be used. Sonnichsen urged evaluators to keep the evaluation on the agenda; someone must remind administrators about the evaluation or it will be forgotten before it becomes relevant.

If some readers feel that these comments reflect a cynical view of managers and program staff, they are misreading our point. It is easy to remember something that fits with our experiences and immediate needs. Unless new information is associated with other experiences, we quickly forget. Consequently, material in evaluations is more likely to be used if it can be related to problems as they become known or to plans as they are made. The best person to watch for application opportunities may be an internal evaluator.

THE EVALUATION ATTITUDE

This text has sought to provide the groundwork for the development of the technical skills necessary to conduct program evaluations in human service, educational, and business settings. Technical skills are only half of the matter, however. Throughout the text we mention the importance of interpersonal relations and the attitude of evaluators as they work with stakeholders. Here we draw several themes together as a way to stress these nontechnical issues.

Humility won't hurt. Evaluators work in agency settings that are not designed to facilitate research. Furthermore, the agency may well have been operating without the help of an evaluator for quite a while. Consequently, evaluators can expect to be seen as providing an optional service. Because we are always working on someone else's turf, any arrogance on our part may nullify the value of superb technical skills.

Impatience may lead to disappointment. Program and facility administrators may have many constituencies, all expecting attention. Program evaluation is only one source of information on which decisions and plans are based. Financial concerns, community pressures, political realities, and bureaucratic inertia are all powerful influences on program planners and administrators. Evaluators with patience are less likely to feel ignored and unloved when their recommendations do not receive immediate attention.

Recognize the importance of the evaluator's perspective. Service staff focus on individuals and often do not understand the overall program. Administrators see an overall perspective, but tend to focus on financial and other practical matters. Evaluators must therefore complement these viewpoints by integrating verification of service delivery, program impact, and resources expended into one package.

Work on practical questions. People working in service organizations are seldom concerned about matters of only theoretical interest. Evaluators can work more effectively when they are oriented toward practical questions about the program being evaluated. Try to remember that helping people change is hard work. Faced with pressing human needs on one hand and with allegations of inefficiency on the other, agency staff desire practical assistance.

Work on feasible issues. If an evaluation is not feasible, do not attempt it. Do not waste your time and that of the program staff. However, although it may not be feasible to work on, say, a cost–benefit analysis, perhaps monitoring activities and outcomes might be feasible and useful to the agency.

Avoid data addiction. It is tempting to seek to gather a great amount of information about the program and those served. Asking for too much information increases the proportion of program participants who will provide no information. And, in fact, evaluators often find themselves under too much time pressure to analyze all the data gathered, thus wasting the efforts of the cooperative participants. If the information is not essential, do not gather it.

Make reports accessible. Using social science jargon and presenting advanced analyses reduce the flow of information to those not trained as evaluators have been. New evaluators often don't realize that few people understand statistical analyses. Save presentations that display the depth of your knowledge and technical skills for professional meetings. To be effective, presentations must be understandable to those who may act on the recommendations.

Seek evaluations of your own work. When evaluation findings and recommendations seem to fall on deaf ears, evaluators will benefit by asking themselves: Was my presentation clear? Did I address the right questions? Were my answers correct? At times the honest answer will be: "Well, I made some mistakes this time." Seek to learn something for the next evaluation. To evaluate the evaluation one might use Scriven's (1991) Key Evaluation Checklist or review the standards for evaluation (Joint Committee on Standards, 1994). Having another evaluator provide feedback on the completed evaluation might suggest ways to improve the next one.

Encourage the development of a learning culture. Ideally, evaluation encourages honest relations among staff, clients, administrators, and program sponsors. Sometimes people act as though all failures could have been avoided. Failures cannot always be avoided. Only the dead make no mistakes; the living fail from time to time. Instead of hiding or condemning failures, help staff and managers to treat honest attempts as experiments and to learn from them.

Summary and Possible Trends for Program Evaluation

Evaluators have become increasingly active in working with agencies and organizations whose programs have been evaluated. No longer do evaluators slip ten copies of a completed report into the mail after preparing a final written report in their offices. Instead, they seek to help the organization make use of an evaluation even when the findings are mixed or negative. The crucial issue is to encourage stakeholders to look upon an evaluation as a development tool to use in making program improvements. The participation of evaluators in planning discussions improves the chances for the appropriate use of feedback on needs, implementation, or outcomes.

The discipline of program evaluation has changed markedly from the 1960s when it began its period of rapid growth. The idea of evaluating the effects of programs and policies is no longer novel or controversial in service agencies and government offices. "Evaluation seems to be almost everywhere these days," report Henry and Mark (2003). Contemporary evaluators are far more sophisticated in methodological skills and in working with organizations than our disciplinary forbears were. And unlike evaluators in the not-very-distant past, we are more likely to expect confusion in program design and limitations in implementation in the field and to recognize the constraints on the activities of the managers of service organizations and government agencies. We also see more clearly that each program setting is unique; what works in one place is not necessarily appropriate for another site or with another population. Evaluators have come to recognize the limitations of evaluation methods as well. The combination of a greater sensitivity to stakeholder needs, a deeper respect for the importance of the context of a program, and a less grandiose view of evaluation methods has resulted, we believe, in better evaluations. Today, we suspect, a smaller proportion of evaluations are inappropriately designed or superficially conducted than in the past. Nevertheless, being useful to organizations and the people served remains a challenge. We have our work cut out for us.

Study Questions

1. Students often seem puzzled by resistance to evaluation findings on the part of stakeholders responsible for providing a service. To develop an understanding of this resistance, imagine something you really worked at—making a high school team, writing an article for a school newspaper, or learning a piece of music, for example. Now imagine one of your parents criticizing you for not doing it perfectly without offering a word of praise. How would you feel? If you can put yourself into this situation, you might better understand the reaction of program personnel toward an insensitive evaluator.

2. If you are up to it, go back and imagine your hypothetical critical parent making a recommendation on how "you should have" reacted on the last football play, or developed the second paragraph differently, or smiled more when you played at your recital. Be sure to recognize that this hypothetical parent has never played football, written a newspaper article, or performed music him/herself. How likely are you to accept the recommendations? Now consider how a police officer or a mental health therapist would react to recommendations from a critical evaluator who has never been ordered to stop and question a possibly dangerous person or tried to counsel a depressed teenager threatening suicide.

3. What aspect of a person's demeanor would encourage you to consider recommendations made for helping you improve your work?

4. Suppose that you completed an evaluation of that sexual assault program mentioned in the first chapter. Suppose that you did make a good effort and learned: (a) that both male and female participants were clearer on the definitions of what is and what is not a sexual assault; (b) that at the follow-up only a few female participants were taking the precautions recommended in the program; and (c) that at the follow-up most men indicated that they thought most sexual assaults were the victims' fault. What implications are suggested by these findings and how can you as the evaluator encourage utilization of your findings?

5. A college committee considered recommending approval of a proposed multidisciplinary program, say, Psychology and Law. What might the committee learn from a needs assessment? What might they use from a study of the jobs or further study of the alumni of the college's undergraduate programs? How could the committee encourage a learning climate among their colleagues in the college when the recommended proposal is presented to a larger, decision-making body?

6. Think of situations in which value polarization might occur. What might be happen if a faculty and student committee considers whether grade inflation is a problem at their college?

Additional Resource

TORRES, R. T., PRESKILL, H. S., AND PIONTEK, M. E. 2004. *Evaluation strategies for communicating and reporting: Enhancing learning in organizations,* rev. ed. Thousand Oaks, CA: Sage.

This is the same resource recommended in the previous chapter. The authors are concerned with both reporting and encouraging utilization of evaluations.

Appendix
Illustrative Program
Evaluation Report

An abbreviated program evaluation report is presented here. McKillip, Lockhart, Eckert, and Phillips (1985) evaluated a media-based program by a university health center to communicate two messages concerning healthy attitudes toward alcohol use. The evaluation was an examination of whether the posters and newspaper ads would get the students' attention. Clearly the outcome desired is for students to discourage friends from driving while intoxicated and to feel free to decline a drink in spite of social pressure. However, it is pointless to mount a media campaign if students don't even notice the messages; this evaluation sought to be sure that the first step toward encouraging healthy attitudes did occur.

Note that this evaluation combined an interrupted time series with switching replications and the control construct design (see McKillip, 1992, for a detailed discussion of the analysis). The use of this design produced an evaluation carefully protected from threats to internal validity. Note the use of multiple sources of data. Finally, note the percentage of students who reported that they had seen the posters *before* the posters went up. These percentages should caution readers about a naive use of self report in evaluations; these evaluators wisely based the evaluation on the change between when the posters were not up and when they were displayed, not on the percentage of students saying they saw the posters.

The content of this illustrative report accurately reflects the findings of the original evaluation. However, the university name has been changed and a few fictional details have been added to better illustrate how a report would be presented to an agency. Reports to agencies are not done in the format used for papers in research journals.

Responsible Alcohol Use Media Campaign: Can We Get College Students' Attention?[1]

An evaluation of the media campaign in the Fall Semester of 2000–2001 sponsored by the Alcohol Education Project of the Student Health Center to encourage social behaviors that counter the prevailing student culture fostering the over-consumption of alcohol

SSU

Jack McKillip, D.C. Lockhart, P. S. Eckert, and J. Phillips

[1]McKillip, J., Lockhart, D. C., Eckert, P.S., and Philips, J., 1985. Adapted with permission.

Contents

Summary   1

Needs to Be Met by the Program   2

Program Description   2
  Target Population   2
  Multi-Media Intervention   2

Evaluation Questions   3

Evaluation Design   3
      Table 1   4

Evaluation Findings   5
  Interviews   5
  Mailed Survey   5
      Figure 1   6
  Media Information Table   7

Conclusions and Implications   8

References   9

Appendices *(buff-colored pages)*   10

SUMMARY

Responsible alcohol use was encouraged by a program sponsored by the Alcohol Education Project at Southern State University. A needs assessment showed that students endorsed moderate drinking, but believed that their friends expected them to do more heavy drinking. The experiences of the Alcohol Education Project (AEP) staff suggested that another problem on campus was drinking and driving. A campaign was planned to encourage students to (1) resist peer pressure to drink heavily and (2) stop friends from driving while drunk. Posters, newspaper ads, an information booth, and a radio call-in show were used by the AEP staff to stress these two themes. There is evidence that those students who are still forming their drinking habits can be influenced by appropriate information; however, information will not be received if the media used to provide the information do not attract the attention of the target audience.

Since the effectiveness of posters, ads, and other methods in attracting student attention was not known, an evaluation was conducted during a ten-week period. A two-week baseline period (with no AEP posters or ads in place) was followed by a two-week emphasis on resisting peer pressure to drink. A second two-week baseline period was followed by a two-week emphasis on keeping friends from driving while drunk. The evaluation ended with a third two-week baseline period. During the two intervention periods, posters, ads, and a radio show stressed one of the themes. For the first four periods (eight weeks) an information table was set up in the student union on Thursdays during the lunch hour. No AEP materials were available during the last two-week period.

Interviews during the ten week evaluation showed that students became aware of the campaign and its themes, student recognition of Theme One increased abruptly during week three, but the level of recognition of Theme Two did not change. When Theme Two materials were available (during weeks seven and eight), recognition of Theme Two increased abruptly. The conclusion that students were aware of the messages was also supported by the numbers and types of material taken from the information table during the weeks of the campaign. Last, a mailed survey during weeks nine and ten showed that the two themes targeted by the campaign were recognized more frequently than the other AEP themes not stressed in this media program.

It was concluded that the media campaign was effective in attracting student attention. Although getting student attention is merely a first step in a chain of events that is hoped to result in responsible alcohol use, it is an essential step. Student services staff members can be confident that using well-placed posters and providing alcohol-related information is an effective use of educational resources.

NEEDS TO BE MET BY THE PROGRAM

Widespread evidence indicates that the rate of abuse of alcoholic beverages on U.S. college campuses is a current problem with implications for the future health of students. Informal observations suggested that alcohol abuse is a problem at Southern State University as well. In addition, answers to mailed surveys to students indicated that although the majority of SSU students viewed moderate drinking as desirable, they believed that their peers expected them to drink heavily. It seemed important for students to be encouraged to hold to their belief in moderate drinking by helping them to resist peer pressures to abuse alcohol. Drinking and driving was also found to be a frequently encountered alcohol-related problem on campus. On the basis of this needs assessment, the SSU Alcohol Education Project staff designed a media-based education program to address alcohol use as related to peer pressure and driving.

PROGRAM DESCRIPTION

Target Population

SSU students, approximately 18,700 undergraduates and 3,300 graduate students, made up the target population of a multimedia campaign to encourage responsible alcohol use.

Multi-Media Intervention

Previous research (Ray, 1973; Rothchild, 1979) has implied that students who are not heavily involved in alcohol abuse and are just forming their alcohol-related attitudes, can be influenced by material strengthening inclinations toward responsible alcohol use. Therefore, the staff of the Alcohol Education Project (AEP) expected that a media-based education project could have positive effects. (Heavy drinkers and those whose drinking patterns are well practiced would probably not be influenced by this approach.)

The two themes for the intervention were selected on the basis of the needs assessment. Theme one was: "It's not rude to refuse a drink." Theme two was: "Friends don't let friends drive drunk."

The program sought to increase student awareness of these themes by (1) putting posters in public places throughout the campus (307 were used for the first theme and 203 for the second); (2) placing half-page ads identical to the posters in the Tuesday and Thursday issues of the campus newspaper; (3) creating a 9.8 square foot window display in the student union concerning the theme being publicized; (4) having an AEP staff member on a radio call-in show during the first week each of the themes was stressed; and (5) providing an information table in the student union during the noon hours of each Thursday stocked with written material on responsible alcohol use with an AEP staff member available to answer questions.

EVALUATION QUESTIONS

The materials could be ignored or they could be attended to by students. Thus, the evaluation sought to assess the degree that the media campaign attracted student attention. Interviews, surveys, and behavioral measures were used to judge whether students were aware of the campaign.

EVALUATION DESIGN

To permit an evaluation of the program, the campaign was divided into five two-week periods as shown in Table 1. The five periods included:

1. A two-week baseline period that only involved the informational table in the student union.
2. A two-week period, weeks three and four, during which the first theme was emphasized using posters, newspaper ads, the window display, and the radio call-in show.
3. A two-week baseline period during which all materials for the first theme had been removed except for the materials at the information table.
4. A two-week period, weeks seven and eight, during which the second theme was emphasized in the same ways used with the first theme.
5. A two-week baseline period in which all campaign materials were removed including the information table.

The use of baseline periods is frequently used in some forms of psychotherapy in order to show that the treatment had an effect. If the present program had an effect, one would expect students to be more aware of the themes of the campaign after the posters, ads, display, and radio show were in place compared to the weeks before. The use of two interventions permitted a replication of the design. That is, if any apparent effects of the first theme of the program were detected by comparing the first period with the second, the pattern could be verified by comparing the first six weeks of the program with the fourth period (weeks seven and eight) using student reactions to the second theme. If the patterns were very similar, one could conclude confidently that the AEP media campaign was responsible for student awareness of the themes. Possible alternative interpretations based on national news reports or alcohol industry ads could be rejected as implausible.

TABLE 1 Timeline for Media Campaign and Evaluation Activities

	WEEK OF SEMESTER									
	1	2	3	4	5	6	7	8	9	10
Media*:										
Theme One	O	O	X	X	O	O	O	O	O	O
Theme Two	O	O	O	O	O	O	X	X	O	O
Measurements:										
Interviews	+	+	+	+	+	+	+	+	+	+
Mailed Survey	a	a	a	a	a	a	a	a	+	+
Media Booth	+	+	+	+	+	+	+	+	a	a

*Includes posters, newspaper advertisements, window displays and radio appearance.

Note: "O" indicates that media related to the theme were not available and "X" indicates that media were available, "+" indicates measurements were taken and an "a" indicates that measurements were not taken. All measurements were relevant to both campaign themes.

EVALUATION FINDINGS

Interviews

Of the 371 students interviewed over the ten weeks, 60 percent were male and 40 percent were female, approximating the composition of the student body. No student was interviewed more than once. During each of the ten weeks approximately 40 students were selected at random during the lunch hour from students at the library, a student union cafeteria, and a busy outdoor walkway. AEP staff members interviewed students concerning the recall of the poster and the newspaper ad. Respondents were shown a facsimile of the newspaper ad/poster for both campaign themes and were asked if they had seen them in the university newspaper or as a poster.

Figure 1 includes the percentages of students reporting that they recalled seeing the poster and the newspaper ad for each of the ten weeks of the campaign. The upper panel of the figure shows the pronounced jump in awareness for Theme One in week three. Note that the lower panel shows that Theme Two was not recognized by as many students during weeks three and four as was the first theme. Since only the first theme was being publicized, these patterns support the interpretation that the campaign was effective in attracting student attention. The difference in the students' reactions to the two themes shows that students were not simply saying that they saw the posters/ad because they thought that is what the interviewers wanted them to say.

In week seven the materials for Theme Two appeared. As expected, awareness of having seen Theme Two material increased abruptly. Recall of Theme One material did not drop to the baseline level since students could remember having seen Theme One material earlier. This replication gave credibility to the interpretation that the multimedia campaign was responsible for student awareness of the program's themes.

Mailed Survey

During the final two-week period, a twelve-page survey on alcohol use was mailed to a random sample of 1,113 students. Usable questionnaires were received from 56.7 percent of this sample. Answers to demographic questions indicated that the respondents accurately reflected the characteristics of the student body.

In addition to questions about alcohol consumption, students were asked which of the seven AEP posters, two from the campaign themes and five not used in this campaign, they had seen. All posters were identified only by their textual content and had been available from AEP since the spring semester of 2002, prior to this fall semester study. The percentage of respondents who recalled having seen each of the posters "more than once" was the measure of program effectiveness. Theme One was recalled by 62 percent of

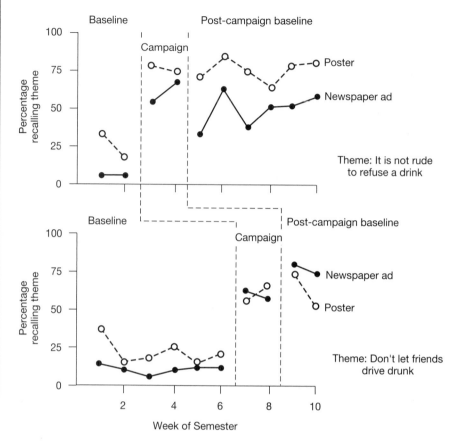

FIGURE 1   Record of percentage of students interviewed reporting recall of poster and newspaper ad containing media campaign themes. Baseline—period before theme's posters or ads were introduced. Campaign—two-week period in which posters and ads for particular theme were displayed about campus and published in campus newspaper. Post-theme baseline—period following campaign, ads for theme were not published and posters for them were taken down.

the respondents and Theme Two by 83 percent. In contrast, the other five AEP (non-campaign) posters were recalled by only 12 to 48 percent of the respondents. The difference between the campaign themes and the other messages was statistically significant ($p = 0.03$). The level of recall was not related to respondent gender, reported college class, or self-described level of alcohol consumption.

Media Information Table

During weeks one through eight the information table was maintained during the Thursday lunch hours in the student union. An AEP staff member answered questions and seven different posters (two campaign theme posters and five others) as well as other materials were available for student use. Overall, more responsible alcohol-use literature was taken during the weeks of the campaign compared to baseline weeks. During the campaign weeks (weeks three, four, seven, and eight) an average of 13.00 campaign theme posters were taken per day compared to an average of 5.33 during the baseline weeks ($t(14) = 2.38$, $p = 0.016$, one-tailed). Furthermore, during the four weeks of the campaign an average of 75 pieces of material were taken compared to 51 pieces during the baseline weeks. This difference is in the direction that one would expect if the campaign had been successful; however, the difference was not statistical significant ($t(14) = 1.42$, $p = 0.089$, one-tailed).

8

Conclusions and Implications

These findings support the use of media, especially multiple media, to publicize responsible alcohol use. Attracting student attention is the essential first step in providing information that may be internalized and may, in turn, result in the development of responsible alcohol use habits.

It is important to note that the point of all health education campaigns is to improve health or prevent loss of health. This evaluation has not demonstrated that the media campaign had an effect on the well-being of students. Although the campaign effectively got the students' attention, there are so many messages endorsing alcohol consumption that the Student Health Center's goals can easily be thwarted. Like any other single health education effort, it would be hard to show a direct connection between the effort and health of the target population. Nevertheless, these data imply that media programs are effective uses of health educational resources.

REFERENCES

RAY, M. 1973. Marketing communication and the hierarchy of effects. In *New models for mass communication research*, ed. P. Clarke. Beverly Hills, CA: Sage.

ROTHCHILD, M. L. 1979. Advertising strategies for high and low involvement situations. In *Attitude research plays for high stakes*, ed. J. Maloney and B. Silverman. New York: American Marketing Association.

*[This page and all pages of the appendices would be
buff colored in the actual report.]*

APPENDICES

1. List of the locations of the posters during the campaign.
2. Reproductions of the posters used.
3. Interview questions.
4. Mailed survey.
5. Means, standard deviations, and sample sizes.

*[It is recommended that a written report also include these items. Many external eval-
uators (but few internal evaluators) also include letters of agreement relevant to the
initiation of the evaluation project. To conserve space neither the items listed above
nor letters of agreement have been included in this illustrative report.]*

References

A citizen's guide to the Federal budget, FY 2002. 2001. Washington, DC: U.S. Government Printing Office (S/N 041-001-00556-1).

ABELSON, P. H. 1977. Commission on federal paperwork. *Science, 197,* 1237.

ABELSON, R. P. 1995. *Statistics as principled argument.* Hillsdale, NJ: Lawrence Erlbaum Associates.

ACKOFF, R. L. 1986. *Management in small doses.* New York: Wiley.

AIKEN, L. S., AND WEST, S. G. 1990. Invalidity of true experiments: Self-report biases. *Evaluation Review, 14,* 374–390.

AIKEN, L. S., WEST, S. G., SCHWALM, D. E., CARROLL, J. L., AND HSIUNG, S. 1998. Comparison of a randomized and two quasi-experimental designs in a single outcome evaluation. *Evaluation Review, 22,* 207–243.

ALEXANDER, H. A. 1986. Cognitive relativism in evaluation. *Evaluation Review, 10,* 259–280.

ALTSCHULD, J. W., AND WITKIN, B. R. 2000. *From needs assessment to action: Transforming needs into solution strategies.* Thousand Oaks, CA: Sage.

AMERICAN EDUCATIONAL RESEARCH ASSOCIATION. 1994. *Ethical standards of the American Educational Research Association.* Washington, DC: Author.

AMERICAN EVALUATION ASSOCIATION GUIDING PRINCIPLES FOR EVALUATORS (www.eval.org/Guiding%20Principles.htm; retrieved May 16, 2005).

AMERICAN PSYCHOLOGICAL ASSOCIATION. 1992. Ethical principles of psychologists and code of conduct. *American Psychologist, 47,* 1597–1611.

AMERICAN SOCIOLOGICAL ASSOCIATION. 1989. *Revised code of ethics.* Washington, DC: Author.

ANDERSON, C.A. 2001. Heat and violence. *Current Directions in Psychological Science, 10,* 33–38.

ANDERSON, J. F., AND BERDIE, D. R. 1975. Effects on response rate of formal and informal questionnaire follow-up techniques. *Journal of Applied Psychology, 60,* 225–257.

ANGELO, T. A., AND CROSS, K. P. 1993. *Classroom assessment techniques: A handbook for college teachers.* Rev. ed. San Francisco: Jossey-Bass.

ANKUTA, G. Y., AND ABELES, N. 1993. Client satisfaction, clinical significance, and meaningful change in psychotherapy. *Professional Psychology: Research and Practice, 24,* 70–74.

ARGYRIS, C. 1985. *Strategy, change, and defensive routines.* Boston: Pitman.

ARGYRIS, C., PUTNAM, R., AND SMITH, D. M. 1985. *Action science: Concepts, methods, and skills for research and intervention.* San Francisco: Jossey-Bass.

ARISTIGUETA, M. P. 1999. *Managing for results in state government.* Westport, CN: Quorum Books.

ARVEY, R. D., AND COLE, D. A. 1989. Evaluating change due to training. In *Training and development in organizations,* eds. I. Goldstein & associates. San Francisco: Jossey-Bass.

ASTIN, A. W. 1971. Two approaches to measuring students' perceptions of their college environment. *Journal of College Student Personnel, 12*(2), 169–172.

ASTIN, A. W. 1993. *Assessment for excellence: The philosophy and practice of assessment and evaluation in higher education.* Phoenix, AZ: Oryx Press.

AVERCH, H. A. 1994. The systematic use of expert judgment. In *Handbook of practical program evaluation,* eds. J. S. Wholey, H. R. Hatry, and K. E. Newcomer. San Francisco: Jossey-Bass.

BABBIE, E. 2003. *Practice of social research,* 10th ed. Belmont, CA: Wadsworth.

BALL, S., AND BOGARTZ, G. A. 1970. *The first year of Sesame Street.* Princeton, NJ: Educational Testing Service.

BARBOUR, G. P., AND WOLFSON, S. M. 1973. Productivity measurement in police crime control. *Public Management, 55,* 16, 18, 19.

BARENDREGT, J. J., BONNEUX, L., AND VAN DER MAAS, P. J. 1997. The health care costs of smoking. *The New England Journal of Medicine, 337,* 1052–1057.

BARZANSKY, A., BERNER, E., AND BECKMAN, C. R. R. 1985. Evaluation of a clinical program: Applying the concept of trustworthiness. *Evaluation & the Health Professions, 8,* 193–208.

Baseline report: strategic development and planning meeting. 2001. Bethesda, MD: National Institutes of Health, National Institute of Diabetes & Digestive & Kidney Diseases.

BAUER, S. M., AND TOMS, K. 1989. Will there be any scientists in the class of 2000? [Summary]. Proceedings of the Annual Meeting of the American Evaluation Association, 26.

BECHTEL, R. B. 1997. *Environment and behavior: An introduction.* New York: Sage.

BERK, R. A. 1977. Discretionary methodology decisions in applied research. *Sociological Methods and Research, 5,* 317–334.

BERK, R. A., AND ROSSI, P. H. 1976. Doing good or worse: Evaluation research politically reexamined. *Social Problems, 23,* 337–349.

BERMAN, J. J. 1978. An experiment in parole supervision. *Evaluation Quarterly, 2,* 71–90.

BERNSTEIN, D. J. 1999. Comments on Perrin's "Effective use and misuse of performance measurement." *American Journal of Evaluation, 20,* 85–93.

BERWICK, D. M. 1989. Continuous improvement as an ideal in health care. *New England Journal of Medicine, 320,* 53–56.

BICKMAN, L. 2000. In *Program theory in evaluation: Challenges and opportunities, New Directions for Program Evaluation, No. 87,* eds. P. J. Rogers, T. A. Hacsi, A. Petrosino, and T. A. Huebner. San Francisco: Jossey-Bass.

BIGELOW, D. Q., AND CIARLO, J. A. 1975. The impact of therapeutic effectiveness data on community mental health center management: The systems evaluation project. *Community Mental Health Journal, 11,* 64–73.

BINGHAM, S. G., AND SCHERER, L. L. 2001. The unexpected effects of a sexual harassment educational program. *The Journal of Applied Behavioral Science, 37,* 125–153.

BINNER, P. R. 1977. Outcome measures and cost analysis. In *Emerging developments in mental health evaluation,* eds. W. Neigher, R. Hammer, and G. Landsberg. New York: Argold Press.

BINNER, P. R. 1991. Needed for mental health management: A new measurement paradigm. *Administration and Policy in Mental Health, 18,* 355–366.

BINNER, P. R. 1993. Information systems and mental health services: Issues for the 90's. *Computers in Human Services, 9*, 47–57.

BOK, S. 1974. The ethics of giving placebos. *Scientific American, 231*(5), 17–23.

BOONE, P. 1994. Down the rathole. *The Economist, 333* (Dec. 10), 69.

BORUCH, R. F. 1997. *Randomized experiments for planning and evaluation: A practical guide.* Thousand Oaks, CA: Sage.

BORUCH, R. F. 1998. Randomized controlled experiments for evaluation and planning. In *Handbook of applied social research methods*, eds. L. Bickman and D. J. Rog. Thousand Oaks, CA: Sage.

BOTCHEVA, L., WHITE, C. R., AND HUFFMAN, L. C. 2003. Learning culture and outcomes measurement practices in community agencies. *American Journal of Evaluation, 22*, 421–434.

BRIGHAM, S. E. 1993. TQM: Lessons we can learn from industry. *Change* (May/June), 42–48.

BRINKERHOFF, R. O. 2003. *The success case method.* San Francisco: Berrett-Koehler.

BROCKNER, J., NATHANSON, S., FRIEND, A., HARBECK, J., SAMUELSON, C., HOUSER, R., BAZERMAN, M. H., AND RUBIN, J. Z. 1984. The role of modeling processes in the "Knee Deep in the Big Muddy" phenomenon. *Organizational Behavior and Human Performance, 33*, 77–99.

BROTMAN, B. 1983. "Workfare": What state terms success others call boondoggle. *Chicago Tribune*, January 2, Sec. 3, pp. 1, 4.

BROWN, F. G. 1984. *Principles of educational and psychological testing.* 3rd ed. New York: Holt, Rinehart, and Winston.

BROWN, J. B., AND ADAMS, M. E. 1992. Patients as reliable reporters of medical care process. *Medical Care, 30*, 400–411.

BRYANT, F. B., AND GUILBAULT, R. L. 2002. "I knew it all along" eventually: The development of hindsight bias in reaction to the Clinton impeachment verdict. *Basic and Applied Social Psychology, 24*, 27–41.

BRYK, A. S., ED. 1983. *Stakeholder-based evaluation.* San Francisco: Jossey-Bass.

BUNDA, M. A. 1983. Alternative ethics reflected in education and evaluation. *Evaluation News, 4*(1), 57–58.

BURTLE, V., ED. 1979. *Women who drink.* Springfield, IL: Charles C. Thomas.

BUSSIGEL, M., AND FILLING, C. 1985. Data discrepancies and their origins: An evaluation of a family practice residency program using a naturalistic inquiry paradigm. *Evaluation & the Health Professions, 8*, 177–192.

CAGLE, L. T., AND BANKS, S. M. 1986. The validity of assessing mental health needs with social indicators. *Evaluation and Program Planning, 9*, 127–142.

CAIDIN, M. 1960. *Let's go flying!* New York: Dutton.

CAMPBELL, D. T. 1969. Reforms as experiments. *American Psychologist, 24*, 409–429.

CAMPBELL, D. T. 1983. The problem of being scientific in program evaluation. Paper presented at the meeting of the Evaluation Research Society. October, Chicago.

CAMPBELL, D. T. 1986. Relabeling internal and external validity for applied social scientists. In *Advances in quasi-experimental design and analysis*, ed. W. M. K. Trochim. San Francisco: Jossey-Bass.

CAMPBELL, D. T. 1987. Guidelines for monitoring the scientific competence of preventive intervention research centers. *Knowledge: Creation, Diffusion, Utilization, 8,* 389–430.

CAMPBELL, D. T., AND ERLEBACHER, A. 1970. How regression artifacts in quasi-experimental designs can mistakenly make compensatory education look harmful. In *Compensatory education: A national debate,* ed. J. Hellmuth. Vol. 3 of *Disadvantaged child.* New York: Brunner-Mazel.

CAMPBELL, D. T., AND STANLEY, J. C. 1963. *Experimental and quasi-experimental designs for research.* Chicago: Rand-McNally.

CANNELL, J. J. 1987. *Nationally normed elementary achievement testing in America's public schools: Now all states are above the national average.* Daniels, WV: Friends of Education.

CARD, J. J., GREENO, C., AND PETERSON, J. L. 1992. Planning an evaluation and estimating its cost. *Evaluation & the Health Professions, 15,* 75–89.

CAREY, R. G. 1974. Emotional adjustment in terminal patients. *Journal of Counseling Psychology, 21,* 433–439.

CAREY, R. G. 1979. Evaluation of a primary nursing unit. *American Journal of Nursing, 79,* 1253–1255.

CAREY, R. G., AND LLOYD, R. C. 1995. *Measuring quality improvement in healthcare: A guide to statistical process control applications.* New York: Quality Resources.

CARLEY, M. 1981. *Social measurement and social behaviors.* London: George Allen & Unwin.

CARTER, D. E., AND NEWMAN, F. L. 1976. *A client-centered system of mental health delivery and program management.* Rockville, MD: National Institute of Mental Health.

CASTNER, L., AND CODY, S. 1999. *Trends in FSP participation rates: Focus on September 1997.* Washington, DC: Mathematica Policy Research.

CAUDLE, S. L. 1994. Using qualitative approaches. In *Handbook of practical program evaluation,* eds. J. S. Wholey, H. P. Hatry, and K. E. Newcomer. San Francisco: Jossey-Bass.

CAULKINS, J. P., RYDELL, C. P., EVERINGHAM, S. S., CHIESA, J., AND BUSHWAY, S. 1999. *An ounce of prevention, a pound of cure: The cost-effectiveness of school-based drug prevention programs.* Santa Monica, CA: Rand.

CENTRA, J. A. 1977. Plusses and minuses for faculty development. *Change, 9*(12), 47, 48, 64.

CHAMBERS, F. 1994. Removing the confusion about formative and summative evaluation: Purpose versus time. *Evaluation and Program Planning, 17,* 9–12.

CHAMPNEY, T. F. 1993. Comments on the use of multiple roles to maximize the utilization of outcome research. *Evaluation and Program Planning, 16,* 335, 336.

CHAN, K-C. 1994. *Vaccines for children: Critical issues in design and implementation* (T-PEMD-94-28). Washington, DC: U.S. General Accounting Office.

CHAN, K-C. 1995. *Vaccines for children: Reexamination of program goals and implementation needed to insure vaccination* (T-PEMD-95-22). Washington, DC: U.S. General Accounting Office.

CHAPMAN, C., AND RISLEY, T. R. 1974. Anti-litter procedures in an urban high-density area. *Journal of Applied Behavioral Analysis, 7,* 377–383.

CHELIMSKY, E. 1997. The coming transformation in evaluation. In *Evaluation for the 21st century: A handbook*, eds. E. Chelimsky and W. R. Shadish. Thousand Oaks, CA: Sage.

CHEN, H. T. 1994. Theory-driven evaluations: Need, difficulties, and options. *Evaluation Practice, 15*, 79–82.

CHEN, H. T., AND ROSSI, P. H. 1989. Issues in the theory-driven perspective. *Evaluation and Program Planning, 12*, 299–306.

Cholesterol screening. 1990. Washington, DC: Office of Inspector General, U. S. Department of Health and Human Services.

CICARELLI, V. G., COOPER, W. H., AND GRANGER, R. L. 1969. *The impact of Head Start: An evaluation of the effects of Head Start on children's cognitive and affective development.* Westinghouse Learning Corporation, OEO Contract No. B89 4536.

CLARK, C. 1989. Clear-cut economies: Should we harvest everything now? *The Sciences, 29*(1), 16–19.

COHEN, J. 1987. *Statistical power analysis for behavioral sciences.* Rev. ed. Hillsdale, NJ: Lawrence Erlbaum.

COLBURN, D. 1987. Who pays? Insurance coverage varies widely. *Washington Post, Health: A weekly journal of medicine, science, and society*, (January 20), 18.

CONNER, R. F., JACOBI, M., ALTMAN, D. G., AND ASLANIAN, C. B. 1985. Measuring need and demand in evaluation research. *Evaluation Review, 9*, 717–734.

COOK, T. D. 2000. The false choice between theory-based evaluation and experimentation. In *Program theory in evaluation: Challenges and opportunities, New Directions for Program Evaluation, No. 87*, eds. P. J. Rogers, T. A. Hacsi, A. Petrosino, and T. A. Huebner. San Francisco: Jossey-Bass.

COOK, T. D., APPLETON, H., CONNER, R. F., SHAFFER, A., TAMKIN, G., AND WEBBER, S. J. 1975. *Sesame Street revisited.* New York: Russell Sage.

COOK, T. D., AND CAMPBELL, D. T. 1979. *Quasi-experimentation.* Chicago: Rand-McNally.

COOK, T. D., AND DEVINE, E. C. 1982. Trying to discover explanatory processes through meta-analysis. Paper presented at the National Meeting of the American Educational Research Association. March, New York.

COOK, T. D., LEVITON, L. C., AND SHADISH, W. R. 1985. Program evaluation. In *Handbook of Social Psychology*, 3rd ed., eds. G. Lindzey and E. Aronson. New York: Random House.

COOK, T. D., AND REICHARDT, C. S., EDS. 1979. *Qualitative and quantitative methods in evaluation research.* Beverly Hills, CA: Sage.

COOK, T. D., AND SHADISH, W. R. 1986. Program evaluation: The worldly science. *Annual Review of Psychology, 37*, 193–232.

COOK, T. D., AND SHADISH, W. R. 1994. Social experiments: Some developments over the past fifteen years. *Annual Review of Psychology, 45*, 545–580.

CORDRAY, D. S. 1986. *Quasi-experimental analysis: A mixture of methods and judgment.* In *Advances in quasi-experimental design, New Directions for Program Evaluation, No. 31*, ed. W. M. K. Trochim. San Francisco: Jossey-Bass.

CRANO, W. D., AND BREWER, M. B. 1986. *Principles and methods of social research.* Newton, MA: Allyn and Bacon.

CRONBACH, L. J. 1980. *Toward reform of program evaluation: Aims, methods, and institutional arrangements.* San Francisco: Jossey-Bass.

CRONBACH, L. J. 1982. *Designing evaluations of educational and social programs.* San Francisco: Jossey-Bass.

CUMMING, G., AND FINCH, S. 2005. Inference by eye: Confidence intervals and how to read pictures of data. *American Psychologist, 60,* 170–180.

CUMMINGS, S. R., RUBIN, S. M., AND OSTER, G. 1989. The cost-effectiveness of counseling smokers to quit. *JAMA, 261,* 75–79.

DARLINGTON, R. B., ROYCE, J. M., SNIPPER, A. S., MURRAY, H. A., AND LAZAR, I. 1980. Preschool programs and later school competence of children from low-income families. *Science, 208,* 202–205.

DATTA, L. 1976. The impact of the Westinghouse/Ohio evaluation on the development of project Head Start. In *The evaluation of social programs,* ed. C. C. Abt. Beverly Hills, CA: Sage.

DATTA, L. 1994. Paradigm wars: A basis for peaceful coexistence and beyond. In *The qualitative-quantitative debate: New perspectives, New Directions for Program Evaluation, No. 61,* eds. C. S. Reichardt and S. F. Rallis. San Francisco: Sage.

DATTA, L. 2000. Seriously seeking fairness: Strategies for crafting non-partisan evaluations in a partisan world. *American Journal of Evaluation, 21,* 1–14.

DAVIS, D. F. 1990. Do you want a performance audit or a program evaluation? *Public Administration Review, 50,* 35–41.

DAWES, R. M. 1994. *House of cards: Psychology and psychotherapy built on myth.* New York: The Free Press.

DAY, C. R., JR. 1981. Solving the mystery of productivity measurement. *Industry Week,* January 26, pp. 61–66.

DE NEUFVILLE, J. I. 1975. *Social indicators and public policy.* Amsterdam: Elsevier Scientific Publishing Company.

DEAN, P. J., RANGE, L. M., AND GOGGIN, W. C. 1996. The escape theory of suicide in college students: Testing a model that includes perfectionism. *Suicide and Life-Threatening Behavior, 26,* 181–186.

DEFRIESE, G. B. 1990. Theory as method. In *Research methodology: Strengthening causal interpretations of nonexperimental data,* eds. L. Sechrest, E. Perrin, and J. Bunker. Rockville, MD: Department of Health and Human Services, Agency for Health Care Policy and Research, (PHS) 90 3454.

DEMING, W. E. 1986. *Out of the crisis.* Cambridge, MA: MIT-CAES.

DEMONE, H. W., JR., AND HARSHBARGER, D. 1973. *The planning and administration of human services.* New York: Behavioral Publications.

DENISTON, O. L., AND ROSENSTOCK, I. M. 1973. The validity of nonexperimental designs for evaluating health services. *Health Services Reports, 88,* 153–164.

DENNIS, M. L. 1994. Ethical and practical randomized field experiments. In *Handbook of practical program evaluation,* eds. J. S. Wholey, H. P. Hatry, and K. E. Newcomer. San Francisco: Jossey Bass.

DENNIS, M. L., INGRAM, P. W., BURKS, M. E., AND RACHAL, J. V. 1994. Effectiveness of streamlined admissions to methadone treatment: A simplified time-series analysis. *Journal of Psychoactive Drugs, 26,* 207–216.

DENNIS, M. L., SODERSTROM, E. J., KONCINSKI, W. S., JR., AND CAVANAUGH, B. 1990. Effective dissemination of energy-related information. *American Psychologist, 45,* 1109–1117.

DENZIN, N. K., AND LINCOLN, Y. S. 2000. *Handbook of qualitative research,* Rev. ed. Thousand Oaks, CA: Sage.

DERBY, A. 1989. Equating death and dollars on the highway. *Business and Society Review, 71*(Fall), 47, 48.

DEVARAJAN, S., DOLLAR, D., AND HOLMGREN, T. 2000. *Aid and reform in Africa: Lessons from ten case studies.* Washington, DC: The World Bank.

DIAL, M. 1994. The misuse of evaluation in educational programs. In *Preventing the misuse of evaluation, New Directions for Program Evaluation, No. 64,* eds. C. J. Stevens and M. Dial. San Francisco: Jossey-Bass.

DIFRANZA, J. R., AND BROWN, L. J. 1992. The Tobacco Institute's "It's the law" campaign: Has it halted illegal sales of tobacco to children? *American Journal of Public Health, 82,* 1271, 1273.

DOBYNS, L., AND CRAWFORD-MASON, C. 1991. *Quality or else: The revolution in world business.* Boston: Houghton-Mifflin.

DONALDSON, S. I. (2003). Theory-driven program evaluation in the new millennium. In *Evaluating social programs and problems: Visions for the new millennium,* eds. S. I. Donaldson and M. Scriven. Mahwah, NJ: Erlbaum.

DONALDSON, S. I., GOOLER, L. E., AND SCRIVEN, M. 2002. Strategies for managing evaluation anxiety: Toward a psychology of program evaluation. *American Journal of Evaluation, 23,* 261–273.

DOR, A., HELD, P. J., AND PAULY, M. V. 1992. The Medicare cost of renal dialysis: Evidence from a statistical cost function. *Medical Care, 30,* 879–891.

DURLAK, J. A., AND FERRARI, J. R., EDS. 1998. *Program implementation in preventive trials.* Binghamton, NY: Haworth Press.

ECKERT, P. A. 1994. Cost control through quality improvement: The new challenge for psychology. *Professional Psychology: Research and Practice, 25,* 3–8.

EDDY, D. M. 1990. Practice policies: Where do they come from? *JAMA, 263,* 1265, 1269, 1272, 1275.

EDDY, D. M., AND BILLINGS, J. 1988. The quality of medical evidence: Implications for quality of care. *Health Affairs, 7*(1), 19–32.

EDMONDSON, A. C. 1996. Learning from mistakes is easier said than done: Group and organizational influences on the detection and correction of human error. *Journal of Applied Behavioral Science, 32,* 5–28.

EDMONDSON, A. C. 2004. Learning from mistakes is easier said than done. *Journal of Applied Behavioral Science, 40,* 66–90.

EGAN, G. 1988a. *Change-agent skills A: Assessing and designing excellence.* San Diego, CA: University Associates.

EGAN, G. 1988b. *Change-agent skills B: Managing innovation and change.* San Diego, CA: University Associates.

EGAN, G., AND COWAN, M. 1979. *People in systems.* Monterey, CA: Brooks/Cole.

EGELHOF, J. 1975. Cop layoffs spur slayings. *Chicago Tribune*, July 10, Sec. 1, p. 2.

EISENBERG, L. 1977. The social imperatives of medical research. *Science, 198,* 1105–1110.

ELLIOTT, E. J. 1989. Accountability in the post-Charlottesville era. *Evaluation Comment* (UCLA Center for the Study of Evaluation), December, pp. 1–4.

ENDICOTT, J., AND SPITZER, R. L. 1975. Designing mental health studies: The case for experimental designs. *Hospital & Community Psychiatry, 26,* 737–739.

EPLEY, N., AND DUNNING, D. 2000. Feeling "holier than thou": Are self-serving assessments produced by errors in self- or social prediction? *Journal of Personality & Social Psychology, 79,* 861–875.

ERICSON, D. P. 1990. Social justice, evaluation, and the educational systems. In *Evaluation and social justice: Issues in public education,* ed. K. A. Sirotnik. San Francisco: Jossey-Bass.

ERS STANDARDS COMMITTEE. 1982. In *Standards for practice,* ed. P. H. Rossi. *New Directions for Program Evaluation, No. 15.* San Francisco: Jossey-Bass, pp. 7–20.

EVANS, B. J., STANLEY, R. O., COMAN, G. J., AND SINNOTT, V. 1992. Measuring medical students' communication skills: Development and evaluation of an interview rating scale. *Psychology and Health, 6,* 213–225.

EVANS, R. G., AND ROBINSON, G. C. 1980. Surgical day care: Measurements of economic payoff. *CMA Journal, 123,* 873–880.

EVANS, R. I., AND RAINES, B. E. 1990. Applying a social psychological model across health promotion interventions. In *Social influence processes and prevention,* eds. J. D. Edwards, R. S. Tindale, L. Health, and E. J. Posavac. New York: Plenum.

FALS-STEWART, W., KLOSTERMANN, K., AND YATES T. 2005. Assessing the costs, benefits, cost-benefit ratio, and cost-effectiveness of marital and family treatments: Why we should and how we can. *Journal of Family Psychology, 19,* 28–39.

FEHR, M. 1999. Management tools in engineering education. *Industry and Higher Education, 13,* April 112–118.

FELSON, M. 1993. Social indicators for criminology. *Journal of Research in Crime and Delinquency, 30,* 400–411.

FELSON, R. B. 1984. The effects of self-appraisal of ability on academic performance. *Journal of Personality and Social Psychology, 47,* 944–952.

FERRISS, A. L. 1988. Uses of social indicators. *Social Forces, 66,* 601–617.

FETTERMAN, D. M. 1991. Auditing as institutional research: A qualitative focus. In *Using qualitative methods in institutional research, New Directions for Institutional Research, No. 72,* ed. D. M. Fetterman. San Francisco: Jossey-Bass.

FETTERMAN, D. M. 1998. Ethnography. In *Handbook of applied social research methods,* eds. L. Bickman and D. J. Rog. Thousand Oaks, CA: Sage.

FETTERMAN, D. M., KAFTARIAN, S. J., AND WANDERSMAN, A. EDS. 1996. *Empowerment evaluation: Knowledge and tools for self-assessment and accountability.* Thousand Oaks, CA: Sage.

FIGUEREDO, A. J. 1993. Critical multiplism, meta-analysis, and generalization: An integrative commentary. *Program evaluation: A pluralistic enterprise, New Directions for Program Evaluation, No. 60,* ed. L. Sechrest. San Francisco: Jossey-Bass.

FINE, M., AND VANDERSLICE, V. 1992. Qualitative activist research: Reflections on methods and politics. In *Methodology in applied social psychology*, eds. F. B. Bryant, J. D. Edwards, R. S. Tindale, E. J. Posavac, L. Heath, Y. Suarez-Balcazar, and E. Henderson. New York: Plenum.

FITCH, R. W. 1995. Accepting the null hypothesis. *Memory & Cognition, 23*, 132–138.

FITZPATRICK, J. 2002. Dialogue with Stewart Donaldson. *American Journal of Evaluation, 23*, 347–365.

FLAY, B. R., AND BEST, J. A. 1982. Overcoming design problems in evaluating health behavior programs. *Evaluation & the Health Professions, 5*, 43–49.

FORK, H. F., WAGNER, R. F., JR., AND WAGNER, K. D. 1992. The Texas Peer Education Sun Awareness Project for Children: Primary prevention of malignant melanoma and nonmelanocytic skin cancers. *Cutis, 50*, 363–364.

FOWLER, F. J., JR. 1998. Design and evaluation of survey questions. In *Handbook of applied social research methods*, eds. L. Bickman and D. J. Rog. Thousand Oaks, CA: Sage.

FREEL, C., AND EPSTEIN, I. 1993. Principles for using management information data for programmatic decision making. *Child and Youth Services, 16*, 77–93.

FREIMAN, J. A., CHALMERS, T. C., SMITH, H., JR., AND KUEBLER, R. R. 1978. The importance of Beta, the Type II error and sample size in the design and interpretation of the randomized control trial. *The New England Journal of Medicine, 299*, 690–694.

FRENCH, M. T. 2000. Economic evaluation of alcohol treatment services. *Evaluation and Program Planning, 23*, 27–39.

FROSS, K., CRACKNELL, B., AND SAMSET, K. 1994. Can evaluation help an organization to learn? *Evaluation Review, 18*, 574–591.

FRY, L. J., AND MILLER, J. 1975. Responding to skid row alcoholism: Self-defeating arrangements in an innovative treatment program. *Social Problems, 22*, 673–687.

FULLER, R. K., BRANCHEY, L., BRIGHTWALL, D. R., DERMAN, R. M., EMRICK, C. D., IBER, F. L., JAMES, K. E., LACOURSIERE, R. B., LEE, K. K., LOWENSTAM, I., MAANY, I., NEIDERHISER, D., NOCKS, J. J., AND SHAW, S. 1986. Disulfiram treatment for alcoholism: A Veterans Administration cooperative study. *JAMA, 68*, 1449–1455.

GABER, J. 2000. Meta-needs assessment. *Evaluation and Program Planning, 23*, 139–147.

GASTON, L., AND SABOURIN, S. 1992. Client satisfaction and social desirability in psychotherapy. *Evaluation and Program Planning, 15*, 227–231.

GERSTEIN, D. R., JOHNSON, R. A., HARWOOD, H. J., FOUNTAIN, D., SUTER, N., AND MALLOY, K. 1994. *Evaluating recovery services: The California drug and alcohol treatment (CALDATA)*. Sacramento, CA: California Department of Alcohol and Drug Programs.

GILBERT, J. P., LIGHT, R. J., AND MOSTELLER, F. 1975. Assessing social innovations: An empirical base for policy. In *Evaluation and experiment*, eds. A. R. Lumsdaine and C. A. Bennett. New York: Academic Press.

GILLMORE, G. M., AND GREENWALD, A. G. 1999. Using statistical adjustment to reduce the biases in student ratings. *American Psychologist, 54*, 518–519.

GLASGOW, R. E., TERBORG, J. R., STRYCKER, L. A., BOLES, S. M., ET AL. 1997. Take Heart II: Replication of a worksite health promotion trial. *Journal of Behavioral Medicine, 20*, 143–116.

GLASER, B., AND STRAUSS, A. L. 1967. *The discovery of grounded truth.* Chicago: Aldine.

GLENMULLEN, J. 2000. *Prozac backlash.* New York: Simon & Schuster.

GOERING, P. N., AND WASYLENKI, D. A. 1993. Promoting the utilization of outcome study results by assuming multiple roles within an organization. *Evaluation and Program Planning, 16,* 329–334.

"Good News—crime is up!" 1983. *Chicago Tribune,* May 8, Sec. 2, p. 2.

GRADUATION RATES FOR ATHLETES AND OTHER STUDENTS WHO ENTERED COLLEGE IN 1992–93. 1999. *Chronicle of Higher Education,* September 10, A60–A62.

GRASSO, A. J., AND EPSTEIN, I., EDS. 1993. *Information systems in child, youth, and family agencies: Planning, implementation, and service enhancement.* New York: The Haworth Press.

GRAY, B. H., COOKE, R. A., AND TANNENBAUM, A. S. 1978. Research involving human subjects. *Science, 201,* 1094–1101.

GREEN, J., AND WINTFELD, N. 1993. How accurate are hospital discharge data for evaluating effectiveness of care? *Medical Care, 31,* 719–731.

GREEN, R. S., AND JERRELL, J. M. 1994. The generalizability of brief ratings of psychosocial functioning. *Evaluation and Program Planning, 17,* 141–151.

GREEN, R. S., AND NEWMAN, F. L. 1999. Total quality management principles promote increased utilization of client outcome data in behavioral health care. *Evaluation and Program Planning, 22,* 179–182.

GREENE, J. C. 1987. Stakeholder participation in evaluation: Is it worth the effort? *Evaluation and Program Planning, 10,* 379–394.

GREINER, J. M. 1994. Use of ratings by trained observers. In *Handbook of practical program evaluation,* eds. J. S. Wholey, H. P. Hatry, and K. E. Newcomer. San Francisco: Jossey-Bass.

GROSS, D. M., AND SCOTT, S. 1990. Proceeding with caution. *Time,* July 16, pp. 56–62.

GRUBER, J., ED. 2001. *Risky behavior among youths: An economic analysis.* Chicago: The University of Chicago Press.

GUBA, E. G., AND LINCOLN, Y. S. 1981. *Effective evaluation.* San Francisco: Jossey-Bass.

GUBA, E. G., AND LINCOLN, Y. S. 1989. *Fourth generation evaluation.* Newbury Park, CA: Sage.

GUILBAULT, R. L., BRYANT, F. B., BROCKWAY, J. H., AND POSAVAC, E. J. 2004. A meta-analysis of research on hind-sight bias. *Basic and Applied Social Psychology, 26,* 103–117.

HANKE, S. H., AND WALKER, R. A. 1974. Benefit-cost analysis reconsidered: An evaluation of the Mid-State project. *Water Resources Research, 10,* 898–908.

HARTOG, J. 1999. Over- and under-education and the relation to vocational training. *Vocational Training: European Journal, 16,* 47–52.

HATRY, H. P. 1994. Collecting data from agency records. In *Handbook of practical program evaluation,* eds. J. S. Wholey, H. P. Hatry, and K. E. Newcomer. San Francisco: Jossey-Bass.

HATRY, H. P., NEWCOMER, K. E., AND WHOLEY, J. S. 1994. Conclusion: Improving evaluation activities and results. In *Handbook of practical program evaluation,* eds. J. S. Wholey, H. P. Hatry, and K. E. Newcomer. San Francisco: Jossey-Bass.

HAVEMAN, R. H., AND WATTS, H. W. 1976. Social experimentation as policy research: A review of negative income tax experiments. In *Evaluation Studies Research Annual*, Vol. 1, ed. G. V. Glass, Beverly Hills, CA: Sage.

HEATH, L., AND PETRAITIS, J. 1986. Television viewing and fear of crime: Where is the scary world? *Basic and Applied Social Psychology, 8,* 97–123.

HEATH, L., TINDALE, R. S., EDWARDS, J. E., POSAVAC, E. J., BRYANT, F. B., HENDERSON-KING, E., SUAREZ-BALCAZAR, Y., AND MEYERS, J., EDS. 1994. *Applications of heuristics and biases to social issues.* New York: Plenum.

Head Start impact study: First year findings. 2005, May. Washington, DC: Administration for Children and Families, USDHHS.

HEDRICK, T. E. 1994. The quantitative-qualitative debate: Possibilities for integration. In *The qualitative-quantitative debate: New perspectives, New Directions for Program Evaluation, No. 61,* eds. C. S. Reichardt and S. F. Rallis. San Francisco: Jossey-Bass.

HEGARTY, T. W., AND SPORN, D. L. 1988. Effective engagement of decisionmakers in program evaluation. *Evaluation and Program Planning, 11,* 335–340.

HEMPHILL, J. F., AND HOWELL, A. J. 2000. Adolescent offenders and stages of change. *Psychological Assessment, 12,* 371–381.

HENDRICKS, M. 1986. A conversation with Michael Wargo. *Evaluation Practice, 7*(6), 23–36.

HENDRICKS, M. 1994. Making a splash: Reporting evaluation results effectively. In *Handbook of practical program evaluation,* eds. J. S. Wholey, H. P. Hatry, and K. E. Newcomer. San Francisco: Jossey Bass.

HENRY, G. T., ED., 1997. Creating effective graphs: Solutions for a variety of evaluation data. *New Directions for Evaluation, No. 73.* San Francisco: Jossey-Bass.

HENRY, G. T., AND MARK, M. M. 2003. Toward an agenda for research on evaluation. In *The practice-theory relationship in evaluation,* No. 97, ed. C. A. Christie. San Francisco: Jossey-Bass.

"High-rise brought low at last." 1998. *The Economist,* July 11, 31–32.

HILKEVITCH, J. 2000. Whistle-blower plan for air safety. *Chicago Tribune,* Jan. 15, Sec. 1, p. 2.

HINE, L. K., LAIRD, N. M., HEWITT, P., AND CHALMERS, T. C. 1989. Meta-analysis of empirical long-term antiarrhythmic therapy after myocardial therapy. *JAMA, 262,* 3037–3040.

HOGAN, R. R. 1985. Response bias in a student follow-up: A comparison of low and high return surveys. *College and Universities, 61,* 17–25.

HORTON, S. V. 1987. Reduction of disruptive mealtime behavior by facial screening. *Behavior Modification, 11,* 53–64.

HOUGLAND, J. G., JR. 1987. Criteria for client evaluation of public programs: A comparison of objective and perceptual measures. *Social Science Quarterly, 68,* 386–394.

HOUSE, E. R. 1976. Justice in evaluation. In *Evaluation Studies Review Annual,* Vol. 1, ed. G. V. Glass. Beverly Hills, CA: Sage.

HOUSE, E. R. 1980. *Evaluating with validity.* Beverly Hills, CA: Sage.

HOUSE, E. R. 1988. *Jesse Jackson and the politics of charisma: The rise and fall of the PUSH/Excel program.* Boulder, CO: Westview Press.

House, E. R. 1990. Methodology and justice. In *Evaluation and social justice: Issues in public education*, ed. K. A. Sirotnik. San Francisco: Jossey-Bass.

House, P. W., and Shull, R. D. 1988. *Rush to policy: Using analytic techniques in public sector decision making*. New Brunswick, NJ: Transaction Books.

Howard, P. K. 1994. *The death of common sense: How law is suffocating America*. New York: Random House.

Hsia, D. C. 2003. Medicare quality improvement: Bad apples or bad systems? *JAMA, 289*, 354–356.

Illich, I. 1976. *Medical nemesis*. New York: Pantheon Books.

Impara, J. C., and Plake, B. S., eds., 1998. *The thirteenth mental measurements yearbook*. Lincoln: University of Nebraska Press.

Ioannidis, J. P. A. 2005. Contradicted and initially stronger effects in highly cited clinical research. *JAMA, 294*(2), 218–228.

Isaacson, W. 1983. The winds of reform. *Time*, March 7, pp. 12–16, 23, 26–30.

Jacobsen, N. S., and Truax, P. 1991. Clinical significance: A statistical approach to defining meaningful change in psychotherapy research. *Journal of Consulting and Clinical Psychology, 59*, 12–19.

Jason, L. A., and Liotta, R. F. 1982. Assessing community responsiveness in a metropolitan area. *Evaluation Review, 6*, 703–712.

Joglekar, P. N. 1984. Cost-benefit studies of health care programs: Choosing methods for desired results. *Evaluations & the Health Professions, 7*, 285–303.

Johnson, P. L. 1990. A conversation with Joseph S. Wholey about the Program for Excellence in Human Services. *Evaluation Practice, 11*(1), 53–61.

Johnston, J. 1983. The status of evaluation as an enterprise. *ERS Newsletter, 7*(2), 1, 7.

Joint Committee on Standards for Educational Evaluation. 1994. *The program evaluation standards: How to assess evaluations of educational programs*. 2nd ed. Thousand Oaks, CA: Sage.

Judd, C. M., and Kenny, D. A. 1981. *Estimating the effects of social interventions*. New York: Cambridge University Press.

Julnes, G., and Mohr, L. B. 1989. Analysis of no-difference findings in evaluation research. *Evaluation Review, 13*, 628–655.

Kahn, J. 2000. Is Harvard worth it? *Fortune, 141*, May 1, 200–204.

Kahneman, D., Slovic, P., and Tversky, A., eds. 1982. *Judgment under uncertainty: Heuristics and biases*. New York: Cambridge University Press.

Kahneman, D., and Tversky, A. 1974. Judgment under uncertainty: Heuristics and biases. *Science, 185*, 1124–1131.

Kane, R. L., and Kane, R. A. 1978. Care of the aged: Old problems in need of new solutions. *Science, 200*, 913–919.

Kapp, S. A., and Grasso, A. J. 1993. BOMIS: A management information system for children and youth service providers. *Child and Youth Services, 16*, 33–47.

Karwath, R. 1990. Jury's out on pregnant teens plan. *Chicago Tribune*, August 28, Sec. 2, p. 4.

Katz, M. M., and Warren, W. L. 1998. *Katz Adjustment Scales Relative Report Form (KAS–R)*. Los Angeles: Western Psychological Services.

KEATING, K. M., AND HIRST, E. 1986. Advantages and limits of longitudinal evaluation research in energy conservation. *Evaluation and Program Planning, 9,* 113–120.

KENT, D. M., FENDRICK, A. M., AND LANGA, K. M. 2004. New and dis-improved: On the evaluation and use of less effective, less expensive medical interventions. *Medical Decision Making, 24,* 282–286.

KERSHAW, D. N. 1972. A negative income tax experiment. *Scientific American, 227,* 19–25.

KIBEL, B. M. 1999. *Success stories as hard data: An introduction to results mapping.* New York: Kluwer Academic.

KING, J. A. 1994. Meeting the educational needs of at-risk students: A cost analysis of three models. *Educational Evaluation and Policy Analysis, 16,* 1–19.

KIRK, R. E. 1982. *Experimental design: Procedures for the behavioral sciences,* 2nd ed. Belmont, CA: Brooks/Cole.

KLITZNER, M., GRUENEWALD, P. J., BAMBERGER, E., AND ROSSITER, C. 1994. A quasi-experimental evaluation of Students Against Drunk Driving. *American Journal of Drug and Alcohol Abuse, 20,* 57–74.

KNAPP, M. 1977. Applying time-series research strategies to program evaluation problems. Paper presented at a meeting of the Evaluation Research Society, October, Washington, DC.

KOLATA, G. B. 1977. Aftermath of the new math: Its originators defend it. *Science, 195,* 854–857.

KRAMER, P. D. 1993. *Listening to Prozac.* New York: Viking.

KRUEGER, R. A. 1994. *Focus groups: A practical guide for applied research,* Rev. ed. Thousand Oaks, CA: Sage.

KRUEGER, R. A., AND CASEY, M. A. 2000. *Focus groups: A practical guide for applied research,* 3rd ed. Thousand Oaks, CA: Sage.

LAVRAKAS, P. J. 1998. Methods for sampling and interviewing for telephone surveys. In *Handbook of applied social research methods,* eds. L. Bickman and D. J. Rog. Thousand Oaks, CA: Sage.

LAWLER, E. E., III, AND HACKMAN, J. R. 1969. Impact of employee participation in the development of pay incentive plans: A field experiment. *Journal of Applied Psychology, 53,* 467–471.

LAZAR, I. 1981. Early intervention is effective. *Educational Leadership,* January, pp. 303–305.

LEE, J., AND WALSH, D. J. 2004. Quality in early childhood programs: Reflections from program evaluation practices. *American Journal of Evaluation, 25,* 351–373.

LEE, S. M. 2001. *Using the racial categories in the 2000 census.* Baltimore, MD: The Annie E. Casey Foundation.

LEEUW, F. L. 2003. Reconstructing program theories: Methods available and problems to be solved. *American Journal of Evaluation, 24,* 5–20.

LEIK, R. K., AND CHALKLEY, M. A. 1990. Parent involvement: What is it that works? *Children Today,* May–June, pp. 34–37.

LENIHAN, K. J. 1977. Telephone and raising bail. *Evaluation Quarterly, 1,* 569–586.

LESLIE, L. A., ANDERSON, E. A., AND BRANSON, M. P. 1991. Responsibility for children. *Journal of Family Issues, 12*, 197–210.

LEVIN, H. M., AND MCEWAN, P. J. 2001. *Cost-effectiveness analysis*, Rev. ed. Thousand Oaks, CA: Sage.

LEVINE, D. I., AND HELPER, S. 1995. A quality policy for America. *Contemporary Economic Policy, 13*, 26–38.

LEVITAN, S. A. 1992. *Evaluation of federal social programs: An uncertain impact.* Washington, DC: Center for Social Policy Studies, The George Washington University.

LEVITON, L. C., AND BORUCH, R. F. 1983. Contributions of evaluation in education programs and policy. *Evaluation Review, 7*, 563–598.

LICHT, M. H. 1979. The Staff-Resident Interaction Chronograph: Observational assessment of staff performance. *Journal of Behavioral Assessment, 1*, 185–198.

LIGHT, R. J., AND PILLEMER, D. B. 1984. *Summing up: The science of reviewing research.* Cambridge, MA: Harvard University Press.

LINCOLN, K. D. 2000. Social support, negative social interactions, and psychological well-being. *Social Service Review, 74*, 231–52.

LINCOLN, Y. S. 1990a. Program review, accreditation processes, and outcome assessment: Pressures on institutions of higher education. *Evaluation Practice, 11*, 13–23.

LINCOLN, Y. S. 1990b. The making of a constructivist: A remembrance of transformations past. In *The paradigm dialog*, ed. E. G. Guba. Newbury Park, CA: Sage.

LINCOLN, Y. S., AND GUBA, E. G. 1985. *Naturalistic inquiry.* Beverly Hills, CA: Sage.

LINN, R. L. 2000. Assessments and accountability. *Educational Researcher, 29*, March, 4–16.

LIPSEY, M. W. 1990. *Design sensitivity: Statistical power for experimental research.* Newbury Park, CA: Sage.

LIPSEY, M. W. 1993. Theory as method: Small theories of treatment. In *Understanding causes and generalizing about them. New Directions in Program Evaluation, No. 57*, eds. L. B. Sechrest and A. G. Scott. San Francisco: Jossey-Bass.

LIPSEY, M. W., AND CORDRAY, D. S. 2000. Evaluation methods for social intervention. *Annual Review of Psychology, 51*, 345–375.

LIPSEY, M. W., CROSSE, S., DUNKLE, J., POLLARD, J. A., AND STOBART, G. 1985. Evaluation: The state of the art and the sorry state of the science. In *Utilizing prior research in evaluation planning, New Directions for Program Evaluation, No. 27*, ed. D. S. Cordray. San Francisco: Jossey-Bass.

LIPSEY, M. W., AND POLLARD, J. A. 1989. Driving toward theory in program evaluation: More models to choose from. *Evaluation and Program Planning, 12*, 317–328.

LIPSEY, M. W., AND WILSON, D. B. 1993. The efficacy of psychological, educational, and behavioral treatment: Confirmation from meta-analysis. *American Psychologist, 48*, 1181–1209.

LOVE, A. J. 1986. Using evaluation to identify service gaps in mental health services to youth. Paper presented at the meeting of the American Evaluation Association. October, Kansas City, MO.

LURIGIO, A. J., AND SWARTZ, J. 1994. Life at the interface: Issues in the implementation and evaluation of a multiphased, multiagency jail-based treatment program. *Evaluation and Program Planning, 17,* 205–216.

MACKENZIE, D. L. 1990, September. Boot camp prisons: Components, evaluations, and empirical issues. *Federal Probation, 54,* 44–52.

MACQUEEN, K. M., AND BUEHLER, J. W. 2004. Ethics, practice, and research in public health. *American Journal of Public Health, 94,* 928–31.

MAGER, R. F. 1972. *Goal analysis.* Belmont, CA: Fearon Publishers.

MALCOLM, M. T., MADDEN, J. S., AND WILLIAMS, A. E. 1974. Disulfiram implantation critically evaluated. *British Journal of Psychiatry, 125,* 485–489.

MALHOTRA, N. K. 2004. *Marketing research: An applied orientation,* 4th ed. Upper Saddle River, NJ: Prentice Hall.

MANGIONE, T. W. 1998. Mail surveys. In *Handbook of applied social research methods,* eds. L. Bickman and D. J. Rog. Thousand Oaks, CA: Sage.

MANOFF, R. K. 1985. *Social marketing: New imperative for public health.* New York: Praeger.

MARGASAK, L. 2001. Pentagon's anti-fraud auditors faked data. *Chicago Tribune,* June 6, Sec. 1, p. 9.

MARK, M. M., AND SHOTLAND, R. L., EDS. 1987. *Multiple methods in program evaluation.* San Francisco: Jossey-Bass.

MARSH, C. 1988. *Exploring data: An introduction to data analysis for social scientists.* New York: Blackwell.

MARSH, H. W. 1998. Simulation study of nonequivalent group-matching and regression-discontinuity designs: Evaluations of gifted and talented programs. *Journal of Experimental Education, 66,* 163–192.

MARSHALL, T. O. 1979. Levels of results. *Journal of Constructive Change, 1*(1), 5.

MARSZALEK-GAUCHER, E., AND COFFEY, R. J. 1993. *Total quality in healthcare: From theory to practice.* San Francisco: Jossey-Bass.

MASSEY, O. T., AND WU, L. 1994. Three critical views of functioning: Comparisons of assessments made by individuals with mental illness, their case managers, and family members. *Evaluation and Program Planning, 17,* 1–7.

MATHISON, S. 1994. Rethinking the evaluator role: Partnerships between organizations and evaluators. *Evaluation and Program Planning, 17,* 299–304.

MAWHINNEY, T. 1992. Total quality management and organizational behavior: An integration for continual improvement. *Journal of Applied Behavioral Analysis, 25,* 525–543.

MAXWELL, G. S. 1985. Problems of being responsive: Reflections on an evaluation of a program for training motorcycle riders. *Evaluation and Program Planning, 8,* 339–348.

MCCARTHY, M. 1978. Decreasing the incidence of "high bobbins" in a textile spinning department through a group feedback procedure. *Journal of Organizational Behavioral Management, 1,* 150–154.

MCCLAVE, T., BENSON, P. G., AND SINCICH, T. 2005. *Statistics for business and economics,* 9th ed. Upper Saddle River, NJ: Prentice Hall.

McClintock, C. C. 1983. Internal evaluation: The new challenge. *Evaluation News*, *4*(1), 61, 62.

McGarrell, E. F., and Sabath, M. J. 1994. Stakeholder conflict in an alternative sentencing program: Implications for evaluation and implementation. *Evaluation and Program Planning, 17*, 179–186.

McIntyre, J. R. 1993. Family treatment of substance abusers. In *Clinical work with substance-abusing clients*, ed. S. L. A. Straussner. New York: Guilford Press.

McKillip, J. 1987. *Need analysis: Tools for human services and education*. Beverly Hills, CA: Sage.

McKillip, J. 1991. Effect of mandatory premarital HIV testing on marriage: The case of Illinois. *American Journal of Public Health, 81*, 650–653.

McKillip, J. 1992. Research without control groups: A control construct design. In *Methodological issues in applied social psychology*, eds. F. B. Bryant, J. Edwards, R. S. Tindale, E. J. Posavac, L. Heath, E. Henderson, and Y. Suarez-Balcazar. New York: Plenum Press.

McKillip, J. 1998. Need analysis: Process and techniques. In *Handbook of applied social research methods*, eds. L. Bickman and D. J. Rog. Thousand Oaks, CA: Sage.

McKillip, J., and Baldwin, K. 1990. Evaluation of an STD education media campaign: A control construct design. *Evaluation Review, 14*, 331–346.

McKillip, J., Lockhart, D. C., Eckert, P. S., and Phillips, J. 1985. Evaluation of a responsible alcohol use media campaign on a college campus. *Journal of Alcohol and Drug Education, 30*(3), 88–97.

McKillip, J., Moirs, K., and Cervenka, C. 1992. Asking open-ended consumer questions to aid program planning: Variations in question format and length. *Evaluation and Program Planning, 15*, 1–6.

McKnight, J. 1995. *The careless society: Community and its counterfeits*. New York: Basic Books.

McMurtrie, B. 2000. Accreditors revamp policies to stress student learning. *Chronicle of Higher Education, 46*, July 7, p. A29–31.

McSweeny, A. J., and Creer, T. L. 1995. Health-related quality-of-life in medical care. *Disease-a-Month, 41*, 1–71.

McWhorter, J. H. 2000. *Losing the race: Self-sabotage in black America*. New York: Free Press.

Meadows, D. L., and Perelman, L. 1973. Limits to growth. In *The future in the making: Current issues in higher education*, ed. D. W. Vermilye. San Francisco: Jossey-Bass.

Meehl, P. E. 1978. Theoretical risks and tabular asterisks: Sir Karl, Sir Ronald, and the slow progress of soft psychology. *Journal of Consulting and Clinical Psychology, 46*, 806–834.

Meehl, P. E. 1990. Appraising and amending theories: The strategy of Lakatosian defense and two principles that warrant it. *Psychological Inquiry, 1*, 108–141.

Meier, S. T. 2004. Improving design sensitivity through intervention-sensitive measures. *American Journal of Evaluation, 25*, 321–334.

Mendez, D., and Warner, K. E. 2000. Smoking prevalence in 2010: Why the Healthy People Goal is unattainable. *American Journal of Public Health, 90*, 401–403.

MIDDLE STATES COMMISSION ON HIGHER EDUCATION. 2000. *Handbook for evaluation teams*, 6th ed. Philadelphia: Author.

MILLENSON, M. L. 1987. System puts doctors, cost cutters at odds. *Chicago Tribune*, June 15, Sec. 1, pp. 1, 11.

MILLER, T. W. 2005. *Data and text mining: A business applications approach.* Upper Saddle River, NJ: Prentice Hall.

MILLSAP, R. E., AND HARTOG, S. B. 1988. Alpha, beta, and gamma change in evaluation research: A structural equation approach. *Journal of Applied Psychology, 73,* 574–584.

MITRA, A. 1994. Use of focus groups in the design of recreation needs assessment questionnaires. *Evaluation and Program Planning, 17,* 133–140.

MOORE, T. J. 1995. *Deadly medicine.* New York: Simon & Schuster.

MORELL, J. A. 2000. Internal evaluation: A synthesis of traditional methods and industrial engineering. *American Journal of Evaluation, 21,* 1098–2140.

MORGAN, M. G., FISCHHOFF, B., BOSTROM, A., LAVE, L., AND ATMAN, C. J. 1992. Communicating risk to the public. *Environmental Science and Technology, 26,* 2048–2056.

MORRIS, M., AND COHN, R. 1993. Program evaluators and ethical challenges: A national survey. *Evaluation Review, 17,* 621–642.

MOSKOP, J. C. 1987, April. The moral limits to federal funding for kidney disease. *Hastings Center Report,* pp. 11–15.

MOSKOWITZ, J. M. 1993. Why reports of outcome evaluations are often biased or uninterpretable: Examples from evaluations of drug abuse prevention programs. *Evaluation and Program Planning, 16,* 1–10.

MOSTELLER, F. 1981. Innovation and evaluation. *Science, 211,* 881–886.

MOWBRAY, C. T., COHEN, E., AND BYBEE, D. 1993. The challenge of outcome evaluation in homeless services: Engagement as an intermediate outcome measure. *Evaluation and Program Planning, 16,* 337–346.

MOWBRAY, C. T., HOLTER, M. C., GREGORY, B., TEAGUE, G. B., AND BYBEE, D. 2003. Fidelity criteria: Development, measurement, and validation. *American Journal of Evaluation, 24,* 315–340.

MURPHY, K. R., AND DAVIDSHOFER, C. O. 2005. *Psychological testing: Principles and applications,* 6th ed. Upper Saddle River, NJ: Prentice Hall.

NAGEL, S. S. 1983a. Nonmonetary variables in benefit-cost evaluation. *Evaluation Review, 7,* 37–64.

NAGEL, S. S. 1983b. Factors facilitating the utilization of policy evaluation research. Paper presented at the meeting of the Evaluation Research Society, October, Chicago.

NATIONAL SAFETY COUNCIL, 1999. *Injury facts.* Itasca, IL: Author.

NEIKIRK, W. 2001. Doubts linger, but time will decide the wisdom of the tax bill. *Chicago Tribune,* May 27, Sec. 1, p. 17.

NEUHAUSER, D. 1991. Parallel providers, ongoing randomization, and continuous improvement. *Medical Care, 29* (7, Supplement), 5–8.

NEWMAN, D. L., AND BROWN, R. D. 1992. Violations of evaluation standards: Frequency and seriousness of occurrence. *Evaluation Review, 16,* 219–234.

NEWMAN, D. L., AND BROWN, R. D. 1996. *Applied ethics for program evaluation.* Thousand Oaks, CA: Sage.

NICKERSON, R. S. 2000. Null hypothesis significance testing: A review of an old and continuing controversy. *Psychological Methods, 5,* 241–301.

NIENSTEDT, B. C., AND HALEMBA, G. J. 1986. Providing a model for agency program evaluation. *State Evaluation Network, 6*(1), 2–4.

NOTEBOOK. 1994, February 2. *Chronicle of Higher Education,* p. A31.

NUNNALLY, J. C. 1975. The study of change in evaluation research: Principles concerning measurement, experimental design, and analysis. In *Handbook of Evaluation Research,* Vol. 1, eds. E. L. Struening and M. Guttentag. Beverly Hills, CA: Sage.

O'DOHERTY, H. 1989. Mediation evaluation: Status report and challenges for the future. *Evaluation Practice, 10*(4), 8–19.

OFFICE OF INSPECTOR GENERAL. 1990. *Technical assistance guides for conducting program evaluations and inspections.* Washington, DC: Department of Health and Human Services.

OFFICE OF THE LEGISLATIVE AUDITOR. 2001. *Insurance for behavioral health care* (PE01-04a). St. Paul, MN: State of Minnesota.

OKRENT, D. 1980. Comment on societal risk. *Science, 208,* 372–375.

ON A DIET? DON'T TRUST YOUR MEMORY. 1989. *Psychology Today,* October, p. 12.

OVERSTREET, E. J., GRASSO, A. J., AND EPSTEIN, I. 1993. Management information systems and external policy advocacy: The Boysville length of stay study. In A. J. Grasso and I. Epstein (eds.), *Information systems in child, youth, and family agencies: Planning, implementation, and service enhancement.* New York: Haworth Press.

PALCA, J. 1990. Trials and tribulations of AIDS drug testing. *Science, 247,* 1406.

PATTON, M. Q. 1980. *Qualitative evaluation methods.* Beverly Hills, CA: Sage.

PATTON, M. Q. 1989. A context and boundaries for a theory-driven approach to validity. *Evaluation and Program Planning, 12,* 375–377.

PATTON, M. Q. 2002. *Utilization-focused evaluation.* 3rd ed. Beverly Hills, CA: Sage.

PAUL, G. L., ED. 1986. *Assessment in residential settings: Principles and methods to support cost-effective quality operations.* Champaign, IL: Research Press.

PAULOS, J. A. 1988. *Innumeracy: Mathematical illiteracy and its consequences.* New York: Hill and Wang.

PEARCE, D., AND MARKANDYA, A. 1988. Pricing the environment. *The OECD Observer,* April/May, pp. 23–26.

PEDHAZUR, E. J., AND SCHMELKIN, L. P. 1991. *Measurement, design, and analysis: An integrated approach.* Hillsdale, NJ: Lawrence Erlbaum Associates.

PENDERY, M. L., MALTZMAN, I. M., AND WEST, L. J. 1982. Controlled drinking by alcoholics? New findings and a reevaluation of a major affirmative study. *Science, 217,* 169–175.

PERRIN, B. 1998. Effective use and misuse of performance measurement. *American Journal of Evaluation, 19,* 367–379.

PETERSON, R. D. 1986. The anatomy of cost-effectiveness analysis. *Evaluation Review, 10,* 29–44.

PETTY, M. M., SINGLETON, B., AND CONNELL, D. W. 1992. An experimental evaluation of an organizational incentive plan in the electric utility industry. *Journal of Applied Psychology*, 77, 427–436.

PION, G. M., CORDRAY, D. S., AND ANDERSON, S. 1993. Drawing the line between conjecture and evidence about the use and benefit of "practice" methodologies. *Professional Psychology: Research and Practice*, 24, 245–249.

POSAVAC, E. J. 1975. *A turning point: Survey of past residents in the Clinical Pastoral Education Program*. Park Ridge, IL: Lutheran General Hospital.

POSAVAC, E. J. 1992. Communication of applied social psychology: An art and a challenge. In *Methodology in applied social psychology*, eds. F. B. Bryant, J. D. Edwards, R. S. Tindale, E. J. Posavac, L. Heath, Y. Suarez-Balcazar, and E. Henderson. New York: Plenum.

POSAVAC, E. J. 1994. Misusing program evaluation by asking the wrong question. In *Preventing the misuse of evaluation, New Directions of Program Evaluation* No. 64., eds C. J. Stevens and M. Dial. San Francisco: Jossey-Bass.

POSAVAC, E. J. 1995. Program quality and program effectiveness: A review of evaluations of programs to reduce excessive medical diagnostic testing. *Program Planning and Evaluation*, 18, 1–11.

POSAVAC, E. J. 1998. Toward more informative uses of statistics: Alternatives for program evaluators. *Evaluation and Program Planning*, 21, 243–254.

POSAVAC, E. J., AND HARTUNG, B. M. 1977. An exploration into the reasons people choose a pastoral counselor instead of another type of psychotherapist. *The Journal of Pastoral Care*, 31, 23–31.

POSAVAC, E. J., AND SINACORE, J. M. 1984. Reporting effect size in order to improve the understanding of statistical significance. *Knowledge: Creation, Diffusion, Utilization*, 5, 503–508.

POSAVAC, E. J., SINACORE, J. M., BROTHERTON, S. E., HELFORD, M., AND TURPIN, R. S. 1985. Increasing compliance to medical treatment regimens. *Evaluation & the Health Professions*, 8, 7–22.

POSAVAC, S. S. 1998. Strategic overbidding in contingent valuation: Stated economic value of public goods varies according to consumers' expectations of funding source. *Journal of Economic Psychology*, 19, 205–214.

Postal service may dump billion-dollar parcel plan. 1990. *Chicago Tribune*, June 14, Sec. 4, p. 1.

Potemkin Factor. 1980. *Time*, February 25, p. 36.

PRAGUE, C. N., IRWIN, M. R., AND REARDON, J. 2004. *Access 2003 Bible*. Hoboken, NJ: Wiley.

PRESKILL, H. 1994. Evaluation's role in enhancing organization learning. *Evaluation and Program Planning*, 17, 291–297.

PRUE, D. M., KRAPFL, J. E., NOAH, J. C., CANNON, S., AND MALEY, R. F. 1980. Managing the treatment activities of state hospital staff. *Journal of Organizational Behavioral Management*, 2, 165–181.

RAJKUMAR, A. S., AND FRENCH, M. T. 1997. Drug abuse, crime costs, and the economic benefits of treatment. *Journal of Quantitative Criminology*, 13, 291–323.

Rawls, J. 2000. *A theory of justice*, Rev. ed.. Cambridge, MA: Harvard University Press.

Ray, M. 1973. Marketing communication and the hierarchy of effects. In *New models for mass communication research*, ed. P. Clarke. Beverly Hills, CA: Sage.

Raykov, T. 1999. Are simple change scores obsolete? An approach to studying correlates and predictors of change. *Applied Psychological Measurement, 23*, 120–126.

Reichardt, C. S. 1979. The statistical analysis of data from nonequivalent group designs. In *Quasi-experimentation*, eds. T. D. Cook and D. T. Campbell. Boston: Houghton Mifflin.

Reichardt, C. S., and Mark, M. M. 1998. Quasi-experimentation. In *Handbook of applied social research methods*, eds. L. Bickman and D. J. Rog. Thousand Oaks, CA: Sage.

Reichardt, C. S., and Rallis, S. F., eds. 1994. *The qualitative-quantitative debate: New perspectives. New Directions for Program Evaluation, No. 61*. San Francisco: Jossey-Bass.

Reichardt, C. S., Trochim, W. M. K., and Cappelleri, J. C. 1995. Reports of the death of regression-discontinuity analysis are greatly exaggerated. *Evaluation Review, 19*, 39–63.

Rezmovic, E. L., Cook, T. J., and Dobson, L. D. 1981. Beyond random assignment: Factors affecting evaluation integrity. *Evaluation Review, 5*, 51–67.

Rice, S. A. 1929. Contagious bias in the interview. *American Journal of Sociology, 35*, 420–423.

Rich, E. C., Gifford, G., Luxenberg, M., and Dowd, B. 1990. The relationship of house staff experience to the cost and quality of inpatient care. *JAMA, 263*, 953–957.

Richmond, F. 1990. Internal evaluation in the Pennsylvania Department of Public Welfare. In The demise of internal evaluation in governmental agencies: Cause for concern or action? N. L. Ross (Chair), panel presented at the meeting of the American Evaluation Association, October, Washington, DC.

Riecken, H. W., and Boruch, R. F., eds. 1974. *Social experimentation: A method for planning and evaluating social intervention*. New York: Academic Press.

Ripsin, C. M., Keenen, J., Van Horn, L., et al. 1992. Oat products and lipid lowering. A meta-analysis. *JAMA, 267*, 3317–25.

Rivlin, A. M. 1990. Evaluation and public policy. Invited address presented at the meeting of the American Evaluation Association, October, Washington DC.

Robinson, E. A. R., and Doueck, H. J. 1994. Implications of the pre/post/then design for evaluating social group work. *Research on Social Work Practice, 4*, 224–239.

Rook, K. S. 1987. Effects of case history versus abstract information on health attitudes and behavior. *Journal of Applied Social Psychology, 17*, 533–553.

Rosenbaum, D. P., and Hanson, G. S. 1998. Assessing the effects of school-based drug education: A six-year multilevel analysis of Project D.A.R.E. *Journal of Research in Crime & Delinquency, 35*, 381–412.

Rosenhan, D. L. 1973. On being sane in insane places. *Science, 179*, 250–258.

Rosenthal, R. 1990. How are we doing in soft psychology? *American Psychologist, 45*, 775–778.

Rosnow, R. L., and Rosenthal, R. 1989. Statistical procedures and the justification of knowledge in psychological science. *American Psychologist, 44*, 1276–1284.

Rossi, P. H. 1978. Issues in the evaluation of human services delivery. *Evaluation Quarterly, 2*, 573–599.

Rossi, P. H., ed. 1982. *Standards for evaluation practice.* San Francisco: Jossey-Bass.

Rossi, P. H. 1994. The war between the quals and the quants: Is a lasting peace possible? In *The qualitative-quantitative debate: New perspectives, New Directions for Program Evaluation, No. 61,* eds. C. S. Reichardt and S. F. Rallis. San Francisco: Sage.

Rossman, G. B., and Wilson, B. L. 1985. Numbers and words: Combining quantitative and qualitative methods in a single large-scale evaluation study. *Evaluation Review, 9,* 627–644.

Roth, J. 1990. Needs and the needs assessment process (reprinted from 1978). *Evaluation Practice, 11,* 141–143.

Rothchild, M. L. 1979. Advertising strategies for high and low involvement situations. In *Attitude research plays for high stakes,* eds. J. Maloney and B. Silverman. New York: American Marketing Association.

Russon, C., and Russon, G., eds. 2005. International perspectives on evaluation standards, *New Directions for Evaluation, No. 104.* San Francisco: Jossey-Bass.

Sabin, E. P. 1998. Perceived need for treatment among drug using arrestees in four cities. *Journal of Offender Rehabilitation, 26,* 47–58.

Sackett, P. R., and Mullen, E. J. 1993. Beyond formal experimental design: Towards an expanded view of the training evaluation process. *Personnel Psychology, 46,* 613–627.

Sanbonmatsu, D. M., Posavac, S. S., and Stasney, R. 1997. The subjective beliefs underlying probability overestimation. *Journal of Experimental Social Psychology, 33,* 276–295.

Sanchez, J. R., and Laanan, F. S. 1997. The economic returns of a community college education: ERIC review. *Community College Review, 25,* Winter, 73–87.

Savaya, R. 1998. The under-use of psychological services by Israeli Arabs: An examination of the roles of negative attitudes and the use of alternative sources of help. *International Social Work, 41,* 195–209.

Schneider, A. L., and Darcy, R. E. 1984. Policy implications of using significance tests in evaluation research. *Evaluation Review, 8,* 573–582.

Schneider, M. J., Chapman, D. D., and Voth, D. E. 1985. Senior center participation: A two-stage approach to impact evaluation. *The Gerontologist, 25,* 194–200.

Schnelle, J. F., Kirchner, R. E., Casey, J. D., Uselton, P. H., Jr., and McNees, M. P. 1977. Patrol evaluation research: A multiple-baseline analysis of saturation police patrolling in a high crime area. *Journal of Applied Behavior Analysis, 10,* 33–40.

Schnelle, J. F., Kirchner, R. E., Macrae, J. W., McNees, M. P., Eck, R. H., Snodgrass, S., Casey, J. D., and Uselton, P. H., Jr. 1978. Police evaluation research: An experimental and cost-benefit analysis of a helicopter patrol in a high crime area. *Journal of Applied Behavior Analysis, 11,* 11–21.

Schreuder, C. 1998. Long lives leading to tough calls. *Chicago Tribune,* March 1, Sec. 1, pp. 1, 13.

Schuh, J. H., and Upcraft, M. L. 2001. *Assessment practice in student affairs: An application manual.* San Francisco: Jossey-Bass.

SCHWARTZ, R., AND MAYNE, J. 2005. Assuring the quality of evaluative information: Theory and practice. *Evaluation and Program Planning, 28*, 1–14.

SCHWARZ, N., AND OYSERMAN, D. 2001. Asking questions about behavior: Cognition, communication, and questionnaire construction. *American Journal of Evaluation, 22*, 127–160.

SCRIVEN, M. 1967. The methodology of evaluation. In *Perspectives of curriculum evaluation*, eds. R. W. Tyler, R. M. Gagne, and M. Scriven. Chicago: Rand-McNally.

SCRIVEN, M. 1973. Goal-free evaluation. In *School evaluation: The politics and the process*, ed. E. R. House. Berkeley, CA: McCutchan.

SCRIVEN, M. 1991. *Evaluation thesaurus.* 4th ed. Newbury Park, CA: Sage.

SCRIVEN, M. 1994. Product evaluation: The state of the art. *Evaluation Practice, 15*, 45–62.

SCRIVEN, M. 1997a. Truth and objectivity in evaluation. In *Evaluation for the 21st century: A handbook*, eds. E. Chelimsky and W. R. Shadish. Thousand Oaks, CA: Sage.

SCRIVEN, M. 1997b. Empowerment evaluation examined. *Evaluation Practice, 18*, 165–175.

SCRIVEN, M. 2003. Evaluation in the new millennium: The transdisciplinary vision. In *Evaluating social programs and problems: Visions for the new millennium*, eds. S. I. Donaldson and M. Scriven. Mahwah, NJ: Erlbaum.

SCRIVEN, M., AND ROTH, J. 1990. Special feature: Needs assessment (reprinted from 1976). *Evaluation Practice, 11*, 135–140.

SECHREST, L. 1984. Social science and social policy. Will our numbers ever be good enough? In *Social science and social policy*, eds. R. L. Shotland and M. M. Mark. Beverly Hills, CA: Sage.

SELIGMAN, C., AND FINEGAN, J. E. 1990. A two-factor model of energy and water conservation. In *Social influence processes and prevention*, eds. J. Edwards, R. S. Tindale, L. Heath, and E. J. Posavac. New York: Plenum.

SHADISH, W. R. 1993. Critical multiplism: A research strategy and its attendant tactics. *Program evaluation: A pluralistic enterprise, New Directions for Program Evaluation, No. 60*, ed. L. Sechrest. San Francisco: Jossey-Bass.

SHADISH, W. R. 1995. Philosophy of science and the quantitative-qualitative debates: Thirteen common errors. *Evaluation and Program Planning, 18*, 63–75.

SHADISH, W. R. 2002. Revisiting field experimentation: Field notes for the future. *Psychological Methods, 7*, 3–18.

SHADISH, W. R., COOK, T. D., AND CAMPBELL, D. T. 2002. *Experimental and quasi-experimental design for generalized causal inference.* Boston: Houghton Mifflin.

SHADISH, W. R., COOK, T. D., AND LEVITON, L. C. 1991. *Foundations of program evaluation: Theories of practice.* Newbury Park, CA: Sage.

SHADISH, W. R., JR., ORWIN, R. G., SILBER, B. G., AND BOOTZIN, R. R. 1985. The subjective well-being of mental patients in nursing homes. *Evaluation and Program Planning, 8*, 239–250.

SHAUGHNESSY, J. J., ZECHMEISTER, E. B., AND ZECHMEISTER, J. S. 2005. *Research methods in psychology*, 6th ed. New York: McGraw-Hill.

SHAW, I. F. 1999. *Qualitative evaluation.* Thousand Oaks, CA: Sage.

SHEPARD, L. A. 1990. "Inflating test score gains": Is it old norms or teaching the test? Los Angeles: UCLA Center for Research on Evaluation, Standards, and Student Teaching, CSE Technical Report 307.

SHIPLEY, R. H. 1976. Effects of companion program on college student volunteers and mental patients. *Journal of Consulting and Clinical Psychology, 4*, 688–689.

SHRAUGER, J. S., AND OSBERG, T. M. 1981. The relative accuracy of self-predictions and judgments by others in psychological assessment. *Psychological Bulletin, 90*, 322–351.

SIEBER, J. E. 1998. Planning ethically responsible research. In *Handbook of applied social research methods*, eds. L. Bickman and D. J. Rog. Thousand Oaks, CA: Sage.

SIEBER, S. D. 1981. *Fatal remedies: The ironies of social intervention.* New York: Plenum.

SILVERMAN, M., RICCI, E. M., AND GUNTER, M. J. 1990. Strategies for increasing the rigor of qualitative methods in evaluation of health care programs. *Evaluation Review, 14*, 57–74.

SILVERMAN, W. A. 1977. The lesson of retrolental fibroplasia. *Scientific American, 236*, June, 100–107.

SILVERMAN, W. K., KURTINES, W. M., GINSBURG, G. S., WEEMS, C. F., LUMPKIN, P. W., AND CARMICHAEL, D. H. 1999. Treating anxiety disorders in children with group cognitive-behavioral therapy: A randomized clinical trial. *Journal of Consulting and Clinical Psychology, 67*, 995–1003.

SINGH, B., GREER, P. R., AND HAMMOND, R. 1977. An evaluation of the use of the Law in a Free Society materials on "responsibility." *Evaluation Quarterly, 1*, 621–628.

SIROTNIK, K. A., ED. 1990. *Evaluation and social justice.* San Francisco: Jossey-Bass.

SLOVIC, P. 1993. Perceived risk, trust, and democracy. *Risk Analysis, 13*, 675–682.

SMITH, M. F. 1989. *Evaluability assessment: A practical approach.* Boston: Kluwer Academic Publishers.

SMITH, M. L. 1994. Qualitative plus/versus quantitative: The last word. In *The qualitative-quantitative debate: New perspectives, New Directions for Program Evaluation, No. 61*, eds. C. S. Reichardt and S. F. Rallis. San Francisco: Jossey-Bass.

SMITH, N. L. 1981. The certainty of judgments in health evaluations. *Evaluation and Program Planning, 4*, 273–278.

SOBELL, M. B., AND SOBELL, L. C. 1978. *Behavioral treatment of alcohol problems.* New York: Plenum.

SOLBERG, L. I., REGER, L. A., PEARSON, T. L., CHERNEY, L. M., O'CONNOR, P. J., FREEMAN, S. L., LASCH, S. L., AND BISHOP, D. B. 1997. Using continuous quality improvement to improve diabetes care in populations. *Journal of Quality Improvement, 23*, 581–592.

SOMMER, R. 1990. Local research. *The Journal of Social Issues, 46*, Spring, 203–214.

SONNICHSEN, R. C. 1994. Evaluators as change agents. In *Handbook of Practical Program Evaluation*, eds. J. S. Wholey, H. Hatry, and K. Newcomer. San Francisco: Jossey Bass.

SONNICHSEN, R. C. 2000. *High impact internal evaluation: A practitioner's guide to evaluating and consulting inside organizations.* Thousand Oaks, CA: Sage.

SPATH, P. 2000. Case management. Making the case for information systems. *MD Computing, 17*(3), May-June, 40–44.

SPEER, D. C., AND TRAPP, J. C. 1976. Evaluation of mental health service effectiveness. *American Journal of Orthopsychiatry, 46*, 217–228.

SPIRING, F. A. 1994. A bill's effect on alcohol-related traffic fatalities. *Quality Progress,* 27(2), 35–38.

SPIRO, S. E., SHALEV, A., SOLOMON, Z., AND KOTLER, M. 1989. Self-reported change versus changed self-report: Contradictory findings of an evaluation of a treatment program for war veterans suffering from post-traumatic stress disorder. *Evaluation Review, 13,* 533–549.

SPORN, D. L. 1989a. A conversation with Gerald L. Barkdoll. *Evaluation Practice, 10*(1), 27–32.

SPORN, D. L. 1989b. A conversation with Michael Hendricks. *Evaluation Practice, 10*(3), 18–24.

Spotlight: Program evaluation and accountability in Minnesota. 1982. State Evaluation Network, 2(5), 2.

SPSS Trends 13.0. 2004. Chicago: SPSS.

Statistical Abstract of the United States: The national data book. 2004-2005. Washington, DC: U.S. Census Bureau.

STEELE, S. 1990. *The content of our character.* New York: St. Martin's Press.

STEIN, S., AND RECKTENWALD, W. 1990. City parks are no place to play. *Chicago Tribune,* November 11, Sec. 1, pp. 1, 18.

STRAUSS, A. L., AND CORBIN, J. M. 1998. *Basics of qualitative research: Techniques and procedures for developing grounded theory,* 2nd ed. Thousand Oaks, CA: Sage.

STUCKER, C. 2004. *Mystery shopper's manual,* 6th ed. Sugar Land, TX: Special Interests Publishing.

Students cheated in college sports. 1990. *Chicago Tribune,* September 10, Sec. 1, p. 12.

STUFFLEBEAM, D. L. 2001. Evaluation models. *New Directions for Program Evaluation, No. 89.* San Francisco: Jossey-Bass.

STUFFLEBEAM, D. L., MADAUS, G. F., AND KELLAGHAN, T. 2000. *Evaluation models,* Rev. ed. Boston: Kluwer.

STYVE, G. J., MACKENZIE, D. L., GOVER, A. R., AND MITCHELL, O. 2000. Perceived conditions of confinement: A national evaluation of juvenile boot camps and traditional facilities. *Law & Human Behavior, 24,* 297–308.

SULLIVAN, J. M., AND SNOWDEN, L. R. 1981. Monitoring frequency of client problems. *Evaluation Review, 5,* 822–833.

SUMMERFELT, W. T. 2003. Program strength and fidelity in evaluation. *Applied Developmental Science, 7,* 55–61.

Survey's overhaul will boost jobless rate. 1993. *Chicago Tribune,* November 17, Sec. 3, p. 7.

SUSSNA, E., AND HEINEMANN, H. N. 1972. The education of health manpower in a two-year college: An evaluation model. *Socio-Economic Planning Science, 6,* 21–30.

SVENSSON, K. 1997. The analysis of evaluation of foreign aid. In *Evaluation for the 21st century: A handbook,* eds. E. Chelimsky and W. R. Shadish. Thousand Oaks, CA: Sage.

SWAIN, J. F., ROUSE, I. L., CURLEY, C. B., AND SACKS, F. M. 1990. Comparison of the effects of oat bran and low-fiber wheat on serum lipoprotein levels and blood pressure. *New England Journal of Medicine, 322,* 147–52.

TAUT, S., AND ALKIN, M. C. 2003. Program staff perceptions of barriers to evaluation and implementation. *American Journal of Evaluation, 24*, 213–226.

TESTA, M. A., ANDERSON, R. B., NACKLEY, J. F., AND HOLLENBERG, N. K. 1993. Quality of life and antihypertensive therapy of men. *New England Journal of Medicine, 328*, 907–913.

THURMAN, Q. C., GIACOMAZZI, A., AND BOGEN, P. 1993. Research note: Cops, kids, and community policing. An assessment of a community policing demonstration project. *Crime & Delinquency, 39*, 554–564.

TIERNEY, W. M., MILLER, M. E., AND MCDONALD, C. 1990. The effect on test ordering of informing physicians of the charges of outpatient diagnostic tests. *The New England Journal of Medicine, 322*, 1499–1504.

TORRES, R. T. 1994. Linking individual and organizational learning: The internalization and externalization of evaluation. *Evaluation and Program Planning, 17*, 327–338.

TORRES, R. T., PRESKILL, H. S., AND PIONTEK, M. E. 2004. *Evaluation strategies for communicating and reporting: Enhancing learning in organizations*, Rev. ed. Thousand Oaks, CA: Sage.

TROCHIM, W. M. K. 1984. *Research design for program evaluation: The regression discontinuity approach*. Beverly Hills, CA: Sage.

TROCHIM, W. M. K., ED. 1986. *Advances in quasi-experimental design and analysis*. San Francisco: Jossey-Bass.

TROCHIM, W. M. K. 1990. The regression-discontinuity design. In *Research methodology: Strengthening causal interpretations of nonexperimental data*, eds. L. Sechrest, E. Perrin, and J. Bunker. Rockville, MD: U.S. Department of Health and Human Services, Agency for Health Care Policy and Research, (PHS) 90 3454.

The trouble with dependent variables. 1990. *Dialogue: Society for Personality and Social Psychology*, Spring, p. 9.

TUKEY, J. W. 1977. *Exploratory data analysis*. Reading, MA: Addison-Wesley.

TURNER, A. J. 1977. Program goal setting in an evaluation system. Paper presented at the Conference on the Impact of Program Evaluation in Mental Health Care, January, Loyola University of Chicago.

TURNER, G. 1999. Peer support and young people's health. *Journal of Adolescence, 22*, 567–572.

TURNER, M. A., AND ZIMMERMAN, W. 1994. Acting for the sake of research: The use of role-playing in evaluation. In *Handbook of practical program evaluation*, eds. J. S. Wholey, H. R. Hatry, and K. E. Newcomer. San Francisco: Jossey-Bass.

TURNER, N. H., O'DELL, K. J., WEAVER, G. D., RAMIREZ, G. Y., AND TURNER, G. 1998. Community's role in the promotion of recovery from addiction and prevention of relapse among women: An exploratory study. *Ethnicity and Disease, 8*, 26–35.

TYSON, T. J. 1985. The evaluation and monitoring of a Medicaid second surgical opinion program. *Evaluation and Program Planning, 8*, 207–216.

ULLMAN, J. B, STEIN, J. A, AND DUKES, R. L. 2000. Evaluation of D.A.R.E (Drug Abuse Resistance Education) with latent variables in context of a Solomon Four Group Design. In *Multivariate applications in substance use research: New methods for new questions*, eds. J. S. Rose, L. Chassin, et al. Mahwah, NJ: Lawrence Erlbaum Associates.

U.S. DEPARTMENT OF EDUCATION. 2003. *Identifying and implementing educational practices supported by rigorous evidence: A user friendly guide.* Washington, DC: Institute of Education Sciences.

VAN DEN EYNDE, J., VENO, A., AND HART, A. 2003. They look good but don't work: A case study of global performance indicators in crime prevention. *Evaluation and Program Planning, 26,* 237–248.

VAN SANT, J. 1989. Qualitative analysis in developmental evaluations. *Evaluation Review, 13,* 257–272.

VEATCH, R. M. 1975. Ethical principles in medical experimentation. In *Ethical and legal issues in social experimentation,* eds. A. M. Rivlan and P. M. Timpane. Washington, DC: Brookings Institute.

VERMILLION, J. M., AND PFEIFFER, S. I. 1993. Treatment outcome and continuous quality improvement: Two aspects of program evaluation. *The Psychiatric Hospital, 24,* 9–14.

VIAVOICE (IBM). 2002. Burlington, MA: ScanSoft.

VISCUSI, W. K. 1992. *Fatal tradeoffs: Public and private responsibilities for risk.* New York: Oxford University Press.

VOJTECKY, M. A., AND SCHMITZ, M. F. 1986. Program evaluation and health and safety training. *Journal of Safety Research, 17,* 57–63.

VROOM, P. I., COLOMBO, M., AND NAHAN, N. 1994. Confronting ideology and self-interest: Misuse of evaluation. In *Preventing the misuse of evaluation, New Directions for Program Evaluation, No. 64,* eds. C. J. Stevens and M. Dial. San Francisco: Jossey-Bass.

W. K. KELLOGG FOUNDATION, 1998. *Evaluation handbook.* Battle Creek, MI: W. K. Kellogg Foundation.

WALDO, G. P., AND CHIRICOS, T. G. 1977. Work release and recidivism: An empirical evaluation of a social policy. *Evaluation Quarterly, 1,* 87–108.

WALLER, B. 2005. *Consider ethics: Theory, readings and contemporary issues.* New York: Longman.

WARHEIT, G. J., BELL, R. A., AND SCHWAB, J. J. 1977. *Needs assessment approaches: Concepts and methods.* Rockville, MD: National Institute of Mental Health.

WASHBURN, G. 2001. 2nd probe also finds cabs shun disabled. *Chicago Tribune,* July 5, Sec. 2, pp. 1, 2.

WEBB, E. J., CAMPBELL, D. T., SCHWARTZ, R. D., SECHREST, L., AND GROVE, J. B. 1981. *Nonreactive measures in the social sciences,* 2nd ed. Boston: Houghton-Mifflin.

WEINREICH, N. K. 1999. *Hands-on social marketing: A step-by-step guide.* Thousand Oaks, CA: Sage.

WEISS, C. H. 1988. If program decisions hinged only on information: A response to Patton. *Evaluation Practice, 9*(3), 15–28.

WEISS, C. H. 1998. Have we learned anything new about the use of evaluation? *American Journal of Evaluation, 19,* 21–33.

WEISS, C. H. 2002. What to do until the random assigner comes. In F. Mosteller and R. Boruch (eds.), *Evidence matters: Randomized trials in education.* Washington, DC: Brookings Institution Press.

WEISS, S. J., JURS, S., LESAGE, J. P., AND IVERSON, D. C. 1984. A cost-benefit analysis of a smoking cessation program. *Evaluation and Program Planning, 7,* 337–346.

WEITZMAN, E. A., AND MILES, M. B. 1995. *Computer programs for qualitative data analysis: A software sourcebook.* Thousand Oaks, CA: Sage.

WHEELER, D. J., AND CHAMBERS, D. S. 1992. *Understanding statistical process control.* 2nd ed. Knoxville, TN: SPC Press.

WHITMORE, E., AND RAY, M. L. 1989. Qualitative evaluation audits: Continuation of the discussion. *Evaluation Review, 13,* 78–90.

WHOLEY, J. S. 1979. *Evaluation: Promise and performance.* Washington, DC: Urban Institute.

WHOLEY, J. S. 1983. *Evaluation and effective public management.* Boston: Little, Brown.

WHOLEY, J. S. 1991. Using program evaluation to improve program performance. *The Bureaucrat,* Sept. pp. 55–59.

WHOLEY, J. S. 1997. Clarifying goals, reporting results. In *Progress and future directions in evaluation: Perspectives on theory, practice, and methods, New Directions for Program Evaluation, No. 87,* eds. D. J. Rog and D. Fournier. San Francisco: Jossey-Bass.

WHOLEY, J. S. 1999. Quality control: Assessing the accuracy and usefulness of performance measurement systems. In H. P. Hatry (ed.), *Performance measurement: Getting results.* Washington, DC: The Urban Institute, 217–239.

WILLIAMS, S. C., SCHMALTZ, S. P., MORTON, D. J., KOSS, R. G., AND LOEB, J. M. 2005. Quality of care in U.S. hospitals as reflected by standardized measures, 2002–2004. *The New England Journal of Medicine, 353*(3), 255–264.

WILLS, K. 1987. A conversation with Joy Frechtling. *Evaluation Practice, 8*(2), 20–30.

WILSON, D. B., GALLAGHER, C. A., AND MACKENZIE, D. L. 2000. A meta-analysis of corrections-based education, vocation, and work programs for adult offenders. *The Journal of Research in Crime and Delinquency, 37,* 347–369.

WINETT, R. A. 1995. A framework for health promotion and disease prevention programs. *American Psychologist, 50,* 341–350.

Winner of the 1988 President's Problem. 1989. *Evaluation Practice, 10*(1), 53–57.

WISLER, C. ED. 1996. *Evaluation and auditing: Prospects for convergence. New Directions for Program Evaluation, No. 71.* San Francisco: Jossey-Bass.

WITKIN, B. R., AND ALTSCHULD, J. W. 1995. *Planning and conducting needs assessments: A practical guide,* Rev. ed. Thousand Oaks: Sage.

WYE, C. G., AND SONNICHSEN, R. C., EDS. 1992. *Evaluation in the federal government: Changes, trends, and opportunities, New Directions for Program Evaluation, No. 55.* San Francisco: Jossey-Bass.

YAMPOLSKAYA, S., NESMAN, T. M., HERNANDEZ, M., AND KOCH, D. 2004. Using concept mapping to develop a logic model and articulate a program theory: A case example. *American Journal of Evaluation, 25,* 191–207.

YATES, B. T. 1994. Toward the incorporation of costs, cost-effectiveness analysis, and cost-benefit analysis into clinical research. *Journal of Consulting and Clinical Psychology, 62,* 729–736.

YATES, B. T. 1999. *Measuring and improving costs, cost-effectiveness, and cost-benefit for substance abuse treatment programs* (NIH Publication Number 99-4518). Bethesda, MD: National Institute on Drug Abuse.

YEATON, W. H., AND SECHREST, L. 1986. Use and misuse of no-difference findings in eliminating threats to validity. *Evaluation Review, 10*, 836–852.

YEATON, W. H., AND SECHREST, L. 1987. Assessing factors influencing acceptance of no-difference research. *Evaluation Review, 11*, 131–142.

ZAMMUTO, R. F. 1982. *Assessing organizational effectiveness.* Albany, NY: SUNY Press.

ZECHMEISTER, E. B., and POSAVAC, E. J. 2003. Data analysis and interpretation in the behavioral sciences. Belmont, CA: Wadsworth.

ZIGLER, E., AND MUENCHOW, S. 1992. *Head Start: The inside story of America's most successful educational experiment.* New York: Basic Books.

ZIGLER, E., AND TRICKETT, P. K. 1978. IQ, social competence, and evaluation of early childhood intervention programs. *American Psychologist, 33*, 789–798.

ZIMRING, F. E. 1975. Firearms and federal law: The Gun Control Act of 1968. *Journal of Legal Studies, 4*, 133–198.

Name Index

Abeles, N., 174
Abelson, P. H., 235
Abelson, R. P., 229, 264
Ackoff, R. L.,136
Adams, M. E., 72
Aiken, L. S., 186, 222
Alexander, H. A., 157
Alkin, M. C., 18, 43
Altman, D. G., 127
Altschuld, J. W., 129, 130
Anderson, C. A., 193
Anderson, E. A., 89
Anderson, J. F., 87
Anderson, R. B., 127
Anderson, S., 60
Angelo, T. A., 101
Ankuta, G. Y., 174
Appleton, H., 33, 107
Argyris, C., 275
Aristigueta, M. P., 172
Arvey, R. D., 186
Aslanian, C. B., 127
Astin, A. W., 11, 20, 41, 50, 84
Atman, C. J., 113
Averch, H. A., 75

Babbie, E., 92, 119, 122
Baldwin, K., 209
Ball, S., 107
Bamberger, E., 226
Banks, S. M., 127
Barbour, G. P., 79
Barendregt, J. J., 244
Barkdoll, G. L., 32
Barzansky, A.,168
Bauer, S. M., 32
Bechtel, R. B., 27
Beckman, C. R. R., 168
Bell, R. A., 120
Benson, P. G., 183
Bentham, J., 108
Berdie, D. R., 87
Berk, R. A., 79
Berman, J. J., 135
Berner, E., 168
Bernstein, D. J., 12, 42
Best, J. A., 218
Bickman, L., 34, 93
Bigelow, D. Q., 268
Billings, J., 219, 220

Bingham, S. G., 107
Binner, P. R., 150, 240, 241
Bogartz, G. A., 107
Bogen, P., 81
Bok, S., 97
Bonneux, L., 244
Boone, P., 127
Bootzin, R. R., 72
Boruch, R. F., 9, 25, 209, 216, 220,
      225, 268, 272
Bostrom, A., 113
Botcheva, 43
Branson, M. P., 89
Brewer, M. B., 204, 222
Brigham, S. E., 6
Brinkerhoff, R. O., 28, 72, 167
Brockner, J., 233
Brockway, J. H., 255
Brotherton, S. E., 34
Brotman, B., 100
Brown, F. G., 180
Brown, J. B., 72
Brown, L. J., 173
Brown, R. D., 109, 110
Bryant, F. B., 187, 255
Bryk, A. S., 30
Buehler, J. W., 109
Bunda, M. A., 108
Burks, M. E., 4
Burtle, V., 97
Bushway, S., 235
Bussigel, M., 157
Bybee, D., 57, 132

Cagle, L. T., 127
Caidin, M., 183
Campbell, D. T., 19, 38, 80, 82, 97, 149, 172,
      181, 191, 193–197, 203, 204, 210, 211,
      214, 216, 219, 226, 230
Cannell, J. J., 59
Cannon, S., 144
Cappelleri, J. C., 208
Card, J. J., 34, 46
Carey, R. G., 6, 12, 103, 132, 144, 194, 220, 262
Carley, M., 117
Carmichael, D. H., 89
Carroll, J. L., 222
Carter, D. E., 88
Casey, M. A., 87, 123
Caudle, S. L., 164

Caulkins, J. P., 235, 264
Cavanaugh, B., 144
Centra, J. A., 182
Cervenka, L. M., 90
Chalkley, M. A., 49
Chalmers, T. C., 106, 219
Chambers, D. S., 194
Chambers, F., 14
Champney, T. F., 278
Chan, K.-C., 4, 125
Chapman, C., 107
Chapman, D. D., 235
Chelimsky, E., 15
Chen, H. T., 28, 61, 79
Chiesa, J., 235
Chiricos, T. G., 274
Ciarlo, J. A., 268
Cicarelli, V. G., 48, 106, 203
Clark, C., 245
Cody, S., 127
Coffey, R. J., 6
Cohen, E., 132
Cohen, J., 179, 225
Cohn, R., 110
Colburn, D., 235
Cole, D. A., 186
Colombo, M., 135
Coman, G. J., 187, 223
Connell, D. W., 205
Conner, R. F., 33, 107, 127
Cook, T. D., 5, 15, 16, 24, 29, 33–35, 41, 42,
    52, 60, 63, 65, 70, 74, 97, 107, 149, 154,
    155, 166, 181, 191, 197, 211, 214, 216,
    223–226, 230
Cooke, R. A., 97
Cooper, W. H., 48, 106
Corbin, J. M., 91, 153
Cordray, D. S., 29, 60, 84, 270, 211
Cowan, M., 129
Cracknell, B., 270
Crano, W. D., 204, 222
Crawford-Mason, C., 6, 12, 25, 42
Creer, T. L., 166
Cronbach, L. J., 3, 18, 44
Cross, K. P., 101
Crosse, S., 34, 79, 102
Cumming, G., 261
Cummings, S. R., 248
Curley, C. B., 106

Darcy, R. E., 106
Darlington, R. B., 106
Datta, L., 100, 168, 203, 223
Davidshofer, C. O., 82, 83, 88, 184
Davis, D. F., 11, 16, 27
Dawes, R. M., 7, 43, 65, 219, 220
Day, C. R., Jr., 239
Dean, P. J., 89

DeFreise, G. B., 60
Deiger, M., 20, 21
Deming, W. E., 6, 18, 149, 219
Demone, H. W., Jr., 231
Deniston, 216
Dennis, M. L., 4, 144, 218, 220, 223, 224, 225
De Neufville, J. I., 118
Denzin, N. K., 169
Devarajan, S., 126
Devine, E. C., 63
Dial, M., 221
DiFranza, J. R., 173
Dobson, L. D., 224
Dobyns, L., 6, 12, 25, 42
Dollar, D., 126
Donaldson, S. I., 20, 28, 31, 61
Dor, A., 235
Douneck, H. J., 187
Dowd, B., 199
Dukes, R. L., 5
Dunkle, J., 34, 79, 102
Dunning, D. 41
Durlak, J. A., 53

Eckert, P. A., 6
Eckert, P. S., 209, 285, 286
Eddy, D. M., 190, 219, 220
Edmondson, A. C., 149, 277
Egan, G., 129
Egelhof, J., 193
Eisenberg, L., 177
Elliott, E. J., 79
Endicott, J., 76
Epley, N., 41
Epstein, I., 133, 148, 149, 151, 269
Ericson, D. P., 99
Erlebacher, A., 203, 204
Evans, B. J., 62, 187, 223
Evans, R. G., 243
Everingham, S. S., 235

Fals-Stewart, W., 231
Fehr, M., 6
Felson, M., 7, 117
Fendrick, A. M., 248
Ferrari, J. R., 53
Ferriss, A. L., 117
Fetterman, D. M., 28, 156, 159, 160
Figueredo, A. J., 278
Filling, C., 157
Finch, S., 261
Fine, M., 116
Finegan, J. E., 62
Fischhoff, B., 113
Fitch, R. W., 274
Fitzpatrick, J., 68
Flay, B. R., 218
Fork, H. F., 174

Fountain, D., 242
Fowler, F. J., 93
Franklin, M., 94, 95, 96
Frechtling, J. 254
Freel, C., 133, 148
Freiman, J. A., 106, 263
French, M. T., 235, 238, 241
Fross, K., 270
Fry, L. J., 168
Fuller, R. K., 225

Gaber, J., 7
Gallagher, C. A., 12
Gaston, L., 272
Gerstein, D. R., 242
Giacomazzi, A., 81
Gifford, G., 199
Gilbert, J. P., 220
Gillmore, G. M., 149
Ginsberg, G. S., 89
Glasser, B., 91
Glasgow, R. E., 62
Glenmullen, J., 55
Goering, P. N., 278
Googin, W. C., 89
Gooler, L. E., 20, 31
Gover, A. R., 275
Granger, R. L., 48, 106
Grasso, A. J., 149, 151, 269
Gray, B. H., 97
Green, J., 75
Green, R. S., 6, 76
Greene, J. C., 169
Greeno, C., 34, 46
Greenwald, A. G., 149
Greer, P. R., 174
Gregory, B., 57
Greiner, J. M., 76, 88, 84
Gross, D. M., 235
Grove, J. B., 80
Gruber, J., 5
Gruenewald, P. J., 226
Guba, E. G., 77, 87, 103, 162, 166, 168, 169
Guilbault, R. L., 187, 255
Gunter, M. J., 166

Hackman, J. R., 213
Halemba, G. J., 16
Hammond, R., 174
Hanke, S. H., 243
Hanson, G. S., 5
Harshbarger, D., 231
Hartog, J., 236
Hartog, S. B., 186
Hartung, 87, 132
Harwood, H. J., 242
Hatry, H. P., 75, 231
Haveman, R. H., 155

Heath, L., 24, 113
Hedrick, T. E., 168
Hegarty, T. W., 250
Heinemann, H. N., 236
Held, P. J., 235
Helford, M., 34
Helper, S., 12
Hemphill, J. F., 89
Hendricks, M., 14, 15, 133, 253, 254
Henry, G. T., 267, 282
Hernandez, M., 61
Hewitt, P., 219
Hilkevitch, J., 149
Hine, L. K., 219
Hirst, E., 182
Hogan, R. R., 72
Hollenberg, N. K., 127
Holmgren, T., 126
Holter, M. C., 57
Horton, S. V., 199
Hougland, J. G., 77
House, E. R., 8, 24, 144
House, P. W., 245
Howard, P. K., 107, 222
Howell, A. J., 89
Hsia, D. C., 12
Hsiung, S., 222
Huffman, L. C., 43

Illich, I., 126
Impara, J. C., 89
Ingram, P. W., 4
Ioannidis, J. P. A., 105
Irwin, M. R., 144, 163
Isaacson, W., 19
Iturrian, A., 276
Iverson, D. C., 244

Jacobi, M., 127
Jacobsen, N. S., 173
Jason, L. A., 76
Jerrell, J. M., 76
Joglekar, P. N., 248
Johnson, P. L., 51
Johnson, R. A., 242
Johnston, J., 13, 20
Judd, C. M., 178
Julnes, G., 273, 274
Jurs, S., 244

Kaftarian, S. J., 28
Kahn, J., 236
Kahneman, D., 24, 122, 182
Kane, R. A., 241
Kane, R. L., 241
Kapp, S. A., 149
Katz, M. M., 76
Keating, K. M., 182

Keenen, J., 106
Kellaghan, T., 24
Kenny, D. A., 178
Kent, D. M., 248
Kershaw, D. N., 222
Kilbel, B. M., 72
King, J. A., 231
Kirchner, R. E., 236
Kirk, R. E., 202
Klitzner, M., 226
Klostermann, K., 231
Knapp, M., 196
Koch, D., 61
Kolata, G. B., 57
Koncinski, W. S., Jr., 144
Koss, R. G., 133
Kotler, M., 186
Kramer, P. D., 55
Krapfl, J. E., 144
Krueger, R. A., 87, 123, 124
Kuebler, R. R., 106
Kurtines, W. M., 89

Laanan, F. S., 236
Laird, N. M., 219
Langa, K. M., 248
Lave, L., 113
Lavrakas, P. J., 87
Lawler, E. E., III, 213
Lazar, L., 49, 105, 106
Lee, J., 15
Lee, S. M., 82
Leeuw, F. L., 34
Leik, R. K., 49
Lenihan, K. J., 189
Lesage, J. P., 244
Leslie, L. A., 89
Levin, H. M., 10, 14, 26, 240,
    242, 249
Levine, D. I., 12
Levitan, S. A., 3
Leviton, L. C., 15, 24, 70, 74, 149, 154,
    268, 272
Light, R. J., 263, 166, 220, 221
Lincoln, Y. S., 7, 13, 20, 77, 87, 103, 162,
    166, 168, 169
Linn, R. L., 59
Liotta, R. F., 76
Lipsey, M. W., 25, 29, 34, 35, 60, 61, 79,
    83–85, 102, 104, 106, 107, 131, 176,
    221, 225, 260, 263, 270, 273
Lloyd, R. C., 6, 12, 132, 144, 194, 262
Lockhart, D. C., 209, 284, 285
Loeb, J. M., 133
Love, A. J., 72, 121
Lumpkin, P. W., 89
Lurigio, A. J., 75
Luxenberg, M., 199

MacKenzie, D. L., 12, 275
MacQueen, K. M., 109
Madaus, G. F., 24
Madden, J. S., 57
Mager, R. F., 82
Malcolm, M. T., 57
Maley, R. F., 144
Malhotra, N. K., 123
Malloy, K., 242
Maltzman, I. M., 97, 105
Mangione, T. W., 87
Manoff, R. K., 126, 127, 128
Margasak, L., 75
Mark, M. M., 169, 198, 282
Markandya, A., 246
Marsh, C., 200
Marsh, H. W., 208
Marshall, E., 94, 104
Marshall, T. O., 53
Marszalek-Gaucher, E., 6
Massey, O. T., 77
Mathison, S., 52, 129
Mawhinney, T., 6
Maxwell, G. S., 166
Mayne, J., 15
McCarthy, M., 199
McClave, T., 183
McClintock, C. C., 20
McDonald, C., 144
McEwan, P. J., 10, 14, 26, 240, 242, 249
McGarrell, E. F., 51, 100
McIntyre, J. R., 97
McKillip, J., 90, 114, 115, 124, 195, 209,
    211, 284, 285
McKnight, J., 6, 116, 126, 177
McMurtrie, B., 11
McNees, M. P., 236
McSweeny, A. J., 166
McWhorter, J. H., 65
Meadows, D. L., 14
Meehl, P. E., 59, 85, 273
Mendez, D., 41
Miles, M. B., 91, 163
Millenson, M. L., 243
Miller, J., 168
Miller, M. E., 144
Miller, T. W., 90
Millsap, R. E., 186
Mitchell, O., 275
Mitra, A., 87, 123, 124
Mohr, L. B., 273, 274
Moirs, K., 90
Moore, T. J., 219
Morell, J. A., 12
Morgan, M. G., 113
Morris, M., 110
Moskop, J. C., 235
Moskowitz, J. M., 270

Mosteller, F., 64, 220
Mowbray, C. T., 57, 132
Muenchow, S., 203
Mullen, E. J., 106, 173
Murphy, R. K., 82, 83, 88, 184
Murray, H. A., 106

Nackley, J. F., 127
Nagel, S. S., 245, 272
Nahan, N., 135
Neikirk, W., 56
Nesman, T. M., 61
Neuhauser, D., 220
Newcomer, K. E., 231, 262
Newman, D. L., 109, 110
Newman, F. L., 6, 88
Nickerson, R. S., 226
Nienstedt, B. C., 16
Nightingale, F., 3
Noah, J. C., 144
Nunnally, J. C., 178

O'Dell, K. J., 89
O'Doherty, H., 41
Okrent, D., 247
Orwin, R. G., 72
Osberg, T. M., 72
Oster, G., 248
Overstreet, E. J., 269
Oyserman, D., 72, 119

Palca, J., 221
Patton, M. Q., 27, 90, 104, 160, 161, 188, 268
Paul, G. L., 88
Paulos, J. A., 187
Pauly, M. V., 235
Pearce, D., 246
Pedhazur, E. J., 84
Pendrey, M. L., 97, 105
Perelman, L., 14
Perkins, C. B., 279
Perrin, B., 12
Peterson, J. L., 34, 46
Peterson, R. D., 239
Petraitis, J., 113
Petty, M. M., 205, 216
Pfeiffer, S. I., 13, 20
Phillips, J., 209, 284, 285
Pillemer, D. B., 166, 221, 263
Pion, G. M., 60
Piontek, M. E., 266, 267, 270, 275, 277, 281, 283
Plake, B. S., 89
Pollard, J. A., 34, 61, 79, 102
Posavac, E. J., 34, 59, 60, 65, 72, 74, 87, 101, 132, 174, 229, 253, 255, 270, 274
Posavac, S. S., 121, 122
Prague, C. N., 144, 163

Preskill, H. S., 254, 266, 267, 270, 275, 277, 281, 283
Prue, D. M., 144
Putnam, R., 275

Rachal, J. V., 4
Raines, B. E., 62
Rajkumar, A. S., 238, 241
Rallis, S. F., 153, 166, 169
Ramirez, G. Y., 89
Range, L. M., 89
Rawls, J., 99
Ray, M., 288, 295
Ray, M. L., 165
Raykov, T., 178
Reardon, J., 144, 163
Recktenwald, W., 134
Reichardt, C. S., 153, 166, 169, 198, 202, 208
Rezmovic, E. L., 224
Ricci, F. M., 166
Rice, S. A., 103
Rich, E. C., 199
Richmond, F., 271
Riecken, H. W., 209, 225
Ripsin, C. M., 106
Risley, T. R., 107
Rivlin, A. M., 129
Robinson, E. A. R., 187
Robinson, G. C., 243
Rog, D. J., 93
Rook, K. S., 124
Rosenbaum, D. P., 5
Rosenhan, D. L., 159
Rosenstock, I. M., 216
Rosenthal, R., 41, 106, 263
Rosnow, R. L., 106
Rossi, P. H., 4, 57, 61, 79, 95, 166, 168
Rossiter, C., 226
Rossman, G. B., 166
Roth, J., 114
Rothchild, M. L., 288, 295
Rouse, I. L., 106
Royce, J. M., 106
Rubin, S. M., 248
Russon, C., 12
Russon, G., 12
Rydell, C. P., 235, 264

Sabath, M. J., 51, 100
Sabin, E. P., 4
Sabourin, S., 272
Sackett, P. R., 106, 173
Sacks, F. M., 106
Samset, K., 270
Sanbonmatsu, D. M., 122
Sanchez, J. R., 236
Savaya, R., 150

Scherer, L. L., 107
Schmaltz, S. P., 133
Schmelkin, L. P., 84
Schmitz, M. F., 103
Schneider, A. L., 106
Schneider, M. J., 235
Schnelle, J. F., 198, 236, 237, 238
Schreuder, C., 235
Schuh, J. H., 11
Schwab, J. J., 120
Schwalm, D. E., 222
Schwartz, R. D., 15, 80
Schwarz, N., 72, 119
Scott, S., 235
Scriven, M., 3, 14, 18, 20, 24–26, 28, 31, 55, 65, 114, 281
Sechrest, L., 79, 80, 273
Seligman, C., 62
Shadish, W. R., 5, 15, 16, 24, 35, 41, 42, 70, 72, 74, 77, 104, 149, 154, 169, 191, 214, 223, 224, 225, 230, 263, 273, 278
Shaffer, A., 33, 107
Shalev, A., 186
Shaughnessy, J. J., 85
Shaw, I. F., 27, 157, 170
Shepard, L. A., 59
Shotland, R. L., 169
Shrauger, J. S., 72
Shull, R. D., 245
Sieber, J. E., 30
Sieber, S. D., 6, 64, 107, 222
Silber, B. G., 72
Silverman, W. A., 219, 166, 226
Silverman, W. K., 89
Sinacore, J. M., 34
Sincich, T., 183
Singh, B., 174
Singleton, B., 205
Sinnott, V., 187, 223
Sirotnik, K. A., 65
Slovic, P., 24, 113
Smith, D. M., 275
Smith, H., Jr., 106
Smith, M. F., 34
Smith, M. L., 172
Snipper, A. S., 106
Snowden, L. R., 77
Sobell, L. C., 96, 97, 105
Sobell, M. B., 96, 97, 105
Soderstrom, E. J., 144
Solberg, L. I., 132
Solomon, Z., 186
Sommer, R., 269
Sonnichsen, R. C., 12, 68, 269, 279
Spath, P., 134
Speer, D. C., 4
Spiring, F. A., 194
Spiro, S. E., 186, 187

Spitzer, R. L., 76
Sporn, D. L., 15, 32, 250
Stanley, J. C., 172, 191, 193, 196, 214
Stanley, R. O., 187, 223
Stasney, R., 122
Steele, S., 65
Stein, J. A., 5
Stein, S., 134
Stobart, G., 102, 34, 79
Strauss, A. L., 91, 153
Strycker, L. A., 62
Stucker, C., 159
Stufflebeam, D. L., 3, 22, 24, 26, 55, 166
Styve, G. J., 275
Sullivan, J. M., 77
Summerfelt, W. T., 104
Sussna, F., 236
Suter, N., 242
Svensson, K., 15
Swain, J. F., 106
Swartz, J., 75, 136

Tamkin, G., 33, 107
Tannenbaum, A. S., 97
Taut, S., 18, 43
Teague, G. B., 57
Terborg, J. R., 62
Testa, M. A., 127
Thurman, Q. C., 81
Tierney, W. M., 144
Toms, K., 32
Torres, R. T., 49, 266, 267, 270, 275, 277, 281, 283
Trapp, J. C., 4
Trickett, P. K., 79
Trochim, W. M. K., 206, 208
Truax, P., 173
Tukey, J. W., 200
Turner, A. J., 79
Turner, G., 62, 89
Turner, M. A., 76
Turner, N. H., 89
Turpin, R., 34, 44, 45
Tversky, A., 24, 122, 182
Tyson, T. J., 209

Ullman, J. B., 5
Upcraft, M. L., 11
Uselton, P. H., Jr., 236

van der Maas, P. J., 244
Vanderslice, V., 116
Van Horn, L., 106
Van Sant, J., 164
Veatch, R. M., 108
Vermillion, J. M., 13, 20
Viscusi, W. K., 246, 247
Vojtecky, M. A., 103

Voth, D. E., 235
Vroom, P. I., 135

Wagner, K. D., 174
Wagner, R. F., Jr., 174
Waldo, G. P., 274
Walker, R. A., 243
Waller, B., 108
Walsh, J., 15
Wandersman, A., 28
Wargo, M. J., 133
Warheit, G. J., 120
Warner, K. E., 41
Warren, W. L., 76
Washburn, G., 76
Wasylenski, D. A., 278
Watts, H. W., 155
Weaver, G. D., 89
Webb, E. J., 80, 33, 107
Weems, C. F., 89
Weinreich, N. K., 128
Weiss, C. H., 113, 131, 264, 269, 272
Weiss, S. J., 244
Weitzman, E. A., 91, 163
West, L. J., 97, 105
West, S. G., 186, 222
Wheeler, D. J., 194

White, C. R., 43
Whitmore, E., 165
Wholey, J. S., 5, 10, 14, 15, 34, 51
Williams, A. E., 57
Williams, S. C., 133
Wills, K., 254
Wilson, B. L., 166
Wilson, D. B., 12, 176, 225, 263
Winett, R. A., 127, 128
Wintfeld, N., 75
Wisler, C., 11, 16, 27
Witkin, B. R., 129, 130
Wolfson, S. M., 79
Wu, L., 77
Wye, C. G., 12

Yampolskaya, S., 61
Yates, B. T., 231, 243
Yeaton, W. H., 273

Zammuto, R. F., 14
Zechmeister, E. B., 85, 174
Zechmeister, J. S., 85
Zigler, E., 79, 203
Zimmerman, W., 76
Zimring, F. E., 269

Subject Index

ABAB design, 199
accountability, 42, 43
accounting, 11
accreditation, 12, 27, 76, 134
acquiescence, 119
advocacy, 94
agricultural extension, 123
alcohol education, 285, 287
alcoholism, 225
alligators, 64
American Evaluation Association, 96
analysis of variance, 201, 202, 212, 216, 217
analysis of covariance, 202, 216, 217
Antabuse, 57
appendix, 258, 260, 264
application form, 140
art criticism, 27
artifacts, 73
assessment, individual, 10
audit, 27
auditors, 16
audits, 10, 11, 20
authentic evaluation, 169
availability bias, 122
avoidable drug errors, 277

basic research, 62, 95, 106, 157
benefit-to-cost ratio, 237, 245
benefits, 66
    future, 241–245, 248
    program, 235, 245
binomial distribution, 183
bloodletting, 177
boot camp prisons, 275
budget, 68, 234, 245

Case Study 1, 80
Case Study 2, 160
Case Study 3, 174, 175
Case Study 4, 205, 206, 216
Case Study 5, 222
Case Study 6, 243, 244, 248
Case Study 7, 274, 275
causal effects, 270
causal hypotheses, 192
ceiling effect, 85
census, 117
change, 186, 187
    cause of, 9
    meaningful, 176, 177

random, 193
scores, 178
systematic, 193
chart, 255
checklists, 88
cholesterol, 57
closed box evaluation. *See* evaluation, black
    box model
cognitive achievement, 88
communication
    plan, 251, 252, 254, 264, 266
    schedule, 253
    skills, 222, 223
community indexes, 73
    members, 101, 102
    policing, 81
comparison group, 201–203
compensatory education, 204
conclusions, evaluative, 164
confidence interval, 193, 228, 261
confidentiality, 75, 99, 102, 110, 121, 260
construct validity, 186
constructivist philosophy, 168
consumer products, 25, 26
Consumer Price Index, 117
Continuous Quality Improvement, 12
control construct, 209, 284
control groups, 29, 39
controlled drinking, 97, 105
correlational techniques, 29
cost analyses, criticism of, 246–248
cost-benefit analysis, 236–238, 240, 243–245,
    246, 248, 249
cost-effectiveness analysis, 10, 238–241, 245,
    246, 248, 249
cost-utility analysis, 240, 249
costs, 9, 14, 33, 229, 231–249
    fixed, 232
    future, 241, 248
    hidden, 233
    incremental, 232
    indirect, 233
    opportunity, 233, 242
    recurring, 233
    sunk, 232, 233
creaming, 28
credibility, 164, 278
crime
    prevention, 85
    reports, 117

criteria,, 47–71
   credible, 69
Cronbach's alpha, 84

DARE, 5
data collection, 153, 156, 223
   costs of, 134
data collectors, 103
deadline for an evaluation, 69
description of clients, 132, 133, 150
descriptions of program, 164
diagnostic laboratory tests, 144, 199, 200
discounting, 242
discrepancies, 29
drug treatment programs, 136

effect size, 175, 176, 225, 226, 228, 262, 263
effectiveness to cost ratio, 238, 239
efficiency, 7, 9, 10, 14, 167
employee
   appraisals, 32
   incentive, 205, 206, 213, 216
empowering, 169
energy conservation, 62
energy use, 144
ERIC, 35
ethical
   principles, 95, 96
   problems in evaluation practice, 110
ethics in program evaluation, 94–112
evaluability assessment, 34, 51
evaluation. *See also* program evaluation
   accountability model, 27
   black box model, 25, 26, 27, 60
   cost of, 80
   definition of, 3
   empowerment model, 28, 29
   expert opinion model, 24–30
   fiscal model, 26, 27
   for accountability, 15
   for development, 15
   for knowledge, 15
   formative, 14, 18, 32, 39, 42
   goal-free model, 26
   improvement-focused, 29,30
   industrial inspection model, 25
   models, 24–30
   naturalistic model, 27, 28
   negative, 42
   objectives-based model, 25, 55, 58, 67
   planning, 23–46
   purpose of, 33
   qualitative model, 27, 28, 39
   quantitative, 39
   questions, 55–68, 289
   reports, 40, 42, 250–267
   social science model, 25
   success case method, 28, 39

summative, 14, 18, 32, 39
theory-driven, 28, 29
traditional model, 24, 25
evaluation attitude, 280, 281
evaluator
   external, 17–19, 43
   internal, 17–19, 33, 34, 40, 43, 45, 51, 270
   personal qualities, 18
evaluator profiles
   Barkdoll, Gerald L., 32
   Deiger, Megan, 21
   Frechtling, Joy, 254
   Hendricks, Michael, 15
   Iturrian, Angelina, 276
   Perkins, Chris Burns, 279
   Turpin, Robin, 44, 45
   Ray, Marilyn L., 164
   Wargo, Michael J., 133
   Whitmore, Elizabeth, 164
   Wholey, Joseph S., 51
evaluators, roles of, 16
experimental
   design, 25
   evaluations, 270
experimentation, objections to, 218–220
experiments in program evaluation, 215–230

fairness, 66
feedback, 14, 144, 145
focus group, 123, 124
food stamps, 127
foreign aid, 126

goals, 26, 52–55
   intermediate, 53, 54, 60, 61, 128, 129
   outcome, 53–55, 58–60, 65, 128, 129
   vague, 153
Government Accountability Office
      (GAO), 16
Government Performance and Results Act
      (GPRA), 172
Government Performance and Results
      Act, 12
graphs, 261, 267
Gross Domestic Product, 117
Gun Control Act, 269

Head Start, 48–50, 105, 106, 203, 223
Health and Psychosocial Instruments
      (HAPI), 88, 89
health education, 294
helicopter police patrol, 198, 236, 237
hindsight bias, 187, 256, 257
HIV (AIDS) testing law, 195
homogeneity, 84
human resources, 21
hypotheses, 59
   testing, 227

immunization, 4, 126
impact model, 35, 36, 63, 64, 128, 169,
    270, 274
impact of program, 272, 273
implementation, 7, 8, 10, 14, 21, 35, 45,
    53–54, 57, 71, 104, 107, 127, 156, 168,
    169, 235, 265, 270, 273
improvement, 49, 158, 169, 265, 277, 278
    practicable, 41
    program, 13
improvement-focused evaluation, 67
informed consent, 97, 98
Institutional Review Boards (IRB), 108–110
inter-item consistency, 83
interaction of threats to internal validity, 185
internal validity, 192, 215, 270. *See also* threats
    to internal validity
Internet sites, 37
interrupted time series, 197
interviewers, 260
interviews, 87, 88, 92, 103, 287, 291
    telephone, 87

job-training, 77
jobless rate, 82
Joint Committee of Standards, 102, 112

key informants, 122–125
Key Evaluation Checklist, 281
kidney dialysis, costs of, 235

learning culture, 275–280
Lowess line, 199, 200

management information system, 132, 133
    problems, 148–150
    reports, 141–143, 145–147
    residential treatment, 148
manufacturing, 25
matching, 203
measures, 71–93
    cost-effective, 85, 86
    multiple, 77, 79, 81, 92
    types of, 86–90
    valid, 81, 82
media campaign, 284–296
medical tests, 101
MEDLINE, 35
merit, 3, 29
methodology, 38, 39
monitoring, 4, 6, 8, 15, 129, 131–151, 155, 227
multiple regression, 208

National Safety Council, 247
need, 167
    assessment of, 14, 113–130, 160
    context of, 126
    definition of, 114, 115

surveys of, 119–121
    unmet, 4, 7, 8, 9, 12, 21, 115, 116, 121, 125,
        130, 260
negative findings, 274
negative side effects, 218
New Hope, 137, 139, 140, 142, 146
noncompliance, 65
nonequivalent control group, 201–206, 209–213
nonreactive measures, 80
novel findings, 188
novel treatments, 96

objective behavior, 82
objectives, 26, 34, 35, 52–55, 67
objectivity, 55
observations, 157–160, 163, 164, 184
    nonparticipant, 157–159
    on-site, 134
    participant, 158–160
    personal, 28, 29
observers
    evaluation staff, 76, 77
    expert, 75, 76
    information from, 75–77
    trained, 76
Office of Inspector General, 27
open forum, 123–125
outcome 4, 5, 7, 8, 9, 10, 14, 29, 34, 38, 42,
    45, 167, 168
    criteria, 260
    evaluation, 171–249, 270
    evaluation
        quasi-experimental, 192–214
        single-group, 171–191
    intermediate, 33, 35, 274
    long-term, 33
outcomes and costs, 231–249

partial correlation, 178–180
peer leadership, 62
Pierre Louis, 177
planners, responsibilities of, 3
planning, 20, 116
posttest, 203
posttest-only design, 173
power tables, 225
presentation, personal, 253–257
pretest-posttest
    design, 172, 173
    nonequivalent control group, 218
prevention, 13
probe, generic, 161
probing, 161, 162
process, 7, 8, 42, 167
program
    costs, 65, 66
    description, 30, 104
    improvement, 110

managers, 100
participants, 7, 30, 35, 39, 41, 101, 135,
    260, 274
  information from, 72, 73
  personnel, 30–32, 34, 39, 40, 43
  planning, 7, 61, 128, 271
  purposes of, 48, 49
  records, 39, 135, 136
  sponsors, 31–33
  staff, information from, 74, 75
  theory, 34, 60–64
    implausible, 63, 64
program evaluation. *See also* evaluation.
  attitudes toward, 40–45
  definition of, 2
  discipline of, 3
  models of, 22, 24–30
  objectivity, 25
  practice of, 2
  purpose of, 14, 18
Program Planning and Evaluation, 7
proposals, 35, 40
proxy variables, 175
pseudoparticipant, 158
PsycINFO, 35
Public Health Service, 41
PUSH/Excel, 8

qualitative
  data, 153
  evaluation, 76
  methods, 152–170, 227
quality
  assurance, 15, 18, 39
  improvement, 6
quantitative methods, 152, 165–169
quasi-experimental
  designs, 192–214
  evaluations, 270

random
  assignment, 29, 39
  sample, 28
rapport, 161
reactivity, 184
recommendations, 264, 265, 270–272, 277
records
  agency, 88, 89
  crime, 82
  program, 75, 82
regression-discontinuity, 206–208
relational database program, 136,
    137, 138
reliability, 49, 82–84. *See also* Cronbach's
    alpha, homogeneity.
  interobserver, 84
  split-half, 83, 84
  test-retest, 84

remedial programs, 184
repeated measures, 85
report
  drafts, 256, 257
  illustrative, 284–296
  outline, 258, 259
  progress, 266
  summary, 250
  written, 257, 258, 264–266
reports, progress, 74
Requests for Proposals, 17
research
  basic, 10, 20
  design, 103
resistance, 31, 49
review panel, 44, 45
role conflicts, 98, 99

SADD, 226
sample
  representativeness of, 38, 39, 119
  snowball, 122
  size, 29, 225, 272, 273
sampling error, 175, 226
SAT, 82, 118
selective control design, 211–213, 216
sensitivity analysis, 242, 243, 248
Sesame Street, 33, 107
side effects, 6, 7, 21, 55, 63, 67, 68, 77, 80,
    156, 243
  negative, 105, 107, 108, 136
significant others, 76
single-group designs, usefulness of, 188–190
smoking cessation, 244
smoothing (a graph), 200, 201
social
  indicators, 117–119
  marketing, 128
social science model, 169
sources of data for evaluation, 71–79
speed crackdown, 194, 195, 209, 210
stakeholders, 28, 29, 30, 32, 39, 40, 45, 50–52,
    54, 98, 99, 128, 156, 164, 223, 250,
    251, 253–255, 258, 264–266, 268–272,
    276, 279, 280, 282
  conflicts among, 155
  needs of, 100–102
standard error of the mean, 83, 84
standard error of measurement, 83
standards, 47–70
statistical analysis, 38–40
statistical power, 227
statistical process control, 194
statistics, 13, 59
stem-and-leaf plot, 263
subjectivist philosophy, 169
subjectivity, 166
success case method, 167

summary, 259
summative evaluation, 270
surveys, 90–92, 287, 288, 290, 291

t test, 216, 226, 227
target population, 38
teaching effectiveness, 101
tests, 88
theories, 10
threats to internal validity, 172, 180–186, 190,
191, 212–214, 226, 227
  attrition, 182, 223, 224
  compensation of the control group, 226
  diffusion of the program, 226
  instrumentality, 185, 213
  history, 181, 202
  local history, 227
  maturation, 180, 181, 202, 204, 212, 216
  regression toward the mean, 182–184, 204,
  210, 216
  resentful demoralization, 226, 227
  selection, 181, 182, 202, 212, 216
  selection-by-maturation, 185
  testing, 184, 202, 213, 216
  rivalry with experimental group, 226

time-series designs, 195–201, 209–211,
213, 284
Total Quality Management, 12
traces, 159
triangulation, 159
trust, 158
Type I error, 105, 106, 187, 188,
273, 274
Type II error, 105–107, 216, 229, 263,
264, 274

utilization, 268–283
  obstacles to, 269–271

validity, 49, 58, 83
validity of evaluations, 102
value of lives, 246, 247
values, 107
volunteer companions, 77

W. K. Kellogg Foundation, 266
work-release program, 274
workfare, 100
worth, 3, 29, 66
written surveys, 86, 87